DESIGN AND ANALYSIS OF
ALGORITHMS

DESIGN AND ANALYSIS OF
ALGORITHMS

V.V. Muniswamy

Director, Annamacharya Institute of Technology &
Sciences, Tirupati - AP

(Formerly Professor of Industrial Engineering &
Computer Science, Sri Venkateswara University, Tirupati)

TECHSAR™

NEW DELHI

Published and Printed by

Techsar Pvt. Ltd.
4435-36/7, Ansari Road, Daryaganj
New Delhi - 110 002 (India)
E-mail : tech_info@techsarworld.com
Website: www.techsarworld.com

ISBN 978-93-80026-73-2

Reprint 2025

Dedicated to my beloved Grandfather
Late Sri Varada Kondappa

PREFACE

This book was motivated by my experience in teaching the course: *Algorithms and Data Structures* in the Computer Engineering program for B.Tech and MCA classes; and *Operations Research* for B.Tech, MBA and M.Tech (Industrial Engineering) curriculum. The successful application of algorithm techniques gives rise to a kind of cognitive unification: Ideas that are disparate and apparently unrelated seem to come together when the appropriate design patterns are used.

This book is designed to provide a comprehensive introduction to the design and analysis of computer algorithms. In terms of the computer science and computer engineering curricula, I have written this book to be primarily focused on the under-graduate course, which is taught as a one-semester course.

There are three main reasons for emphasis on algorithm design techniques. First, these techniques provide a student with tools for designing algorithms for new problems. This makes learning algorithm design techniques a very valuable endeavour from the practical standpoint. Second, they seek to classify multitudes of known algorithms according to an underlying design idea. Learning to see such structure among algorithms from different application areas should be a major goal of computer science education. Third, in my opinion, algorithm design techniques have considerable utility as general problem solving strategies, applicable to problems beyond computing.

This book is intended to be used as a textbook for a university course in Design and Analysis of Algorithms, typically taught in the second or third year of a Computer Science and Information Technology curriculum. However, it is also designed for professional programmers and for anyone else who needs to take the next step up from merely knowing a programming language. Because it is easy to understand, it is also appropriate as a supplemental text to a more formal course. It assumes that the student has completed an elementary course in C or C++ and data structures.

Once we have learned to program, we run into real-world problems that require more than a programming language alone to solve. Design and Analysis of Algorithms is a soft absorption into the most practical ways to make data do what we want it to do. The book starts at the very beginning with an introduction to algorithms.

Typical computer science textbooks are full of theory, mathematical formulas, and complex examples of computer code. This book, on the other hand, focus on simple explanations of techniques. I avoided complex proofs and heavy mathematics. There are lots of figures to augment the text.

The book covers a broad range of algorithms making their design and analysis accessible to all levels of readers. Each chapter is relatively self-contained and can be used as a unit of study. The algorithms are described in a pseudocode designed to be readable by anyone who has done a little programming. The explanations have been kept elementary without sacrificing depth of coverage or mathematical rigor.

The first chapter gives an overview of algorithms. This provides an insight to complexity of algorithms. The topics include: performance analysis, asymptotic notation (big-Oh, omega, and theta), recurrence relations, probabilistic analysis, and amortized analysis.

The purpose of chapter-2 is to give an introduction to disjoint set operations and spanning trees (dfs, bfs, connected and biconnected components). Chapters 3 to 7 present algorithm design techniques – divide and conquer, greedy method, dynamic programming, backtracking, and branch-and-bound. Chapter-8 introduces the NP-complete problems with examples of some intractable problems, P and NP classes, NP-hard and NP-completeness, and Cook's theorem.

Chapter summary is given at the end of each chapter; and a set of multiple-choice (self-test quiz) questions and exercises (includes questions from GATE for Computer Science & Engineering, and Information Technology). The quizzes and exercises are designed to consolidate the concepts presented in the text. These exercises, generally, require the student to extend the implementation given in the text. Appendix-A provides the key to self-test quizzes. Appendix-B gives the solutions or hints to the exercises.

I am a firm believer in the old adage, "a picture is worth 1024 words:" So you will find extensive illustrations throughout the book.

I am grateful for the help I have received on this work from my friends and colleagues. I would like to thank K. Venkateswara Rao, Systems Administrator, Computer Center, R. Devarajulu Reddy, English faculty, N. Venkata Siva Kumar, C. Bhanu Prakash and D. Murali Krishna, Computer Science faculty, Annamacharya Institute of Technology & Sciences, Tirupati-AP for their assistance in preparation of this book. Finally, I would like to thank Mr. C. Gangi Reddy, Honorary Secretary, Annamacharya Educational Trust, for using Computer Center facilities of the college.

I would appreciate hearing from readers about my shortcomings or strengths. My email address is vvms@yahoo.com.

Other miscellaneous *uncovered topics* in the chapters are given in the Appendix-B.

Tirupati (AP) *V. V. Muniswamy*
June 2009

CONTENTS

CHAPTER 1

INTRODUCTION TO ALGORITHMS

The design and analysis of algorithms is one of the essential key topics in computer science. We often encounter several algorithms for the same problem, and we must decide which is best. This leads us to the interesting and all-important field of *analysis of algorithms* whose overall goal is an understanding of the complexity of algorithms. The general idea is to take a particular algorithm and determine its quantitative behaviour.

To get started, we will design and analyze a simple algorithm for multiplying integers using only addition. Though this might sound like a trivial exercise, it is actually quite tricky to design an efficient multiplication algorithm. Such an algorithm is important because computers do not just magically know how to multiply numbers; we must tell them how to multiply using more primitive operations like addition that it already knows how to perform. The simplest algorithm for multiplying integers m and n is to simply add n to 0 exactly m times.

```
Algorithm 1.1: product(m, n)
    Input: m ≥ 0 and n ≥ 0 are integers.
    Output: the product of m and n.
    p = 0
    for i = 1 to m do
        p = p + n
    return p
```

Can we determine the number of additions that the algorithm uses to find the product of m and n? It should not be too difficult to see that it uses m additions. Can we use fewer? Notice that when $m > n$, product(n, m) uses n additions whereas product(m, n) uses m which is greater than n additions. The following algorithm makes sure that we always use min(m, n) additions:

```
Algorithm 1.2: product(m, n)
    If m > n then swap(m, n)
    p = 0
    for i = 1 to m do
        p = p + n
    return p
```

This algorithm is certainly better than Algorithm 1.1. We still might be able to improve efficiency by redefining multiplication recursively, that is, like this (we will assume that $m \le n$):

$$m \times n = \begin{cases} 0 & \text{if } m = 0 \\ n + (m-1) \times n & \text{otherwise} \end{cases}$$

This definition is recursive because we use multiplication to define multiplication.

Algorithm 1.3: product(m, n)

```
If m = 0 then
    return 0
Else
    return n + product(m − 1, n)
```

To understand how this algorithm works, consider the example of multiplying 3 by 5:

1. Calling product(3, 5) returns 5 + product(2, 5),
2. Calling product(2, 5) returns 5 + product(1, 5),
3. Calling product(1, 5) returns 5 + product(0, 5) and
4. Calling product(0, 5) returns 0.

Therefore:

1. product(1, 5) returns 5 + 0 = 5,
2. product(2, 5) returns 5 + (5 + 0) = 10 and
3. product(3,5) returns 5 + (5 + (5 + 0)) = 15.

As we can see, having the algorithm calls itself is not a problem because it calls itself with a smaller m each time. Eventually, we have $m = 0$ in which case the algorithm does not call itself.

Consider another simple algorithm for finding the largest of three numbers. Algorithm 1.4 takes seven instructions (3 comparisons and 4 assignments), whereas Algorithm 1.5 uses five instructions (2 comparisons + 3 assignments). Hence, we can say that Algorithm 1.5 is better than Algorithm 1.4.

Algorithm 1.4: max(a, b, c)

```
If a > b, then
    If a > c, then m = a
    Else m = c
    Endif
Else
    If b > c, then m = b
    Else m = c
    Endif
Endif
return m
```

Algorithm 1.5: max(a, b, c)

```
m = a
If b > m, then
    m = b
Endif
If c > m, then
    m = c
Endif
return m
```

1.1 ALGORITHM

An algorithm, named after the ninth century scholar *Abu Jafar Muhammad Ibn Musu Al-Khowarizmi*, is defined as follows: Roughly speaking:

- An algorithm is a set of rules for carrying out calculation either by hand or on a machine.
- An algorithm is a finite step-by-step procedure to achieve a required result.
- An algorithm is a sequence of computational steps that transform the input into the output.
- An algorithm is a sequence of operations performed on data that have to be organized in data structures.
- An algorithm is an abstraction of a program to be executed on a physical machine (model of Computation).

The most famous algorithm in history dates well before the time of the ancient Greeks: this is *Euclid*'s algorithm for calculating the greatest common divisor of two integers.

Algorithmic is a branch of computer science that consists of designing and analyzing computer algorithms. The "design" pertains to the description of algorithm at an abstract level by means of a pseudo language, and proof of correctness that is, the algorithm solves the given problem in all cases. The "analysis" deals with performance evaluation (complexity analysis).

We start with defining the model of computation, which is usually the Random Access Machine (RAM) model, but other models of computations can be used such as PRAM. PRAM stands for Parallel Random Access Machine, an abstract machine for designing the algorithms applicable to parallel computers. In the RAM model, we assume that all memory locations are equally expensive to access, no concurrent operations are performed, all reasonable instructions take unit time (except, of course, function calls), constant word size is used (unless we are explicitly manipulating bits). Once the model of computation has been defined, an algorithm can be described using a simple language (or pseudo language) whose syntax is close to programming language such as C or java.

An algorithm[§] is a finite sequence of instructions, each of which has a clear meaning and can be performed with a fine amount of effort in a finite length of time. An integer assignment statement such as: $x = a + b$ is an example of an instruction that can be executed in a finite amount of effort. In an algorithm, instructions can be executed any number of times, provided the instructions themselves indicate the repetition. However, we require that, no matter what the input values may be, an algorithm terminates executing a finite number of instructions. Thus, a program is an algorithm as long as it never enters an infinite loop on any input.

Definition of algorithm states that each instruction of an algorithm must have a "clear meaning" and must be executable with a "finite amount of effort". Now what is clear to one person may not be clear to another, and it is often difficult to prove strictly that an instruction can be carried out in a finite amount of time. It is often difficult as well to prove that on any input, a sequence of instructions terminates.

What kinds of problems are solved by algorithms?[♣]

[§] Aho, Hopcroft and Ullman "Data Structures and Algorithms", Pearson Education, 2001.

[♣] Cormen, Leiserson, Rivest, and Stein "Introduction to Algorithms", MIT Press, 2002.

Suppose computers were infinitely fast and computer memory was free. Would we have any reason to study algorithms? The answer is yes, if for no other reason than that we would still like to demonstrate that our solution method terminates and does so with the correct answer. If computers were infinitely fast, any correct method for solving a problem would do. We would probably want our implementation to be within the bounds of good software engineering practice (i.e., well designed and documented), but we would most often use whichever method was the easiest to implement.

Sorting is by no means the only computational problem for which algorithms have been developed. Practical applications of algorithms are everywhere and include the following examples:

- The Human Genome Project has the goals of identifying all the 100,000 genes in human DNA, determining the sequences of the 3 billion chemical base pairs that make up human DNA, storing this information in databases, and developing tools for data analysis. Each of these steps requires sophisticated algorithms.
- The Internet enables people all around the world to quickly access and retrieve large amounts of information. In order to do so, clever algorithms are employed to manage and manipulate this large volume of data. Examples of problems which must be solved include finding good routes on which the data will travel, and using a search engine to quickly find pages on which particular information resides.
- Electronic commerce enables goods and services to be negotiated and exchanged electronically. The ability to keep information such as credit card numbers, passwords, and bank statements is essential if electronic commerce is to be used widely. Public-key cryptography and digital signatures are among the core technologies used and are based on numerical algorithms and number theory.
- In manufacturing and other commercial settings, it is often important to allocate scarce resources in the most beneficial way. An oil company may wish to know where to place its wells in order to maximize its expected profit. An airline may wish to assign crews to flights in the least expensive way possible, making sure that each flight is covered and that government regulations regarding crew scheduling are met. An Internet service provider may wish to determine where to place additional resources in order to serve its customers more effectively.

1.2 PSEUDOCODE

Pseudocode (derived from pseudo and code) is a compact and informal high-level description of a computer programming algorithm that uses the structural conventions of some programming language. But, it typically omits details that are not essential for the understanding of the algorithm, such as functions (or subroutines), variable declarations and system-specific code. Pseudocode is an artificial and informal language that helps programmers develop algorithms. Pseudocode is a "text-based" detail (algorithmic) design tool.

The purpose of using pseudocode is that it may be easier to read than conventional programming languages, and that it may be a compact description of the key principles of an algorithm. No standard for pseudocode syntax exists, as a program in pseudocode is not an executable program.

Flowcharts can be thought of as a graphical alternative to pseudocode. A *flowchart* is a schematic representation of an algorithm, or the step-by-step solution of a problem, using suitably interpreted geometric figures (called flowchart symbols) connected by flow-lines for the purpose of designing or documenting a program.

As the name suggests, pseudocode generally does not actually obey the syntax rules of any particular language; there is no systematic standard form, although any particular writer will generally borrow style and syntax for example control structures from some conventional programming language. Popular syntax sources include C language. Variable declarations are typically omitted. Function calls and blocks of code, for example code contained within a loop, is often replaced by a one-line natural language sentence. Depending on the writer, pseudocode may therefore vary widely in style, from a near-exact imitation of a real programming language at one extreme, to a description approaching formatted prose at the other.

Example 1.1: To find the sum of the digits of an integer.

Algorithm in pseudocode

sumOfDigits(n)
1. *sum* = 0
2. Repeat steps 3 to 5, while $n \neq 0$
3. *digit* = n mod 10
4. add *digit* to *sum*
5. divide n by 10 // *integer division*
6. return *sum*

Function in C language

```
int sumDigits(int n)
{   sum = 0;
    while( n!= 0 )
    {  digit = n % 10;
       sum = sum + digit;
       n = n / 10;
    }
    return sum;
}
```

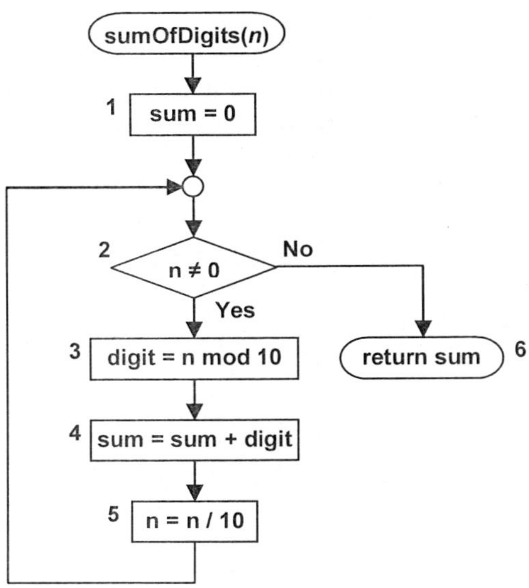

Figure 1.1: Sum of digits of an integer

Example 1.1 shows how pseudocode differs from regular code in C language. Figure 1.1 illustrates a flowchart for finding the sum of digits of an integer. The sequence of instructions of an algorithm in a flowchart can easily be understood by the learners of programming. The flowcharts can also be used for documentation of algorithms.

Pseudocode is independent of any programming language. Pseudocode cannot be compiled nor executed, and there are no real formatting or syntax rules. It is simply one step - an important one - in producing the final code. The benefit of pseudocode is that it enables the programmer to concentrate on the algorithms without worrying about all the syntactic details of a particular programming language. In fact, one can write pseudocode without even knowing what programming language one will use for the final implementation.

1.2.1 Pseudocode Conventions

The structured part of pseudocode is a notation for representing specific structured programming constructs: SEQUENCE, WHILE, IF-THEN-ELSE, REPEAT-UNTIL, FOR, and CASE. Each of these constructs can be embedded inside any other construct. These constructs represent the logic, or flow of control in an algorithm.

It has been proven that three basic constructs for flow of control are sufficient to implement any appropriate algorithm. SEQUENCE is a linear succession where one instruction is performed sequentially after another. WHILE is a loop (repetition) with a simple conditional test at its beginning. IF-THEN-ELSE is a decision (selection) in which a choice is made between two alternative courses of action. Although these constructs are sufficient, it is often useful to include three more constructs: REPEAT-UNTIL is a loop with a simple conditional test at the bottom. CASE is a multi-way branch (decision) based on the value of an expression. CASE is a generalization of IF-THEN-ELSE. FOR is a "counting" loop.

SEQUENCE

Sequential control is indicated by writing one instruction after another, each instruction on a line by itself, and all instructions aligned with the same indent. The instructions are performed in the sequence (top to bottom) that they are written. Several keywords are often used to indicate common input, output, and processing operations.

Input: READ, OBTAIN, GET
Output: PRINT, DISPLAY, SHOW
Compute: COMPUTE, CALCULATE, DETERMINE
Initialize: SET, INIT
Add one: INCREMENT
Subtract one: DECREMENT

IF-THEN-ELSE

Binary choice on a given Boolean condition is indicated by the use of four keywords: IF, THEN, ELSE, and ENDIF. The general form is:

```
IF condition THEN
    Sequence-1
```

```
ELSE
    Sequence-2
ENDIF
```

The ELSE keyword and sequence-2 are optional. If the condition is true, sequence-1 is performed; otherwise sequence-2 is performed. Consider the following example:

```
IF subjectMarks > or = 40, THEN
    Print "passed in the subject"
ELSE
    Print "failed in the subject"
ENDIF
```

WHILE

The WHILE construct is used to specify a loop with a test at the top. The beginning and ending of the loop are indicated by two keywords WHILE and ENDWHILE. The general form is:

```
WHILE condition
    sequence
ENDWHILE
```

The loop is entered only if the condition is true. The sequence is performed for each iteration. At the end of each iteration, the condition is evaluated and the loop continues as long as the condition is true. The following example illustrates use of WHILE loop for finding the sum of first 10 natural numbers:

```
SET number, sum to zero
WHILE number < 10
    INCREMENT number
    ADD number to sum
ENDWHILE
DISPLAY sum
```

CASE

A CASE construct indicates a multi-way branch based on conditions that are mutually exclusive. Four keywords, CASE, OF, OTHERS, and ENDCASE, and conditions are used to indicate the various alternatives. The general form is:

```
CASE expression OF
    condition-1: sequence-1
    condition 2: sequence-2
    ...
    condition-n: sequence-n
    OTHERS: default sequence
ENDCASE
```

The OTHERS clause with its default sequence is optional. Conditions are normally numbers or characters indicating the value of expression, but they can be statements or some other notation that specifies the condition under which the given sequence is to be performed. A certain sequence may be associated with more than one condition. The following CASE statement displays the name of month for a given month in number.

```
CASE month OF
    1: print "January"
    2: print "February"
    ...
    12: print "December"
    OTHERS: print "None"
ENDCASE
```

REPEAT-UNTIL

This loop is similar to the WHILE loop except that the test is performed at the bottom of the loop instead of at the top. Two keywords, REPEAT and UNTIL are used. The general form is:

```
REPEAT
    sequence
UNTIL condition
```

The sequence in this type of loop is always performed at least once, because the test is performed after the sequence is executed. At the end of each iteration, the condition is evaluated, and the loop repeats if the condition is false. The loop terminates when the condition becomes true.

FOR

The FOR-loop is a specialized construct for iterating a specific number of times, often called a "counting" loop. Two keywords, FOR and ENDFOR are used. The general format is:

```
FOR iteration bounds
    sequence
ENDFOR
```

In cases where the loop constraints can be obviously inferred it is best to describe the loop using problem domain vocabulary. Observe the following example.

```
SET sum to zero
FOR number = 1 to 10
    ADD number to sum
ENDFOR
```

NESTED CONSTRUCTS

The constructs can be embedded within each other, and this is made clear by use of indenting. Nested constructs should be clearly indented from their surrounding constructs. Example:

```
SET sum to zero
REPEAT
    READ number
    IF number is odd THEN
        ADD number to sum
    ENDIF
UNTIL number < zero
Display sum
```

In the above example, the IF construct is nested within the REPEAT construct, and therefore is indented.

1.3 PERFORMANCE ANALYSIS

In software engineering, performance analysis is the investigation of a program's behaviour using information gathered as the program runs. The goal of performance analysis is to determine which parts of a program to optimize for speed and memory usage. The notion of an algorithm is central to all of the computer programming, so we should begin with a careful analysis of this concept.

Optimization of a program relates to the algorithm efficiency. Every algorithm must use some of a computer's resources to complete its task. The resources most relevant to efficiency are *central processor time* (CPU time) and *internal memory* (RAM). In other words, the two important ways to characterize the effectiveness of an algorithm are its space complexity and time complexity.

We are generally concerned with "good" solutions to the problems. Good algorithms usually have the following qualities and capabilities:

- They are simple but powerful and general solutions.
- They can be easily understood by others, that is, the implementation is clear.
- They can be easily modified if necessary.
- They can work correctly according to the specifications of the task.
- They are economical in the utilization of computer time and computer storage.
- They are documented well enough to be used by others.
- They are independent of computer and its operating system.
- They are able to support for sub-functions.
- The solution of an algorithm is correct and satisfying to its designer.

The computing time and storage requirements of an algorithm have a more direct relationship to performance.

1.3.1 Space Complexity

The space complexity of an algorithm (for a given input) is the number of elementary objects that this algorithm needs to store during its execution. This number is computed with respect to the size of the input data. The space occupied by an algorithm is determined by the number and sizes of the variables and data structures used by the algorithm.

The space complexity of a problem is a related concept that measures the amount of space, or memory required by the algorithm. An informal analogy would be the amount of scratch paper needed while working out a problem with pen and paper. Space complexity is measured with Big-O notation (to be introduced in the next section).

The better the time complexity of an algorithm is, the faster the algorithm will carry out the work in practice. Apart from time complexity, its space complexity is also important: This is essentially the number of memory cells which an algorithm needs. A good algorithm keeps this number as small as possible. There is often a time-space-tradeoff involved in a problem, that is, it cannot be solved with few computing time and low memory consumption. One then has to make a compromise and to exchange computing time for memory consumption or vice versa, depending on which algorithm one chooses and how one parameterizes it.

The way in which the amount of storage space required by an algorithm varies with the size of the problem it is solving. Space complexity is normally expressed as an order of magnitude, e.g. $O(n^2)$ means that if the size of the problem (n) doubles then four times as much working storage will be needed. The following examples elucidate the space complexity.

Example 1.2: Algorithm 1.5 finds the largest of three numbers. The problem is characterized by the specific values of four variables: a, b, c, and m. In addition to these four memory cells, the algorithm requires its instruction space.

Example 1.3: Algorithm 1.6 finds the maximum element in the given array of size n. The algorithm returns the maximum element in the array. Here, the storage requirements are the number of elements of the array (a), array size (n), array index (i), variable *max*, and the instruction space. The required total space is = (n+3+ instruction space).

Algorithm 1.6: arrayMax(a[1..n], n)

```
max = a[1]
For i = 2 to n do
    If a[i] > max, then
        max = a[i]
    Endif
Endfor
Return max
```

Example 1.4: Algorithm 1.7 computes the factorial of an integer, n recursively. The space instances are characterized by n. The recursion stack space consists of the formal parameters, the local variables, and the return address.

Algorithm 1.7: Factorial(n)

```
If n = 0, then
      Return 1
Else
      Return n x Factorial(n-1)
Endif
```

We conclude that the space required by an algorithm is the sum of a fixed size and a variable part whose size depends on the problem instance being solved. An *instance* is the actual data for which the problem needs to be solved.

1.3.2 Time Complexity

The number of machine instructions which a program executes during its running time is called its *time complexity*. This number depends primarily on the size of the program's input. Time taken by a program is the sum of the compile time and the run time. In time complexity, we consider run time only. The time required by an algorithm is determined by the number of elementary operations.

We may be able to reduce space requirements by increasing the run time, or conversely, reduce time requirements by increasing memory space. This situation is referred to as the *space-time tradeoff*. We will restrict our analysis to the run time of an algorithm, and we will assume that there is sufficient memory space to implement the algorithm. With the current technology, computer memory is typically abundant and cheap in relation to the processor.

We would make judgments regarding the merit of an algorithm independent of a specific software implementation on a specific hardware. In this type of analysis, we assume some general model of computation. We evaluate the algorithms by using RAM model. This model assumes the existence of a single generic processor, random access memory, and a set of basic operations that the processor can execute. It is then assumed that the algorithm is implemented as a computer program that will execute on this RAM model. This model executes instructions one after another, with no concurrent operations. Now, to determine the run time of an algorithm we must determine the time required by each basic (primitive) operation, and multiply that by how many times the operation is used when implementing the algorithm on the RAM model.

We define the following set of primitive operations that are independent from the programming language used and can be identified also in the pseudocode.

- Assigning a value to a variable
- Calling a function
- Performing an arithmetic operation
- Comparing two variables
- Indexing into an array or following a pointer reference
- Returning from a function

We now show how to count the number of primitive operations executed by an algorithm.

Example 1.5: Consider the simple Algorithm 1.5 for finding the largest of three numbers. This algorithm is again given below for ease of understanding.

```
Algorithm 1.5: max(a, b, c)
1.  m = a
2.  If b > m, then
3.      m = b
4.  Endif
5.  If c > m, then
6.      m = c
7.  Endif
8.  return m
```

We examine the following three cases:

(1) When a is the maximum of a, b, and c. The count of primitive operations is 4. One assignment at line 1, two comparisons at lines 2 and 5, and one return statement are executed.

(2) When b > a and c > a or c < a, the number of primitive operations is 5. Two assignments at lines 1 and 3 and, two comparisons at lines 2 and 5, and one return statement are executed.

(3) When c > a, c > b and b > a, the number of primitive operations is 6. Three assignments at lines 1, 3 and 6 and, two comparisons at lines 2 and 5, and one return statement are executed.

The primitive operations of the Algorithm 1.5 vary from 4 to 6.

Example 1.6: Consider the problem of finding the sum of squares of first n natural numbers.

```
Algorithm 1.8: Sum(n)
1.  sum = 0
2.  For i = 1 to n do
3.      sum = sum + i * i
4.  Endfor
5.  Return sum
```

The analysis of the Algorithm 1.8 is simple. Statements 1 and 5 count for one unit each. Line 3 counts for three units per time executed (one multiplication, one addition, and one assignment) and is executed n times, for a total of $3n$ units. Line 2 has the hidden costs of initializing i, testing $i \leq n$, and incrementing i. The total of all these is 1 to initialize, $n+1$ for all the tests, and n for all the increments, which is $2n+2$. Thus, the run time of this algorithm is given by:

$$T(n) = 5n + 4$$

Example 1.7: Algorithm 1.9 searches a target item (*key*) in the given list of size *n*. The algorithm returns the location (index) of the list where *key* is found; otherwise null.

```
Algorithm 1.9: LinearSearch(a[1..n], n, key)
1.  For i = 1 to n do
2.      If a[i] = key, then
3.          Return i            // search is successful
4.      Endif
5.  Endfor
6.  Return null                 // search is unsuccessful
```

The following analysis can be carried out looking at the LinearSearch algorithm:

- Best case: $a[1] = key$. When the key is found at the first location, the number of primitive operations is 5 (irrespective of list size, *n*). Line 1: assigning 1 to *i* at the beginning of for loop – this action corresponds to executing one primitive operation. Condition $i \leq n$ is tested before entering the body of the for loop. This action contains one primitive operation. Line 2: $a[i]$ is compared with *key* (two primitive operations – indexing and comparing), and at line 3, Return *i* corresponds to one primitive operation.

- Worst case: When the key is not found in the list, the total number of primitive operations is $5n+5$. Line 1: assigning 1 to *i* at the beginning of for loop – this action corresponds to executing one primitive operation (only once). Condition $i \leq n$ is tested before entering the body of the for loop. This action contains one primitive operation. Index *i* is incremented: $i=i+1$ (two primitive operations – summing and assigning). These three primitive operations (testing $i \leq n$ and incrementing index) are performed $n+1$ times. Line 2: $a[i]$ is compared with *key* (two primitive operations – indexing and comparing) - these two primitive operations are performed *n* times. Two more primitive operations are considered – that is, one initialization and one return null (line 6). Therefore, $T(n) = 1 + 3(n+1) + 2n + 1 = 5n+5$.

Example 1.8: We analyze the Algorithm 1.6: *arrayMax* similar to Example 1.7.

- Best case ($T(n) = 5n$) occurs when $a[1]$ is the maximum element, so that variable *max* is never reassigned.

- Worst case ($T(n) = 7n\text{-}2$) occurs when the maximum element happens to be the last element (in case of array is sorted in ascending), so that the variable *max* is reassigned at each iteration of the for loop.

1.4 ASYMPTOTIC NOTATION

Asymptotic analysis of algorithms is a means of comparing relative performance. Time complexity of an algorithm concerns determining an expression of the number of primitive operations (i.e., step count) needed as a function of the problem size. Since the step count measure is somewhat rough, one does not aim at obtaining an exact step count. Instead, one attempts only to get asymptotic bounds on the step count. Asymptotic analysis makes use of the

O (Big-Oh) notation. Two other notational constructs used in the analysis of algorithms are Θ (Big-Theta) notation and Ω (Big-Omega) notation.

In general, each step in the algorithm corresponds to a small number of primitive operations that does not depend on the input size. Thus, we can perform simplified analysis that estimates the number of primitive operations executed up to a constant factor. Algorithm *LinearSearch* executes $5n+5$ primitive operations in the worst-case. Let $T(n)$ be worst-case time of *LinearSearch.* Then

$$a(5n+5) \leq T(n) \leq b(5n+5)$$

where a is the time taken by the fastest primitive operation, and b is the time taken by the slowest primitive operation. Hence, the running time $T(n)$ is bounded by two linear functions.

The change of hardware/software environment affects $T(n)$ by a constant factor, but does not alter the growth rate of $T(n)$. The linear growth rate of the running time $T(n)$ is an inherent property of algorithm *LinearSearch.*

The growth rate is not affected by constant factors or lower-order terms. For example, $7n + 15$ is a linear function and $5n^2 + 8n$ is a quadratic function.

1.4.1 Big-Oh Notation

Given functions $f(n)$ and $g(n)$, we say that $f(n)$ is $O(g(n))$ if there are positive constants $c > 0$ and $n_0 \geq 1$ such that

$$f(n) \leq cg(n) \quad \text{for all } n, n \geq n_0$$

This definition is referred to as the "big-Oh" notation. Alternatively, we can also say "$f(n)$ is *order* of $g(n)$". This definition is illustrated in Figure 1.2 (the value of $f(n)$ always lies on or below $cg(n)$).

The big-Oh notation gives an upper bound on the growth rate of a function. The statement "$f(n)$ is $O(g(n))$" means that the growth rate of $f(n)$ is no more than the growth rate of $g(n)$.

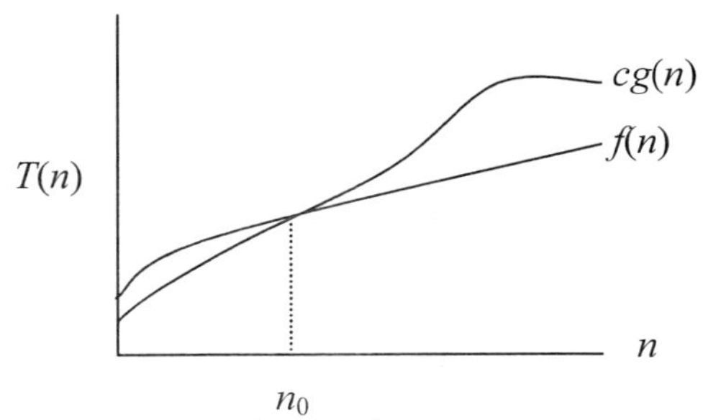

Figure 1.2: $f(n)$ is $O(g(n))$, for $f(n) \leq cg(n)$ when $n \geq n_0$

The following example illustrates that $f(n)$ is $O(g(n))$, for $f(n) \leq cg(n)$ when $n \geq n_0$.

Let $f(n) = 4n^2 + 7n + 12$, and

$g(n) = n^2$
For $n > 8$ and $c = 5$, $f(n) \le 5g(n)$
We verify this by substituting for $n = 9$, we have

$$4(9^2) + 7(9) + 12 \le 5(9^2)$$
$$399 \le 405$$

For large enough n, $f(n)$ is bounded above by $5g(n)$.
We write $f(n) = O(g(n))$
$4n^2 + 7n + 12 = O(n^2)$.

Example 1.9: $2n + 10$ is $O(n)$.
By O-notation, we need to find a real constant $c > 0$ and an integer constant $n_0 \ge 1$, such that $2n + 10 \le cn$.

$$2n + 10 \le cn$$
$$(c-2)\, n \ge 10$$
$$n \ge 10 / (c-2)$$

A possible choice is $c = 3$ and $n_0 = 10$. This is one of the many choices.

Example 1.10: n^2 is not $O(n)$.

$n^2 \le cn$
$n \le c$ (after dividing by n on both sides)

This inequality cannot be satisfied since c must be a constant.

Example 1.11: $(n+1)^2 = n^2 + 2n + 1$ is $O(n^2)$.

$$(n+1)^2 \le cn^2$$

This needs $c > 0$ and $n_0 \ge 1$ such that $(n+1)^2 \le cn^2$ for $n \ge n_0$.
This is true for $c = 4$ and $n_0 = 1$ → $(1+1)^2 \le 4(1)^2$

Example 1.12: $3n^3 + 20n^2 + 5$ is $O(n^3)$.
This needs $c > 0$ and $n_0 \ge 1$ such that $3n^3 + 20n^2 + 5 \le cn^3$ for $n \ge n_0$.
This is true for $c = 4$ and $n_0 = 21$ → $3(21)^3 + 20(21)^2 + 5 \le 4(21)^3$
$36608 \le 37044$

Example 1.13: $\log n + \log\log n$ is $O(\log n)$. Note: $\log n$ is $\log_2 n$
This needs $c > 0$ and $n_0 \ge 1$ such that $\log n + \log\log n \le c\log n$ for $n \ge n_0$.
This is true for $c = 4$ and $n_0 = 2$ → $\log(2) + \log(\log(2)) \le 4(\log(2))$
$1 + \log(1) \le 4(1)$ ($\log_2 2 = 1$)
$1 + 0 \le 4$

Big-Oh Rules:

- If $f(n)$ is a polynomial of degree k, then $f(n)$ is $O(n^k)$, i.e., drop lower-order terms and constant factors (see Example 1.11).
- Use the smallest possible class of functions - say "$2n$ is $O(n)$" instead of "$2n$ is $O(n^2)$".

- Use the simplest expression of the class - say "$3n + 5$ is $O(n)$" instead of "$3n + 5$ is $O(3n)$".

In computing, we categorize the algorithms according to their asymptotic run-time functions. The run-time behaviour of most algorithms falls into one of only about seven primary categories: $O(1)$, $O(\log n)$, $O(n)$, $O(n \log n)$, $O(n^2)$, $O(n^3)$, and $O(2^n)$. These are known as *complexity classes* or *asymptotic growth classes.*

Figure 1.3 shows the relative growth rates of seven orders in the order hierarchy. This figure indicates why *Big-Oh* differences eventually dominate other factors in estimating the behaviour of functions.

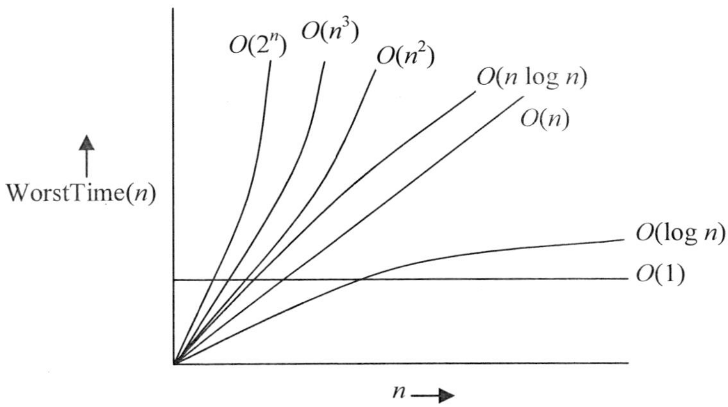

Figure 1.3: Comparison of WorstTime(n) for seven orders of functions

Typical Running Times of Algorithms

- $O(1)$ - *constant*: The running time of the algorithm is constant.

  Example: Retrieve an element from an array, given its index. Since the index provides direct access into the array, the time it takes to complete this task is independent of the size n of the array.

- $O(\log n)$ - *logarithmic*: Typically achieved by dividing the problem into smaller segments and only looking at one input element in each segment.

  Example: Binary search

- $O(n)$ - *linear*: Typically achieved by examining each element in the input once.

  Example: Find the minimum element of an array.

- $O(n \log n)$ – *linear-logarithmic*: Typically achieved by dividing the problem into sub-problems, solving the sub-problems independently, and then combining the results. Unlike the $\log n$ algorithms, each element in the sub-problems must be examined.

  Example: Merge sort

- $O(n^2)$ - *quadratic*: Typically achieved by examining all pairs of data elements.

  Example: Selection Sort

- $O(n^3)$ - *cubic*: Often achieved by combining algorithms with a mixture of the previous running times.

  Example: Matrix Multiplication - Each item in the result matrix is obtained by multiplying together two vectors of size n. This requires n time. Since there are n^2 elements in the resulting matrix, it takes n^3 time to compute the entire resulting matrix.

- $O(2^n)$ - *exponential*: Any exponential function with a base strictly greater than 1 grows faster than any polynomial function (n^2 or n^3). Fibonacci numbers grow exponentially.

  Example: A brute-force approach to solve the longest common subsequence problem requires exponential time.

1.4.2 Big-Omega Notation

As O-notation provides an asymptotic *upper* bound on a function, Ω-notation provides an *asymptotic lower bound.* Given functions $f(n)$ and $g(n)$, we say that $f(n)$ is $\Omega(g(n))$ if there are positive constants $c > 0$ and $n_0 \geq 1$ such that

$$f(n) \geq cg(n) \quad \text{for all } n, n \geq n_0$$

This definition is referred to as the "big-Omega" notation and is illustrated in Figure 1.4: for all values n to the right of n_0, the value of $f(n)$ is on or above $cg(n)$.

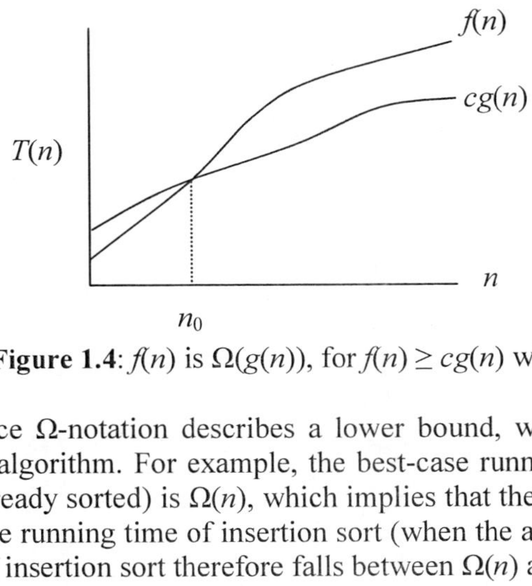

Figure 1.4: $f(n)$ is $\Omega(g(n))$, for $f(n) \geq cg(n)$ when $n \geq n_0$

Example 1.14: Since Ω-notation describes a lower bound, we use it to bound the best-case running time of an algorithm. For example, the best-case running time of insertion sort (when the input array is already sorted) is $\Omega(n)$, which implies that the running time of insertion sort is $\Omega(n)$. The worst-case running time of insertion sort (when the array is in reverse order) is $O(n^2)$. The running time of insertion sort therefore falls between $\Omega(n)$ and $O(n^2)$, since it falls anywhere between a linear function of n and a quadratic function of n.

1.4.3 Big-Theta Notation

Let $f(n)$ and $g(n)$ be two asymptotically positive real-valued functions. We say that $f(n)$ is $\Theta(g(n))$ if there is an integer n_0 and positive real constants c_1 and c_2 such that $c_1g(n) \leq f(n) \leq c_2g(n)$ for all $n \geq n_0$ (to the right of n_0 the value of $f(n)$ always lies between $c_1g(n)$ and $c_2g(n)$ inclusive).

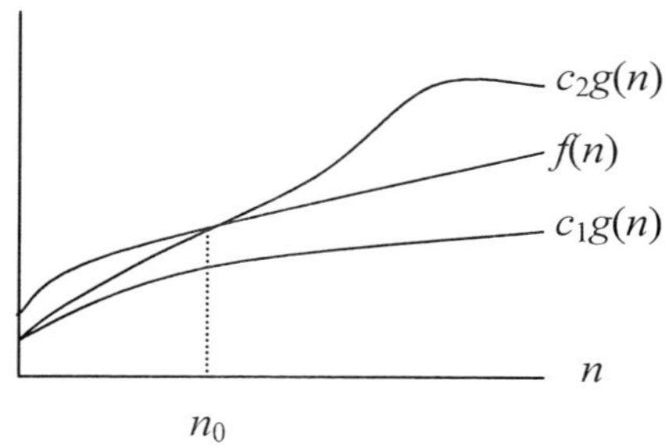

Figure 1.5: $f(n)$ is $\Theta(g(n))$, for $c_1g(n) \le f(n) \le c_2g(n)$ when $n \ge n_0$

Example 1.15: $f(n) = 3n^2 + 7n - 5$.
For large values of n, $7n - 5$ is insignificant compared to $3n^2$, so we would expect that $f(n)$ is $\Theta(3n^2)$. In fact, since constant multiples are not significant, we expect that $f(n)$ is $\Theta(n^2)$. We could note that for $n \ge 1$, $7n - 5 \ge 0$ and so $3n^2 + 7n - 5 \ge 3n^2$. And we could note that for $n \ge 7$,

$$3n^2 + 7n - 5 \le 3n^2 + 7n \le 3n^2 + n^2 \le 4n^2.$$

$$3(7^2)+7(7)-5 \le 3(7^2)+7(7) \le 3(7^2)+7^2 \le 4(7^2)$$

$$191 \le 196 \le 196 \le 196$$

So we have, taking $g(n) = n^2$, that $3g(n) \le f(n) \le 4g(n)$ for all $n \ge 7$.
Taking $n_0 = 7$, $c_1 = 3$, and $c_2 = 4$ in the definition, we have proved that $f(n)$ is $\Theta(n^2)$.

In practice, we will almost always work informally, using the two rules that a constant multiple can be ignored and that lower order terms in a summation can be ignored. Using these rules, we can say immediately, for example, that $7n^3 - 2n^2 + 12n$ is $\Theta(n^3)$.

1.4.4 Little-oh Notation

The asymptotic upper bound provided by O-notation may or may not be asymptoti-cally tight. The bound $2n^2 = O(n^2)$ is asymptotically tight, but the bound $2n = O(n^2)$ is not. We use o-notation to denote an upper bound that is not asymptotically tight.

Suppose $f(n)$ and $g(n)$ are real valued functions defined for all $n > n_0$ (where n_0 is a fixed positive real). We write

$f(n)$ is $o(g(n))$

if and only if

$$\lim_{n\to\infty} \frac{f(n)}{g(n)} = 0$$

That is, if eventually $f(n)/g(n)$ becomes less than any given positive number. "$f(n) = o(g(n))$" means for all $c > 0$ there exists some $n_0 > 0$ such that $0 \le f(n) < cg(n)$ for all $n \ge n_0$. The value of

n_0 must not depend on n, but may depend on c. For example, $2n = O(n^2)$, but $2n^2 \neq o(n^2)$. Examples: $10000n = o(n^2)$, $\log(n) = o(n)$, Notice that $f(n) = o(g(n))$ implies, and is stronger than, $f(n) = O(g(n))$. Little-o is like big-O, but it gives an upper bound that is not asymptotically tight.

Alternatively, "$f(n)$ is little o of $g(n)$" if and only if $f(n) = O(g(n))$, but $f(n) \neq \Theta(g(n))$.

We often use the little-oh notation this way:

$$f(n) = g(n) + o(h(n)).$$

This intuitively means that the error in using $g(n)$ to approximate $f(n)$ is negligible in comparison to $h(n)$.

Little-omega is like Big-Omega, but it gives a lower bound that is not asymptoti-cally tight. If $f(n)$ is $\omega(g(n))$, then the growth rate of $f(n)$ is greater than the growth rate of $g(n)$. $f(n)$ is $\omega(g(n))$ if and only if there exist positive constants c and n_0 such that $f(n) > cg(n)$, for all $n \geq n_0$. Alternatively, $f(n)$ is $\omega(g(n))$, if and only if

$$\lim_{n\to\infty} \frac{f(n)}{g(n)} = \infty$$

Example 1.16: The function $f(n) = 12n^2 + 6n$ is $o(n^3)$ and $\omega(n)$.
Let us verify that $f(n)$ is $o(n^3)$. Let $c > 0$. We take $n_0 > 12$ (or $n_0 \geq 13$).

$$12n^2 + 6n < cn^3$$
$$12(13^2) + 6(13) < c(13^3)$$
$$2106 \quad < \quad c(2197)$$

For $c = 1, 2, 3, \ldots$, the above "less than" inequality satisfies. Hence, $f(n)$ is $o(n^3)$ – that is, $f(n) < cg(n)$.

To show that $f(n)$ is $\omega(n)$, let $c > 0$. If we take $n_0 = c/12$, then, for $n \geq n_0$.

$$12n^2 + 6n > cn$$
$$12(c^2/12^2) + 6(c/12) > c(c/12)$$
$$(c/12)(c + 6) > (c/12)c$$
$$c + 6 > c$$

Hence, $f(n)$ is $\omega(n)$ – that is, $f(n) > cg(n)$.

1.5 RECURRENCE RELATIONS

An algorithm is recursive if it can call itself. Recursive algorithms generally solve a problem by reducing the problem to an in instance of the same problem with smaller input. Often times, a recursive solution to a problem is the most natural, and therefore gives the simplest procedure. We note the following two points:

- Always identify the base case and associated result first.
- Make sure the recursive call is for a smaller problem (one closer to the base case).

When an algorithm contains a recursive call to itself, its running time can often be described by a recurrence. A recurrence relation is an equation or inequality that describes a function in terms of its value on smaller inputs. What we must now do is associate with each recursive algorithm an unknown time function $T(n)$, where n measures the size of the arguments to the algorithm. We can then get a recurrence for $T(n)$, that is an equation for $T(n)$ in terms of $T(k)$ for various values of k.

Here we shall present how to analyze a simple recursive algorithm. Let us consider the classical example of computing the factorial of a number.

Example 1.17: The factorial function is given as, $f(n)$:

$n! = n \times (n-1) \times (n-2) \times \ldots \times 2 \times 1$, where n is an integer.

Algorithm 1.7 computes the factorial of an integer, n recursively. An appropriate size measure for this function is the value of n. Let $T(n)$ be the running time for Factorial(n). Running time for lines 1 and 2 is $O(1)$, and for line 4 it is $O(1)+T(n-1)$. The Factorial(n) is called (n-1) times. Thus, for some constants c and d,

$$T(n) = \begin{cases} d, & if \quad n = 1 \\ c + T(n-1), & if \quad n > 1 \end{cases} \qquad (1.1)$$

We substitute in (1.1) for $n = 1, 2, 3, \ldots, (n-2), (n-1)$.

$T(1) = d$ for $n = 1$
$T(2) = c + T(1) = c + d$ for $n > 1$
$T(3) = c + T(2) = c + (c + d) = 2c + d$ for $n > 2$
$T(4) = c + T(3) = c + (2c + d) = 3c + d$ for $n > 3$
. . .
$T(n-2) = c + T((n-2)-1) = c + T(n-3)$ by substituting n-2 for n
$T(n-1) = c + T((n-1)-1) = c + T(n-2) = c + (c + T(n-3)) = 2c + T(n-3)$
$T(n) = c + T(n-1) = c + (2c + T(n-3)) = 3c + T(n-3)$ if $n > 3$

and so on. In general,

$T(n) = ic + T(n-i)$ if $n > i$

Finally, when $i = n-1$, we get

$T(n) = ic + T(n-i) = (n-1)c + T(n-(n-1)) = c(n-1) + T(1)$

$T(n) = c(n-1) + d$ (1.2)

From (1.2), we can conclude that $T(n)$ is $O(n)$.

The general method for solving recurrence equations, as illustrated by Example 1.17, is repeatedly to replace terms $T(k)$ on the right side of the equation by the entire right side with k substituted for n, until we obtain a formula in which T does not appear on the right as in (1.2). Often we must then sum a series or, if we cannot sum it exactly, we get a close upper bound on the sum to obtain an upper bound on $T(n)$.

Example 1.18: Another classical example used to demonstrate the power of recursion in problem solving is the Towers of Hanoi puzzle. In this puzzle, we are given three pegs labeled

A, *B*, and *C*. Initially, a tower of '*n*' disks of different sizes is stacked on peg *A* in order of decreasing size. That is, the largest disk is on the bottom, and the smallest disk is on the top of the tower as shown in Figure 1.6. The objective is to transfer the entire '*n*' disks on peg *A* to peg *C* (using peg *B* as an auxiliary tower), moving only one disk at a time, and never moving a larger disk on top of a smaller disk.

Consider the case of $n = 2$. We can solve this puzzle by first moving the top disk on peg *A* to peg *B*, then moving the lone remaining disk on peg *A* to peg *C*, and finally moving the disk on peg *B* to peg *C*. The two disks on peg *A* has now been moved from peg *A* to peg *C*, without violating any of the constraints in the puzzle. This has taken three moves which is a minimum. This solution demonstrates two important topics: (1) recursive functions and stacks, and (2) recurrence relations.

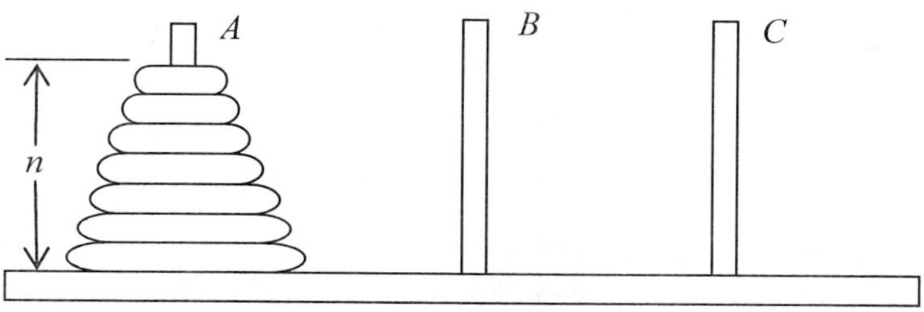

Figure 1.6: Initial setup for the Towers of Hanoi puzzle

Algorithm 1.10: Hanoi(*n*, *A*, *B*, *C*)

```
1.  If n = 1, then
2.      Move from A to C
3.  Else
4.      Hanoi(n-1, A, C, B)
5.      Move from A to C
6.      Hanoi(n-1, B, A, C)
```

For $n = 3$, the algorithm translates into the following 7 moves. An example of a recursion tree that illustrates the recursive procedure calls used by Hanoi() when $n = 3$ is given in Figure 1.7.

1. Move from *A* to *C*
2. Move from *A* to *B*
3. Move from *C* to *B*
4. Move from *A* to *C*
5. Move from *B* to *A*
6. Move from *B* to *C*
7. Move from *A* to *C*

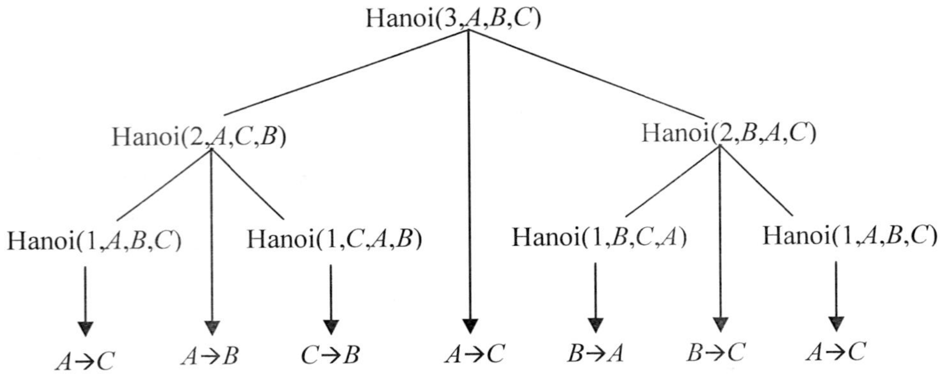

Figure 1.7: Recursion tree that results when Towers of Hanoi algorithm is invoked with Hanoi(3, *A*, *B*, *C*)

Notice that any activation of Hanoi() when $n > 1$ will involve the initiation of two recursive calls, one on line 4 and one on line 6. The recursion tree can often be used to visualize two recursive calls.

If we let $T(n)$ represent the number of moves needed to solve the Towers of Hanoi puzzle when there are n disks, then it is easy to see that for the Hanoi() algorithm,

$$T(n) = \begin{cases} 1 & \text{if } n = 1 \\ 2T(n-1)+1 & \text{if } n > 1 \end{cases} \qquad (1.3)$$

Specifically, if $n > 1$ our solution requires the moving of two stacks of n-1 disks (line 4 and line 6), each requiring $T(n\text{-}1)$ moves, plus one additional disk (line 5).

Given the equation (1.3), we can calculate $T(n)$ for any value of n by first calculating $T(1)$ given $T(0)$, and the calculating $T(2)$ from $T(1)$, and so on, until we reach $T(n)$. We later prove that the following equation (1.4) gives the same results as equation (1.3):

$$T(n) = 2^n - 1 \qquad \text{for } n \geq 1 \qquad (1.4)$$

Equation (1.4) is the closed form of recurrence relation (1.3). The closed form means that we can compute the result by using a fixed number of operations. The advantage of closed form expressions for recurrence relations is that they give us a better understanding of the behaviour of the algorithm that the recurrence relation describes.

One of the most useful methods for solving a recurrence relation is to make an educated guess at the closed form, and then prove that this guess is correct. This involves examining the recurrence for small values of n, and then concluding a guess at the closed form. We consider the recurrence relation (1.3) and observe $T(n)$ for small values of n (n = 1, 2, 3, 4, 5):

$$\begin{aligned}
T(1) &= 1 && \rightarrow 2^1 - 1 \\
T(2) &= 2T(n\text{-}1) + 1 = 2T(1) + 1 = 2(1) + 1 = 3 && \rightarrow 2^2 - 1 \\
T(3) &= 2T(n\text{-}1) + 1 = 2T(2) + 1 = 2(3) + 1 = 7 && \rightarrow 2^3 - 1 \\
T(4) &= 2T(n\text{-}1) + 1 = 2T(3) + 1 = 2(7) + 1 = 15 && \rightarrow 2^4 - 1 \\
T(5) &= 2T(n\text{-}1) + 1 = 2T(4) + 1 = 2(15) + 1 = 31 && \rightarrow 2^5 - 1
\end{aligned}$$

From this sequence, it shows that $T(n)$ is always one less than a power of 2. That is:

$$T(n) = 2^n - 1 \qquad \text{for } n \geq 1 \qquad (1.5)$$

This appears to be a good guess at the closed form. We have already shown that (1.5) is correct for $0 \leq n \leq 5$, but does this prove that the proposed closed form is correct for all n? We can now test this by *mathematical induction*.

The induction hypothesis is that $T(\alpha) = 2^\alpha - 1$ for $1 \leq \alpha \leq n\text{-}1$. At $n = 1$, we have $T(1) = 2^1 - 1 = 1$, which agrees with the recurrence relation for the base case. By substituting the induction hypothesis into equation (1.3), we get:

$$\begin{aligned} T(n) &= 2T(n\text{-}1) + 1 \\ &= 2(2^{n\text{-}1} - 1) + 1 \qquad \text{(because } T(n) = 2^n - 1\text{, and } T(n\text{-}1) = 2^{n\text{-}1} - 1\text{)} \\ &= 2(2^{n\text{-}1}) - 2 + 1 \\ &= 2^n - 1 \end{aligned}$$

We have proven that equation (1.5) is true for all $n \geq 1$.

Recurrence relations are particularly well suited for solution by mathematical induction; however, it requires that we make an appropriate guess.

Bounding Recurrence Relations: When analyzing a recurrence relation that depicts the resources used by an algorithm, we are interested in finding the tightest possible asymptotic bound on the closed form. Thus, instead of determining the exact closed form, and then expressing this solution using asymptotic notation, it is often easier to make a guess directly at the asymptotic form of the solution, and then verify this guess using induction. This technique is known as *constructive induction* because it allows us to fill the missing specifications necessary to prove some assertion (or statement).

Example 1.19: Consider the recurrence relation:

$$T(n) = \begin{cases} 1 & \text{if } n = 1 \\ T(n-1) + n & \text{if } n > 1 \end{cases} \qquad (1.6)$$

If we wish to prove that $T(n) = O(n^2)$, then it is sufficient to show that $T(n) \leq cn^2$ for some positive constant $c > 0$, and for all values of $n > n_0$ (n_0 is a positive constant). First, we will assume that $T(\alpha) \leq c\alpha^2$ for $1 \leq \alpha \leq n\text{-}1$. Then we will use this induction hypothesis to show that $T(n) \leq cn^2$. By substituting the induction hypothesis into equation (1.6), we get the following steps:

$$\begin{aligned} T(n) &= T(n - 1) + n \\ &\leq c(n - 1)^2 + n \qquad \text{if } T(n) \leq cn^2\text{, then } T(n - 1) \leq c(n - 1)^2 \\ &= c(n^2 - 2n + 1) + n \\ &= cn^2 - 2cn + c + n \\ &\leq cn^2 \end{aligned}$$

$T(n) \leq cn^2$ holds for all $n \geq 1$ when $c = 1$. This means that $n_0 \geq 1$. From (1.6), we have that $T(1) = 1$, and from the induction hypothesis $T(1) = c(1)^2$. Choosing $c = 1$ will also satisfy this base case, and hence $T(n) = O(n^2)$.

Backward Substitution and Iteration: In this method we simply continue to substitute back until we see a pattern of some sort. We then deduce a formula from the pattern. Once we discover a likely formula we prove that the formula actually solves the relation.

Example 1.20: Solve the following recurrence using iteration.

$$T(n) = \begin{cases} 1 & \text{if } n = 1 \\ 2T(n/2) + n & \text{if } n > 1 \end{cases} \quad (1.7)$$

Since $T(n/2) = 2T(n/4) + n/2$, we have

$$T(n) = 2(2T(n/4) + n/2)) + n = 4T(n/4) + 2n$$

Substituting for $T(n/4)$, we obtain

$$T(n) = 4(2T(n/8) + n/4)) + 2n = 8T(n/8) + 3n$$

Continuing in this manner, we find that

$$T(n) = 2^k T(n/2^k) + kn$$

After $\log_2 n$ substitutions ($k = \log_2 n$), we have

$$T(n) = 2^{\log_2 n} \times T(n/2^{\log_2 n}) + \log_2 n \times n$$

Noting that $2^{\log_2 n} = n$, we have

$$T(n) = n \times T(n/n) + \log_2 n \times n$$

$$T(n) = n \times T(1) + \log_2 n \times n$$

$$T(n) = n + n\log_2 n \qquad \text{because } T(1) = 1$$

1.5.1 The Master Method

The master method provides a "cookbook" method for solving recurrences of the form:

$$T(n) = aT(n/b) + f(n) \qquad (1.8)$$

where $a \geq 1$ and $b > 1$ are constants and $f(n)$ is an asymptotically positive function. The master method requires memorization of three cases, but then the solution of many recurrences can be determined quite easily.

The recurrence (1.8) describes the running time of an algorithm that divides a problem of size n into 'a' subproblems, each of size n/b, where a and b are positive constants. The 'a' subproblems are solved recursively, each in time $T(n/b)$. The cost of dividing the problem and combining the results of the subproblems is described by the function $f(n)$.

As a matter of technical correctness, the recurrence is not actually well defined because n/b might not be an integer. Replacing each of the a terms $T(n/b)$ with either $T(\lfloor n/b \rfloor)$ or $T(\lceil n/b \rceil)$ does not affect the asymptotic behavior of the recurrence, however. We normally find it convenient, therefore, to omit the floor and ceiling functions when writing divide-and-conquer recurrences of this form.

The master theorem: Let $a \geq 1$ and $b > 1$ be constants, let $f(n)$ be a function, and let $T(n)$ be defined on the nonnegative integers by the recurrence

$$T(n) = aT(n/b) + f(n)$$

where we interpret n/b to mean either $\lfloor n/b \rfloor$ or $\lceil n/b \rceil$. Then $T(n)$ can be bounded asymptotically as follows.

1. If $f(n) = O(n^{\log_b a-\varepsilon})$ for some constant $\varepsilon > 0$, then $T(n) = \Theta(n^{\log_b a})$.
2. If $f(n) = \Theta(n^{\log_b a})$, then $T(n) = \Theta(n^{\log_b a} \log_2 n)$.
3. If $f(n) = \Omega(n^{\log_b a+\varepsilon})$ for some constant $\varepsilon > 0$, and if $af(n/b) \le cf(n)$ for some constant $c < 1$ and all sufficiently large n, then $T(n) = \Theta(f(n))$.

Before applying the master theorem to some examples, let us spend a moment trying to understand what it says. In each of the three cases, we are comparing the function $f(n)$ with the function $n^{\log_b a}$. Intuitively, the solution to the recurrence is determined by the larger of the two functions. If, as in case 1, the function $n^{\log_b a}$ is the larger, then the solution is $T(n) = \Theta(n^{\log_b a})$. If, as in case 3, the function $f(n)$ is the larger, then the solution is $T(n) = \Theta(f(n))$. If, as in case 2, the two functions are the same size, we multiply by a logarithmic factor, and the solution is $T(n) = \Theta(n^{\log_b a} \log_2 n) = \Theta(f(n)\log_2 n)$.

Example 1.21: To use the master method, we simply determine which case (if any) of the master theorem applies and write down the answer. Consider the recurrence:

$$T(n) = 9T(n/3) + n.$$

For this recurrence, we have $a = 9$, $b = 3$, $f(n) = n$, and thus we have that

$$n^{\log_b a} = n^{\log_3 9} = n^{\log_3 3^2} = \Theta(n^2).$$

Since $f(n) = O(n^{\log_3 9-\varepsilon})$, where $\varepsilon = 1$, we can apply case 1 of the master theorem and conclude that the solution is $T(n) = \Theta(n^2)$.

Example 1.22: Consider the following recurrence:

$$T(n) = T(2n/3) + 1,$$

in which $a = 1$, $b = 3/2$, $f(n) = 1$, and $n^{\log_b a} = n^{\log_{3/2} 1} = n^0 = 1$ (note: log(1) to any base is 0). Case 2 applies, since $f(n) = \Theta(n^{\log_b a}) = \Theta(1)$, and thus the solution to the recurrence is given by:

$$\begin{aligned} T(n) &= \Theta(n^{\log_b a} \log_2 n) \\ &= \Theta(1 \text{ x } \log_2 n) \\ &= \Theta(\log_2 n). \end{aligned}$$

Example 1.23: Consider the following recurrence:

$$T(n) = 3T(n/4) + n\log_2 n.$$

We have $a = 3$, $b = 4$, $f(n) = n\log_2 n$, and $n^{\log_b a} = n^{\log_4 3} = O(n^{0.793})$. Since $f(n) = \Omega(n^{\log_4 3+\varepsilon})$, where $\varepsilon \approx 0.2$, case 3 applies for $f(n)$. For sufficiently large n, $af(n/b) = 3(n/4)\log_2(n/4) \leq (3/4)n\log_2 n = cf(n)$ for $c = 3/4$. Consequently, by case 3, the solution to the recurrence is $T(n) = \Theta(f(n)) = \Theta(n\log_2 n)$.

The following table shows some common recurrence relations (d indicates a constant):

Table 1.1: Some Common Recurrences

Recurrence	*Solution*
$T(n) = T(n/2) + d$	$T(n) = O(\log_2 n)$
$T(n) = T(n/2) + n$	$T(n) = O(n)$
$T(n) = 2T(n/2) + d$	$T(n) = O(n)$
$T(n) = 2T(n/2) + n$	$T(n) = O(n \log_2 n)$
$T(n) = T(n\text{-}1) + d$	$T(n) = O(n)$

1.6 PROBABILISTIC ANALYSIS

In analysis of algorithms, there are two measures of performance that are usually considered. These are the worst-case and average-case behaviour of the algorithm. These two measures can be applied to both the time and space complexity of an algorithm. The worst-case complexity for a given problem size n corresponds to the maximum complexity among all problems of size n. Determination of the worst-case complexity for many algorithms is relatively easy.

In many practical applications, it is important to have a measure of the *expected complexity* of a given algorithm rather than the worst-case behaviour. The expected complexity gives a measure of the behaviour of the algorithm *averaged* over all possible problems of size n. Computation of average complexity of an algorithm involves complex and sophisticated mathematical analysis.

Probabilistic analysis of algorithms is an approach to estimate the complexity of an algorithm. It starts from an assumption about a probabilistic distribution of the set of all possible inputs. This assumption is then used to design an efficient algorithm or to compute an expected running time of a known algorithm. The following is a simple example on probabilistic average-case analysis.

Example 1.24: Consider Algorithm 1.9 LinearSearch which searches a target element, x in the given list of size n. In the worst-case, the algorithm will examine all n elements in the list before terminating. The average-case situation is somewhat different. For a probabilistic average-case analysis, it is generally assumed that all possible terminations are equally likely – that is, the probability that x will be found at position 1 is $1/n$, at position 2 is $1/n$, and so on. The average search cost is therefore the sum of all possible search costs each multiplied by their associated probability. For instance, if $n = 5$, we would have:

$$\text{Average search cost} = \frac{1}{5}(1+2+3+4+5) = 3$$

In general case, we have:

$$\text{Average search cost} = \frac{1}{n}\left(\frac{n(n+1)}{2}\right) = \frac{n+1}{2}$$

Example 1.25: Consider a slightly complicated example of binary search Algorithm 1.11. Given an element x and an ordered list (in ascending order), find whether or not x is present in the list of size, n. What we wish to establish in this analysis is the *average number of iterations* of the search loop that are required before the algorithm terminates in a *successful* search. The algorithm terminates as soon as the search value, x is found in the list, a. The associated binary search tree for an array of size 15 is given in Figure 1.8.

Algorithm 1.11: BinarySearch(a[1..n], n, x)

```
low = 1
high = n
While (low ≤ high)
    mid = (low + high) / 2
    If (a[mid] > x)
          high = mid – 1
    else If (a[mid] < x)
          low = mid + 1
    else
          return mid          // found
    Endif
Endwhile
return -1                     // not found
```

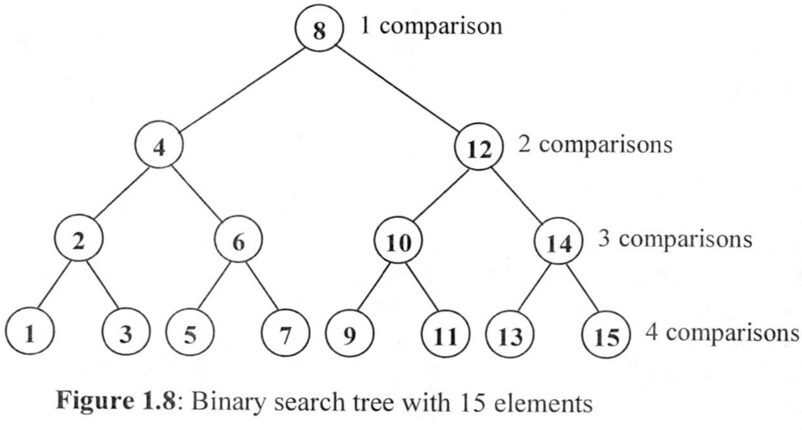

Figure 1.8: Binary search tree with 15 elements

Referring to the binary search tree, we infer that 1 element can be found with 1 comparison, 2 elements with 2 comparisons, 4 elements with 3 comparisons, and so on – that is, sum over all possible elements = 1 + 2 + 2 + 3 + 3 + 3 + 3 + 4 + ... In general, 2^i elements require i+1 comparisons. We assume that all elements present in the array are equally likely to be found – that is, search follows a uniform probability distribution. Then, their probability of retrieval is $1/n$, and the average search cost is the sum over all possible search costs, each multiplied by their associated probability. That is (lg n represents $\log_2 n$):

$$\text{Average search cost} = \frac{1}{n}\sum_{i=0}^{\lfloor \lg n \rfloor}(i+1)\times 2^i = \frac{1}{n}\left\{\sum_{i=0}^{\lfloor \lg n \rfloor} i\times 2^i + n\right\} \qquad (1.9)$$

This formula is exact only when n is one less than a power of 2. Some calculus is required to evaluate the sum:

$$\text{sum} = \sum_{i=0}^{\lfloor \lg n \rfloor} i\times 2^i$$

We may recognize that this sum is a geometric progression and we know that in general:

$$1 + x + x^2 + x^k = \frac{x^{k-1}-1}{x-1}$$

We may also note that:

$$i\times 2^i = \frac{d}{dx}(2x^i) \qquad x = 2$$

It follows that to compute this sum, we can take the derivative of $(x^{k-1} - 1)/(x-1)$ multiplied by 2 and evaluating at x=2 where $k = \lfloor \lg n \rfloor$. When this is done, we get:

$$\text{sum} = \sum_{i=0}^{\lfloor \lg n \rfloor} i\times 2^i = (n+1)(\lfloor \lg n \rfloor - 1) + 2 = (n+1)(\lfloor \lg n \rfloor + 1)$$

And, after substituting for the sum in the average search cost expression (1.9), we find:

$$\text{Average search cost} = \frac{(n+1)\lfloor \lg n \rfloor + 1}{n} \approx \lfloor \lg n \rfloor \qquad \text{for sufficiently large } n.$$

1.7 AMORTIZED ANALYSIS

Webster's dictionary defines "amortize" as "to put money aside at intervals for gradual payment of a debt, etc". This term is adapted for computational complexity, meaning by it "to average the running times of operations in a sequence over the sequence".

Amortized analysis refers to finding the average running time per operation over a worst-case sequence of operations. Amortized analysis differs from average-case performance in that probability is not involved; amortized analysis guarantees the time per operation over worst-case performance.

The method requires knowledge of which series of operations are possible. This is most commonly the case with data structures, which have state that carries on between operations. The basic idea is that a worst-case operation can alter the state in such a way that the worst-case cannot occur again for a long time, thus "amortizing" its cost.

As a simple example, in a specific implementation of the dynamic array, we double the size of the array each time it fills up. Because of this, array reallocation may be required, and in the worst-case an insertion may require $O(n)$. However, a sequence of n insertions can always be done in $O(n)$ time, so the amortized time per operation is $O(n)/n = O(1)$.

Notice that average-case analysis and probabilistic analysis are not the same thing as amortized analysis. In average-case analysis, we are averaging over all possible inputs; in probabilistic analysis, we are averaging over all possible random choices; in amortized analysis, we are averaging over a sequence of operations. Amortized analysis assumes worst-case input and typically does not allow random choices.

There are several techniques used in amortized analysis:

- *Aggregate analysis* determines the upper bound $T(n)$ on the total cost of a sequence of n operations, then calculates the average cost to be $T(n)/n$.
- *Accounting method* determines the individual cost of each operation, combining its immediate execution time and its influence on the running time of future operations. Usually, many short-running operations accumulate a "debt" of unfavourable state in small increments, while rare long-running operations decrease it drastically.
- *Potential method* is like the accounting method, but overcharges operations early to compensate for undercharges later.

1.7.1 Accounting Method

Since running time of an operation is thought of as having a monetary value with approach, we will use the terms *amortized running time* and *amortized cost* interchangeably.

With the accounting method, if the amortized cost of an operation exceeds its actual cost, the positive difference is recorded as a credit on a balance sheet; else the negative difference is recorded as a debit. Accumulated credits can later be used to help pay for operations that register debits on the balance sheet. The deficit spending is allowed. However, any such deficits must ultimately be paid off using the credits allocated to other operations in the sequence. If this condition is met, then the sum of the amortized costs of the operations in the sequence will provide an upper bound on the actual cost of the sequence.

If we let c_i and $\hat{c}_i$ denote the actual and amortized running times of the i-th operation in a sequence of n operations, then the actual and amortized running times of the sequence are $\sum_{i=1}^{n} c_i$ and $\sum_{i=1}^{n} \hat{c}_i$, respectively. The key idea to amortized complexity analysis involves upper bounding the actual running time of the sequence by amortized running time of the sequence. Specifically, we will want to ensure that

$$\sum_{i=1}^{n} c_i \geq \sum_{i=1}^{n} \hat{c}_i \qquad (1.10)$$

Example 1.26: Consider a simple example based on the *stack* ADT using accounting method. The *Push* and *Pop* operations can be implemented in $\Theta(1)$ time using a linked list. We also include the *MakeEmpty* operation to make the analysis nontrivial. The *MakeEmpty* requires $\Theta(n)$ time for a stack containing $n \geq 0$ elements. The actual costs of these operations are proportional to:

Operation	Actual Cost (c)
Push	1
Pop	1
MakeEmpty	n

We assume that *Pop* will not be applied to an empty stack.

If we perform a sequence of m operations, then in the worst case each would be a *MakeEmpty* operation requiring $\Theta(n)$ time, and the running time for an entire sequence would be $\Theta(mn)$. It is obvious that this worst-case analysis ignores the correlated effects of the stack ADT operations. The *MakeEmpty* operation takes $\Theta(n)$ time only if there are n elements on the stack. Using the accounting method, we can incorporate this information into our analysis. Specifically, an element cannot be removed from a stack using a *Pop*, unless it has been previously placed on the stack using *Push*. The same restriction applies to *MakeEmpty*. Thus, whenever a *Push* operation is performed, we add an extra credit to the balance sheet. This credit can be used later to pay for the element's removal during either a *Push* or *MakeEmpty* operation. Therefore, let us assign the following amortized costs to the stack ADT operations:

Operation	Amortized Cost ($\hat{c}$)
Push	2
Pop	0
MakeEmpty	0

It is not difficult that, stating with an empty stack, any sequence of stack operations can be paid for using these amortized costs. According to the actual costs and to the choices for the amortized costs, if the stack is initially empty, the balance sheet can become negative.

Given that any sequence of operations can be paid for by the amortized costs shown above, all that remains is to determine the amortized cost of a worst-case sequence of m operations. This will occur if all m are *Push* operations, yielding a worst-case amortized cost of $2m$. In conclusion, since we have previously shown that the amortized cost of such a sequence provides an upper bound on the actual cost of the sequence. We now know that any sequence of m stack operations can be performed in $\Theta(m)$ time, and that the average cost of each operation is given by $2m/m = \Theta(1)$.

1.7.2 Potential Method

Given a data structure D, let us denote its initial configuration (i.e., its configuration before any operations have been applied) using D_0, and its i-th configuration (i.e., its configuration after the i-th operation) as D_i. Next let us define a potential function Φ, which performs the mapping Φ: $D \rightarrow \mathbb{R}$. That is, a potential function maps a data structure configuration into a real number. The potential method then works as follows: The amortized running time of an operation on data structure D is defined with respect to Φ as

$$\hat{c} = c + \Delta\Phi(D)$$

where $\Delta\Phi(D)$ represents the change in potential that resulted from operation c. Therefore, the amortized running time of a sequence of m operations is

$$\sum_{i=1}^{m} \hat{c}_i = \sum_{i=1}^{m} (c_i + \Phi(D_i) - \Phi(D_{i-1}))$$

$$= \sum_{i=1}^{m} (c_i + \Phi(D_m) - \Phi(D_0)) \qquad (1.11)$$

From equation (1.11), it is easy to see that the amortized running time of the sequence will bound the actual running time of the sequence (i.e., condition (1.10) will be satisfied) as long as $\Phi(D_m) \geq \Phi(D_0)$. Furthermore, a sufficient (but not necessary) condition for satisfying equation (1.10) is that $\Phi(D_i) \geq \Phi(D_{i-1})$ for $i = 1, 2, 3, \ldots, m$.

CHAPTER SUMMARY

- *Design and analysis of algorithms* is one of the essential key areas in computer science. The *design* pertains to the description of algorithm at an abstract level by means of a pseudo language, and proof of correctness that is, the algorithm solves the given problem in all cases. The *analysis* deals with performance evaluation.
- An *algorithm* is a finite sequence of steps, each of which has a clear meaning and can be performed with a fine amount of effort in a finite length of time.
- *Pseudocode* (derived from pseudo and code) is a compact and informal high-level description of a computer programming algorithm that uses the structural conventions of some programming language.
- *Performance analysis* is the investigation of a program's behaviour using information gathered as the program runs. The goal of performance analysis is to determine which parts of a program to optimize for speed and memory usage.
- Two important ways to characterize the effectiveness of an algorithm are its *space complexity* and *time complexity*.

- *Space complexity* of an algorithm is the number of elementary objects that this algorithm needs to store during its execution. The space occupied by an algorithm is determined by the number and sizes of the variables and data structures used by the algorithm.
- Number of machine instructions which a program executes during its running time is called *time complexity*.
- *Asymptotic analysis* of algorithms is a means of comparing relative performance. Time complexity of an algorithm concerns determining an expression of the number of primitive operations needed as a function of the problem size.
- Asymptotic analysis makes use of the O, Θ and Ω notations.
- O-notation: Given functions $f(n)$ and $g(n)$, we say that $f(n)$ is $O(g(n))$ if there are positive constants $c > 0$ and $n_0 \geq 1$ such that $f(n) \leq cg(n)$ for all n, $n \geq n_0$. Big-Oh notation gives an upper bound on the growth rate of a function.
- Ω-notation: Given functions $f(n)$ and $g(n)$, we say that $f(n)$ is $\Omega(g(n))$ if there are positive constants $c > 0$ and $n_0 \geq 1$ such that $f(n) \geq cg(n)$ for all n, $n \geq n_0$. Big-Omega notation gives a lower bound on the growth rate of a function.
- Θ-notation: Let $f(n)$ and $g(n)$ be two asymptotically positive real-valued functions. We say that $f(n)$ is $\Theta(g(n))$ if there is an integer n_0 and positive real constants c_1 and c_2 such that $c_1 g(n) \leq f(n) \leq c_2 g(n)$ for all $n \geq n_0$.
- Little-oh notation denotes an upper bound that is not asymptotically tight. Suppose $f(n)$ and $g(n)$ are real valued functions defined for all $n > n_0$ (where n_0 is a fixed positive real). We write $f(n)$ is $o(g(n))$ if and only if
$$\lim_{n \to \infty} \frac{f(n)}{g(n)} = 0$$
- Little-omega gives a lower bound that is not asymptotically tight. If $f(n)$ is $\omega(g(n))$, then the growth rate of $f(n)$ is greater than the growth rate of $g(n)$. $f(n)$ is $\omega(g(n))$ if and only if there exist positive constants c and n_0 such that $f(n) > cg(n)$, for all $n \geq n_0$. Alternatively, $f(n)$ is $\omega(g(n))$, if and only if
$$\lim_{n \to \infty} \frac{f(n)}{g(n)} = \infty$$
- When an algorithm contains a recursive call to itself, its running time can often be described by a recurrence. A *recurrence relation* is an equation or inequality that describes a function in terms of its value on smaller inputs.
- *Master method* provides a "cookbook" method for solving recurrences of the form: $T(n) = aT(n/b) + f(n)$ where $a \geq 1$ and $b > 1$ are constants and $f(n)$ is an asymptotically positive function.
- *Probabilistic analysis of algorithms* is an approach to estimate the complexity of an algorithm. It starts from an assumption about a probabilistic distribution of the set of all

possible inputs. This assumption is then used to design an efficient algorithm or to compute an expected running time of a known algorithm.

- *Amortized analysis* refers to finding the average running time per operation over a worst-case sequence of operations. The method requires knowledge of which series of operations are possible. This is most commonly the case with data structures, which have state that carries on between operations.

SELF-TEST QUIZ

1.1 The step-by-step description of a process is called as

(a) algorithm (b) pseudocode (c) flowchart (d) program

1.2 Pseudocode is

(a) refined version of program
(b) language independent code
(c) outcome of compilation process
(d) code developed using the syntax of a specific language

1.3 Experimental methods are used in

(a) performance analysis
(b) performance measurements
(c) efficiency
(d) performance analysis and performance measurements

1.4 The time taken by the program P is the sum of

(a) the run time and loading time
(b) liking time and loading time
(c) liking time and compilation time
(d) compilation time and the run time

1.5 The components of time complexity are

(a) the compiler used.
(b) the target computer.
(c) the computer options.
(d) the compiler, the computer options, the target computer

1.6 The approaches used to determine the performance of a program are

(a) Analytical
(b) analytical and experimental
(c) analytical and theoretical
(d) experimental

1.7 The most popular asymptotic notations is

(a) big-oh (b) theta (c) little-oh (d) omega

1.8 $\sum_{1 \le k \le n} O(n)$, where $O(n)$ stands for order n is

(a) $O(n)$ (b) $O(n^2)$ (c) (b) $O(n^3)$ (d) (b) $O(3n^2)$

1.9 What is the running time to retrieve an element from an array of size n?

(a) $O(n\text{-}1)$ (b) $O(n)$ (c) $O(n/2)$ (d) $O(1)$

1.10 Retrieval from a linked list of size n has running time:

(a) $O(n\text{-}1)$ (b) $O(n)$ (c) $O(n/2)$ (d) $O(1)$

1.11 Suppose we want to arrange the n numbers stored in any array such that all negative values occur before all positive ones. Minimum number of exchanges required in the worst-case is

(a) n-1 (b) n (c) n+1 (d) $n/2$

1.12 If n is a power of 2, then the minimum number of multiplications needed to compute x^n is

(a) $\log_2 n$ (b) $\sqrt{n}$ (c) n-1 (d) n

1.13 Which one of the following shows the correct relationship among some of the more common time complexities for the algorithms?

(a) $O(\log_2 n) < O(n) < O(n\log_2 n) < O(2^n) < O(n^2)$
(b) $O(n) < O(\log_2 n) < O(n\log_2 n) < O(2^n) < O(n^2)$
(c) $O(n) < O(\log_2 n) < O(n\log_2 n) < O(n^2) < O(2^n)$
(d) $O(\log_2 n) < O(n) < O(n\log_2 n) < O(n^2) < O(2^n)$

1.14 For what values of n is $10 \times n \times \log_2 n > 2n^2$?

(a) Only $n \geq 32$ (b) Only $0 < n \leq 20$
(c) Only $20 \leq n \leq 32$ (d) Only $n \geq 0$

1.15 Let $f(n) = n^2 \lg n$ and $g(n) = n(\lg n)^{10}$ be two positive functions of n. Which one of the following statements is correct?

(a) $f(n) = O(g(n))$ and $g(n) \neq O(f(n))$
(b) $g(n) = O(f(n))$ and $f(n) \neq O(g(n))$
(c) $f(n) \neq O(g(n))$ and $g(n) \neq O(f(n))$
(d) $f(n) = O(g(n))$ and $g(n) = O(f(n))$

1.16 The solution to the recurrence equation $T(2^k) = 3T(2^{k-1})+1$, $T(1) = 1$ is

(a) 2^k (b) $(3^{k+1}-1)/2$ (c) $3^{\log_2 k}$ (d) $2^{\log_3 k}$

1.17 Consider the following algorithm for searching a given number x in an unsorted array $A[1...n]$ having n distinct values.

1. Choose an i uniformly at random from $1...n$;
2. If $A[i] = x$, then stop else go to 1;

Assuming x is present in A, what is the expected number of comparisons made by the algorithm before it terminates?

(a) n (b) n-1 (c) $2n$ (d) $n/2$

1.18 The running time of the following algorithm

```
Procedure A(n)
If n ≤ 2 return 1;
Else return A(ceil(√n));
```

is best described by

(a) $O(n)$ (b) $O(\log_2 n)$ (c) $O(\log \log_2 n)$ (d) $O(1)$

1.19 Consider the following three claims:

I $(n+k)^m = \Theta(n^m)$ where k and m are constants
II $2^{n+1} = O(2^n)$
III $2^{2n+1} = O(2^n)$

Which of these claims are correct?

(a) I and II (b) I and III (c) II and III (d) I, II, and III

1.20 Consider the following recurrence relation

$T(1) = 1$
$T(n+1) = T(n) + \lfloor \sqrt{n+1} \rfloor$ for all $n \geq 1$

The value of $T(m^2)$ for $m \geq 1$ is

(a) $\frac{m}{6}(21m - 39) + 4$ (b) $\frac{m}{6}(4m^2 - 3m + 5)$

(c) $\frac{m}{2}(m^{2.5} - 11m + 20) - 5$ (d) $\frac{m}{6}(5m^3 - 34m^2 + 137m - 104) + \frac{5}{6}$

1.21 The tightest lower bound on the number of comparisons, in the worst-case, for comparison-based sorting is of the order of

(a) n (b) n^2 (c) $n \log n$ (d) $n \log^2 n$

1.22 What does the following algorithm approximate? Assume $m > 1$ and $\varepsilon > 0$.

```
x = m;
y = 1;
while(x - y > ε)
{   x = (x + y)/2;
    y = m / x;
}
```

```
print(x);
```

(a) $\log_2 m$ (b) m^2 (c) $m^{1/2}$ (d) $m^{1/3}$

1.23 Let $A[1..n]$ be an array storing a bit (0 or 1) at each location, and $f(m)$ is a function whose time complexity is $\Theta(m)$. Consider the following algorithm fragment:

```
counter = 0;
for( i = 0; i < n;  i++ )
{
    if(A[i] == 1) counter++;
    else {  f(counter);  counter = 0;  }
}
```

The complexity of this algorithm fragment is

(a) $\Omega(n^2)$ (b) $\Omega(n \log n)$ and $O(n^2)$ (c) $\Theta(n)$ (d) $o(n)$

1.24 The time complexity of the following function is (assume $n > 0$)

```
int recursive(int n)
{   if( n == 1 ) return(1);
    else return(recursive(n-1) + recursive(n-1));
}
```

(a) $O(n)$ (b) $O(n \log n)$ (c) $O(n^2)$ (d) $O(2^n)$

1.25 The following recurrence equation evaluates to

$T(1) = 1$ for $n = 1$
$T(n) = 2T(n\text{-}1) + n$ for $n \geq 2$

(a) $2^{n+1}\text{-}n\text{-}2$ (b) $2^n\text{-}n$ (c) $2^{n+1}\text{-}2n\text{-}2$ (d) $2^n\text{+}n$

1.26 Suppose $T(n) = 2T(n/2) + n$, $T(0) = T(1) = 1$.
Which one of the following is false?

(a) $T(n) = O(n^2)$ (b) $T(n) = \Theta(n \log n)$
(c) $T(n) = \Omega(n^2)$ (d) $T(n) = O(n \log n)$

1.27 Consider the following program fragment in which i, j, and n are integer variables.

GATE-2006

```
for( i = n, j=0;  i > 0;  i /= 2, j += i );
```

Let val(j) denote the value stored in the variable j after termination of the for loop. Which one of the following is true?

(a) val(j) = $\Theta(\log n)$ (b) val(j) = $\Theta(\sqrt{n})$
(c) val(j) = $\Theta(n)$ (d) val(j) = $\Theta(n \log n)$

1.28 Consider the following program segment:

GATE-2007

```
int j, n;
j = 1;
while( j <= n )
    j = j*2;
```

The number of comparisons made in the execution of the loop for any $n > 0$ is:

(a) $\lceil \log_2 n \rceil + 1$ (b) n (b) $\lfloor \log_2 n \rfloor$ (d) $\lfloor \log_2 n \rfloor + 1$

1.29 In the following algorithm, let $n \geq m$.

GATE-2007

```
int gcd(n, m)
{   if( n % m == 0 ) return m;
    n = n % m;
    return gcd(m, n);
}
```

How many recursive calls are made by this method?

(a) $\Theta(\log_2 n)$ (b) $\Theta(n)$ (c) $\Theta(\log_2 \log_2 n)$ (d) $\Theta(\sqrt{n})$

1.30 What is the time complexity of the following recursive algorithm?

GATE-2007

```
int doSomething(int n)
{   if( n <= 2 )
        return 1;
    else
        return (doSomething(floor(sqrt(n))) + n);
}
```

(a) $\Theta(n^2)$ (b) $\Theta(n\log_2 n)$ (c) $\Theta(\log_2 n)$ (d) $\Theta(\log_2 \log_2 n)$

1.31 Consider the following code segment:

GATE-2007

```
int isPrime(int n)
{   int i;
    for( i = 2;   i <= sqrt(n);   i++ )
        if( n % i == 0 )
        {   printf("Not Prime");  return 0;  }
    return 1;
}
```

Let $T(n)$ denote the number of times the *for* loop is executed by the program on input n. Which of the following is *true*?

(a) $T(n) = O(\sqrt{n})$ and $T(n) = \Omega(\sqrt{n})$
(b) $T(n) = O(\sqrt{n})$ and $T(n) = \Omega(1)$
(c) $T(n) = O(n)$ and $T(n) = \Omega(\sqrt{n})$

(d) None of the above.

1.32 The minimum number of comparisons required to determine if an integer appears more than $n/2$ times in a sorted array of n integers is

GATE-2008

(a) $\Theta(n)$ (b) $\Theta(\log n)$ (c) (d) $\Theta(1)$

EXERCISES

1.1 What is an algorithm? Explain various criteria used for judging an algorithm.

1.2 What is a pseudocode? Mention the pseudocode specifications.

1.3 How do you say one algorithm is better than another algorithm for solving the same problem?

1.4 Describe the performance analysis in detail.

1.5 Design an algorithm that reads a list of numbers and makes a count of the number of negatives, and the number of positives in the set.

1.6 For the given x and n, write an algorithm to compute $x^n /n!$, and compute the running time.

1.7 Design an algorithm to determine whether or not a number n is a factorial number.

1.8 Design an algorithm to simulate multiplication by addition. The program should accept as input two integers (they may be zero, positive, or negative).

1.9 Devise an algorithm that inputs three integers and outputs them in ascending order.

1.10 Write an algorithm to evaluate a polynomial using Horner's rule.

1.11 Differentiate between profiling and debugging.

1.12 Differentiate between priori analysis and posteriori analysis.

1.13 Define omega notation. Explain the terms involved in it. Give an example.

1.14 Define time complexity. Describe different notations used to represent there complexities.

1.15 Write the non-recursive algorithm for finding the Fibonacci sequence and derive its time complexity.

1.16 Write an algorithm to compute x^n for any real number x and integer n (where n is an integral power of 2). Prove that the running time of this algorithm is $\Theta(\log_2 n)$.

1.17 Derive the function $f(n) = 12n^2 + 6n$ is $o(n^3)$ and $\omega(n)$.

1.18 Show that $n^3 \log n$ is $\omega(n^3)$.

1.19 Explain how time complexity of an algorithm is computed.

1.20 Explain the asymptotic notations used in algorithm analysis.

1.21 Consider a polynomial in n of the form

$$f(n) = \sum_{i=0}^{m} a_i n^i = a_m n^m + a_{m-1} n^{m-1} + a_2 n^2 + a_1 n + a_0 \text{ where } a_m > 0,$$

then $f(n) = \Omega(n^m)$.

1.22 Show that $f(n) = 8n+128 = O(n^2)$.

1.23 Is $2^{n+1} = O(2^n)$? Is $2^{2n} = O(2^n)$?

1.24 Show that $f(n)+g(n) = O(n^2)$ where $f(n) = 3n^2 - n + 4$ and $g(n) = n\log n+5$.

1.25 Show that $f(n) = 4n^2 - 64n + 288 = \Omega(n^2)$.

1.26 Show that $f_1(n) + f_2(n) = O(\max(g_1(n), g_2(n)))$ where $f_1(n) = O(g_1(n))$ and $f_2(n) = O(g_2(n))$.

1.27 Show that $f_1(n) \times f_2(n) = O((g_1(n) \times g_2(n))$ where $f_1(n) = O(g_1(n))$ and $f_2(n) = O(g_2(n))$.

1.28 Prove that $f(n) = O(h(n))$ where $f(n) = O(g(n))$ and $g(n) = O(h(n))$.

1.29 Let $f(n)$ and $g(n)$ be asymptotically nonnegative functions. Using the basic definition of Θ-notation, prove that $\max(f(n), g(n)) = \Theta(f(n) + g(n))$.

1.30 Let $f(n)$ and $g(n)$ be asymptotically positive functions. Prove or disprove each of the following conjectures.

(a) $f(n) = O(g(n))$ implies $g(n) = O(f(n))$.

(b) $f(n) + g(n) = \Theta(\min(f(n), g(n)))$.

(c) $f(n) = O(g(n))$ implies $\log_2(f(n)) = O(\log_2(g(n)))$, where $\log_2(g(n)) \geq 1$ and $f(n) \geq 1$ for all sufficiently large n.

(d) $f(n) = O(g(n))$ implies $2^{f(n)} = O(2^{g(n)})$.

(e) $f(n) = O((f(n))^2)$.

(f) $f(n) = O(g(n))$ implies $g(n) = \Omega(f(n))$.

(g) $f(n) = \Theta(f(n/2))$.

(h) $f(n) + o(f(n)) = \Theta(f(n))$.

1.31 Use mathematical induction to show that when n is an exact power of 2, the solution of the recurrence

$$T(n) = \begin{cases} 2 & \text{if } n = 2 \\ 2T(n/2) + n & \text{if } n = 2^k \text{ for } k > 1 \end{cases}$$

is $T(n) = n \log_2 n$.

1.32 Show that the solution of $T(n) = T(\lceil n/2 \rceil) + 1$ is $O(\lg n)$.

1.33 Determine a good asymptotic upper bound on the recurrence

$T(n) = 3T(\lfloor n/2 \rfloor) + n$.

1.34 Develop a probabilistic algorithm to find the value of integral $\int_0^2 \sqrt{4 - x^2}\, dx$.

1.35 Give a Monte Carlo algorithm for finding the majority element in an array.

1.36 Can amortized analysis be used to show that any sequence of m list ADT operations can be implemented in $\Theta(m)$ time when using a linked list?

1.37 A sequence of m operations is performed on a data structure. The running time of the i-th operation is given by:

$$c_i = \begin{cases} i, & \text{if } i = 2^k, \text{ integer } k \\ 1, & \text{otherwise} \end{cases}$$

Determine the amortized running time per operation.

CHAPTER 2

DISJOINT SETS

Two or more sets are said to be *disjoint* if they have no element in common. For example, {1, 2, 3} and {4, 5, 6} are disjoint sets, while sets {1, 2, 3} and {2, 4, 5, 6} are not. The elements of a set are letters, numbers, or any other objects. For example, the elements of the set {a, b, c} are the letters a, b, and c.

Formally, two sets A and B are disjoint, if their intersection is the empty set, that is if $A \cap B = \Phi$. This definition extends to any collection of sets. A collection of sets is pairwise disjoint or mutually disjoint if any two distinct sets in the collection are disjoint. Formally, let I be an index set, and for each i in I, let A_i be a set. Then, the family of sets $\{ A_i : i \in I\}$ is pairwise disjoint if for any i and j in I with $i \neq j$, $A_i \cap B_j = \Phi$. For example, the collection of sets {{1}, {2}, {3} ...} is pairwise disjoint. If $\{A_i\}$ is a pairwise disjoint collection (containing at least two sets), then clearly its intersection is empty.

2.1 UNION-FIND OPERATIONS

A *disjoint-set data structure* is a collection of disjoint dynamic sets that supports *union-find* operations. A union-find operation is an algorithm that performs two useful operations on such a data structure:

- *Find*: Determine which set a particular element is in. Also useful for determining if two elements are in the same set.
- *Union*: Combine or merge two sets into a single set.

Because it supports these two operations, a disjoint-set data structure is sometimes called a *union-find data structure*. *MakeSet* is other important operation, which makes a set containing only a given element (a singleton), is generally trivial. With these three operations, many practical partitioning problems can be solved.

In order to define these operations more precisely, some way of representing the sets is needed. One common approach is to select a fixed element of each set, called its representative, to represent the set as a whole. Then, *Find*(x) returns the representative of the set that x belongs to, and *Union* takes two set representatives as its arguments.

Suppose x and y are two elements in two different sets. We want to support the following operations:

MakeSet(x) creates a new set whose only member is x. Thus, x is representative of the set. Since the sets are disjoint, we require that x not already be in some other set.

Union(x, y) unites sets containing x and y. The two sets are assumed to be disjoint prior to the operation. The representative of the resulting set is any member of the two sets (x or y).

Find(x) returns a pointer to representative of set containing x.

2.1.1 Applications

Disjoint set data structures have lots of applications. For instance, Kruskal's minimum spanning tree algorithm relies on such a data structure to maintain the components of the intermediate spanning forest. Another application might be maintaining the connected components of a graph as new vertices and edges are added. In both these applications, we can use a disjoint-set data structure, where we keep a set for each connected component, containing that component's vertices.

Example 2.1: One application of disjoint-set data structure is to determine the connected components of an undirected graph. Figure 2.1 shows a graph with three connected components. The edges are added dynamically and we need to maintain the connected components as each edge is added. Let V denote the set of vertices and E the set of edges of the graph.

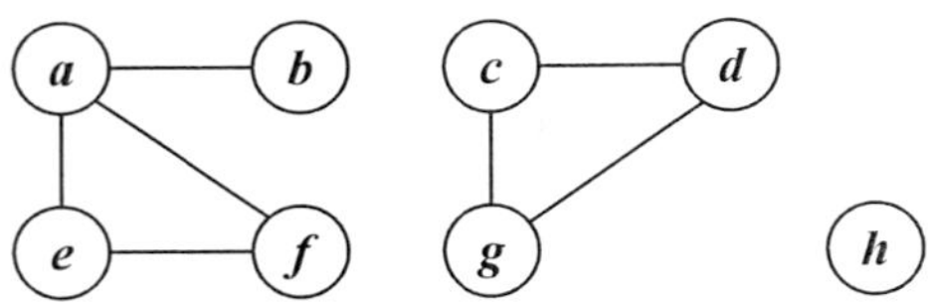

$V = \{a, b, c, d, e, f, g, h\}$
$E = \{ (a, b), (a, e), (a, f), (e, f), (c, d), (c, g), (g, d) \}$

Figure 2.1: Undirected graph with three connected components

The following steps illustrate the collection of disjoint sets after each edge is processed:

Initial sets:	$\{a\}$ $\{b\}$ $\{c\}$ $\{d\}$ $\{e\}$ $\{f\}$ $\{g\}$ $\{h\}$
Process (a, b):	$\{a, b\}$ $\{c\}$ $\{d\}$ $\{e\}$ $\{f\}$ $\{g\}$ $\{h\}$
Process (a, e):	$\{a, b, e\}$ $\{c\}$ $\{d\}$ $\{f\}$ $\{g\}$ $\{h\}$
Process (a, f):	$\{a, b, e, f\}$ $\{c\}$ $\{d\}$ $\{g\}$ $\{h\}$
Process (e, f):	$\{a, b, e, f\}$ $\{c\}$ $\{d\}$ $\{g\}$ $\{h\}$
Process (c, d):	$\{a, b, e, f\}$ $\{c, d\}$ $\{g\}$ $\{h\}$
Process (c, g):	$\{a, b, e, f\}$ $\{c, d, g\}$ $\{h\}$
Process (g, d):	$\{a, b, e, f\}$ $\{c, d, g\}$ $\{h\}$

Initially, each vertex is placed in its own set. Then, the edge (a, b) unites the sets containing a and b, edge (a, e) unites the sets containing a and e, and so on. After all the edges are processed, two vertices are in the same connected component if and only if the corresponding objects are in the same set.

Union-find applications also involve manipulating objects of all types.

- Computers in a network.
- Web pages on the Internet.
- Transistors in a computer chip.
- Variable name aliases.
- Pixels in a digital photo.

2.1.2 Linked List Representation

A simple way to implement a disjoint-set data structure is to represent each set by a linked list. The first object in each linked list serves as its set's representative. Each object in the linked list contains a set member, a pointer to the object containing the next set member, and a pointer back to the representative. Each list maintains pointers to the representative. Figure 2.2 shows two sets $\{a, b, c, d\}$, and $\{e, f, g\}$ represented as doubly linked lists. Within each linked list, the objects may appear in any order (subject to our assumption that the first object in each list is the representative).

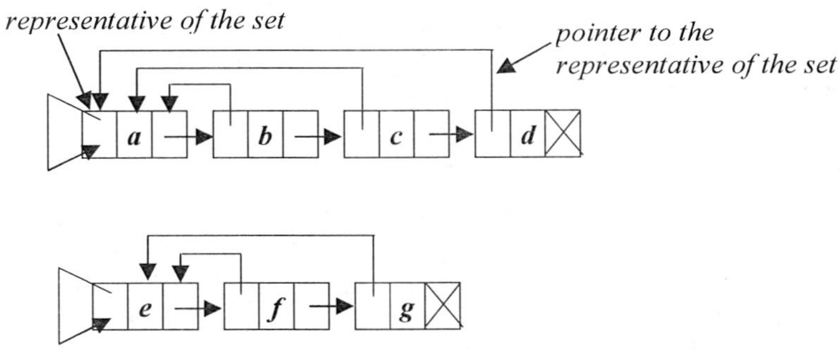

Figure 2.2: Linked list representation of disjoint sets

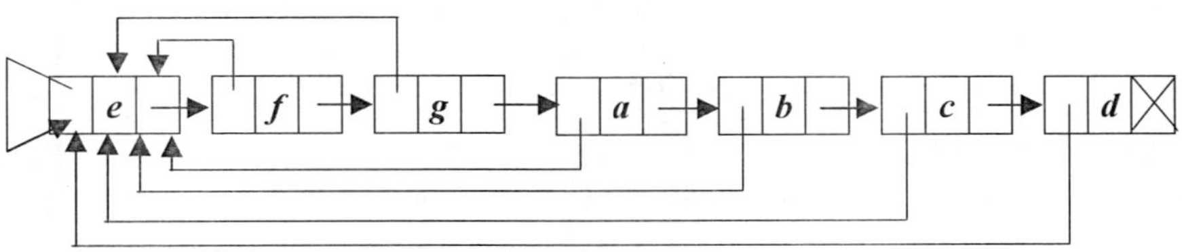

Figure 2.3: Result of *Union(a, e)*. Representative of the resulting set is '*e*'

With this linked-list representation, both *MakeSet* and *Find* are easy, requiring constant time: $O(1)$ time. To carry out *MakeSet*(a), we create a new linked list whose only object is 'a'. For *Find*(a), we just return the pointer from 'a' back to the representative – here 'a' is the representative.

The *Union* operation takes significantly more time than *MakeSet* and *Find*. As Figure 2.3 shows, we perform *Union*(a, e) by appending a's list onto the end of e's list. The representative of the new set is the element that was originally the representative of the set containing 'e'. But, we must update the pointer to the representative for each object originally on a's list, which takes time *linear* in the length of a's list.

Find(e) takes O(1) time – representative head of the list. *Union* needs updating of pointers: *MakeSet*(a), *MakeSet*(b), ..., *MakeSet*(g), and *Union*(a, b), *Union*(b, c), ..., *Union*(f, g). Suppose we have m operations that included n *MakeSet* operations, *MakeSet* and *Find* take $O(1)$ time each, and *Union* requires [$O(1)$ + time of head pointer update].

At 1st *Union* operation, it needs 1 update.
At 2nd *Union* operation, it needs 2 updates.
. . .
At ith *Union* operation, it needs i updates.
Total for n–1 *Union* operations = $\sum_{i=1}^{n-1} i = n(n-1)/2$.

Hence, n *Union* operations run in $O(n^2)$ time.

We execute the sequence of n *MakeSet* operations followed by n–1 *Union* operations, so that $m = 2n-1$. We spend $O(n)$ time performing the n *MakeSet* operations. The total number of operations is $2n-1$, and so each operation on average requires $O(n)$ time. That is, the *amortized time* of an operation is $O(n)$.

2.1.3 Weighted-Union Heuristic

In the worst case, the above implementation of the *Union* procedure requires an average of $O(n)$ time per call because we may be appending a longer list onto a shorter list; we must update the pointer to the representative for each member of the longer list. Suppose instead that each representative also includes the size of the set, we can now append the smaller set to the longer one, with ties broken arbitrarily. A single *Union* can still take $O(n)$ time, if both sets have m members, however, a sequence of m *MakeSet*, *Union*, and *Find* operations takes $O(m+n\log_2 n)$ instead of $O(n)$ time.

How many times can the reference to the representative of the set be modified, for each single object x, in a set of size n? The x's reference to the representative of the set is modified when its set is the smaller in a *Union* operation.

In 1st update, the resulting set must contain at least 2 members.
In 2nd update, the resulting set must contain at least 4 members.
. . .
In $\lceil \log_2 k \rceil$ update, the resulting set must contain at least k members.

Since the set has n elements, each object in the set has been updated at most $\lceil \log_2 n \rceil$ over all the *Union* operations. Hence, the total time used in updating the n elements is $O(n\log_2 n)$. Each *MakeSet* and *Find* operation takes $O(1)$ time, and there are $O(m)$ of them (upper bound). The total time for the entire sequence is thus $O(m+n\log_2 n)$.

Since n *Union* operations take $O(n\log_2 n)$, the amortized time of a *Union* operation is $O(\log_2 n)$ (i.e., $O(n\log_2 n)/n$). Since m *MakeSet* and *Find* operations take $O(m)$ time, the amortized time of *MakeSet* and *Find* is $O(m)/m = O(1)$.

2.1.4 Tree Representation

A faster implementation of disjoint sets is through the rooted trees, with each node containing one member and each tree representing one set. Each member in the tree has only one parent. The root is the representative and every node points to its parent while the root points to itself. A collection of disjoint sets is represented by a forest which is a collection of trees.

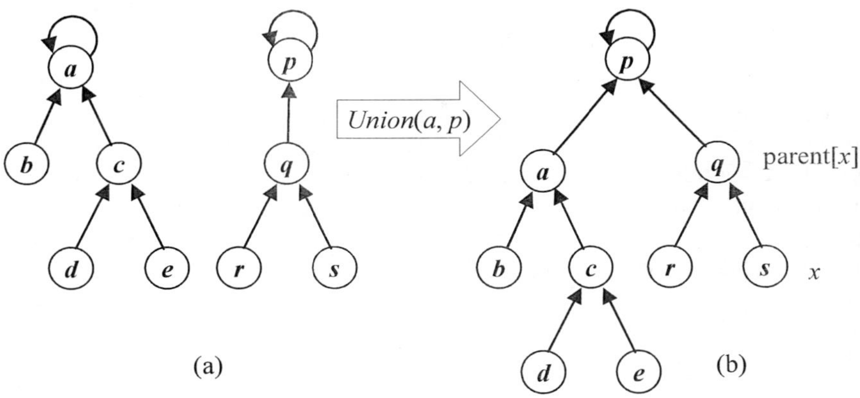

Figure 2.4: Rooted tree representation of disjoint sets

Figure 2.4(a) is a disjoint-set forest representing two sets $\{a, b, c, d, e\}$ and $\{p, q, r, s\}$. The representative of first set is a, and that of second one is p. Figure 2.4(b) shows the *Union*(a, p). Since we have linked the nodes from children to parent, we make one of the trees as a subtree of the other. To obtain the union of two sets, we set the root of one tree to point to the root of the other. The following set of algorithms is the simplified *Union-find*. The parent of a vertex x is denoted by parent[x]. *Find*(x) traces the path from x to the root.

```
MakeSet(x)              Find(x)                      Union(x, y)
    parent[x] = x           while x ≠ parent[x]          x' = Find(x)
                                x = parent[x]            y' = Find(y)
                            return x                     parent[y'] = x'
```

2.1.5 Heuristics for Disjoint Set Operations

The implementation of disjoint set forest does not alone improve the running time. It is similar to the linked list implementation. A sequence of *Union* operations may create a tree of size n that is a linear chain of n nodes (we obtain a degenerate tree). The worst-case running time is linear (see Figure 2.5). We use *union-by-rank* and *path compression* heuristics to improve the running time.

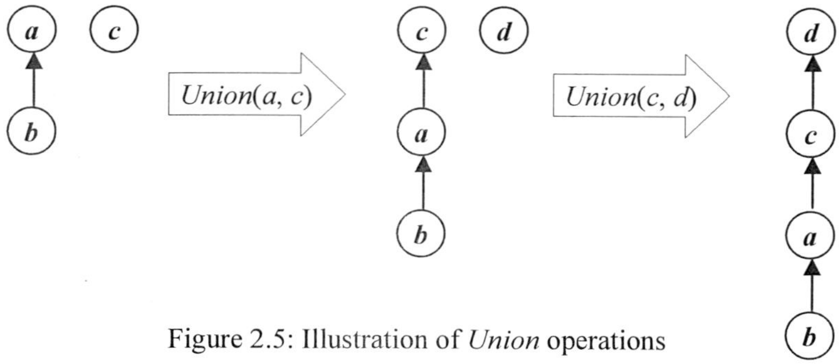

Figure 2.5: Illustration of *Union* operations

Union-by-rank: When performing *Union*, if we make the root of the larger tree as the root of the resulting tree, we can save some time. For each node, we maintain a *rank* that approximates the logarithm of the subtree size (n), and is also an upper bound of the height of a tree ($\log_2 n$). The union-by-rank on its own gives $O(\log_2 n)$ *Find* time. A tree of rank, r contains at least 2^r elements. In union-by-rank, the tree with a smaller rank is made to point to the root of the tree with a higher rank. This is illustrated in the following figure.

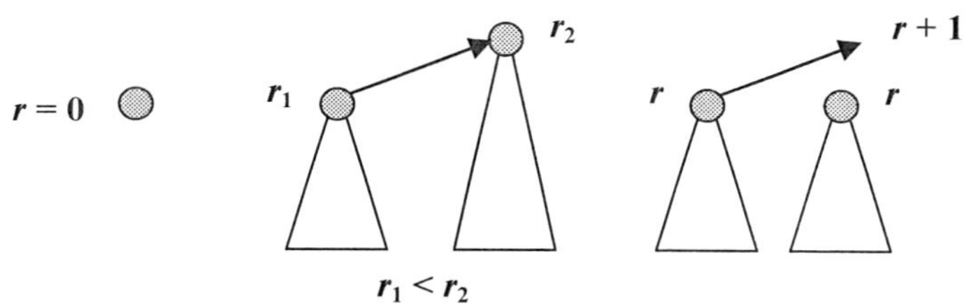

Figure 2.6: Illustration of Union-by-rank

When applying *Union* to two trees, there are two cases, depending on whether the roots have equal rank. If the roots have unequal rank, we make the root of higher rank the parent of the root of lower rank, but the ranks themselves remain unchanged. If, instead, the roots have equal ranks, we arbitrarily choose one of the roots as the parent and increment its rank. The *Link* procedure called by *Union*, takes pointers to two roots as inputs. This method is implemented by pseudocode as follows:

```
MakeSet(x)
1. parent[x] = x      // self loop
2. rank[x] = 0        // upper bound of height of tree

Union(x, y)
1. if(Find(x) ≠ Find(y)), then
2.       Link(Find(x), Find(y))
```

```
Link(x, y)                              // with Union-by-rank
if (rank[x] > rank[y]), then
        parent[y] = x
else
        parent[x] = y
        if (rank[x] = rank[y]), then        // need to update rank
                rank[y] = rank[y]+1
```

```
Find(x)
if (x ≠ parent[x]), then
        parent[x] = Find(parent[x])
return parent[x]
```

Path compression: When doing *Find*, we can speed-up any subsequent queries on the find path by compressing the path: we make each node on the path to the root point directly to the root. Any subsequent queries on any of the nodes on the path will be done in just one step. Path compression is also known as *collapsing rule*.

During a *Find* operation, when following a path from some node to the root, make each node encountered along the path be a child of the root. First, find the root, and then re-traverse the same path, making each node a child of the root.

Example 2.2: Figure 2.7(a) shows a tree before executing a *Find* operation on the node for element g and Figure 2.7(b) shows the result after f and g are made children of the root. Nodes a and c on the path are not moved because a is the root, and c is already a child of the root.

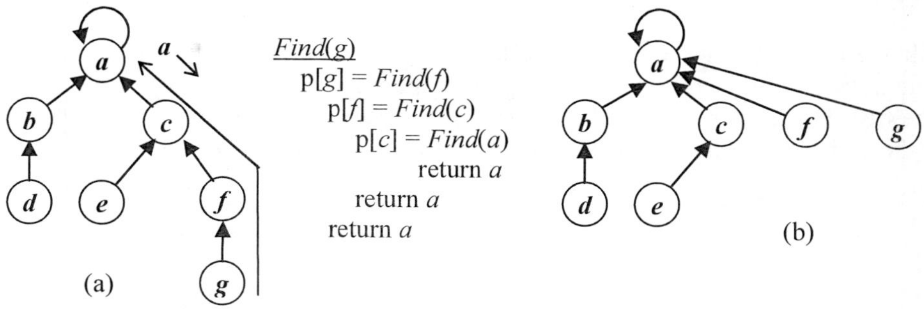

Figure 2.7: Path compression during *Find*(g) operation

Path compression takes place during the *Find* operation. This works by recursion from the given input node up to the root of the tree, forming a path. Then the root is returned and assigned as the parent for each node in path. The parent of g after *Find*(g) is a.

When we use either union by rank or path compression, the running time is improved. Alone, union-by-rank yields the same worst-case running time of the weighted union heuristic: $O(m\log_2 n)$. When we use both heuristics, the running time is further improved to $O(m\alpha(n))$ where m is the total number of operations, and n is the number of *MakeSet* operations. The $\alpha(n)$ is a very slowly growing function, which has a value of at most 4 for any feasible value of n. Thus, we can view the running time as linear in m in all practical situations.

2.2 SPANNING TREES

A *spanning tree* of an undirected graph of n nodes is a set of n-1 edges that connects all nodes. Every node is reachable from every other node. In undirected graph, edges do not have an associated direction. A graph may have many spanning trees; for instance the complete graph on four vertices. We use vertices and nodes of a graph interchangeably. Figure 2.8 shows an undirected graph with four of its spanning trees. Note that each of the four spanning trees contains three edges.

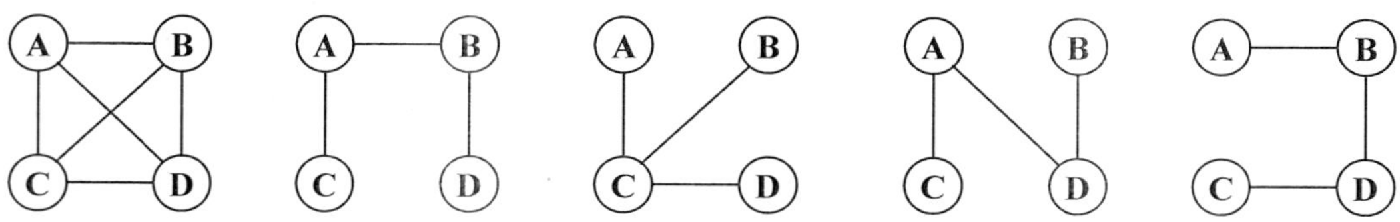

Figure 2.8: Undirected graph and four of the spanning trees of the graph

Properties of spanning trees:

- There is no cycle – a cycle needs n edges in an n-node graph.
- There is exactly one path between any two nodes – there is at least one path between any two nodes because all nodes are connected. Further, there is not more than one path between a pair of nodes.
- Adding a non-tree edge creates a cycle – Suppose a non-tree edge (x, y) is added to a spanning tree. Now there are two distinct paths between (x, y), the added edge and the path in the tree. Hence there is a cycle. For example, if we add an edge (A, D) to the spanning tree shown in the last part of the Figure 2.8, then we will have a cycle (A, B, D, A).

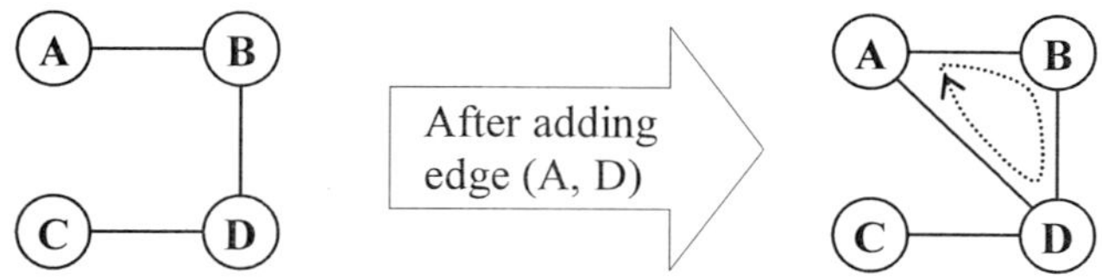

Figure 2.9: Adding a non-tree edge creates a cycle

- Removing an edge from a cycle as above creates a spanning tree: after removal of the edge there are (n-1) edges. All nodes of the graph are connected: suppose edge (x, y) is removed that belonged to the original graph. The nodes x and y are still connected because x and y were on a cycle. For other node pairs, in the path in the original graph replace the edge (x, y) by the path between x and y. Removing the edge (B, D) from the cycle (A, B, D, A) creates the spanning tree.

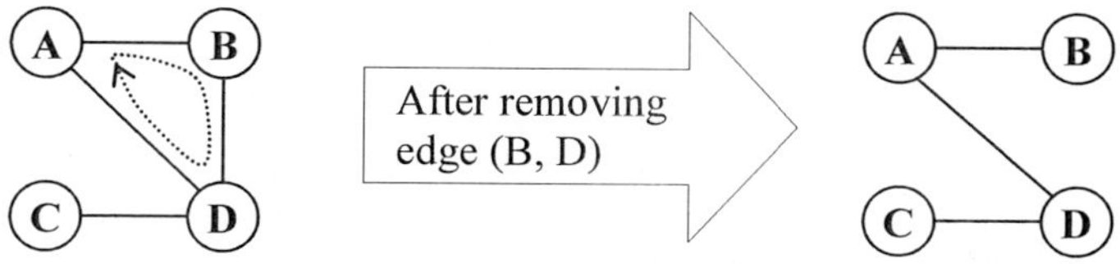

(a) Not a spanning tree (b) A spanning tree

Figure 2.10: Removing one edge from graph creates a spanning tree

Applications: Spanning trees have applications to the design of communication networks. If nodes represent cities and edges represent distances, and we need to run power lines to each city, the spanning trees are useful. For routing problems (mail routes, school buses, and traveling salesmen), and other path types, spanning trees provide a better approach.

Depth First Search (DFS) and Breadth First Search (BFS) are powerful methods to explore a graph in a systematic way. We can obtain spanning trees by using these techniques. Both methods start in a node *v* of an undirected graph and visit all nodes that can be reached from *v*. Figure 2.11 shows an undirected graph and its DFS and BFS spanning trees (obtained starting from node A). The methods differ in the order in which they visit the nodes:

- DFS first explores the edges out of the node most recently reached, that is, it tries to go as deep as possible first.
- BFS explores the edges in the order in which their source node is reached. It explores all edges out of the current node first and then goes to the next node.

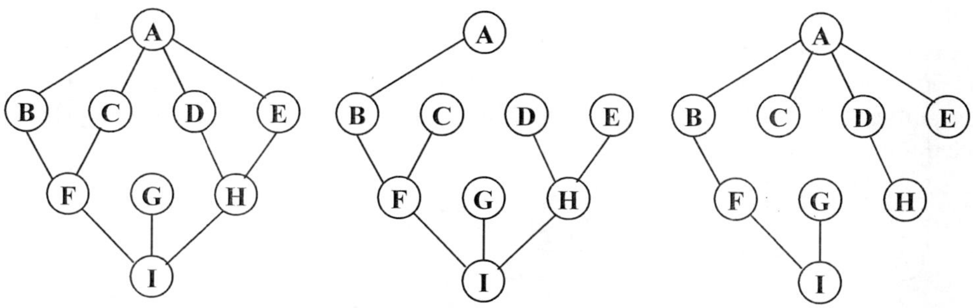

(a) An undirected graph (b) DFS spanning tree (c) BFS spanning tree

Figure 2.11: An undirected graph and its DFS and BFS spanning trees

2.2.1 Depth-First Search

A primary problem concerning the graphs is the reachability. A number of graph problems involves traversal of a graph. Traversal of a graph means visiting each of its nodes exactly once. This is accomplished by visiting the nodes in a systematic manner. Two commonly used techniques of graph traversal are depth-first search (DFS) and breadth-first search (BFS). These algorithms work for both directed and undirected graphs.

Depth-first search is a generalization of the preorder traversal of a tree. DFS can serve as a structure around which many other efficient graph algorithms can be built.

Suppose we have an undirected graph G in which all nodes are initially marked *unvisited.* DFS works by selecting one node v of G as a start (head) node; v is marked *visited.* The each unvisited node adjacent to v is searched in turn, using DFS recursively. Once all nodes that can be reached from v have been visited, the search of v is complete. If certain nodes remain unvisited, we select an unvisited node as a new start node. We repeat this process until all nodes of G have been visited.

This technique is called depth-first search because it continues searching in the forward (*deeper*) direction as long as possible. For example, suppose x is the most recently visited node. DFS selects some unexplored edge (x, y) coming from x. If y has not been visited, then the procedure marks y visited and initiates a new search at y. After completing the search through all paths beginning at y, the search returns to x the node from which y was first visited. The process of selecting unexplored edges coming from x is then continued until all edges from x have been explored.

An adjacency list, *adj*[v] can be used to represent the nodes adjacent to node v, and an array *mark*, whose elements are chosen from (*visited, unvisited*), can be used to determine whether a node has been previously visited. The recursive procedure DFS is outlined in Algorithm 2.1. To use it on an n-node graph, we initialize *mark* to *unvisited* and then commence a depth-first search from each node that is still unvisited when its turn comes.

The n nodes of a graph are represented as n linked lists. There is one list for each node in the graph. Each *node* in the adjacency list, *adj*[] contains two fields: *vertex* (*node label*) and *next* (a *link* field pointing to next node). This is a self-referential object. The w denotes a pointer variable pointing to this *node*. Before invoking DFS algorithm with start (head) node, initialize all nodes unvisited - that is, *mark*[i] = *unvisited,* for i = 1 to n. The adjacency lists for an undirected graph is shown in Figures 2.12.

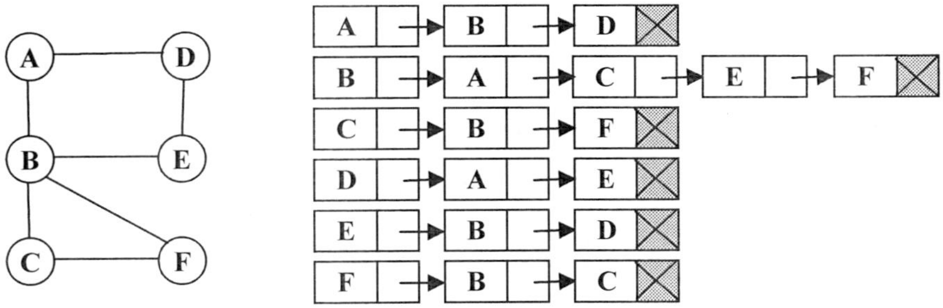

Figure 2.12: An undirected graph and its adjacency list

```
Algorithm 2.1: DFS(v: head node)
1.  Mark v visited                          // mark[v] = visited
2.  Print v
3.  Assign the address of head node of      // w = adj[v]
    adjacency list to w
4.  While w ≠ null
5.      Assign adjacent node to v           // v = w→vertex
6.      If node v is unvisited, then        // if (mark[v] = unvisited)
7.          call DFS(v)                     //     DFS(v)
8.      Get next adjacent node              // w = w→next
9.  Endwhile
10. Return
```

Example 2.3: As an example of DFS, suppose in the graph of Figure 2.12 we start at node A. The steps of DFS are shown in the Table 2.1 and illustrated in Figure 2.13. The order of nodes visited by DFS is A, B, C, F, E, and D.

Table 2.1: Trace of DFS

#	*mark* A	B	C	D	E	F	*Description of the process*
1	1	0	0	0	0	0	Mark A as visited
2	1	0	0	0	0	0	Call DFS(B) recursively
3	1	1	0	0	0	0	DFS(B) marks B as visited
4	1	1	0	0	0	0	A is already visited
5	1	1	0	0	0	0	Call DFS(C) recursively
6	1	1	1	0	0	0	DFS(C) marks C as visited
7	1	1	1	0	0	0	B is already visited
8	1	1	1	0	0	0	Call DFS(F) recursively
9	1	1	1	0	0	1	DFS(F) marks F as visited
10	1	1	1	0	0	1	B, C already visited; no recursive calls
11	1	1	1	0	0	1	DFS(D) returns to DFS(C), and then DFS(B). DFS(B) sees A, C, E, F adjacent, and ignores already visited A, C, F, and finds unseen node E, and thus calls DFS(E).
12	1	1	1	0	1	1	DFS(E) marks E as visited, ignores B, and calls DFS(D).
13	1	1	1	1	1	1	DFS(D) marks D as visited, ignoring A, E; returns to DFS(E). DFS(E) ignores B and returns to DFS(B). DFS(B) returns to DFS(A) ignoring A, B, F. Finally, DFS(A) ignores B and returns.

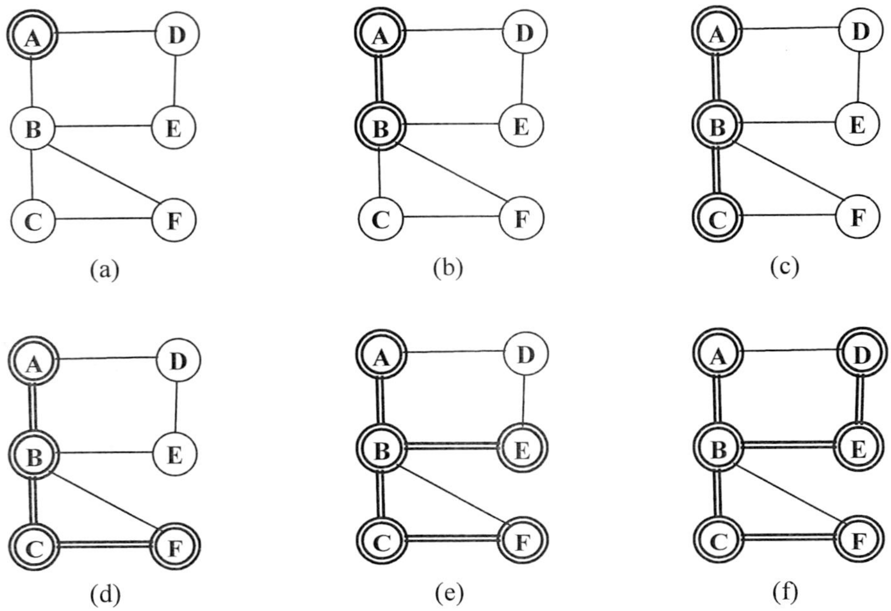

Figure 2.13: Trace of DFS for an undirected graph

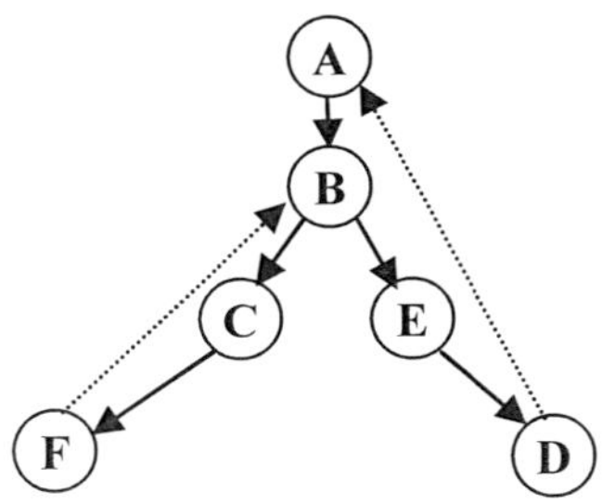

Figure 2.14: DFS spanning tree of graph of Figure 2.12

The most natural result of a depth first search of a graph is a spanning tree of the vertices reached during the search. Figure 2.14 shows the DFS spanning tree for the undirected graph (Figure 2.12). The root of the tree is A, the first node visited. In fact, we can select any one of the nodes as a root. Dashed lines represent back edges. The back edges in a graph are those that connect some descendent node in a tree to an ancestor node in the same tree. It can be shown that if the graph is undirected then all of its edges are tree edges or back edges. DFS on a graph with n vertices and m edges takes $O(n + m)$ time.

2.2.2 Breadth-First Search

Another systematic way of visiting the nodes is called *breadth-first search* (BFS). The approach is called "breadth-first" because from each node v that we visit we search as broadly as possible by next visiting all nodes adjacent to v.

As for depth-first search, we can build a spanning forest when we perform a BFS. In this case, we consider edge (x, y) a tree edge if node y is first visited from node x in the inner loop of the search procedure BFS (Algorithm 2.2).

It turns out that for BFS of an undirected graph, every edge that is not a tree is a cross edge, that is, it connects two nodes neither of which is an ancestor of the other.

The BFS algorithm inserts a node into a queue, which we assume is initially empty. Every entry in the array *mark* is assumed to be initialized to the value *unvisited.* If the graph is not connected, BFS must be called on a node of each connected component. Note that in BFS we must mark a node visited before inserting it into the queue, to avoid placing it on the queue more than once. The algorithm terminates when the queue becomes empty.

We assume the graph is represented by an adjacency list. The algorithm depends on the availability of an implementation of a queue.

Algorithm 2.2: BFS(v: *head* node)

```
Mark v visited
Print v
Insert v into queue
While queue is not empty
      Delete an item from the queue and assign it to v.
      Assign the address of adjacency list of v to adj.
      While adj ≠ null
            Assign node of adj to v.
            If node v is unvisited, then
                  Mark v visited
                  Print v
                  Insert v into the queue
            Endif
            Assign the next node of adjacency list to adj.
      Endwhile
Endwhile
Return
```

Example 2.4: We simulate the BFS algorithm using the undirected graph and its adjacency list shown in Figure 2.12. We start at node A. The steps of BFS are presented in the Table 2.2. The order of nodes visited is A, B, D, C, E, and F. BFS spanning tree is shown in Figure 2.16.

Table 2.2: Trace of BFS

#	Node	*Queue* 1 2 3 4 5 6	*mark* A B C D E F	*Description of the process*
1	A	A □ □ □ □ □	1 0 0 0 0 0	Mark A *visited*; insert A into queue.
2	B	B □ □ □ □ □	1 1 0 0 0 0	Delete A from queue. B is adjacent to A. (A→B→D→ null). Insert B into queue; mark B *visited.*
3	D	B D □ □ □ □	1 1 0 1 0 0	D is adjacent to B. Insert D into queue; mark D *visited.* Now the end of adjacency list (A→B→D→ null) is reached.
5	C	□ D C □ □ □	1 1 1 1 0 0	Delete B from queue. A is adjacent to B (B→A→C→E→F). A is already marked *visited.* Next one is C. As C is *unvisited*, mark C *visited.* Insert C into queue. Next node is E in this adj-list. As E is *unvisited*, mark E *visited.*
6	E	□ D C E □ □	1 1 1 1 1 0	Next node is E in this adjacency list. As E is *unvisited*, mark E *visited*, and insert E into queue.
7	F	□ D C E F □	1 1 1 1 1 1	F is next adjacent node in this adj-list (B→A→C→E→F→ null). As F is *unvisited*, mark F *visited*, and insert F into queue. Null is encountered by traversing this adjacent list.
8	--	□ □ C E F □	1 1 1 1 1 1	Delete D. Adj-list starting with D is (D→A→E→ null). Nodes D, A, E are already *visited.* We encounter null. Inner while-loop is terminated
9	--	□ □ □ □ □ □	1 1 1 1 1 1	Delete C, E, F one-by-one and repeat the above steps for each node. Finally queue is *empty.* Exit from the algorithm.

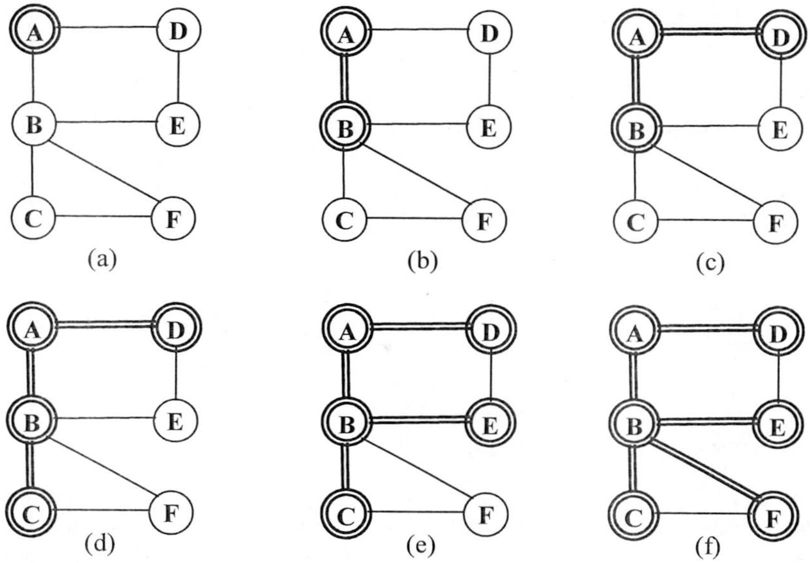

Figure 2.15: Trace of BFS

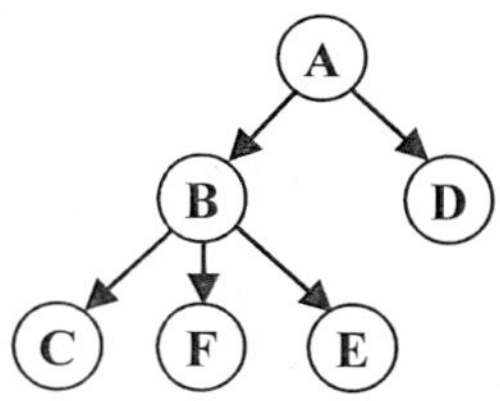

Figure 2.16: BFS spanning tree of graph of Figure 2.12

Breadth-First Search of a graph is the generalization of the level-order traversal. The BSF tree is a shortest path tree starting from its root. Every vertex has a path to the root, with path length equal to its level, and no path can skip a level so this really is a shortest path.

Although we have discussed DFS and BFS for undirected graphs, the same search algorithms work essentially unmodified for directed graphs. The only difference is that when exploring a vertex v, we only want to look at edges (v, w) going out of v; we ignore the other edges coming into v.

For BFS in directed graphs, each edge of the graph either connects two vertices at the same level, goes down exactly one level, or goes up any number of levels. For DFS, each edge either connects an ancestor to a descendant, a descendant to an ancestor, or one node to a node in a previously visited subtree. It is not possible to get "forward edges" connecting a node to a subtree visited later than that node. We will use this property to test if a directed graph is strongly connected (every vertex can reach every other one). The running time of BFS on a graph with n vertices and m edges is $O(n + m)$.

2.2.3 Connected Components

A graph is said to be *connected* if at least one path exists between every pair of vertices in the graph. Alternatively, two vertices are defined to be in the same *connected component* if there exists a path between them. The undirected graph in Figure 2.17 is connected, while the graph shown in Figure 2.18 is not connected. In Figure 2.17, the node A has paths (A, C, D, B), (A, C), and (A, C, D), connecting the nodes B, C, and D, respectively. For example, a path does not exist between B and D in graph of Figure 2.18.

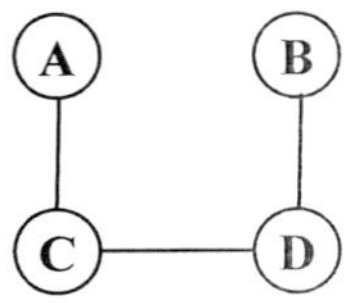

Figure 2.17: Connected graph

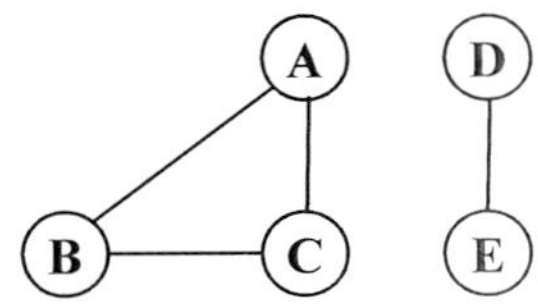

Figure 2.18: A graph that is not connected

A directed graph is said to be *strongly connected* if every two nodes in the graph are reachable from each other. For example, the digraph shown in Figure 2.19 is strongly connected, since A is connected to B and C, B to A and C (via A), and C to B and A (via B). The digraph in Figure 2.20 is not strongly connected since C is not reachable from either A or B.

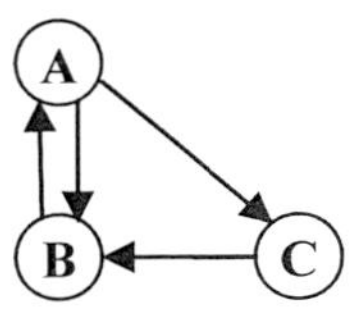

Figure 2.19: A digraph that is strongly connected

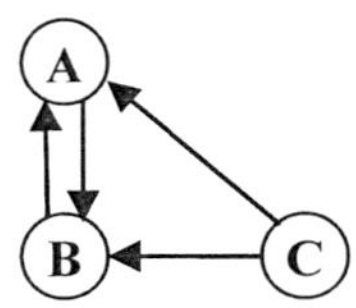

Figure 2.20: A digraph that is not strongly connected

Connectivity in undirected graphs is rather straightforward. A graph that is not connected is naturally and obviously decomposed in several connected components (Figure 2.21). DFS does this easily. Each restart of the algorithm marks a new connected component.

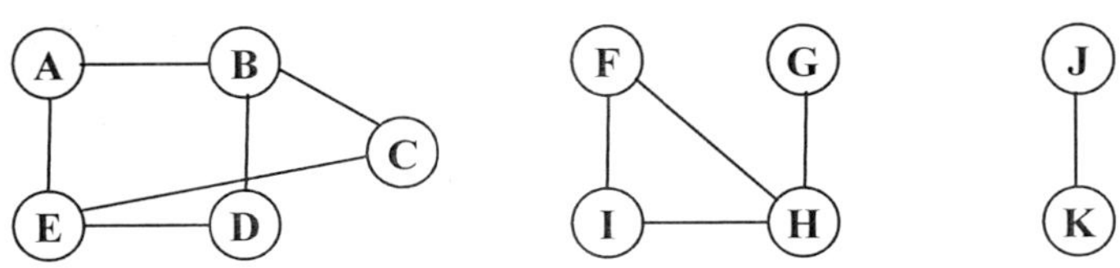

Figure 2.21: Connected components of undirected graphs

In directed graphs, connectivity is more restrained. The digraph in Figure 2.22 is not connected, in that there is no path from node 12 to 6, or from 6 to 1. Connectivity in digraphs is defined as:

Let two nodes u and v of a directed graph $G = (V, E)$ connected if there is a path from u to v, and one from v to u. This relation between nodes is reflexive, symmetric, and transitive, so it is an equivalence relation on the nodes. As such, it partitions V into disjoint sets, called the strongly connected components of the graph. In the directed graph of Figure 2.22, there are four strongly connected components.

A cycle in a directed graph is a circular path. Figure 2.22 has quite a few of them, for example, 10 → 11 → 12 → 10. A graph without cycles is acyclic. A directed graph has a cycle if and only if its DFS reveals a back edge.

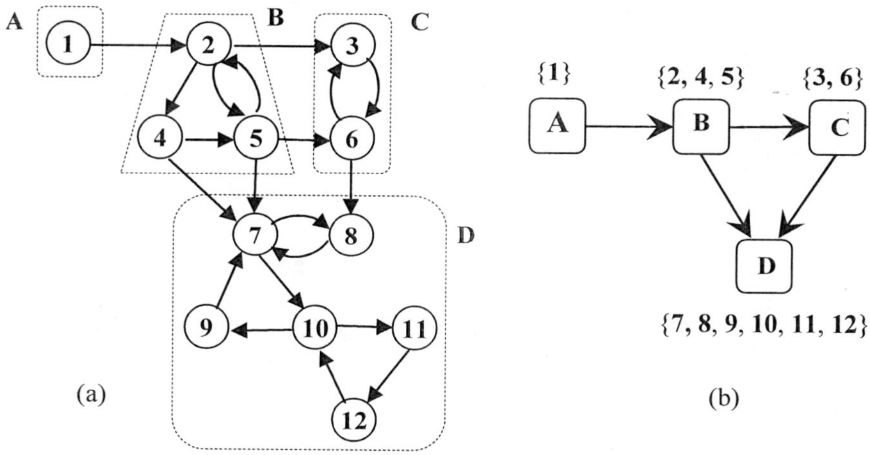

Figure 2.22: A directed graph and its strongly connected components

If we shrink each of these strongly connected components down to a single node, and draw an edge between two of them if there is an edge from some node in the first to some node in the second, the resulting directed graph has to be a directed acyclic graph (DAG) – that is, it can have no cycles (see Figure 22.2(b)). The reason is simple: A cycle containing several strongly connected components would merge them all into a single strongly connected component. We can restate this observation as follows: Every directed graph is a DAG of its strongly connected components. In Figure 2.22, A, B, C, and D are marked as the connected components. For example, there is an edge from node 2 to node 3 connecting B and C components.

2.2.4 Biconnected Components

In many applications involving transportation or communication networks, it is important to identify points through which all network traffic must flow (such as, for example, the Vijayawada railway junction).

An *articulation point* (*cutvertex*) of a graph is a vertex v such that when we delete v and all edges incident upon v, we break a connected component of the graph into two or more pieces (connected components). A connected graph with no articulation points is said to be *biconnected*. Alternatively, a biconnected component of a connected graph G is a maximal biconnected subgraph of G. Note that all the edges in a cycle will be in the same biconnected component.

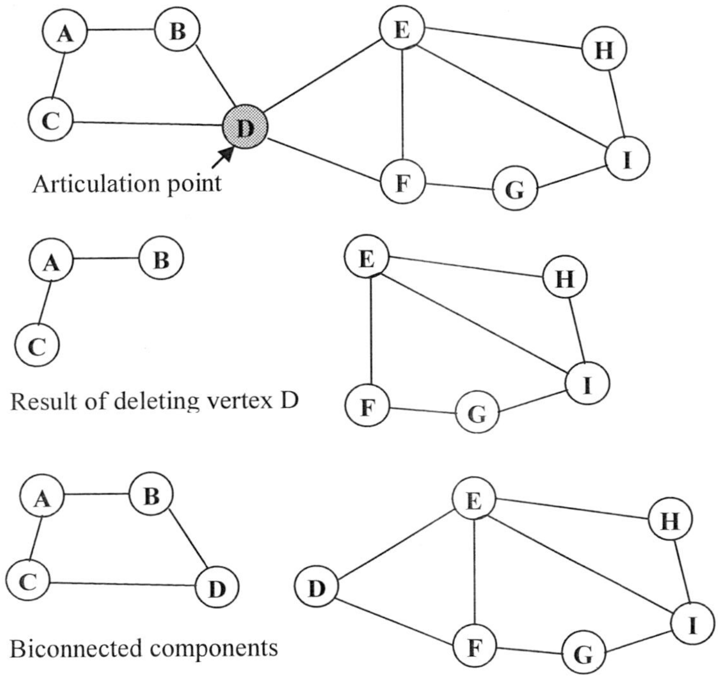

Figure 2.23: An undirected graph and its biconnected components

The following observations are made on biconnected components:

- Two biconnected components of the same graph can have at most one vertex in common. For example, vertex D is common for the two biconnected components :{ A, B. C, D} and (D, E, F, G, H, I).
- No edge can be in two or more biconnected components. Notice that edge (B, D) is in biconnected component {A, B. C, D}.
- The biconnected components of graph *G* partition the edges of *G*.
- The biconnected components of a connected, undirected graph *G* can be found by using any depth-first spanning tree of *G*.
- A nontree edge (*u*, *v*) is a back edge with respect to a spanning tree *T* if and only if either *u* is an ancestor of *v* or *v* is an ancestor of *u*. Observe the DFS spanning tree shown in Figure 2.24, the nontree edge (C, D) is a back edge since D is an ancestor of C.
- A nontree edge that is not back edge is called a cross edge. In Figure 2.24, the nontree edge (B, E) is a cross edge since it is not the back edge.
- No graph can have cross edges with respect to any of its depth-first spanning trees. This can be observed from the undirected graph and its DFS spanning tree shown in Figures 2.23 and 2.24.

- The root of the depth-first spanning tree is an articulation point if and only if it has at least two children. Root D is an articulation point, because D has two children B and E.

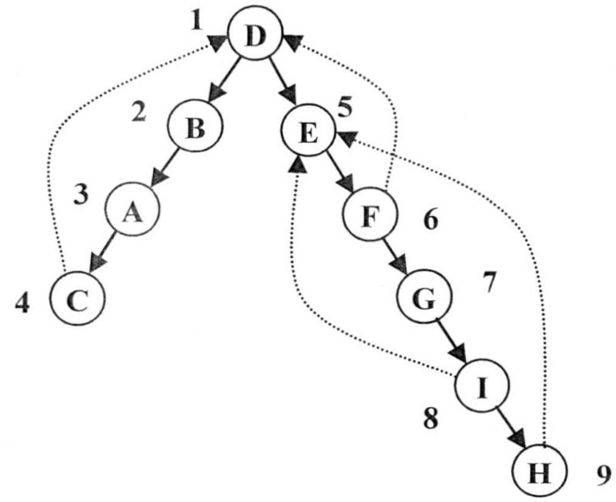

Figure 2.24: DFS Spanning tree of undirected graph (Fig 2.23)

We shall here present a DFS algorithm to find all the articulation points of a connected graph, and thereby test by their absence whether the graph is biconnected.

We number the nodes of a graph in the order in which we first mark them visited during a depth-first search. We call this the *depth-first numbering* (*dfn*) of a graph. In Figure 2.24, these numbers are given against each node. The *df-numbers* (*dfn*) orders the nodes in a preorder traversal of the DFS spanning tree. For every vertex w in the DFS spanning tree, we compute the lowest-numbered vertex, $low(w)$, that is reachable from w by taking zero or more tree edges and then possibly one back edge (in that order). The $low(w)$ is defined as the lowest depth-first number that can be reached from w using a path of descendants followed by, at most, one back edge.

$$low(w) = \min\{dfn(w), \min\{low(x) \mid x \text{ is a child of } w\}, \min\{dfn(x) \mid (w, x) \text{ is a back edge}\}\}$$

Example 2.5: The *dfn* and *low* are computed for the undirected graph of Figure 2.23 in Figure 2.24. As an example of the computation of *low*, the postorder traversal visits C first. At C, there is a back edge (C, D), so $low(C) = \min\{dfn(C), dfn(D)\} = \min\{4, 1\} = 1$. Then A is visited, and $low(A) = \min\{dfn(A), low(\text{child of A})\} = \min\{dfn(A), low(C)\} = \{3, 1\} = 1$. The *low* values of remaining nodes are calculated as follows (Table 2.3 shows the summary of *dfn* and *low* values against their nodes):

$low(B) = \min\{dfn(B), low(\text{child of B})\} = \min\{dfn(B), low(A)\} = \{2, 1\} = 1.$

$low(D) = \min\{dfn(D), low(\text{child of D})\} = \min\{dfn(D), low(B)\} = \{1, 1\} = 1.$

$low(H) = \min\{dfn(H), dfn(E)\} = \min\{9, 5\} = 5.$ → (H, E) is a back edge.

$low(I) = \min\{dfn(I), dfn(E)\} = \min\{8, 5\} = 5.$ → (I, E) is a back edge.

$low(G) = \min\{dfn(G), low(\text{child of G})\} = \min\{dfn(G), low(I)\} = \{7, 5\} = 5.$

$low(F) = \min\{dfn(F), low(\text{child of F}), dfn(D)\}$ → (F, D) is a back edge.

= min{*dfn*(F), *low*(G), *dfn*(D)} = min{ 6, 5, 1} = 1.

low(E) = min{*dfn*(E), *low*(child of E)} = min{*dfn*(E), *low*(F)} = {5, 1} = 1.

Table 2.3: Summary of *dfn* and *low* values generated by DFS

Node	A	B	C	D	E	F	G	H	I
dfn	3	2	4	1	5	6	7	9	8
low	1	1	1	1	1	1	5	5	5

Let DFS spanning tree, *T* be empty and *count* be 1. Mark each vertex "unvisited". Also initialize a STACK of edges, initially empty. Choose an initial *v* arbitrarily. Then call BICONSEARCH(*v*).

Algorithm 2.3: BICONSEARCH(*v*)

```
Mark v "visited"
dfn[v] = count
Add 1 to count
For each vertex w in adjlist(v) do
        If (v, w) is not on the STACK, push (v, w)
            ( (v, w) is on STACK if either
                v < w and w already "visited" or
                v > w and w = parent[v]  )
        Endif
        If w is "unvisited" then
            add (v, w) to T; set parent(w) = v;
            BICONSEARCH(w)
            If low[w] ≥ dfn[v] then a biconnected component
                        has been found;
                    pop the edges up to and including
                    (v, w); these are the component.
            Endif
            low[v] = min (low[v], low[w])
        Else If w is not parent[v] then
            low[v] = min(low[v], dfn[w])
        Endif
Endfor.
```

After computing *low*, we consider each node. The root, D is an articulation point because it has two children B and E (see Figures 2.23 and 24). Alternatively, $low(B) \geq dfn(D)$ or $low(E) \geq dfn(D)$.

The time taken by the algorithm 2.3 on *n*-node graph of *m* edges and $n \leq m$ is $O(m)$. A constant amount of time is attributed to any node or edge in any pass. Thus, the total time is $O(n + m)$.

CHAPTER SUMMARY

- A *disjoint set* data structure maintains a collection $S = \{S_1, S_2, . . ., S_n\}$ of disjoint dynamic sets. It supports the creation and merging of sets, is known as *Union-Find*. It may be implemented in different ways. *Union*() requires a constant time, $O(n)$. *Find*() takes $O(n^2)$.
- The total running time for the disjoint sets with weighted-union heuristic is $O(m+n\log_2 n)$.
- A faster implementation of disjoint sets is through the rooted trees, with each node containing one member and each tree representing one set.
- By using *union-by-rank* and *path compression* heuristics, we can improve the running time of disjoint set operations.
- A *spanning tree* of an undirected graph of n nodes is a set of n-1 edges that connects all nodes. Every node is reachable from every other node.
- We can obtain spanning trees by using DFS and BFS.
- DFS first explores the edges out of the node most recently reached, that is, it tries to go as deep as possible first.
- BFS is called "breadth-first" because from each node v that we visit we search as broadly as possible by next visiting all nodes adjacent to v.
- Running time of DFS or BFS on a graph with n vertices and m edges is $O(n + m)$.
- A graph is said to be *connected* if at least one path exists between every pair of vertices in the graph.
- Partitioning the set of vertices (in directed graph) into disjoint sets is called the *strongly connected* components of the graph.
- *Articulation point* (or cut vertex) is any vertex whose removal (together with the removal of any incident edges) results in a disconnected graph.
- A graph is *biconnected* if it contains no articulation points.
- DFS finds all the articulation points of a connected graph, and thereby test by their absence whether the graph is biconnected.

SELF-TEST QUIZ

2.1 Two sets A and B are disjoint, if their ________ is the empty set.

(a) union (b) difference (c) intersection (d) inversion

2.2 Suppose we have three sets, $A = \{a, b, e, f\}$, $B = \{b, g, h\}$, and $C = \{c, d, g, h\}$, which of these two sets form the disjoint sets.

(a) B & C (b) C & A (c) A & B (d) None of these

2.3 What is a general data structure known that supports the creation and merging of sets?

(a) union-find (b) disjoint set
(c) make and join (d) either (a) or (b)

2.4 What is the total time required to process the n union operations in *Union-Find* structure?

(a) $O(n)$ (b) $O(\log_2 n)$ (c) $O(1)$ (d) $O(n^2)$

2.5 What is total time needed to process the n find operations in *Union-Find* structure?

(a) $O(n)$ (b) $O(\log_2 n)$ (c) $O(1)$ (d) $O(n^2)$

2.6 In weighted-union heuristic of disjoint sets, ___ ___ ___.

(a) the smaller set is appended to the longer one.
(b) the longer set is appended to the smaller one.
(c) two equal sets are merged.
(d) either (b) or (c).

2.7 The worst-case running time of weighted-union heuristic of disjoint sets, for m operations and n elements is

(a) $O(mn)$ (b) $O(n\log_2 n)$ (c) $O(m+n\log_2 n)$ (d) $O(n^2)$

2.8 In weighted-union heuristic of disjoint sets, for m operations and n elements, the amortized time of *MakeSet* and *Find* is

(a) $O(n)$ (b) $O(\log_2 n)$ (c) $O(1)$ (d) $O(n^2)$

2.9 In weighted-union heuristic of disjoint sets, the amortized time of *Union* is

(a) $O(n)$ (b) $O(\log_2 n)$ (c) $O(1)$ (d) $O(n^2)$

2.10 Disjoint-set forests are represented by

(a) linked lists (b) graphs (c) trees (d) arrays

2.11 In union-by-rank heuristic (disjoint-set forests), the root with smaller rank is made to point to the root with larger rank during a ______ operation.

(a) *Find* (b) *MakeSet* (c) *Union* (d) any one of these

2.12 Assume that we start with a disjoint-set forest of trees, each having one node. Let T be a tree with n nodes created by a sequence of unions using union-by-rank heuristic. The height of T is no greater than _____.

(a) n (b) $\log_2 n$ (c) $n-1$ (d) $n+1$

2.13 In disjoint-set forest, the worst-case running time by path compression takes place during the ______ operation.

(a) *Find* (b) *MakeSet* (c) *Union* (d) any one of these

2.14 In disjoint-set forest, the worst-case running time by path compression is (m: number of operations, and n: number of nodes in the tree)

(a) $O(m+\log_2 n)$ (b) $O(m\log_2 n)$
(c) $O(m+n\log_2 n)$ (d) $O(n\log_2 n)$

2.15 If j is a node on the path from i to its root and parent[i] $\neq$ root[i], then set parent[j] to root[i]. In disjoint sets, this is known as

(a) weighted-union heuristic (b) union-by-rank heuristic
(c) path compression (d) union-by-rank and path compression

2.16 Insertion of an edge to a spanning tree forms a

(a) circuit (b) cycle (c) open path (d) binary tree

2.17 A *spanning tree* of an undirected graph of n nodes is a set of _____ edges that connects all nodes.

(a) n-1 (b) n-2 (c) n (d) n+1

2.18 In a spanning tree, there is at least _______ path between any two nodes.

(a) three (b) two (c) one (d) none of these

2.19 In ____________ traversal the adjacent nodes of a node are visited first.

(a) Inorder (b) Postorder
(c) Breadth First Search (d) Depth First Search

2.20 Using the depth first search the edges are traversed by search algorithm to make a tree called as

(a) breadth first spanning tree (b) depth first spanning tree
(c) spanning tree (d) Weighted graph

2.21 If the starting node is 'a', the DFS of the following graph is

(a) a-b-c-e-d
(b) b-e-d-a-c
(c) b-e-a-d-c
(d) a-c-b-d-e

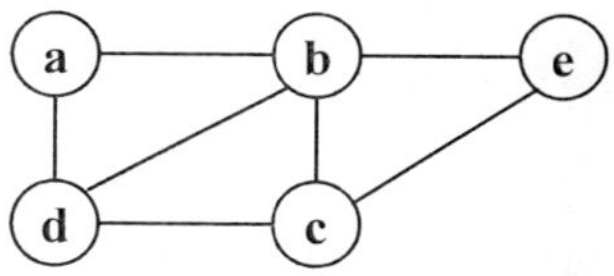

2.22 In the implementation of DFS _______ data structure is mostly used.

(a) Stack (b) File (c) Array (d) Queue

2.23 DFS on a graph with n vertices and m edges takes _____ time.

(a) $O(mn)$ (b) $O(n + m)$ (c) $O(m\text{-}n)$ (d) $O(m\text{-}n\text{+}1)$

2.24 The running time of BFS on a graph with n vertices and m edges is $O(n + m)$.

(a) $O(mn)$ (b) $O(n + m)$ (c) $O(m\text{-}n)$ (d) $O(m\text{-}n\text{+}1)$

2.25 The number of edges that must be removed from a connected graph with n vertices and m edges to produce a spanning tree is

(a) m (b) $n - m$ (c) $m - n + 1$ (d) $m - n$

2.26 The minimum number of edges in a connected cyclic graph on n vertices is

(a) n-1 (b) n (c) n+1 (d) none of these

2.27 A directed graph has a cycle if and only if its depth-first search reveals a _____ edge.

(a) tree (b) forward (c) cross (d) back

2.28 If there exists at least one path between every pair of vertices in a graph, it is known as

(a) complete graph (b) acyclic graph (c) connected graph (d) Euler graph

2.29 Which of the following is useful in traversing a graph by breadth-first search?

(a) stack (b) set (c) list (d) queue

2.30 Let T be a depth first search tree in an undirected graph G. Vertices u and v are leaves of this tree T. The degrees of both u and v in G are at least 2. Which one of the following statements is true? *GATE-2006*

(a) There must exist a vertex w adjacent to both u and v in G.
(b) There must exist a vertex w whose removal disconnects u and v in G.
(c) There must exist a cycle in G containing u and v.
(d) There must exist a cycle in G containing u and all its neigbours in G.

2.31 Consider the following graph: *GATE-2003*

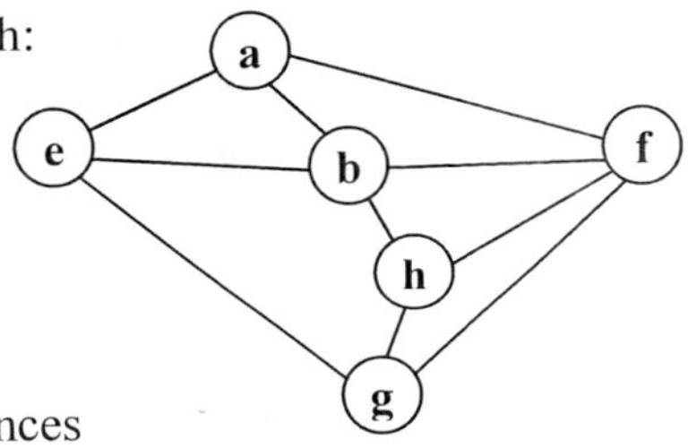

Among the following sequences

I. a b e g h f II. a b f e h g III. a b f h g e IV. a f g h b e

which are depth first traversals of the above graph?

(a) I, II and IV only (b) I and IV only
(c) II, III and IV only (d) I, III and IV only

Consider the following undirected graph to answer the questions: 2.32, 2.33, and 2.34

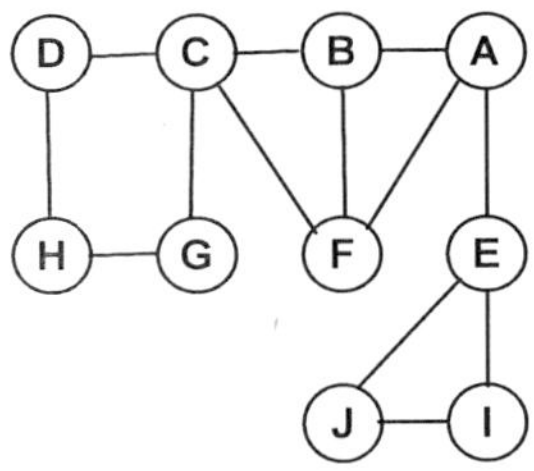

2.32 The articulation points of the above graph are ______________ vertices.

(a) A, C (b) E, C (c) A, C, E (d) A, E

2.33 How many biconnected components are there in the above graph?

(a) 2 (b) 3 **(c) 4** (d) 5

2.34 Which of the following are the biconnected components?

I. (A, E) II. (A, B, C, F) III. (C, D, G, H) IV. (E, I, J)

(a) I and II (b) II, III, and IV (c) III and IV (d) I, II, III, and IV

2.35 If (v, w) is a back edge, then in the spanning forest of G, ______________.

(a) v is an ancestor of w.
(b) w is an ancestor of v.
(c) v and w are siblings.
(d) either (a) or (b)

2.36 For any connected graph G, any ______ distinct biconnected components have at most one vertex in common.

(a) one (b) two (c) three (d) four

EXERCISES

2.1 What is a disjoint set? Mention its applications.

2.2 Explain union/find algorithm with an example.

2.3 Initially, we have the following disjoint sets consisting of distinct elements: $\{a\}$, $\{b\}$, $\{c\}$, $\{d\}$, $\{e\}$, $\{f\}$, $\{g\}$, $\{h\}$. Show the result of the following sequence of operations (using disjoint-set forest): *Union*(a, b), *Union*(e, f), *Union*(g, h), *Union*(e, g), *Union*(d, e). When unions are:

(a) Performed arbitrarily,
(b) Performed union-by-rank, and
(c) Perform a *Find* with path compression on the deepest node.

2.4 Consider the following disjoint-set forest, perform *Find*(9) operation. Draw the resulting tree after path compression.

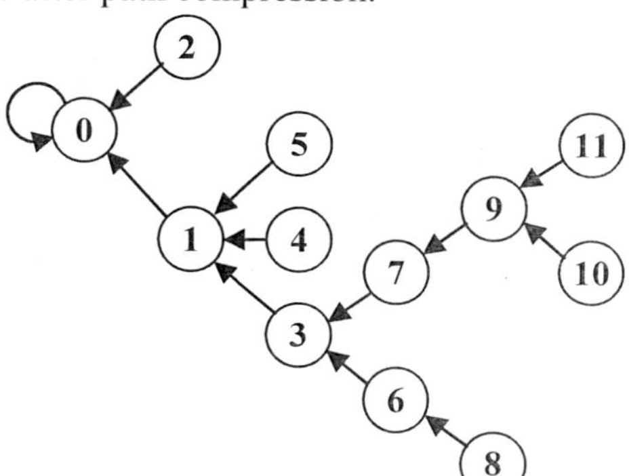

2.5 Using union-by-height (or rank), show that a tree with k nodes has a height of at most $\log_2 k + 1$.

2.6 Show that if $m = n^2$, then the running time of m union/find operations is $O(m)$.

2.7 Show that if $m = n\log_2 n$, then the running time of m union/find operations is $O(m)$.

2.8 Suppose we start with n sets, each containing a distinct element.

(a) Show that if u unions are performed, then no set contains more than u+1 elements.

(b) Show that at most n-1 unions can be performed before number of sets becomes 1.

(c) Show that if fewer than $\lceil n/2 \rceil$ unions are performed, then at least one set with a single element in it remains.

2.9 What is a spanning tree? Show that a simple graph is connected if it has a spanning tree.

2.10 Find the DFS and BFS spanning trees for the following two graphs.

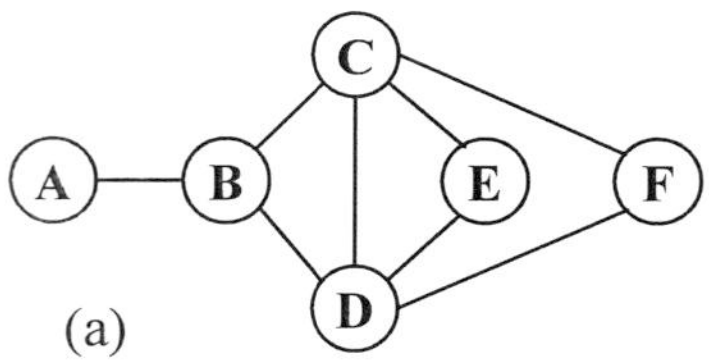

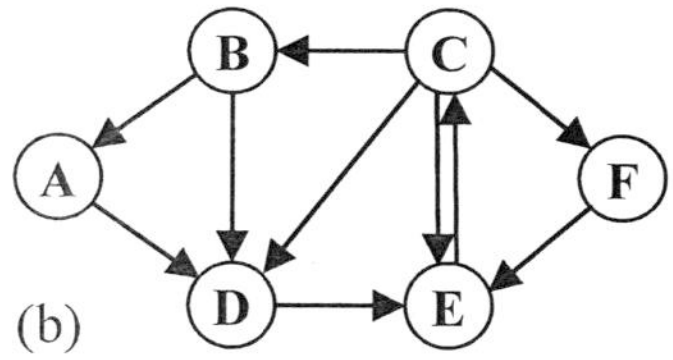

2.11 Explain biconnected components? What is the relation between depth first search and biconnected components of an undirected graph?

2.12 Show that if G is a connected undirected graph, then no edge of G can be in two different biconnected components.

2.13 Find all the articulation points of the graph shown in Figure-A. Show the depth-first spanning tree and the values of *df-number* and *low* for each node.

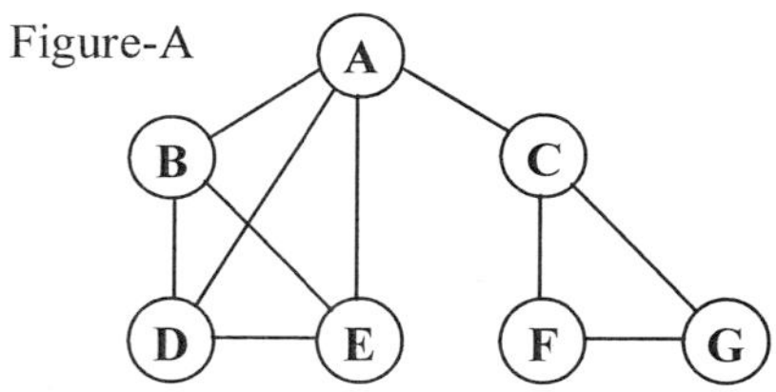

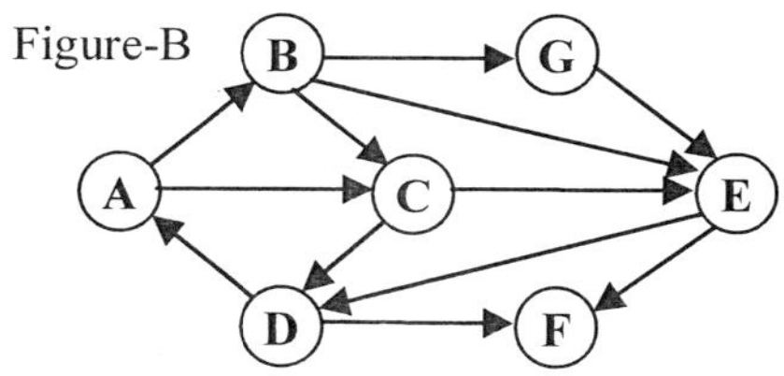

2.14 Find the strongly connected components of the directed graph (Figure-B).

CHAPTER 3

DIVIDE AND CONQUER

In computer science, divide and conquer is an important algorithm design paradigm. It works by recursively breaking down a problem into two or more sub-problems of the same type, until these become simple enough to be solved directly. The solutions to the sub-problems are then combined to give a solution to the original problem. A divide and conquer algorithm is closely tied to a type of recurrence relation between functions of the data in question; data is "divided" into smaller portions and the result calculated thence. The divide-and-conquer algorithms consist of three steps:

1. Breaking the problem into several sub-problems that are similar to the original problem but smaller in size,
2. Solve the sub-problem recursively (successively and independently), and then
3. Combine these solutions to subproblems to create a solution to the original problem.

The technique is named "divide and conquer" because a problem is conquered by dividing it into several smaller problems. This technique yields elegant, simple and quite often very efficient algorithms. For example, if the work of splitting the problem and combining the partial solutions is proportional to the problem's size n, there are a bounded number b of sub-problems of size n/b at each stage, and the base cases require $O(1)$ (constant-bounded) time, then the divide-and-conquer algorithm will have $O(n \log n)$ complexity. This is used for problems such as sorting to reduce the complexity from $O(n^2)$, although in general there may also be other approaches to designing efficient algorithms.

Divide and conquer algorithms typically have a time complexity recurrence relations of the form:

$$T(1) = c$$
$$T(n) = aT(n/b) + cn^k$$

such that a problem of size n is split into "a" subproblems, each of size n/b. And cn^k is the cost of combining the solutions. The closed form solution for this recurrence depends on the relation between a, and b^k (n is a power of b: i.e., $n = b^k$)

If $a > b^k$, then $T(n) = O(n^{\log_b a})$
If $a = b^k$, then $T(n) = O(n^k \log n)$

If $a < b^k$, then $T(n) = O(n^k)$

The master theorem gives us the running times of most of the divide-and-conquer procedures. For example, merge sort is a typical divide and conquer algorithm, where the list to be sorted is split into two equal subproblems and it takes $O(n)$ time to put the two sorted sublists back together. Thus, the recurrence relation will be:

$T(n) = 2T(n/2) + n$ where $a = 2$, $b = 2$, and $k = 1$.

Applying the above theorem, merge sort has a time complexity of $O(n \log_2 n)$.

What is a *recurrence relation*?* A recurrence relation is a function that is defined in terms of itself. It is a means of generating an integer sequence. One starts with a small number of initial values, and then applies a recurrence rule. For example, a function to generate the Fibonacci numbers is defined as:

General case: $F(n) = F(n - 1) + F(n - 2)$, for $n \geq 2$
Base cases: $F(0) = 0$, $F(1) = 1$

One use of recurrence relations is in determining the complexity of algorithms.

This technique is the basis of efficient algorithms for all kinds of problems, such as sorting (quick sort, merge sort), binary search, powering a number, Fibonacci numbers, matrix multiplication and so on.

3.1 BINARY SEARCH

A binary search algorithm is a technique for finding a particular value in a sorted list. It makes progressively better guesses, and closes in on the sought value by selecting the median element in a list, comparing its value to the target value (key), and determining if the selected value is greater than, less than, or equal to the target value. A guess that turns out to be too high becomes the new top of the list, and a guess that is too low becomes the new bottom of the list. Pursuing this approach iteratively, it narrows the search by a factor of two each time, and finds the target value. The binary search consists of the following steps:

1. Search a sorted array by repeatedly dividing the search interval in half.
2. Begin with an interval covering the whole array.
3. If the value of the search key is less than the item in the middle of the interval, narrow the interval to the lower half. Otherwise narrow it to the upper half.
4. Repeatedly check until the value is found or the interval is empty.

The most straightforward implementation is recursion, which recursively searches the sub-array dictated by the comparison:

* Refer Section 1.5 for detailed explanation of recurrence relation.

Algorithm 3.1: BinarySearch(*arr*[1..*n*], *value*, *low*, *high*)

```
If (high < low)
        return -1              // not found
Endif
mid = (low + high) / 2
If (arr[mid] > value)
        return BinarySearch(arr, value, low, mid-1)
Else If (arr[mid] < value)
            return BinarySearch(arr, value, mid+1, high)
      Else
            return mid         // found
      Endif
Endif
```

The algorithm is invoked with initial *low* and *high* values of 1 and *n*. We can eliminate the recursion above and convert this to an iterative implementation. Iterative one is presented in Algorithm 1.11. Figure 3.1 illustrates trace of the algorithm to find the target *value* of 65.

mid = (*low* + *high*)/2 = (1+9)/2 = 5
arr[*mid*] < *value*   (55 < 65)
low = *mid*+1 = 5+1 = 6
high = 9

mid = (*low* + *high*)/2 = (6+9)/2 = 7
arr[7] > *value*   (75 > 65)
high = *mid*–1 = 7–1 = 6

mid = (*low* + *high*)/2 = (6+6)/2 = 6
arr[6] > *value*   (65 > 65) → false
arr[6] < *value*   (65 < 65) → false
arr[6] = *value*   (65 = 65) → true
Found at *mid* = 6.

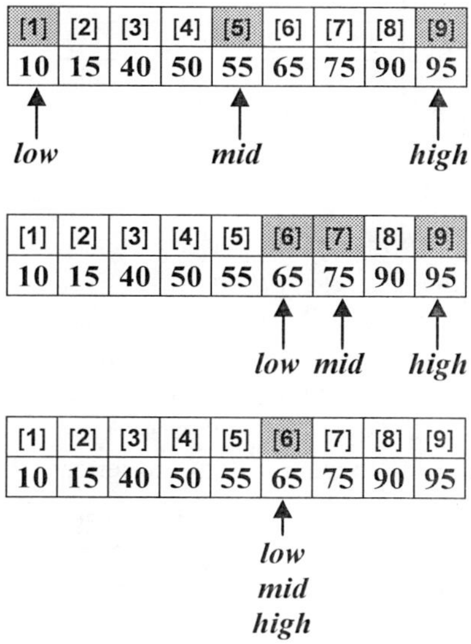

Figure 3.1: Trace of binary search

Binary search is a logarithmic algorithm and runs in $O(\log_2 n)$ time. Specifically, $1+\log_2 n$ iterations are needed to return an answer. In most cases it is considerably faster than a linear search. It can be implemented using recursion or iteration, as shown above.

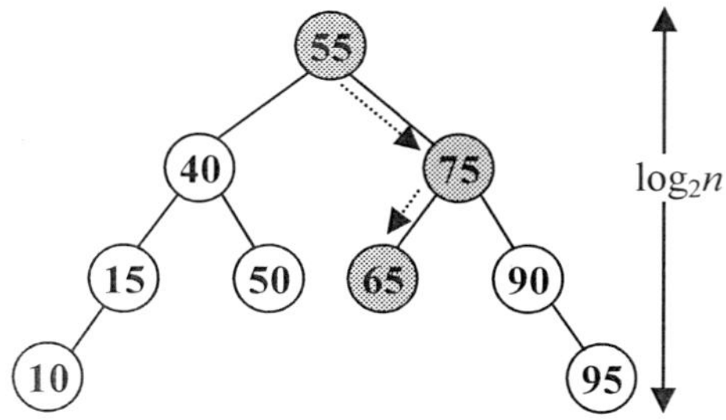

Figure 3.2: Trace of binary search algorithm to find 65

Let us verify the height (or depth) of the binary search tree with $\log_2 n$ values. Notice the following table. Binary search tree of Figure 3.2 has $n = 9$ nodes. Hence, its height is $\lfloor \log_2 9 \rfloor$ = 3. Note that this is an upper bound.

Table 3.1: $\log_2 n$ values for different sizes of binary search tree

n	1	2	3	4	5	6	7	8	9
$\log_2 n$	0.00	1.00	1.58	2.00	2.32	2.58	2.81	3.00	3.17
$\lfloor \log_2 n \rfloor$	0	1	1	2	2	2	2	3	3

n	15	16	17	31	32	33	64	65	128
$\log_2 n$	3.91	4.00	4.09	4.95	5.00	5.04	6.00	6.02	7.00
$\lfloor \log_2 n \rfloor$	3	4	4	4	5	5	6	6	7

3.2 MERGE SORT

Merge sort is an $O(n \log n)$ comparison-based sorting algorithm. In most implement-tations it is stable, meaning that it preserves the input order of equal elements in the sorted output. It is an example of the divide and conquer algorithmic paradigm.

Sorting by merging is a recursive, divide-and-conquer strategy. In the base case, we have a sequence with exactly one element in it. Since such a sequence is already sorted, there is nothing to be done. To sort a sequence of elements ($n > 1$):

- divide the sequence into two sequences of length $\lceil n/2 \rceil$ and $\lfloor n/2 \rfloor$,
- recursively sort each of the two subsequences; and then,
- merge the sorted subsequences to obtain the final result.

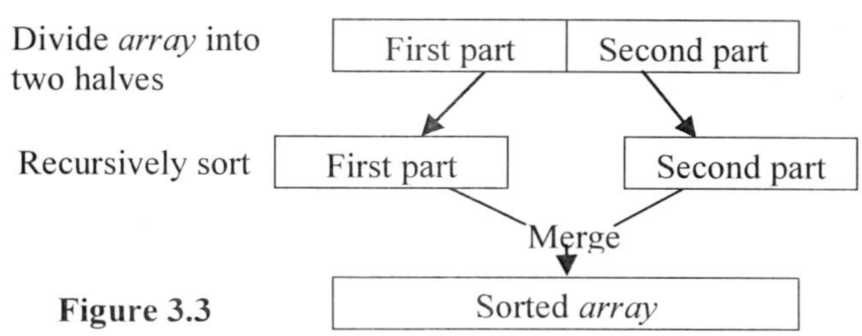

Figure 3.3

Figure 3.3 shows the idea of merge sort. Figure 3.4 illustrates the operation of the two-way merge sort algorithm. We assume to sort the given array $a[n]$ into ascending order. We split it into two subarrays: $a[1]...a[\lceil n/2 \rceil]$ and $a[\lceil n/2 \rceil+1]...a[n]$. Each subarray is individually sorted, and the resulting sorted subarrays are merged to produce a single sorted array of n elements. Consider an array of nine elements: {75, 40, 10, 90, 50, 95, 55, 15, 65}. The *mergeSort* algorithm divides the array into subarrays and merges them into sorted subarrays by *merge*() algorithm as illustrated in the Figure 3.4 (Dashed-line arrows indicate the process of splitting and the regular arrows the merging process).

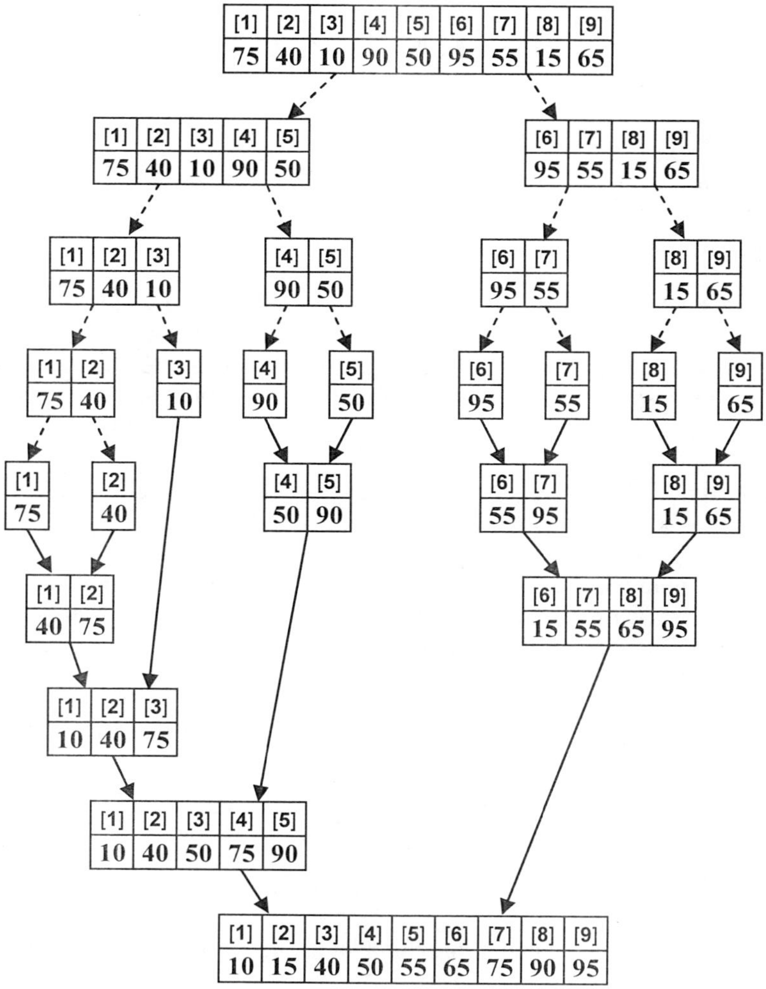

Figure 3.4: Two-way merge sort

First, left half of the array with five elements is being split and merged; and next second half of the array with four elements is processed (Notice how the splitting continues until subarrays containing a single element are produced). Figure 3.4 represents the sequence of recursive calls that are produced by *mergeSort* when it is applied to nine elements.

Since merge operations cannot be done in place, a second temporary array, *tmp*[] is needed, in addition to the main array, *a*[].

The *merge*() algorithm takes three integer parameters: *left*, *mid* (middle), and *right*. The relationship among these parameters is:

$left \leq mid < right$

It is assumed that the two subsequences of the array, *a*[]:

a[*left*], *a*[*left*+1], . . ., *a*[*mid*],

and

a[*mid*+1], *a*[*mid*+2], . . ., *a*[*right*],

are both sorted. The *merge*() method merges the two sorted subarrays using the temporary array, *tmp*[]. It then copies the merged and sorted sequence into the array at

a[*left*], a[*left*+1], . . ., *a*[*right*]

The *mergesort*() algorithm implements the recursive divide-and-conquer by taking two parameters: *left* and *right* (Initially, $left = 1$, $right = n$). These parameters specify the two subsequences of the array, *a*[] to be sorted. If the sequence to be sorted contains more than one element, the sequence is split in two, each half is recursively sorted, and then two sorted halves are merged by calling *merge*() algorithm. We assume that the two arrays *a*[] and *tmp*[] are *globally* declared.

In *merge* algorithm, the total number of iterations of the two while-loops, in the worst case, is $right - left$. The number of iterations of the third for-loop is the same. Since all the loops do a constant amount of work, the total running time for the *merge* method is $O(n)$, where $n = right - left$. This is the total number of elements in the two sub-arrays that are merged.

We analyze the worst-case running time of *mergesort* on n elements. Merge sort on just one element takes constant time. When we have $n > 1$ elements, we break down the running time as follows.

- *Divide:* The divide step just computes the middle of the subarray, which takes constant time, $O(1)$.
- *Conquer:* We recursively solve two subproblems, each of size $n/2$, which contributes $T(n/2) + T(n/2)$ to the running time.
- *Combine:* The *merge* procedure on an n-element subarray takes time $O(n)$.

We add a function that is $O(n)$ and a function that is $O(1)$. This sum is a linear function of n, that is, $O(n)$. Adding it to the $2T(n/2)$ term from the "conquer" step gives the recurrence for the worst-case running time $T(n)$ of *mergesort*:

$T(1) = O(1)$ for $n = 1$

$T(n) = 2T(n/2) + O(n)$ for $n > 1$

This can be solved by repeated substitutions. Finally,

$T(n) = n\log_2 n + n$

Therefore, the running time of merge sort is $O(n\log_2 n)$. The solution is explained in Example 1.20.

Algorithm 3.2: *megresort(left, right)*

```
If(left < right)
        mid = (left + right)/2          // Divide problem into subproblems
        mergesort(left, mid)            // Solve first subproblem
        mergesort(mid+1, right)         // Solve second subproblem
        merge(left, mid, right)         // Combine the solutions
Endif
```

Algorithm 3.3: *merge(left, mid, right)*

```
i = j = left;    k = mid + 1
While j ≤ mid and k ≤ right
    If a[j] < a[k]
        tmp[i] = a[j];  Increment i and j
    Else
        tmp[i] = a[k];  Increment i and k
    Endif
Endwhile
While j ≤ mid
    tmp[i] = a[j];  Increment i and j
Endwhile
For i = left to k
    a[i] = tmp[i]
Endfor
```

3.3 QUICK SORT

As its name implies, *quicksort* is the fastest known sorting algorithm in practice. The algorithm solely depends on the data it receives. If the data has certain properties, *quicksort* is one of the fastest, if not, *quicksort* can be very slow. *Quicksort* can perform quite fast, on average about $O(n\log n)$, but its worst case is a degrading $O(n^2)$. For *quicksort*, the worst case is usually when the data is already sorted.

Quicksort sorts by using a divide and conquer strategy to divide a list into two sub-lists. Quicksort is naturally recursive. We partition the array into two sub-arrays, and then re-start the algorithm on each of these sub-arrays. The partition procedure involves choosing some object (usually, already in the array - *pivot*); If some other object is greater than the chosen object, it is added to one of the sub-arrays, if it is less than the chosen object, it is added to another subarray. Thus, the entire array is partitioned into two sub-arrays, with one sub-array having everything that is larger than the chosen object, and the other sub-array having everything that is smaller. A general algorithm based on a recursive method follows:

Variable *a* is an integer array of size, *n*. The *left* and *right* invoke procedure and they are initialized with 1 and *n* respectively; and are the current lower and upper bounds of the sub-arrays. The indices *newleft* and *newright* are used to select certain elements during the processing of each sub-array. Variable *amid* (pivot) is the element which is placed in its final location in the array.

Algorithm 3.4: Quicksort(*a*, *left*, *right*)

```
newleft = left;   newright = right.
amid = a[(left + right)/2]                    // pivot
While newleft ≤ newright     // Partition
      While( a[newleft] < amid and newleft < right )    // while-loop-1
            Increment newleft
      Endwhile
      While( amid < a[newright] and newright > left )  // while-loop-2
            Decrement newright
      Endwhile
      If newleft ≤ newright, then
            Swap ( a[newleft], a[newright] )
            Increment newleft and Decrement newright
      Endif
Endwhile    // Partition ends
If left < newright, then
      Call Quicksort(a, left, newright )   //sort left sub-array
Endif
If newleft < right, then
      Call Quicksort(a, newleft, right )  // sort right sub-array
Endif
```

Index *left* scans the list from left to right, and index *right* scans the list from right to left. A swap is performed when left is at an element larger than the *pivot* and right is at an element smaller than the *pivot*. A final swap with the pivot completes the divide step. The *pivot* element is placed in its final proper position in the array. We take the *pivot* as the middle element of the array (or sub-array). We consider an unsorted array of size 12 to sort the array in ascending order: {65, 35, 15, 90, 75, 45, 40, 60, 95, 25, 85, 55}.

left = 1, *right* = 12, *newleft* = *left*, *newright* = *right*, *mid* = (*newleft* + *newright*)/2 = 6, *amid* = *a*[*mid*] = *a*[6] = 45. The middle element of the array is 45 which acts as a *pivot*. Now, left sublist is 1 to 5 and right sublist is 7 to 12. The while-loop-1 scans left sublist from left to right - as the element 65 is greater than *pivot* (45), 65 is to be shifted to right sublist. The *newleft* = 1. The while-loop-2 scans right sublist from right to left - as the element 25 is less than *pivot* (45), The *newright* = 10. The elements in the *newleft* and *newright* are interchanged.

a_1	a_2	a_3	a_4	a_5	a_6	a_7	a_8	a_9	a_{10}	a_{11}	a_{12}	*newleft*	*newright*
65	35	15	90	75	**45**	40	60	95	25	85	55	1	10

The subsequent steps are illustrated as follows (complete trace of the algorithm is given in Table 3.2.

a_1	a_2	a_3	a_4	a_5	a_6	a_7	a_8	a_9	a_{10}	a_{11}	a_{12}	*newleft*	*newright*
25	35	15	90	75	**45**	40	60	95	65	85	55	4	7

a_1	a_2	a_3	a_4	a_5	a_6	a_7	a_8	a_9	a_{10}	a_{11}	a_{12}	*newleft*	*newright*
25	35	15	40	75	**45**	90	60	95	65	85	55	5	6

a_1	a_2	a_3	a_4	a_5	a_6	a_7	a_8	a_9	a_{10}	a_{11}	a_{12}	*newleft*	*newright*
25	35	15	40	**45**	75	90	60	95	65	85	55	6	5

As *left* < *newright* (1 < 5), the following recursive call is made to sort the left sublist:

Quicksort(*a*, *left*, *newright*).

Table 3.2: Trace of Quick sort

step	a_1	a_2	a_3	a_4	a_5	a_6	a_7	a_8	a_9	a_{10}	a_{11}	a_{12}	*left*	*right*	*pivot*
0	65	35	15	90	75	45	40	60	95	25	85	55	1	12	45
1	25	35	15	40	45	75	90	60	95	65	85	55	1	5	15
2	15	35	25	40	45	75	90	60	95	65	85	55	2	5	25
3	15	25	35	40	45	75	90	60	95	65	85	55	3	5	40
4	15	25	35	40	45	75	90	60	95	65	85	55	6	12	95
5	15	25	35	40	45	75	90	60	55	65	85	95	6	11	60
6	15	25	35	40	45	55	60	90	75	65	85	95	6	7	55
7	15	25	35	40	45	55	60	90	75	65	85	95	8	11	75
8	15	25	35	40	45	55	60	65	75	90	85	95	10	11	90
9	15	25	35	40	45	55	60	65	75	85	90	95	sorted array		

The best-case behaviour of the quicksort algorithm occurs when in each recursion step the partitioning produces two parts of equal length. In order to sort n elements, in this case the running time is in $O(n\log_2 n)$. This is because the recursion depth is $\log_2(n)$ and on each level there are n elements to be treated (Figure 3.5(a)).

The worst-case occurs when in each recursion step an unbalanced partitioning is produced, namely that one part consists of only one element and the other part consists of the rest of the elements (Figure 3.5(c)). Then the recursion depth is n-1 and quicksort runs in time $O(n^2)$. In the average case a partitioning as shown in Figure 3.5(b) is to be expected. Both the best-case and the average case are the same - that is, $O(n\log_2 n)$.

Figure 3.5: Recursion depth of quicksort (a) best-case, (b) average-case, (c) worst-case

The choice of the comparison element (*amid*) determines which partition is achieved. Suppose that the first element of the sequence is chosen as comparison element. This would lead to the worst-case behaviour of the algorithm when the sequence is initially sorted. Therefore, it is better to choose the element in the middle of the sequence as comparison element.

Even better would it be to take the n/2-th greatest element of the sequence (the median). Then the optimal partition is achieved. Actually, it is possible to compute the median in linear time. This variant of quicksort would run in time $O(n\log_2 n)$ even in the worst-case.

However, the beauty of quicksort lies in its simplicity. And it turns out that even in its simple form quicksort runs in $O(n\log_2 n)$ on the average. Moreover, the constant hidden in the O-notation is small. Therefore, we trade this for the (rare) worst-case behaviour of $O(n^2)$.

3.4 STRASSEN'S MATRIX MULTIPLICATION

The core of many equation solvers is a matrix multiplication routine. The time complexity of calculating the matrix product $C = AB$ where A, B, and C are n x n matrices, using traditional matrix multiplication, is $O(n^3)$. Strassen's matrix multiplication algorithm is able to perform this calculation in time $O(n^{2.81})$. Thus one might be able to speed up the code by using Strassen's algorithm instead of the traditional algorithm.

The traditional algorithm follows directly from the definition of matrix multiplication. To compute Cij, we compute the dot product of the ith row in A with the jth column in B. Figure 3.5 makes it more visual.

$$Cij = \sum_{k=1}^{n} A_{ik} B_{kj}$$

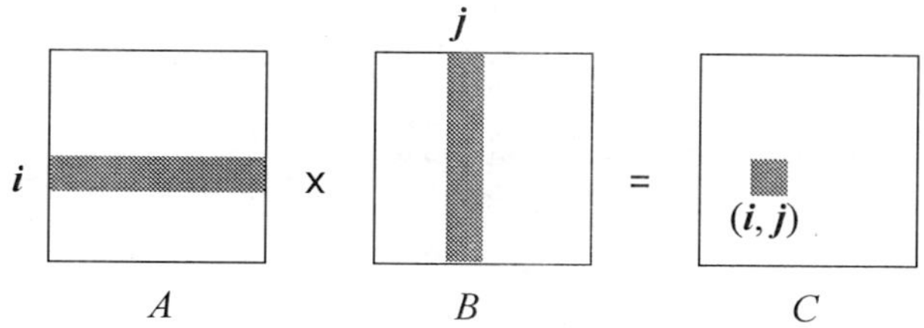

Figure 3.5: Matrix multiplication

is as follows ($O(n^3)$ multiplications):

Algorithm 3.5: multi(A, B, C)

```
For i = 1 to n
        For j = 1 to n
                C[i][j] = 0
                For k = 1 to n
                        C[i][j] = C[i][j] + A[i][k] x B[k][j]
                Endfor
        Endfor
Endfor
```

It is based on a recursive divide and conquer scheme. Given n x n matrices A and B we wish to calculate C=AB. To see how this algorithm works we first divide the matrices as follows (decomposing C=AB into four blocks):

$$\begin{bmatrix} C_{11} & C_{12} \\ C_{21} & C_{22} \end{bmatrix} = \begin{bmatrix} A_{11} & A_{12} \\ A_{21} & A_{22} \end{bmatrix} \times \begin{bmatrix} B_{11} & B_{12} \\ B_{21} & B_{22} \end{bmatrix}$$

If the matrices A and B are not of type 2^n x 2^n, we fill the missing rows and columns with zeros. The elements of C are given by:

$$C_{11} = A_{11}B_{11} + A_{12}B_{21}$$
$$C_{12} = A_{11}B_{12} + A_{12}B_{22}$$
$$C_{21} = A_{21}B_{11} + A_{22}B_{21}$$
$$C_{22} = A_{21}B_{12} + A_{22}B_{22}$$

As an example, to perform the multiplication of A and B

$$AB = \begin{bmatrix} 1 & 2 & 3 & 4 \\ 0 & 6 & 0 & 3 \\ 4 & 1 & 1 & 2 \\ 0 & 3 & 5 & 0 \end{bmatrix} \begin{bmatrix} 1 & 4 & 2 & 7 \\ 3 & 1 & 3 & 5 \\ 2 & 0 & 1 & 3 \\ 1 & 4 & 5 & 1 \end{bmatrix}$$

We define the following eight $n/2$ by $n/2$ matrices:

$$A_{11} = \begin{bmatrix} 1 & 2 \\ 0 & 6 \end{bmatrix} \quad A_{12} = \begin{bmatrix} 3 & 4 \\ 0 & 3 \end{bmatrix} \quad B_{11} = \begin{bmatrix} 1 & 4 \\ 3 & 1 \end{bmatrix} \quad B_{12} = \begin{bmatrix} 2 & 7 \\ 3 & 5 \end{bmatrix}$$

$$A_{21} = \begin{bmatrix} 4 & 1 \\ 0 & 3 \end{bmatrix} \quad A_{22} = \begin{bmatrix} 1 & 2 \\ 5 & 0 \end{bmatrix} \quad B_{21} = \begin{bmatrix} 2 & 0 \\ 1 & 4 \end{bmatrix} \quad B_{22} = \begin{bmatrix} 1 & 3 \\ 5 & 1 \end{bmatrix}$$

Strassen showed how the matrix C can be computed using only 7 block multiplications and 18 block additions or subtractions (12 additions and 6 subtractions):

$$P_1 = (A_{11} + A_{22}) \times (B_{11} + B_{22})$$
$$P_2 = (A_{21} + A_{22}) \times B_{11}$$
$$P_3 = A_{11} \times (B_{12} - B_{22})$$
$$P_4 = A_{22} \times (B_{21} - B_{11})$$
$$P_5 = (A_{11} + A_{12}) \times B_{22}$$
$$P_6 = (A_{21} - A_{11}) \times (B_{11} + B_{12})$$
$$P_7 = (A_{12} - A_{22}) \times (B_{21} + B_{22})$$
$$C_{11} = P_1 + P_4 - P_5 + P_7$$
$$C_{12} = P_3 + P_5$$
$$C_{21} = P_2 + P_4$$
$$C_{22} = P_1 + P_3 - P_2 + P_6$$

The correctness of the above equations is easily verified by substitution.

$$P_1 = (A_{11} + A_{22}) \times (B_{11} + B_{22}) = \begin{bmatrix} 1 & 2 \\ 0 & 6 \end{bmatrix} + \begin{bmatrix} 1 & 2 \\ 5 & 0 \end{bmatrix} \times \begin{bmatrix} 1 & 4 \\ 3 & 1 \end{bmatrix} + \begin{bmatrix} 1 & 3 \\ 5 & 1 \end{bmatrix}$$

$$= \begin{bmatrix} 2 & 4 \\ 5 & 6 \end{bmatrix} \times \begin{bmatrix} 2 & 7 \\ 8 & 2 \end{bmatrix} = \begin{bmatrix} 36 & 22 \\ 58 & 47 \end{bmatrix}$$

$$P_2 = (A_{21} + A_{22}) \times B_{11} = \begin{bmatrix} 14 & 23 \\ 14 & 23 \end{bmatrix}$$

$$P_3 = A_{11} \times (B_{12} - B_{22}) = \begin{bmatrix} -3 & 12 \\ -12 & 24 \end{bmatrix}$$

$$P_4 = A_{22} \times (B_{21} - B_{11}) = \begin{bmatrix} -3 & 2 \\ 5 & -20 \end{bmatrix}$$

$$P_5 = (A_{11} + A_{12}) \times B_{22} = \begin{bmatrix} 34 & 18 \\ 45 & 9 \end{bmatrix}$$

$$P_6 = (A_{21} - A_{11}) \times (B_{11} + B_{12}) = \begin{bmatrix} 3 & 27 \\ -18 & -18 \end{bmatrix}$$

$$P_7 = (A_{12} - A_{22}) \times (B_{21} + B_{22}) = \begin{bmatrix} 18 & 16 \\ 3 & 0 \end{bmatrix}$$

$$C_{11} = P_1 + P_4 - P_5 + P_7 = \begin{bmatrix} 17 & 22 \\ 21 & 18 \end{bmatrix}$$

$$C_{12} = P_3 + P_5 = \begin{bmatrix} 31 & 30 \\ 33 & 33 \end{bmatrix}$$

$$C_{21} = P_2 + P_4 = \begin{bmatrix} 11 & 25 \\ 19 & 3 \end{bmatrix}$$

$$C_{22} = P_1 + P_3 - P_2 + P_6 = \begin{bmatrix} 22 & 38 \\ 14 & 30 \end{bmatrix}$$

$$C = \begin{bmatrix} 17 & 22 & 31 & 30 \\ 21 & 18 & 33 & 33 \\ 11 & 25 & 22 & 38 \\ 19 & 3 & 14 & 30 \end{bmatrix}$$

The elements of matrix C can be verified with naïve Algorithm 3.5.

Algorithm 3.6 gives the Strassen's matrix multiplication after dividing matrices into sub-matrices and recursively multiply sub-matrices.

We perform seven $n/2$ by $n/2$ matrix multiplications and eighteen $n/2$ by $n/2$ matrix additions. The matrix additions take $O(n^2)$ time. If the matrix multiplications are done recursively, then the running time satisfies

$$T(n) = 7T(n/2) + O(n^2)$$

The solution of this recurrence is $T(n) = O(n^{\log_2 7}) = O(n^{2.81})$.

```
Algorithm 3.6: matmul(A, B, C, n)
If n = 1, then                          // base case
    C = C + A * B
Else
    matmul(A, B, C, n/4)
    matmul(A, B+(n/4), C+(n/4), n/4)
    matmul(A+2*(n/4), B, C+2*(n/4), n/4)
    matmul(A+2*(n/4), B+(n/4), C+3*(n/4), n/4)
    matmul(A+(n/4), B+2*(n/4), C, n/4)
    matmul(A+(n/4), B+3*(n/4), C+(n/4), n/4)
    matmul(A+3*(n/4), B+2*(n/4), C+2*(n/4), n/4)
    matmul(A+3*(n/4), B+3*(n/4), C+3*(n/4), n/4)
Endif
```

CHAPTER SUMMARY

- *Divide-and-conquer* algorithms consist of three steps: *Divide* the problem into sub-problems, *Conquer* the sub-problems by solving them recursively, and *Combine* sub-problem solutions.
- The complexity of divide-and-conquer algorithm is $O(n \log n)$.
- Applications of divide-and-conquer strategy are sorting, searching, powering a number, Fibonacci numbers, matrix multiplication and so on.
- *Binary search* uses the technique of divide-and-conquer, and performs in $O(\log n)$.
- Sorting by *merging* is a recursive, divide-and-conquer strategy. Merge sort is an $O(n\log n)$ comparison-based sorting algorithm.
- *Quicksort* is the fastest known sorting algorithm in practice. If the data has certain properties, quicksort is one of the fastest, if not, quicksort can be very slow. Quicksort can perform quite fast, on average about $O(n \log n)$, but its worst-case is a degrading $O(n^2)$. Quicksort sorts by using a divide and conquer strategy.
- *Strassen's matrix multiplication* algorithm is able to perform the calculations in time $O(n^{2.81})$. It is based on a recursive divide and conquer scheme.

SELF-TEST QUIZ

3.1 What are the three sequential steps of divide-and-conquer algorithms?

(a) Combine-Conquer-Divide
(b) Divide-Combine-Conquer
(c) Divide-Conquer-Combine
(d) Conquer-Divide- Conquer

3.2 The divide and conquer algorithm is closely tied to a type of recurrence relation. What is the base-case complexity of divide-and-conquer algorithm?

(a) $O(n)$ (b) $O(\log n)$ (c) $O(n \log n)$ (d) $O(1)$

3.3 The divide-and-conquer algorithm will have __________ complexity.

(a) $O(n)$ (b) $O(\log n)$ (c) $O(n \log n)$ (d) $O(n^2)$

3.4 The divide-and-conquer strategy is used for problems such as sorting to reduce the complexity from __________.

(a) $O(n)$ (b) $O(\log n)$ (c) $O(n \log n)$ (d) $O(n^2)$

3.5 The average successful search time taken by binary search on a sorted array of 10 elements is

(a) 2.6 (b) 2.7 (c) 2.8 (d) 2.9

3.6 Binary search executes in ________ time.

(a) $O(n)$ (b) $O(\log n)$ (c) $O(n \log n)$ (d) $O(n^2)$

3.7 Given two sorted lists of size m and n respectively. The number of comparisons needed in the worst case by the merge sort algorithm is

(a) mn (b) $\max(m, n)$ (c) $\min(m, n)$ (d) m+n-1

3.8 Merge sort performs in two phases: sort and merge. What is the expected time for merging?

(a) $O(n)$ (b) $O(\log n)$ (c) $O(n \log n)$ (d) $O(n^2)$

3.9 What is the running time of merge sort?

(a) $O(n)$ (b) $O(\log n)$ (c) $O(n \log n)$ (d) $O(n^2)$

3.10 The running time of an algorithm $T(n)$, where n is the input size, is given by

$T(n) = p$ for $n = 1$

$T(n) = 8T(n/2) + qn$ for $n > 1$

where p and q are constants. What is the order of this algorithm?

(a) n (b) n^2 (c) n^3 (d) n^n

3.11 Merge sort uses

(a) Divide and conquer strategy
(b) Backtracking approach
(c) Heuristic approach
(d) Greedy method

3.12 Which one of the following is useful in implementing quicksort?

(a) stack (b) set (c) list (d) queue

3.13 The recurrence relation that arises in relation with the complexity of binary search is (where k is a constant)

(a) $T(n) = T(n/2) + k$ (b) $T(n) = 2T(n/2) + k$
(c) $T(n) = T(n/2) + \log(n)$ (d) $T(n) = T(n/2) + n$

3.14 Which one of the following algorithm design techniques is used in the quicksort?
(a) Dynamic programming
(b) Backtracking approach
(c) Divide and conquer strategy
(d) Greedy method

3.15 Quicksort runs in _______ worst-case time.
(a) $O(n)$ (b) $O(\log n)$ (c) $O(n \log n)$ (d) $O(n^2)$

3.16 The average running time of quicksort is
(a) $O(n)$ (b) $O(\log n)$ (c) $O(n \log n)$ (d) $O(n^2)$

3.17 Which one of the following algorithm design techniques is used in Strassen's matrix multiplication algorithm?
(a) Dynamic programming
(b) Backtracking approach
(c) Divide and conquer strategy
(d) Greedy method

3.18 Strassen's algorithm is able to perform matrix multiplication in time ___.
(a) $O(n^{2.61})$ (b) $O(n^{2.71})$ (c) $O(n^{2.81})$ (d) $O(n^3)$

3.19 In Strassen's matrix multiplication algorithm ($C = AB$), if the matrices A and B are not of type 2^n x 2^n, the missing rows and columns are filled with _____.
(a) 0's (b) 1's (c) -1's (d) 2's

3.20 In Strassen's matrix multiplication algorithm ($C = AB$), the matrices A and B are decomposed into ____ blocks.
(a) 2 (b) 4 (c) 8 (d) 16

3.21 In Strassen's matrix multiplication algorithm ($C = AB$), the matrix C can be computed using only 7 block multiplications and 18 block additions or subtractions. How many additions and how many subtractions are there out of 18?
(a) 9 and 9 (b) 6 and 12 (c) 12 and 6 (d) none of these

Consider the following program that attempts to locate an element x in an array Y[] using binary search. Program is erroneous. Answer the questions 3.22 and 3.23.

GATE-2008

```
/* 1 */  func(int Y[10], int x) {
/* 2 */      int i, j, k;
/* 3 */      i = 0; j = 9;
/* 4 */      do  {
/* 5 */              k = (i + j)/2;
/* 6 */              if( Y[k] < x ) i = k;  else j = k;
/* 7 */          } while( (Y[k] != x) && (i < j) );
/* 8 */      if(Y[k] == x) printf ("x is in the array");
/* 9 */      else printf("x is not in the array");
/* 10 */ }
```

3.22 On which of the following contents of Y and x does the program fail?

(a) Y is [1 2 3 4 5 6 7 8 9 10] and $x < 10$
(b) Y is [1 3 5 7 9 11 13 15 17 19] and $x < 1$
(c) Y is [2 2 2 2 2 2 2 2 2 2] and $x > 2$
(d) Y is [2 4 6 8 10 12 14 16 18 20] and $2 < x < 20$ and x is even

3.23 The correction needed in the program to make it work properly is

(a) Change line 6 to: if($Y[k] < x$) $i = k+1$; else $j = k-1$;
(b) Change line 6 to: if($Y[k] < x$) $i = k-1$; else $j = k+1$;
(c) Change line 6 to: if($Y[k] <= x$) $i = k$; else $j = k$;
(d) Change line 7 to: } while(($Y[k] == x$) && ($i < j$));

3.24 The median of n elements can be found in $O(n)$ time. Which one of the following is correct about the complexity of quick sort, in which median is selected as pivot?

GATE-2006

(a) $\Theta(n)$ (b) $\Theta(n \log_2 n)$ (c) $\Theta(n^2)$ (d) $\Theta(n^3)$

EXERCISES

3.1 Write and explain the control abstraction for Divide and conquer.

3.2 Explain the divide and conquer method with an example.

3.3 Write a binary search algorithm. Derive its time complexity.

3.4 Explain the different stages of binary search algorithm to locate 90 in the following ordered list: 10, 15, 35, 40, 50, 55, 65, 75, 90, 95.

3.5 Suppose a binary tree has leaves $\ell_1, \ell_2, \ldots, \ell_m$ at depths $d_1, d_2, \ldots, d_m$ respectively. Prove that $\sum_{i=1}^{m} 2^{-d_i} \leq 1$ and determine when the equality is true.

3.6 Modify the normal binary search algorithm so that in case of unsuccessful search it returns the index i such that $A[i] < key < A[i+1]$.

3.7 Devise a binary search algorithm which splits the set not into two sets of equal sizes but into two sets one-third and two-thirds. How does this algorithm compare with binary search?

3.8 The input is an n by n matrix of numbers that is already in memory. Each individual row is increasing from left to right. Each individual column is increasing from top to bottom. Give an $O(n)$ worst-case algorithm that decides if a number x is in the matrix.

3.9 Design a divide-and-conquer algorithm to find the maximum and minimum of an array A of n elements, and prove that the algorithm makes at most $3n/2$ element-to-element comparisons.

3.10 Write an algorithm to sort n numbers in ascending order using mergesort, and compute its time complexity.

3.11 What is a stable sorting method? Is mergesort a stable sorting method?

3.12 Determine the running time of mergesort for
(i) sorted input
(ii) reverse-ordered input
(iii) random-ordered input

3.13 Suggest refinements to mergesort to make it in-place.

3.14 Trace the Quicksort algorithm to sort the list C, O, L, L, E, G, E in alphabetical order. Give an instance, where the Quicksort algorithm has worst case complexity.

3.15 Write the Quicksort algorithm. Analyze the worst-case time complexity.

3.16 Is Quicksort stable sorting method? Justify your answer.

3.17 Show how Quicksort sorts the following sequence of keys in ascending order.
22, 55, 33, 11, 99, 77, 55, 66, 54, 21, 32.

3.18 List some of the relative advantages and disadvantages of the partition algorithm.

3.19 One way to sort a file of n records is to scan the file first merging consecutive pairs of size of one, then merging pairs of size two, etc. Write an algorithm which carries out this process. Show how this algorithm works on data set keys (10, 30, 45, 15, 35, 25, 20, 40).

3.20 Explain the Strassen's matrix multiplication.

3.21 Use Strassen's matrix multiplication algorithm to multiply the following two matrices.

$$A = \begin{bmatrix} 3 & 2 \\ 4 & 8 \end{bmatrix} \qquad B = \begin{bmatrix} 1 & 5 \\ 9 & 6 \end{bmatrix}$$

CHAPTER 4

GREEDY METHOD

Many of the problems that computer algorithms are designed to solve have involve optimization or finding a "best" solution. That is, some operation can be performed in a number of different ways, all meeting some basic constraints, and the problem is to find the way that is optimal. It means that it maximizes or minimizes the value of some desirable quantity.

In many optimization problems, there are two types of solutions: feasible solutions, and optimal solutions. When applying an algorithm design method to a problem, we may get an unacceptable solution - a feasible solution that is clearly not optimal and/or a feasible solution that is close to an optimal solution.

The greedy method is one of the simplest approaches to solve the optimization problem in which we want to determine the global optimum of a given function by a sequence of steps where at each stage we can make a choice among a class of possible decisions. In the greedy method, the choice of the optimal decision is made on the information at hand without worrying about the effect these decisions may have in the future. The "greedy-choice property" and "optimal substructure/subproblem" are two ingredients in the problem that lend to a greedy strategy. It says that a globally optimal solution can be arrived at by making a locally optimal choice.

Greedy algorithms are easy to invent, easy to implement and most of the time quite efficient. However, there are many problems that cannot be solved correctly by the greedy approach. The principal advantage of greedy algorithms is that they are usually straightforward, easy to understand and easy to code. Their main disadvantage is that for many problems there is no greedy algorithm. More precisely, in many cases there is no guarantee that making locally optimal improvements in a locally optimal solution yields the optimal global solution.

"The one with maximum benefit from multiple choices is selected" is the basic idea of greedy method. A greedy method arrives at a solution by making a sequence of choices, each of which simply looks the best at the moment. Algorithm 4.1 describes the details of greedy method.

Algorithm 4.1: greedy(partial solution S, sub-problem P)

```
Generate all candidate choices as list L for current sub-problem P.
While (L is not empty or other finish condition is not met)
    Compute the feasible value of each choice in L;
    Modify S and P by taking choice with the highest feasible value;
    Update L according to S and P;
Endwhile
Return the resulting complete solution.
```

For an optimization problem, what remains is called a sub-problem after making one or several steps of greedy choice. For problem or sub-problem P, let S be the partial solution, and L be the list of candidate choices at the current moment. To order or prioritize the choices, some evaluation criteria are used to express the feasible value. According to the Algorithm 4.1, the candidate choice with the highest feasible value is selected, and the partial solution is updated accordingly. This procedure is repeated step by step until a resulting complete solution is obtained.

The representation of the Algorithm 4.1 can be illustrated by a search tree as shown in Figure 4.1. Each node in the search tree corresponds to a partial solution, and a line between two nodes represents the decision to add a candidate choice to the existing partial solution. Consequently, leaf nodes at the end of tree correspond to complete solutions. The black circle at level 1 denotes an initial partial solution. At level 2, there are five candidate choices for current partial solution, which denotes by five nodes. In order to select the best node, promise of each node should be determined. After some evaluation function has been employed, the second node with highest benefit (the circle in gray at level 2) is selected. Then, the partial solution and sub-problem are updated accordingly.

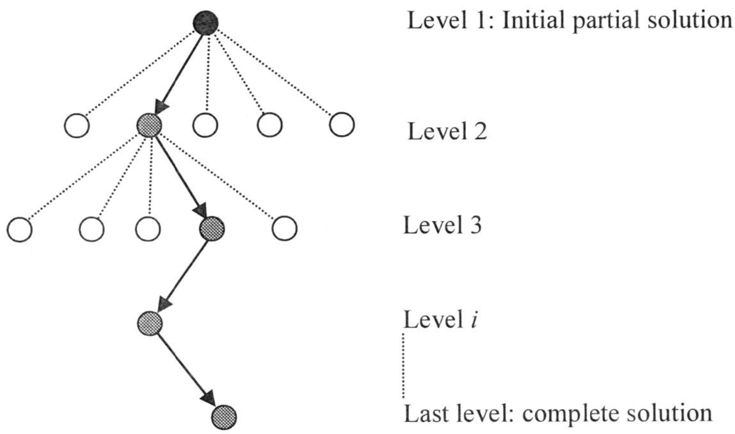

Figure 4.1: Representation of greedy algorithm

Example 4.1 illustrates the essence of greedy algorithm which depends on the selection policy.

Example 4.1: Given a set S of n items, with each item i having

p_i = profit on ith item
w_i = weight of ith item
x_i = amount of ith item to maximize profit
Objective: Choose the items with maximum total profit but with weight $\leq W$.

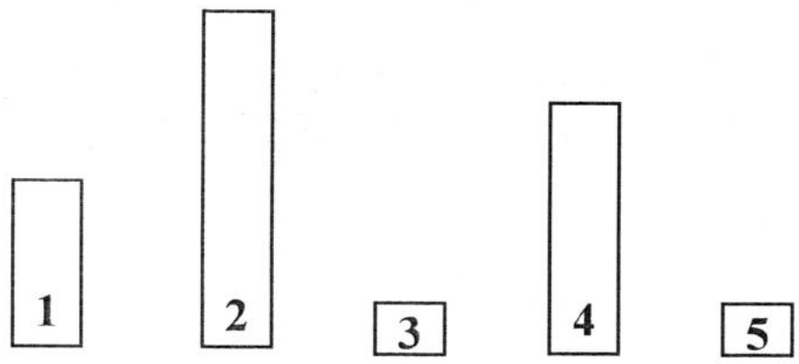

Items:	1	2	3	4	5
Weight (gms):	**4**	**8**	**2**	**6**	**1**
Profit (Rs):	**12**	**32**	**40**	**30**	**50**
Value (Rs/gm):	**3**	**4**	**20**	**5**	**50**

Figure 4.2: Example of greedy method

This problem can be defined as follows:

Objective is to maximize $\sum_{i \in S} p_i x_i$

subject to the constraint $\sum_{i \in S} x_i \leq W$

We need $W \leq 10$ gms with maximum profit. 5th item has maximum profit (Rs 50): select 5th item and its weight is 1 gm (W = 1 gm). The subsequent phases are shown below, taking maximum profit with total weight restriction.

Table 4.1: Greedy method example

Item (i)	Profit (p_i)	Total Profit	Weight (w_i)	Total weight (W)
5	50	50	1	1
3	40	90	2	3
4	30	120	6	9
2	32	152	1	10

The initial partial solution is item 5 with weight 1 gm, having a profit of Rs 50, subject to a total weight of 10 gms. The remaining partial solutions with their sub-problems are shown in the above table.

The greedy method technique has many applications: such as selection sort, optimal merge patterns, knapsack problem, minimum spanning trees, shortest paths problem, job sequencing, and so on.

4.1 JOB SEQUENCING WITH DEADLINES

The arrangement of jobs on a single processor with deadline constraints is named as *job sequencing with deadlines*. We arrange n jobs on a processor in a sequence to obtain maximum profit subject to deadlines. The sequencing problem is stated as follows:

- Each ith job is associated with a deadline ($d_i \geq 0$), and a profit ($p_i > 0$).
- For any ith job, the profit p_i is earned, if job is completed by its deadline.
- To complete a job, it is processed on a processor for one unit of time.
- Only one processor is available for processing all jobs.
- Not all jobs have to be scheduled.

A feasible solution for this problem is a subset *list* of jobs such that each job in this subset can be completed by its deadline. The value of a feasible solution is the sum of the profits of the jobs in *list* ($\sum p_i$, where *list* contains ith job). An optimal solution is a feasible solution with maximum profit. The following example illustrates the sequencing problem.

Example 4.2: Consider a sequencing problem where the four jobs have a profit of (10, 30, 60, 40) and corresponding deadlines (2, 3, 1, 3).

Here, $n = 4$,

$(p_1, p_2, p_3, p_4) = (10, 30, 60, 40)$, and

$(d_1, d_2, d_3, d_4) = (2, 3, 1, 3)$.

The following sketch illustrates the deadlines of four jobs, and Table 4.2 lists feasible solutions.

```
            1  2  3 ←— units of time
            —  —  —    ('◄' indicates deadline)
Job1 →      —  ◄       (Job1 has a slack time of 1 unit)
Job2 →      —     ◄    (Job2 has a slack time of 2 units)
Job3 →      —◄         (Job3 has no slack time)
Job4 →      —     ◄    (Job4 has a slack time of 2 units)
```

Table 4.2: List of feasible solutions (Example 4.2)

Sno	*Feasible solution list*	*Processing sequence*	*Total profit* $\sum_{i \in J} p_i$
1	{1, 2}	1 → 2 (Process 2nd job after 1st job)	40
2	{1, 3}	3 → 1 (Process 1st job after 3rd job)	70
3	{1, 4}	1 → 4	50
4	{2, 3}	3 → 2	90
5	{2, 4}	2 → 4 or 4 → 2	70
6	{3, 4}	3 → 4	100
7	{1, 2, 3}	3 → 1 → 2	100
8	{1, 2, 4}	1 → 2 → 4 or 2 → 1 → 4 or 4 → 1 → 2	80
9	{1, 3, 4}	3 → 1 → 4	110
10	{2, 3, 4}	3 → 2 → 4 or 3 → 4 → 2	130
11	{1}	1	10
12	{2}	2	30
13	{3}	3	60
14	{4}	4	40

Solution 10 is optimal yielding a total profit of 130. The optimal job sequence is either (3, 2, 4) or (3, 4, 2). The two sequences are shown below:

```
1  2  3      units of time
—  —  —      (◄ indicates deadline)
3 ◄ 2 4 ◄
3 ◄ 4 2 ◄
```

We realize a greedy algorithm to get an optimal solution. We must formulate an optimization measure to determine how the next job is selected. We have to maximize the objective function, $\sum p_i$ (that is, total profit is the optimization measure). Using this measure, the next job to include is that increases total profit the most, subject to a resulting feasible solution, *list*. This requires considering the jobs in decreasing order of the p_i's. Let us apply this criterion to the Example 4.2.

Ordering the jobs in decreasing order of profit:

Profits = (60, 40, 30, 10)
Job # = (3, 4, 2, 1)
Deadlines = (1, 3, 3, 2)

The formal algorithm is as follows:

Step-1: Sort p_i into decreasing order. After sorting $p_1 \geq p_2 \geq p_3 \ldots p_i$.

Step-2: Add the next *i*th job to the solution set *list* if *i*th job can be completed by its deadline, d_i. Assign *i*th job to the *k*th vacant time slot in the *list*. If *list*[*k*] = 0, then *k*th time slot is empty. If *k*th time slot is not vacant, then search the preceding slot, (*k*-1), and so on, meeting its deadline constraint.

Step-3: Stop if all jobs are examined. Otherwise, go to step-2.

- The greedy method described above always obtains an optimal solution to the job sequencing problem.

The solution of Example 4.2 is presented in the following Table 4.3.

Table 4.3: Trace of Algorithm 4.2 (Example 4.2)

job (*i*)	p_i	d_i	profit	operation	*list*[1..4] initialized to 0
3	60	1	60	Assign job 3 to slot 1.	3 | 0 | 0 | 0
4	40	3	100	Assign job 4 to slot 3.	3 | 0 | 4 | 0
2	30	3	130	Assign job 2 to slot 2, because slot 3 is not empty.	3 | 2 | 4 | 0
1	10	2	130	Reject job 1, because it violates its deadline.	3 | 2 | 4 | 0

Optimal job sequence is 3 → 2 → 4 with maximum profit of 130.

Algorithm 4.2: JobSequence(*job*[1..*n*], *p*[1..*n*], *d*[1..*n*], *list*[1..*n*], *n*)

```
1.   Initialize list with zeros.        // make all n time slots empty
2.   profit = 0;                        // profit = total profit
3.   For i = 1 to n do
4.       k = d[i];                      // set ith job's deadline to k
5.       While( k > 0 )
6.           If( list[k] = 0 )                // if kth slot is vacant,
7.               list[k] = job[i];            // assign ith job to kth slot
8.               add p[i] to profit;          // accumulate total profit
9.               go to step 3;                // exit from while-loop (break)
10.          Endif
11.          Decrement k by 1;                // otherwise get preceding slot
12.      Endwhile
13.  Endfor
14.  Print list
```

Time complexity: Sorting (sort p_i into decreasing order) and selection of jobs takes $O(n \log n)$ time in total. Consider n jobs in turn. For each job, inserting the job into the partial solution using its deadline takes $O(n)$ time. Checking whether the new solution is still feasible takes $O(n)$ time. Hence, total running time, in worst-case, is $O(n^2)$.

4.2 KNAPSACK PROBLEM

The 0-1 Knapsack problem is defined as follows: Given a knapsack of capacity c and n items of weights $\{ w_1, w_2 \ldots w_n\}$ and profits $\{ p_1, p_2 \ldots p_n\}$, the objective is to choose a subset of n objects that fits into the knapsack and that maximizes the total profit.

Consider a knapsack (bag) with a capacity of c. We select items from a list of n items. Each item has both a weight of w_i and a profit of p_i. In a feasible solution, the sum of the weights must not exceed knapsack capacity (c), and an optimal solution is both feasible and reaches the maximum profit.

An optimal packing is a feasible solution one with a maximum profit:

$$p_1x_1 + p_2 x_2 + p_3 x_3 + \ldots + p_n x_n = \sum_{i=1}^{n} p_i x_i$$

subject to constraints: $w_1x_1 + w_2 x_2 + w_3 x_3 + \ldots + w_n x_n = \sum_{i=1}^{n} w_i x_i \leq c$

and $x_i = 1$ or 0, $1 \leq i \leq n$

We have to find the values of x_i where $x_i = 1$ if ith item is packed into the knapsack and $x_i = 0$ if ith item is not packed.

Greedy strategies for the knapsack problem are:

(1) From the remaining items, select the item with maximum profit that fits into the knapsack.

(2) From the remaining items, select the item that has minimum weight and also fits into the knapsack.

(3) From the remaining items, select the one with maximum p_i/w_i that fits into the knapsack.

Example 4.3: There are four items that have a profit and weight list below. The knapsack capacity is 4 kgs. We apply the above three greedy strategies.

item (i)	p_i	w_i
1	5	1
2	9	3
3	4	2
4	8	2

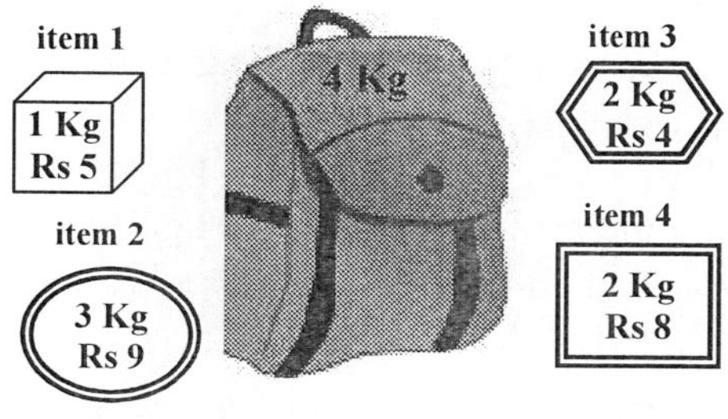

Figure 4.3: A Knapsack problem

Method 1 chooses the item with maximum profit. First choose the item 2 which has a maximum profit of Rs 9 with weight 3 kgs. If we next select item 4, then total profit will be Rs 17. But, it violates the capacity constraint of 4 kgs.

Method 2 selects the item that has minimum weight. First select item 1, and next item 4. If we select third one as item 3, the total weight will be 5 kgs (1+2+2). This violates the 4 kgs constraint.

Method 3 chooses the item with maximum p_i/w_i that fits into the knapsack. We first compute p_i/w_i and make the following table.

item (i)	p_i	w_i	p_i/w_i
1	5	1	5
2	9	3	3
3	4	2	2
4	8	2	4

Sort items in decreasing order of p_i/w_i →

item (i)	p_i	w_i	p_i/w_i
1	5	1	5
4	8	2	4
2	9	3	3
3	4	2	2

The order of items selected is 1 and 4. If we include item 2, then it violates the capacity constraint.

These three methods do not guarantee an optimal solution. This example illustrates the 0-1 knapsack problem which exhibits no greedy choice property and hence no greedy algorithm exists. Only dynamic programming algorithm exists.

4.2.1 Fractional Knapsack Problem

In this version of a problem, the items can be broken into smaller piece, so that we pack only a fraction x_i of item i, where $0 \le x_i \le 1$. Item i contributes $x_i w_i$ to the total weight in the knapsack, and $x_i p_i$ to the total profit. Knapsack capacity is c.

The fraction knapsack problem can be stated as follows:

Maximize $\sum_{i=1}^{n} p_i x_i$ subject to constraint $\sum_{i=1}^{n} w_i x_i \le c$

It is clear that an optimal solution must fill the knapsack exactly, for otherwise we could add a fraction of one of the remaining items and increase the total profit. Thus in an optimal solution

$$\sum_{i=1}^{n} w_i x_i = c \cdot$$

The fractional knapsack problem has the greedy-choice property.

Let us continue the Example 4.3.

(1) Include all of item 1, $x_1 = 1$, $x_1 w_1 = 1$ kg.
(2) Include all of item 4, $x_4 = 1$, $x_4 w_4 = 2$ kg.
(3) Include 1/3 of item 2, $x_2 = 1/3$, $x_2 w_2 = 1$ kg.
Now the total weight is 4 kg = c.

The solution is: $x_1 = 1$, $x_2 = 1/3$, $x_3 = 0$, $x_4 = 1$; and maximum profit = $\sum_{i=1}^{n} p_i x_i$

$= 5 + 0 + 9(1/3) + 8 =$ Rs 16.

Algorithm 4.3: GreedyFractionalKnapsack ($p[1..n]$, $w[1..n]$, $x[1..n]$, c)

```
Initialize x[] with zeros.
profit = 0;                // total profit of items filled in knapsack
weight = 0;                // total weight of items packed in knapsack
i = 1;
While( weight < c )        // c: knapsack capacity
     If( weight+w[i] ≤ c )
          x[i] = 1;
          weight = weight + w[i];
     Else
          x[i] = (c - weight) / w[i];
          weight = c;
     Endif
     profit = profit + p[i]*x[i];
     i++;
Endwhile
```

One way to prove the correctness of the above algorithm is to prove the greedy choice property and optimal substructure property. It consists of two steps. First, prove that there exists an optimal solution begins with the greedy choice given above. The second part prove that if A is an optimal solution to the original problem S, then A-a is also an optimal solution to the problem S-s where a is the item included as in the greedy choice and S-s is the subproblem after the first greedy choice has been made. The second part is easy to prove since the more profitable items have less weight. Note that if $p`/w`$, is not it can replace any other because $w` < w$, but it increases the profit because $p` > p$.

The fractional knapsack problem has the greedy-choice property. Let the ratio $p`/w`$ is maximal. This supposition implies that $p`/w` \geq p/w$ for any pair (p, w), so $p`p/w > p$ for any $(p, w)$. Now, suppose a solution does not contain the full $w`$ weight of the best ratio. Then by replacing an amount of any other w with more $w`$ will improve the value.

Time complexity: If the items are already sorted into decreasing order of p_i/w_i, then the while-loop takes a time in $O(n)$. Therefore, the total time including the sort is in $O(n \log n)$.

4.3 MINIMUM-COST SPANNING TREES

The trees are the special cases of graphs. A tree may be defined as a connected graph without any cycle. A tree defined as a special case of a graph does not have a special node (vertex) called the *root*. In fact, any node may be chosen as the root.

Let $G = (V, E)$ be an undirected connected graph (where V is a set of vertices or nodes, and E is a set of edges). A sub-graph $T = (V, E')$ of G is a spanning tree of G if T is a tree. A spanning tree of a graph is an undirected tree consisting of only those edges necessary to connect all nodes in the original graph.

Suppose we are asked to network a collection of computers by linking selected pairs of them. This converts into a graph problem in which nodes are computers, undirected edges are potential links, and the goal is to pick enough of these edges that the nodes are connected. But this is not all; each link also has a maintenance cost, reflected in that edge's weight. What is the cheapest possible network?

One immediate observation is that the optimal set of edges cannot contain a cycle, because removing an edge from this cycle would reduce the cost without compromising connectivity: *removing a cycle edge cannot disconnect a graph.*

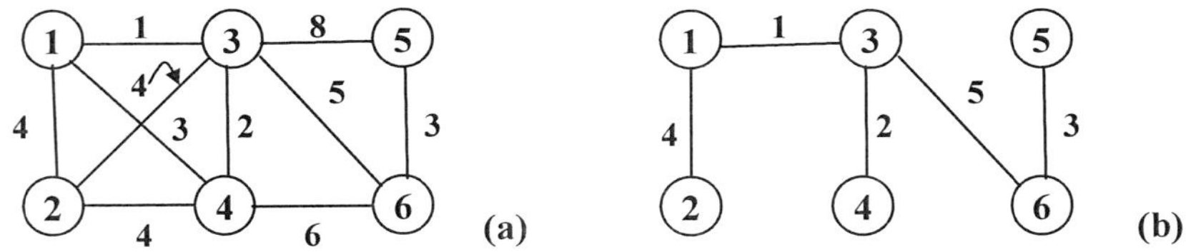

Figure 4.4: An undirected weighted graph and its minimum spanning tree. Cost of minimum spanning tree is 15.

In practical situations, the edges have weights assigned to them. These weights may represent the cost of construction, the length of the link, and so on. Given such a weighted graph, one would then wish to select nodes to have minimum total cost or minimum total length. In either case the links selected have to form a tree (assuming all weights are positive). If this is not so, then the selection of links contains a cycle. Removal of any one of the links on this cycle results in a link selection of less cost connecting all cities. We are therefore interested in finding a spanning tree of G with minimum cost. The cost of a spanning tree is the sum of the costs of the edges in that tree. Figure 4.4 shows a graph and one of its minimum-cost spanning trees. Since the identification of a minimum-cost spanning tree involves the selection of a subset of edges, this problem fits the subset model.

There are several different ways to construct a minimum-cost spanning tree. Many of these methods use the following property of minimum-cost spanning trees, which we call the *MST property*. Let $G = (V, E)$ be a connected graph with a cost function defined on the edges. Let U be some proper subset of the set of vertices V. If (u, v) is an edge of the lowest cost such that $u \in U$ and $v \in V-U$, then there is a minimum-cost spanning tree that includes (u, v) as an edge.

4.3.1 Prim's Algorithm

There are two popular techniques that exploit the *MST* property to construct a minimum-cost spanning tree from a weighted graph. One such method is known as *Prim*'s algorithm. The second one is *Kruskal*'s algorithm. *Prim* and *Dijkstra* discovered independently for creating a minimum-cost spanning tree for a weighted graph.

The minimum spanning tree grows in successive stages. At any stage, we can make out that we have a set of nodes that have already been included in the tree, the remainder of the nodes have not. The Prim's algorithm then finds a new node to be included in the tree by choosing the edge (u, v). The edge (u, v) has the minimum weight (cost) among all edges, where u is in the tree and v is yet to be added to the tree. The algorithm starts by selecting a node arbitrarily, and then in each stage, we include an edge (by adding an associated node) in the tree.

Using greedy technique, the Prim's algorithm builds the minimal spanning tree by iteratively adding nodes into a working tree (n = number of nodes in the graph). A tree on n nodes has n-1 edges.

1. Start with a tree which contains only one node.
2. Identify a node (outside the tree) which is closest to the tree and add the minimum cost edge from that node to some node in the tree and incorporate the additional node as a part of the tree.
3. If there are less then n-1 edges in the tree, go to step 2

Figure 4.5 illustrates the stages of the Prim's algorithm on graph of Figure 4.4(a). We start with an empty graph and then add edges in increasing order of weights (ties are broken arbitrarily).

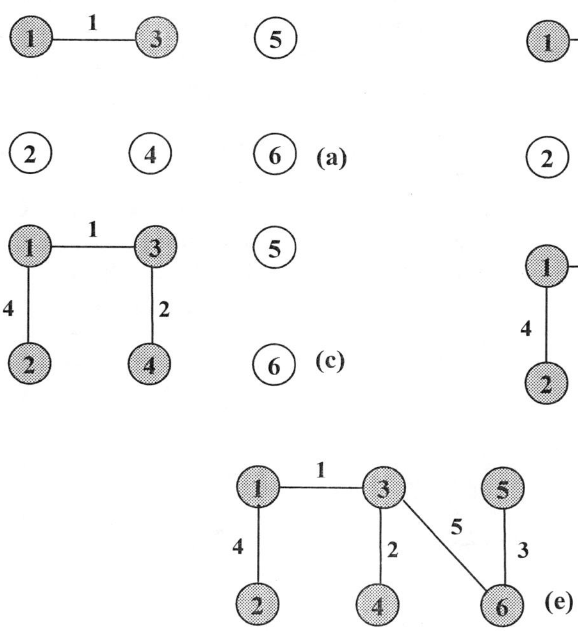

Figure 4.5: Stages in Prim's algorithm

We represent a weighted graph by an adjacency matrix to store the set of edges. An entry (i, j) in an adjacency matrix contains information on the edge that goes from node i to node j. Each matrix entry contains the weight of the corresponding edge. An infinity value, ∞ is used to denote an edge that is missing from the graph. Table 4.4 is an adjacency matrix for the weighted undirected graph shown in Figure 4.4(a).

Table 4.4: Adjacency matrix of Figure 4.4(a)

	1	*2*	*3*	*4*	*5*	*6*
1	∞	4	1	3	∞	∞
2	4	∞	4	4	∞	∞
3	1	4	∞	2	8	5
4	3	4	2	∞	∞	6
5	∞	∞	8	∞	∞	3
6	∞	∞	5	6	3	∞

The Prim's algorithm is implemented using the adjacency matrix of a graph. This matrix is denoted by *adjMatrix*[*i*, *j*] where *i* and *j* operate from 1 to *n* for *n*-node weighted undirected graph. We assume that the [*i*, *j*] element of the adjacency matrix is infinity if there is no edge between the nodes *i* and *j*. The *selected* is an integer array. The elements of *selected* contain either 0's or 1's. (0 represents not included in the minimum spanning tree and 1 included). Algorithm 4.4 builds the *MST* for a weighted graph.

Prim's algorithm runs in $O(n^2)$ time, where *n* is the number of nodes in the graph. To see this, it takes a sum of $O(|E|)+\Theta(1)$ time for finding the minimum cost edge, where $|E|$ is the number of edges. Total time of the for-loops is $O(n^2)$. Hence, Prim runs in $O(n^2)$ time.

Prim's algorithm always yields a *MST*. We can prove it by induction. Let T_0 be a part of any *MST* which consists of a single vertex. Assume that T_{i-1} is a part of *MST*. We need to prove that T_i, generated by T_{i-1} by Prim's algorithm is a part of a *MST*. Assume that no *MST* of the graph can contain T_i.

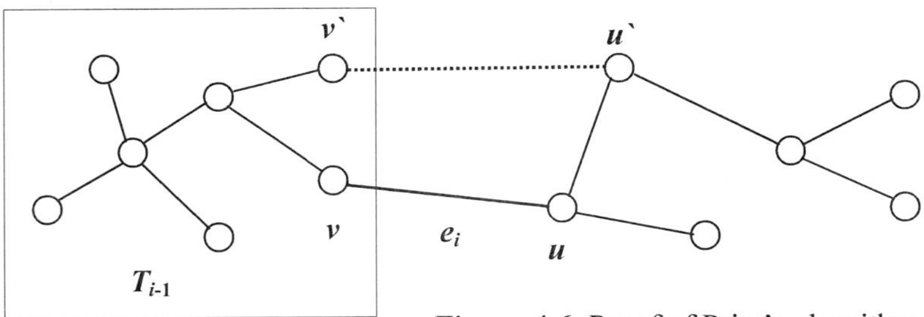

Figure 4.6: Proof of Prim's algorithm

Let $e_i = (u, v)$ be a minimum weight edge from a vertex in T_{i-1} to a vertex not in T_{i-1} used by Prim's algorithm to expand T_{i-1} to T_i. By out assumption, if we add e_i to *T*, a cycle must be formed. In addition to e_i, the cycle must contain another edge (*v*`, *u*`). If we delete the edge e_k (*v*`, *u*`), then we obtain another spanning tree. Now we have $w_{ei} \leq w_{ek}$. So, weight of new spanning tree is less than or equal to *T*. New spanning tree is a minimum spanning tree which contradicts the assumption that no minimum spanning tree contains T_i.

Algorithm 4.4: Prim(*adjMatrix*[1..*n*] [1..*n*])

```
n = Number of nodes in the graph.
nEdges = Current number of edges included in the MST.
min = Minimum weight (cost) of edge.
row, col indicate the row and column of the edge included in the MST.
sum = Total minimum weight (cost) of the edges included in the MST.
Initialize selected[] with zeros.
selected[1] = 1;        // To start with, node 1 is included in MST
nEdges = 1;             // Make one count of edges to be included in MST
sum = 0;
While( nEdges < n )
    min = ∞;
    /* Repeat following steps to cover all nodes from 1 to n */
    For i = 1 to n do
        If( selected[i] = 1 )
        /*  If node i is included in MST, then repeat to get
            min-cost node j to connect to i  */
        For j = 1 to n do
            If( selected[j] = 0 )          // Select the min-cost edge
                If( min > adjMatrix[i][j] )
                    min = adjMatrix[i][j];
                    row = i;  col = j;
                Endif
            Endif
        Endfor
        Print row, col, adjMatrix[row][col];
    Endfor
    selected[col] = 1; // Once i and j  form a min-edge, mark 1 selected
    nEdges++;
    sum = sum + adjMatrix[row][col];
Endwhile.
Print sum;      // Total Min-Cost
```

4.3.2 Kruskal's Algorithm

Like Prim's algorithm, *Kruskal's algorithm* also constructs the minimum spanning tree of a graph by adding edges to the spanning tree one-by-one. At all points during its execution, the set of edges selected by Prim's algorithm forms exactly one tree. On the other hand, the set of edges selected by Kruskal's algorithm forms a forest of trees.

Kruskal's algorithm is conceptually quite simple. The edges are selected and added to the spanning tree in increasing order of their weights. An edge is added to the tree only if it does not create a cycle. The beauty of Kruskal's algorithm is the way that potential cycles are detected.

Let us illustrate the Kruskal's algorithm by considering the graph G shown in Figure 4.4(a). The edges of the graph are arranged in increasing order of weights as shown in Table 4.5. Initially the spanning tree, T is empty. We select the edge with smallest weight and include it in T. If the selected edge creates a cycle, then it will be removed from T. We repeat these two steps until the tree T contains n-1 edges (where n is the number of nodes in the graph G). If the tree T contains less than n-1 edges and the edge list is empty, then no spanning tree T is possible for the graph G. These steps are illustrated in Figure 4.7 (see also Table 4.5).

First, the minimum edge 1-3 is included in the empty tree, T. In step (c), next minimum edge 3-4 is added. After the step (c), if we include minimum edge 1-4 in the tree T, then a cycle (1-3-4-1) will be formed. Next edge 5-6 with weight 3 is added in step (d). In step (e), edge 1-2 is included in T. Addition of edge 2-3 also creates a cycle. Next minimum edge 2-4 forms a cycle (2-4-3-1-2). Finally, edge 3-6 is added to obtain the minimum spanning tree, T.

Table 4.5: Minimum spanning tree using Kruskal's algorithm

Edge:	1-3	3-4	1-4	5-6	1-2	2-3	2-4	3-6	4-6	3-5
Weight:	1	2	3	3	4	4	4	5	6	8
Include:	yes	yes	no	yes	yes	no	no	yes	no	no

The Kruskal's algorithm 4.5 will return a set of edges that forms the minimum spanning tree, T for the given weighted, connected, undirected graph, G.

Algorithm 4.5: Kruskal(set of edges of graph G)

```
    S: contains edges in G sorted by increasing weight.
    n: number nodes in G.
    T: contains the edges of minimum spanning tree – initially empty.
    nEdges: current number of edges included in the MST.
While nEdges ≤ n-1
    E = {x, y}          // min weight edge in S not yet checked.
    xroot = find(x);  // find the current root of the tree that the node x is in
    yroot = find(y);  // find the current root of the tree that the node y is in
    If (xroot ≠ yroot ), // x, y are not in the same connected component.
        merge(xroot, yroot);    // merge two nodes' trees
        T = T union {E};        // add min edge to T
        nEdges++;
    Endif
Endwhile.
```

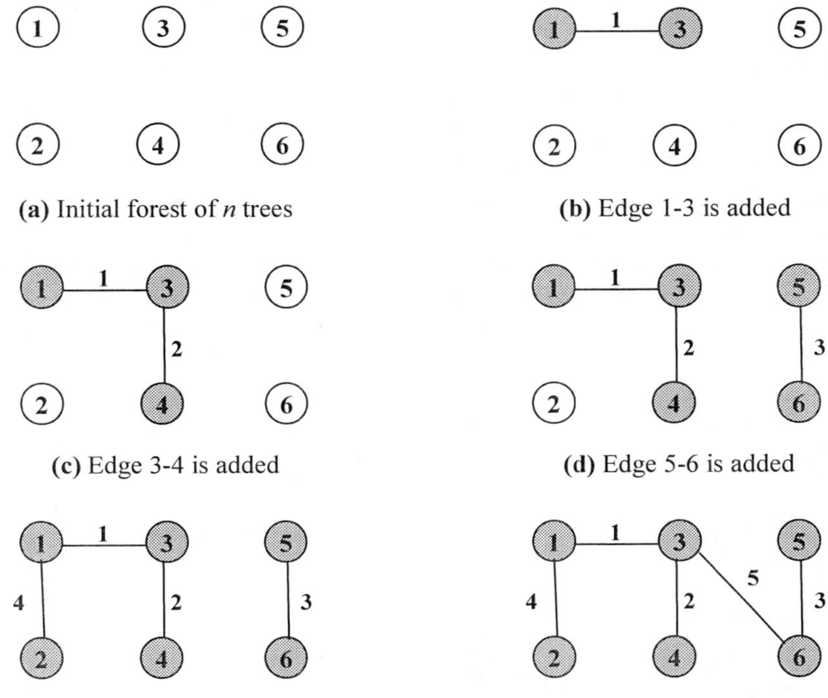

(a) Initial forest of n trees

(b) Edge 1-3 is added

(c) Edge 3-4 is added

(d) Edge 5-6 is added

(e) Edge 1-2 is added

(f) Edge 1-3 is added

Figure 4.7: Kruskal's minimum spanning tree

For finding and deleting the min-cost edge, we use a *minheap* where its nodes are the labels + costs of the graph edges. For cycle detection, note that T is a forest at any given time, adding an edge eliminates two trees from the forest and replaces them by a new tree containing the union of the nodes of the two old trees, and edge $e = (u, v)$ creates a cycle if both u and v belong to the same tree in the forest. Union-Find data structure is perfect to tell if an edge creates a cycle, and to keep track of what nodes belong to each tree in the forest. Time complexity of the Kruskal's algorithm is as follows:

$O(m)$ to build the heap (m is the number of edges in G)
up to m calls to *Union*-and-*Find*, taking $O(m \log n)$ time
up to m calls to delete-min, taking $O(m \log m)$ time.
Therefore, the total time is $O(m \log m)$.

4.4 SINGLE-SOURCE SHORTEST PATHS PROBLEM

A minimum spanning tree gives no indication about the shortest path between two vertices. Rather only the overall cost or weight is minimized. In real life, we are required to find the shortest path between two cities. For example, one would be interested in finding most economical route between any two cities in a given railways network.

We are given a directed graph G in which every edge has a weight, and our problem is to find a path from one vertex v to another vertex w such that the sum of the weights on the path is as minimal as possible. We shall call such a path a *shortest path*, even though the weights may represent costs, time, or some other quantity other than distance.

We can think of G as a map of railway routes, for example, with each vertex representing a city and the weight on each edge the cost of traveling from one city to the second. Our problem is then to find a route from city v to city w such that the total cost is a minimum. Consider the directed graph shown in Figure 4.8. The shortest path from node 1 to node 5 is 1→4→3→5 and has a total cost of 12 (6+4+2), compared to the cost of 20 for the edge directly from 1 to 5 and the cost of 14 for the path 1→2→3→5.

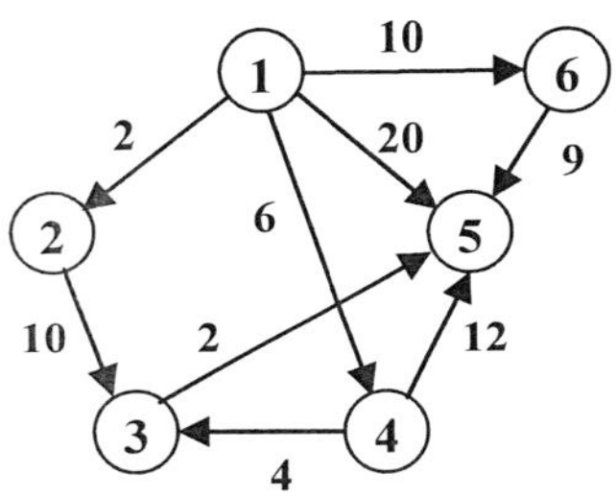

	1	*2*	*3*	*4*	*5*	*6*
1	∞	2	∞	6	20	10
2	∞	∞	10	∞	∞	∞
3	∞	∞	∞	∞	2	∞
4	∞	∞	4	∞	12	∞
5	∞	∞	∞	∞	∞	∞
6	∞	∞	∞	∞	9	∞

Figure 4.8: A weighted directed graph and its adjacency matrix

It turns out that it is just easy to solve the more general problem of starting at one node, called the *source*, and finding the shortest path to every other node, instead of to just one destination node. For simplicity, we take the source to be node 1, and our problem then consists of finding the shortest path from node 1 to every other node in the graph.

4.4.1 Dijkstra's Algorithm

The solution we will show for the shortest-path problem is called Dijkstra's Algorithm, after Edsger Dijkstra, who first described it in 1959. This algorithm is based on the adjacency matrix representation of a graph. Somewhat surprisingly, it finds not only the shortest path from one specified vertex to another, but the shortest paths from the specified vertex to all the other vertices.

We are given a directed graph $G = \{V, E\}$ in which each edge has a cost (weight, distance, time, or any other appropriate measurement), and vertex is specified as the *source*. Our aim is to find the cost of the shortest path from the source to every vertex in V, where the length of a path is just the sum of the costs of the edges on the path. This is called the *single-source shortest paths* problem.

Dijkstra's Algorithm is called as *greedy* technique. The algorithm works by maintaining a set S of vertices whose shortest distance from the source is already known. Initially, S contains only the source vertex. At each step, we add to S a remaining vertex v whose distance from the source is as short as possible. Then we can find a shortest path from the source to v that passes only through vertices in S. At each step of the algorithm, we use an array d to record the length of the shortest path to each vertex. Once S includes all vertices, d will hold the shortest distance from the source to each vertex.

The Algorithm 4.6 assumes that a weighted digraph $G = \{V, E\}$ is given, where $V = \{1, 2, \ldots n\}$ and vertex 1 is the source. The "a" is a 2-dimensional array of weights, where $a[i][j]$ is the distance or cost from vertex i to vertex j on edge $i \rightarrow j$. If there is no edge $i \rightarrow j$, then we assume $a[i][j]$ is ∞, some value much larger than any actual distance or cost. At each step, $d[i]$ contains the length of the current shortest path from source 1 to vertex i.

Let us apply Dijkstra to the digraph of Figure 4.8. Initially, $S = \{1\}$, $d[2] = 2$, $d[3] = \infty$, $d[4] = 6$, $d[5] = 20$, and $d[6] = 10$. In the first iteration of the for-loop of lines 8 to 13 (Algorithm 4.6), as $d[2]$ is minimum, $w = 2$ is selected. Then we set $d[3] = \min(\infty, 2+10) = 12$. $d[4]$, $d[5]$, and $d[6]$ do not change, because reaching them from 1 directly is shorter than going through vertex 2. After each iteration, the sequence of d-values is shown in Table 4.6 and Figure 4.10 illustrates the stages of the algorithm.

In addition to adjacency matrix, *adjMat*[], d[], and S[], a boolean array *found*[] is used. If *found*[v] = true, then the shortest distance from source 1 to v found; else not found. In other words, *found*[v] is true if v is in the set S.

To estimate the running time of Dijkstra's algorithm, we note that the main loop (lines 6 to 23 of Algorithm 4.6) is executed n-1 times, where n is the number of vertices. There are other two loops within the main loop – each is executed n-1 times. These loops contribute a multiple of $(n-1)^2$ iterations. Statements done outside the loops contribute only $O(n)$, so the running time of the algorithm is $O(n^2)$.

Correctness of Dijkstra's algorithm: It is based on the greedy method. It adds vertices by increasing distance. Suppose it did not find all shortest distances. Let f be the first wrong vertex the algorithm processed. When the previous node, d, on the true shortest path was considered, its distance was correct. But the edge (d, f) was relaxed at that time. Thus, as long as distance[f] $\geq$ distance[d], f's distance cannot be wrong. That is, there is no wrong vertex.

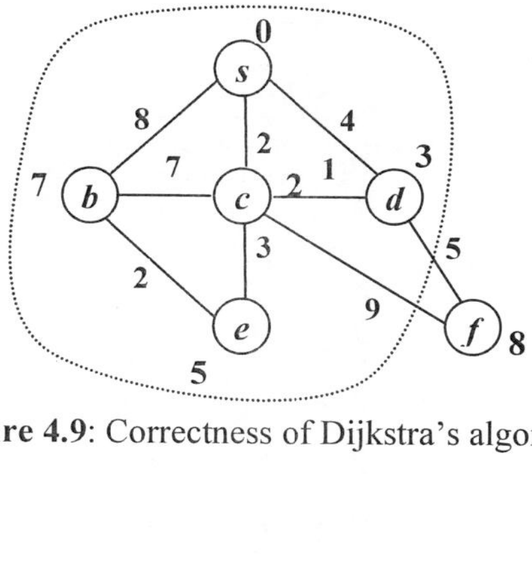

Figure 4.9: Correctness of Dijkstra's algorithm

Algorithm 4.6: Dijkstra(*adjMat*[1..*n*][1..*n*])

```
found[1] = true;  d[1] = 0;    S[1]=1;
For v = 2 to n do        // initialize found and d
    found[v] = false;
    d[v] = adjMat[1][v];
Endfor
For i = 2 to n do        // add one vertex v to S on each pass
    min = ∞;
    For w = 2 to n do  // find the closest vertex v to source 1
        If( found[w] = true and d[w] < min )
            v = w;
            min = d[w];
        Endif
    Endfor
    found[v] = true;        // add v to the set S
    S[i] = v;
    For w = 2 to n do      // update the remaining distances in d
        If( found[w] = true )
            If( min + adjMat[v][w] < d[w])
                d[w] = min + adjMat[v][w];
            Endif
        Endif
    Endfor
Endfor.
For i = 2 to n do   // print shortest path from vertex 1 to other vertices
    print d[i];
Endfor
```

Table 4.6: Computation of Dijkstra on digraph (Figure 4.8)

Iteration	*S*	*w*	*d*[2]	*d*[3]	*d*[4]	*d*[5]	*d*[6]
(initial)	{1}	–	2	∞	6	20	10
(1)	{1, 2}	2	2	12	6	20	10
(2)	{1, 2, 4}	4	2	10	6	18	10
(3)	{1,2, 4, 3}	3	2	10	6	12	10
(4)	{1, 2, 4, 3, 6}	6	2	10	6	12	10
(5)	{1, 2, 4, 3, 6, 5}	5	2	10	6	12	10

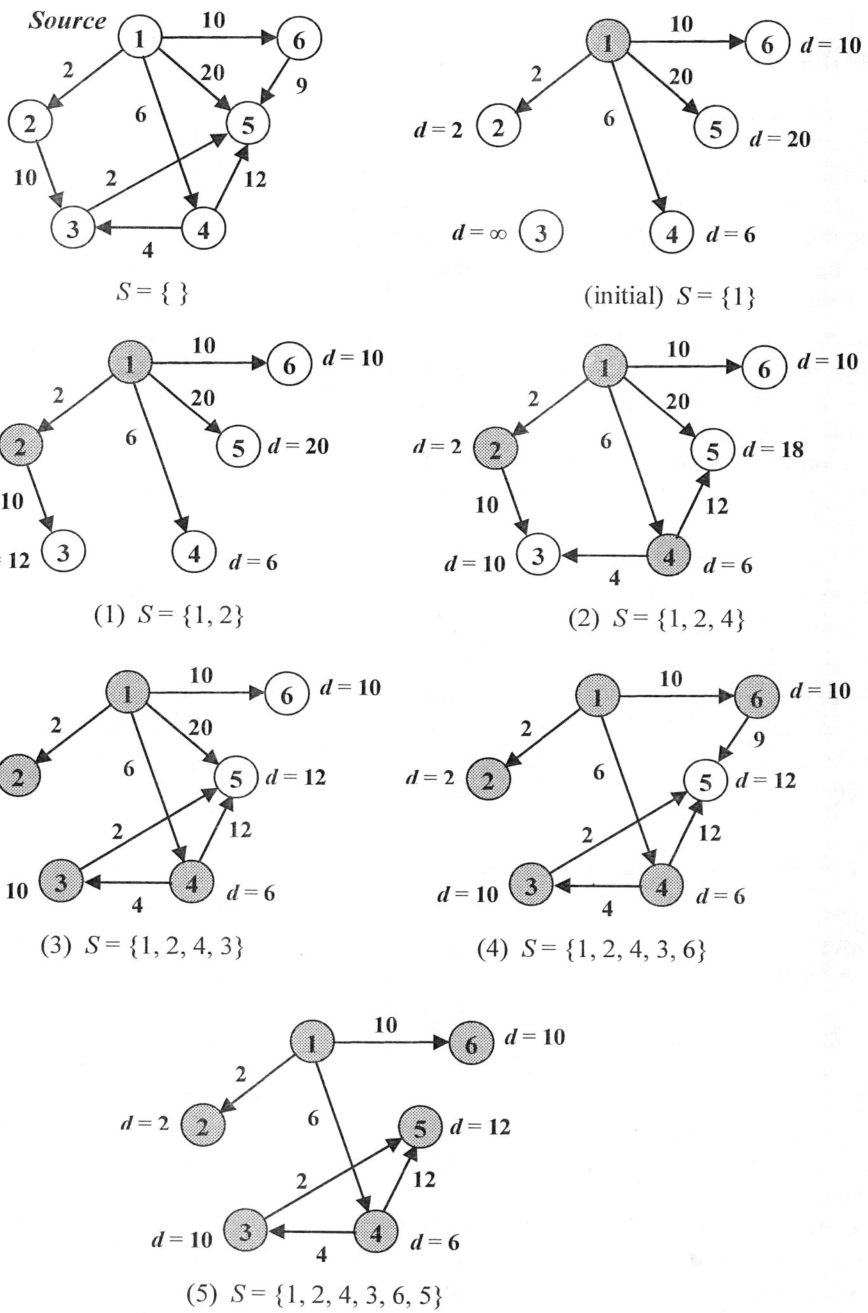

Figure 4.10: Stages of Dijkstra's algorithm

4.5 HUFFMAN CODES

Data compression is useful in any situation where we are communicating over a low-bandwidth channel, such as a modem line or infrared connection, and we wish to minimize the time needed to transmit the data. Likewise, data compression is also useful for storing collections of large documents more efficiently, so as to allow for a fixed-capacity storage device to contain as many documents as possible. For example, we are given a string X defined over some alphabet, such as the ASCII or Unicode character sets, and we want to efficiently encode X into a small binary string Y (using only the bits 0 and 1).

The method for data compression explored in this section is the *Huffman code*. Standard encoding schemes, such as the ASCII and Unicode systems, use fixed-length binary strings to encode characters (with 8 bits in the ASCII system and 16 in the Unicode system). A Huffman code, on the other hand, uses a variable-length encoding optimized for the string X. The optimization is based on the use of character frequencies, where we have, for each character 'c', a count of the number of times 'c' appears in the string X. The Huffman code saves space over a fixed-length encoding by using short code-word strings to encode high-frequency characters and long code-word strings to encode low-frequency characters.

Suppose character 'A' appears 50 times in a text, but 'B' appears only 10 times. ASCII coding assigns 8 bits per character, so total bits for 'A' and 'B' is 60 x 8 = 480. If 'A' gets a 4-bit code and 'B' gets 8-bit code, total is 50 x 4 + 10 x 8 = 280.

Huffman codes are a widely used and very effective technique for compressing data; savings of 20% to 90% are typical, depending on the characteristics of the data being compressed. Huffman's greedy algorithm uses a table of the frequencies of occurrence of the characters to build up an optimal way of representing each character as a binary string.

4.5.1 The Huffman Coding Algorithm

This algorithm assigns binary codes to letters so that the most frequently occurring letters have the shortest codes. This results in a minimal length encoding of a text document. In 1952, David Huffman discovered an optimal algorithm for encoding documents. Huffman codes are used in a wide variety of practical applications, including fax machines, modems, computer networks, and high-definition televisions.

A *Huffman code* for a document is generated from a priority queue (implemented by a heap tree) that has one leaf for each different character in the document. A code for each character is then determined by the root-to-leaf path to that character. The left branches are labeled "0" and the right branches are labeled "1". For example, a root-to-leaf path that goes right-left-right gives the code 101.

The Huffman tree (Figure 4.11) assigns 00 to C, 01 to A, 100 to B, 101 to D, and 11 to E. This is a correct Huffman code for any text document that contains only these five characters, and in which the relative frequencies of those characters determine this particular Huffman tree. We shall see how these relative frequencies are used to construct the tree.

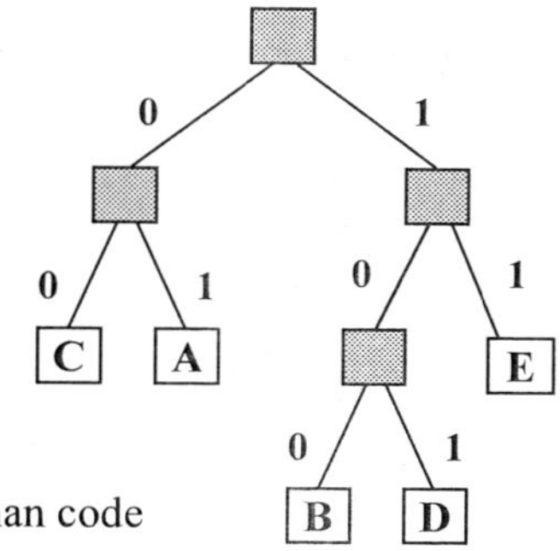

Figure 4.11: A Huffman code

For example, a document contains the letters "A" through "E" with the frequencies (in percentage) is as follows:

A:22, B:13, C:18, D:16, E:31

The construction of binary min-heap tree is illustrated as follows (inserted in this order one by one as a pair of letter and frequency: A:22, B:13, C:18, D:16, E:31):

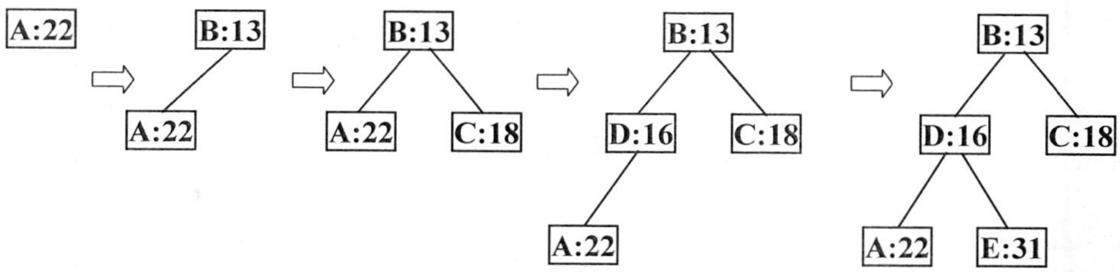

Figure 4.12: Construction of a min-heap

The min-heap (Figure 4.12) represents a priority queue. The Huffman tree is built by deleting top node of the heap one by one. These steps are illustrated as follows (*Note*: In a Huffman tree, each internal node is the sum of its children, and the weighted external path length is minimal. The weighted external path length of a binary tree of integers is the sum of the products of each leaf and its level):

(a) Delete B:13 and D:16 from the heap, and insert into the empty Huffman tree.

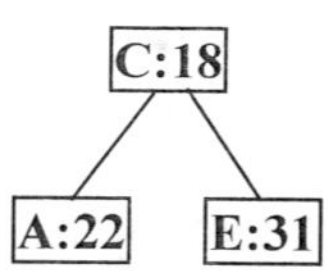

Heap after deletion of B and D

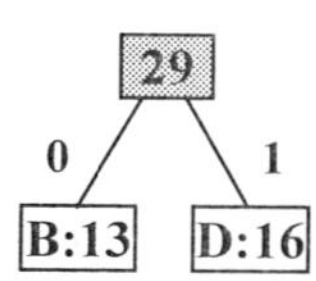

Huffman tree after insertion of B and

(b) Remove C:18 and A:22 from the heap, and add them to the Huffman tree.

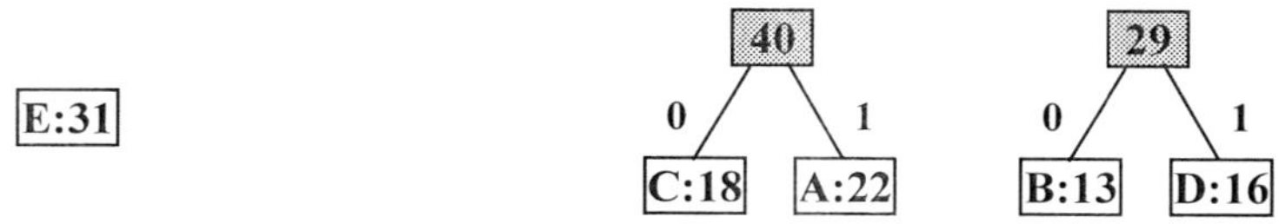

Heap after deletion of C and A   Huffman trees after insertion of C and A

(c) Remove E:31 from the heap, and insert it into the Huffman tree.

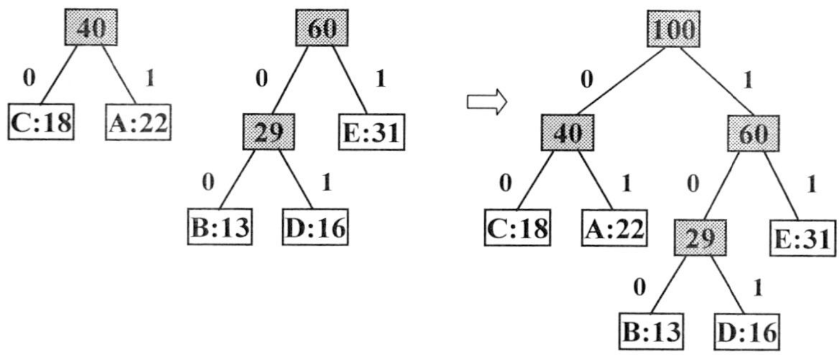

Letter	Code
A	01
B	100
C	00
D	101
E	11

Huffman tree   Huffman Code

Figure 4.13: Combining Huffman trees

Once the Huffman tree is derived, the document can be encoded and decoded uniquely. For example, with the code from the Huffman tree in Figure 4.13, the word ACE would be encoded as 010011. The first digit is 0, so, starting at the root, we move to the left child of the root. The second digit is 1, so we move to the right child and reach leaf 'A'. So we output 'A' and start at the root again. The next two digits are 00, so we move to left twice and reach the leaf node 'C'. We therefore output 'C' and return to the root. The next two digits are 11, so we move right twice and arrive at leaf node 'E'. Finally, ACE has been written and we touch the end of the encoded text, ACE.

It is significant that, by using a Huffman tree, no character's code is a prefix of any other character's code. This *unique prefix property* guarantees the uniqueness of the decoding. For example, we cannot have 'A' map to 10 (2-bit) and 'B' map to 100 (3-bit), because 10 is a prefix (the start of) 100.

In Huffman algorithm, each iteration of the while-loop can be implemented in $O(\log n)$ time using a priority queue represented with a heap, where n is number of distinct characters in the file. In addition, each iteration takes two nodes out of PQ and adds one in, a process that will be repeated n-1 times before exactly one node is left in PQ. Thus, this algorithm runs in $O(n \log n)$ time.

Algorithm 4.7: Huffman()

1. Find the frequency of each character in the file to be compressed.
2. For each distinct character create a one-node binary tree containing the character and its frequency as its priority.
3. Insert the one-node binary trees in a priority queue (*PQ*) in increasing order of frequency.
4. While (there are more than one tree in *PQ*)
   // dequeue two trees t_1 and t_2; Create a tree t that contains t_1 as its
   // left subtree and t_2 as its right subtree;
5. $PQ(t) = PQ(t_1) + PQ(t_2)$;
6. Insert t in its proper location in *PQ*;
7. Endwhile.
8. Assign 0 and 1 weights to the edges of the resulting tree, such that the left and right edge of each node do not have the same weight.

CHAPTER SUMMARY

- The *greedy method* is one of the simplest approaches to solve the optimization problem in which we want to determine the global optimum of a given function by a sequence of steps where at each stage we can make a choice among a class of possible decisions.
- The *greedy-choice property* is a globally-optimal solution that can always be found by a series of local improvements from a starting configuration.
- The arrangement of jobs on a single processor with deadline constraints to obtain maximum profit is named as *job sequencing with deadlines.*
- The *knapsack problem* is to fill the knapsack (bag) with items to maximize the total value subject to its capacity.
- A *minimum cost spanning tree* of a weighted graph is an undirected tree that has minimum total cost or minimum total length.
- *MST property*: $G = (V, E)$ is a connected graph with a cost function defined on the edges. U is some proper subset of the set of vertices V. If (u, v) is an edge of the lowest cost such that $u \in U$ and $v \in V–U$, then there is a minimum-cost spanning tree that includes (u, v) as an edge.
- *Prim*'s and *Kruskal*'s are the two popular algorithms that exploit the *MST* property to construct a minimum-cost spanning tree from a weighted graph.
- Prim's algorithm runs in $O(n^2)$ time, where n is the number of nodes in the graph. Kruskal's algorithm takes a total time of $O(|E|\log |E|)$.

- The *single-source shortest path problem* is to find shortest paths from a source vertex v to all other vertices in the graph.
- *Dijkstra*'s algorithm finds the shortest paths from a single source to all other nodes of a weighted directed graph with positive weights.
- A *Huffman code* for a text document is an optimal encoding of its characters so that more frequent characters have shorter codes.
- The Huffman algorithm first tabulates the frequencies of the characters in the document, and inserts those character-frequency pairs into a min heap. From that, it builds the Huffman tree for the data. Then the binary code for each character is read from the root-to-leaf path to the character in the Huffman tree.
- In a Huffman tree, each internal node is the sum of its children, and the weighted external path length is minimal.

SELF-TEST QUIZ

4.1 The *greedy method* is a general algorithm design paradigm, built on the following elements:

(a) different choices and collections
(b) configurations and objective function
(c) different choices, collections, or values to optimize
(d) all of the above

4.2 The greedy-choice property is a globally-optimal solution that can be found by a series of ______ improvements from a starting configuration.

(a) local (b) global
(c) local or global (d) local and global

4.3 Greedy solutions exist for

(a) no problems (b) no optimization problems
(c) some problems (d) all problems

4.4 The approach to algorithm design for optimization problems that makes direct use of the fact that the most apparent next component of a solution is part of the optimal solution is

(a) divide and conquer (b) greedy
(c) brute force (d) dynamic programming

4.5 The essence of greedy algorithm is the _______ policy.

(a) maximization (b) minimization
(c) selection (d) either (a) or (b)

4.6 If you have a problem that can be solved by a greedy algorithm, then it must be true that:

(a) the problem has optimal substructure.
(b) the problem can also be solved by a divide and conquer algorithm.
(c) the problem cannot usually also be solved by dynamic programming.
(d) none of the above.

4.7 An undirected graph G has n nodes. Its adjacency matrix is given by an n x n square matrix whose (i) diagonal elements are 0's, and (ii) non-diagonal elements are 1's. Which one of the following is true? *GATE 2005*

(a) Graph G has no minimum spanning tree (*MST*).
(b) Graph G has a unique *MST* of cost n-1.
(c) Graph G has multiple distinct *MST*s, each of cost n-1.
(d) Graph G has multiple spanning trees of different costs.

4.8 Let w be the minimum weight among all edge weights in an undirected connected graph. Let e be a specific edge of weight and w. Which of the following statements is false? *GATE 2007*

(a) There is a minimum spanning tree containing e.
(b) If e is not in minimum spanning tree T, then in the cycle formed by adding e to T, all edges have the same weight.
(c) Every minimum spanning tree has an edge of weight w.
(d) e is present in every minimum spanning tree.

4.9 Minimum spanning tree is an attribute of __________.

(a) arrays (b) weighted graphs
(c) unweighted graphs (d) sets of points

4.10 Prim's algorithm runs in ________ time, where n is the number of nodes in the graph.

(a) $O(n)$ (b) $O(n^2)$ (c) $O(n^3)$ (d) $O(\log n)$

4.11 Prim's algorithm can efficiently be implemented by ________.

(a) binary search tree (b) *AVL* tree
(c) splay tree (d) red-black tree

4.12 In Kruskal's algorithm, the edges are selected and added to the spanning tree in ________ order of their weights.

(a) increasing (b) increasing or decreasing
(c) decreasing (d) increasing and decreasing

4.13 What is the total running time of Kruskal's algorithm, where $|E|$ is the number of edges and n number of nodes in a graph?

(a) $O(|E|)$ (b) $O(|E|\log n)$ (c) $O(|E|\log |E|)$ (d) $O(n\log |E|)$

4.14 Dijkstra's algorithm runs in ______ time.

(a) $O(n)$ (b) $O(n^2)$ (c) $O(n^3)$ (d) $O(n \log n)$

4.15 The shortest-path problem is called _________ algorithm.

(a) Dijkstra's (b) Prim's
(c) Kruskal's (d) Graph

4.16 The single-source shortest path problem has a good well-known solution of the type

(a) brute force (b) greedy
(c) depth-first search (d) divide-and-conquer

4.17 The Kruskal, Prim, and Dijkstra algorithms have what approach to algorithm design in common?

(a) divide and conquer (b) greedy
(c) dynamic programming (d) probabilistic

4.18 Consider the following graph:

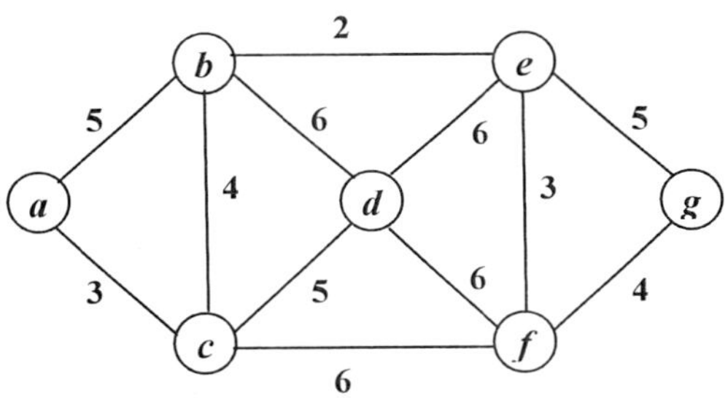

Which one of the following is NOT the sequence of edges added to the minimum spanning tree using Kruskal's algorithm?

(a) (b, e) (e, f) (a, c) (b, c) (f, g) (c, d)
(b) (b, e) (e, f) (a, c) (f, g) (b, c) (c, d)
(c) (b, e) (a, c) (e, f) (b, c) (f, g) (c, d)
(d) (b, e) (e, f) (b, c) (a, c) (f, g) (c, d)

4.19 Consider a sequencing problem where the four jobs (J1, J2, J3, J4) have a profit of (10, 30, 60, 40) and corresponding deadlines (2, 3, 1, 3). Which one of the following sequences of jobs is the optimal solution?

(a) {J3, J4, J2} (b) {J3, J1, J2}
(c) {J3, J1, J4} (d) {J3, J4}

4.20 Which of the following algorithmic techniques did you use to solve the fractional knapsack problem?

(a) Divide and Conquer.
(b) Greedy.
(c) Dynamic Programming.
(d) Branch and Bound.

4.21 Huffman's algorithm is

(a) divide and conquer
(b) greedy
(c) dynamic programming
(d) probabilistic

4.22 Characters that occur more frequently have ________ Huffman codes.

(a) shorter (b) longer
(c) shorter or longer (d) average

4.23 No Huffman code is the ______ of any other Huffman codes so that decoding is unambiguous.

(a) prefix (b) suffix (c) prefix or suffix (d) average

4.24 Huffman uses variable-length bit coding. It enables ________ unambiguous decoding.

(a) right-to-left
(b) left-to-right
(c) left-to-middle
(d) middle-to-left

4.25 Symbols *A*, *B*, *C*, *D* are being produced by the information source with probabilities 1/2, 1/4, 1/8, 1/8 respectively. What is the binary Huffman code?

(a) A = 0, B = 01, C = 011, D = 111
(b) A = 00, B = 01, C = 10, D = 11
(c) A = 0, B = 10, C = 110, D = 111
(d) A = 1, B = 01, C = 000, D = 001

EXERCISES

4.1 Explain the general characteristics of a greedy method.

4.2 Explain the terms feasible solution, optimal solution, and objective function.

4.3 With the help of a control abstraction, explain the greedy method.

4.4 Applying the greedy strategy, find the solution for optimal storage on tapes for the problem instance $n = 3$, $(\ell_1, \ell_2, \ell_3) = (5, 10, 3)$.

4.5 Write a greedy algorithm to the job sequencing with deadlines.

4.6 Explain "job sequencing with deadlines" algorithm. Using this algorithm, find the solution for the instance $n = 7$, $(p_1...p_7) = (3, 5, 20, 18, 1, 6, 30)$ and $(d_1...d_7) = (1, 3, 4, 3, 2, 1, 2)$.

4.7 Explain the algorithm for job sequencing with deadlines. Using this algorithm, find the solution for the instance $n = 4$, $(p_1, p_2, p_3, p_4) = (100, 10, 15, 27)$ and $(d_1, d_2, d_3, d_4) = (2, 1, 2, 1)$.

4.8 Suggest a greedy algorithm for knapsack problem. What are the various strategies chosen to incorporate the greediness?

4.9 Find an optimal solution to the knapsack instance $n = 7$, $M = 15$, $(p_1...p_7) = (10, 5, 15, 7, 6, 18, 3)$ and $(w_1...w_7) = (2, 3, 5, 7, 1, 4, 1)$.

4.10 Prove that greedy knapsack generates optimal solution to the given instance of knapsack problem, when the profit-weight ratio is arranged in non-increasing order.

4.11 Write an algorithm for greedy knapsack and analyze its time complexity.

4.12 Let $S = \{a, b, c, d, e, f, g\}$ be a collection of objects with benefit-weight values as follows: a: (12, 4), b: (10, 6), c: (8, 5), d: (11, 7), e: (14, 3), f: (7, 1), and g: (9, 6). What is the optimal solution to the fractional knapsack problem for S assuming we have a knapsack that can hold objects with total weight 18? What is the complexity of this method?

4.13 Explain the 0/1 knapsack problem with greedy method. Show that this strategy does not necessarily yield optimal solution.

4.14 Develop a counterexample to show that the greedy algorithm developed for the fractional knapsack problem does not work for the 0/1 knapsack problem.

4.15 What is a minimum spanning tree? What are its applications?

4.16 What is a spanning tree? Explain the Prim's algorithm with an example.

4.17 Explain the Kruskal's algorithm with an example and analyze its time complexity.

4.18 Prove that the edge with the smallest weight will be part of every minimum spanning tree.

4.19 State whether the following statements are true or false. Justify the answer.

(a) If e is a minimum weight edge in a connected weighted graph, it must be among the edges of at least one minimum spanning tree of the graph.

(b) If e is a minimum weight edge in a connected weighted graph, it must be among the edges of each one minimum spanning tree of the graph.

(c) If edge weights of a connected weighted graph are all distinct, the graph must have exactly one minimum spanning tree.

(d) If edge weights of a connected weighted graph are not all distinct, the graph must have more than one minimum spanning tree.

4.20 Write Prim's algorithm under the assumption that the graphs are represented by adjacency lists. Analyze the computing time and space requirements of this new version of Prim's algorithm using adjacency lists.

4.21 Obtain the minimum spanning tree of the following graph, using Prim's algorithm under the assumption that the graphs are represented by adjacency lists.

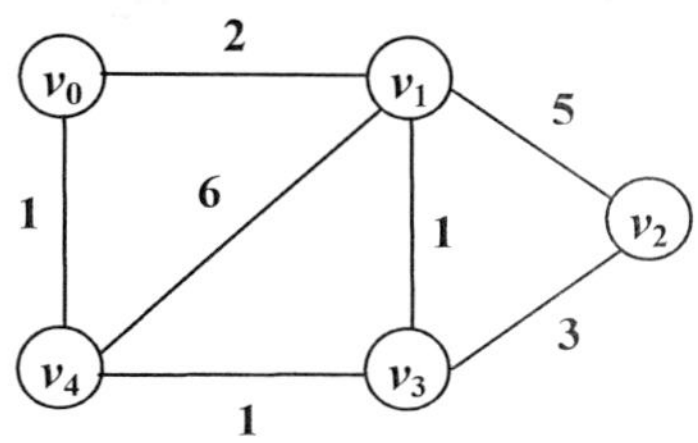

4.22 Prove that if the weights on edges of a connected undirected graph are distinct, then there is a unique minimum spanning tree.

4.23 How many comparisons of edge weights will be done by the minimum spanning tree algorithm, in total, if the input is a complete undirected graph with n vertices and v is the start vertex?

4.24 What is the basic difference between Prim's and Kruskal's approaches to obtain minimum spanning trees? Illustrate the results for the following graph:

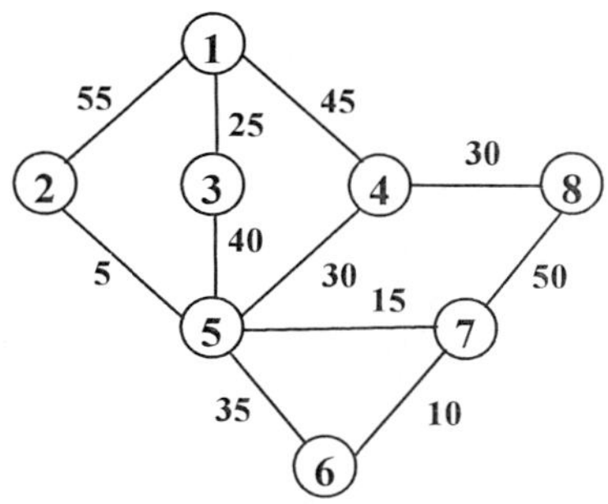

4.25 Write a greedy algorithm to generate the shortest path.

4.26 Design a linear-time algorithm for solving the single source shortest path algorithm for directed acyclic graphs represented by their adjacency linked lists.

4.27 Information to be transmitted over the internet contains the following characters with their associated frequencies as shown in the following table:

Characters:	A	E	L	N	O	S	T
Frequency:	45	65	13	45	18	22	53

Use Huffman technique to answer the following questions:

(a) Build the Huffman code tree for the message and find the codeword for each character.
(b) If the data consists of only these characters, what is the total number of bits to be transmitted? What is the percentage saving if the data is sent with 8-bit ASCII values without compression?
(c) Verify that your computed Huffman codewords are correct.

4.28 Symbols *A*, *B*, *C*, *D*, *E*, *F* are being produced by the information source with probabilities (in percentages) 30, 40, 6, 10, 10, 4 respectively. What is the binary Huffman code?

CHAPTER 5

DYNAMIC PROGRAMMING

Algorithms designed using *dynamic programming* are similar to those developed using divide-and-conquer. Both solve a problem by breaking it down into several subproblems that can be solved recursively. The difference between the two is that in the dynamic programming approach, the results obtained from solving smaller sub-problems are *reused* in the calculation of larger subproblems. Thus, dynamic programming is a *bottom-up* technique that usually begins by solving the smaller sub-problems, saving these results, and then reusing them to solve larger subproblems until the solution to the original problem is obtained. This is in contrast to the divide-and-conquer approach, which solves problems in a *top-down* method.

It is important to realize that dynamic programming is justified if there is some degree of overlap in the subproblems. The basic idea is to avoid computing the same result twice or more. This is usually accomplished by constructing a table in memory, and filling it with known results as they are calculated. These results are then used to solve larger subproblems. Retrieving a given result from this table requires $O(1)$ time.

The problem of calculating the nth Fibonacci number does, however, exhibit overlapping subproblems. The recursive implementation would be:

```
fib(n)
{   if (n = 0) return 0;
    if (n = 1) return 1;
    return fib(n-1) + fib(n-2);
}
```

The problem of calculating $fib(n)$ thus depends on both $fib(n\text{-}1)$ and $fib(n\text{-}2)$. To see how these subproblems overlap look at how many times *fib* is called and with what arguments when we try to calculate $fib(5)$:

$fib(5)$
$fib(4) + fib(3)$
$[fib(3)+fib(2)] + [fib(2)+fib(1)]$
$[[fib(2) + fib(1)] + [fib(1) + fib(0)]] + [[fib(1) + fib(0)] + fib(1)]$
$[[[fib(1) + fib(0)] + fib(1)] + [fib(1) + fib(0)]] + [[fib(1) + fib(0)] + fib(1)]$

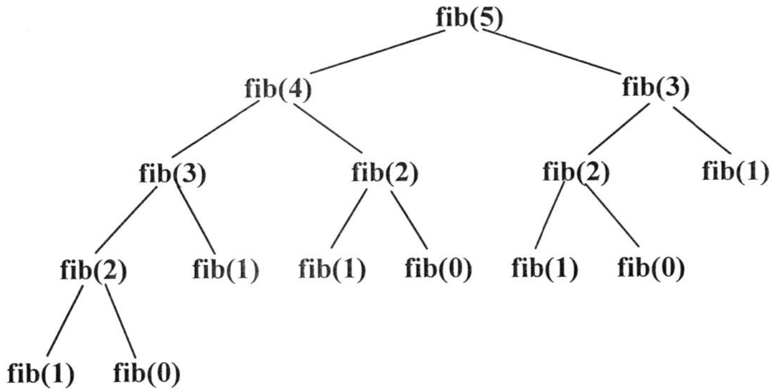

Figure 5.1: Recursive computation of Fibonacci numbers

Using this brute-force approach, the final result is obtained by adding together *fib*(n) values of 1. That is, this procedure must perform at least *fib*(n)-1 additions. The running time of this brute-force method is super-polynomial. One thing that should be noticed about this solution is that many of intermediate values are repeatedly calculated. For example, *fib*(2) is computed thrice to obtain *fib*(5) (see Figure 5.1).

At the kth stage we only need to know the values of *fib*(k-1) and *fib*(k-2), but we wind up calling each multiple times. Starting from the bottom and going up we can calculate the numbers we need for the next step, removing the massive redundancy.

The dynamic programming approach to the direct computation of the nth Fibonacci number avoids the recalculation of intermediate values by storing them in a table when they are initially calculated. A one-dimensional array *fib*[0..n] containing n+1 locations is set up, and the value of Fibonacci number is stored in *fib*[i] for i = 0, 1, 2, ..n. Then, *fib*[i] is computed by adding together *fib*[i-2] and *fib*[i-1] for i = 2, 3, ..n. Since *fib*[i-2] and *fib*[i-1] can be retrieved from the table and added together in a constant time, the computation of each *fib*[i] is accomplished in O(1) time, and entire computation requires $O(n)$ time as well as $O(n)$ space. The purpose of this example is to demonstrate how dynamic programming can be applied.

```
fib2(n)
{   fib[0] = 0, fib[1] = 1;
    for(i = 2;  i < n;  i++)
        fib[i] = fib[i-2] + fib[i-1];
    return fib[i];
}
```

In Big-O notation the *fib*() function takes $O(c^n)$ time, that is, exponential in n, while the *fib*2() function takes $O(n)$ time (c is a constant).

The above problem is one of the first examples of the performance issues surrounding recursion versus iteration. In fact, the Fibonacci example leads people to believe that recursion is inherently slow. This is not true, but in cases where we can define a problem with overlapping subproblems recursively using the above technique will always reduce the execution time.

Optimal substructure

A problem is said to have optimal substructure if the globally optimal solution can be constructed from locally optimal solutions to subproblems. The general form of problems in which optimal substructure plays a roll goes something like this. Let us say we have a collection of objects called A. For each object ob in A we have a "cost," $c(ob)$. Now find the subset of A with the maximum (or minimum) cost, perhaps subject to certain constraints.

The brute-force method would be to generate every subset of A, calculate the cost, and then find the maximum (or minimum) among those values. But if A has n elements in it we are looking at a search space of size 2^n if there are no constraints on A. Oftentimes n is huge making a brute-force method computationally infeasible. Let us take a look at an example.

Example 5.1: Maximum subarray sum

Let us say we are given an array of integers. What (contiguous) subarray has the largest sum? For example, if our array is [1, 2, -5, 4, 7, -2] then the subarray with the largest sum is [4, 7] with a sum of 11. One might think at first that this problem reduces to finding the subarray with all positive entries, if one exists, that maximizes the sum. But consider the array [1, 5, -3, 4, -2, 1]. The subarray with the largest sum is [1, 5, -3, 4] with a sum of 7.

First, consider the brute-force solution. Because of the constraints on the problem, namely that the subsets under consideration are contiguous, we only have to check $O(n^2)$ subarrays.

Let us see if we cannot find an optimal substructure to exploit. We are given an input array $a[0..n\text{-}1]$. Let us say we know the subarray of $a[0..i\text{-}1]$ with the largest sum (and that sum). Using just this information, can we find the subarray of $a[0..i]$ with the largest sum?

Let $a[j..k]$ be the optimal subarray, t the sum of $a[j..i\text{-}1]$, and s the optimal sum. If $t+a[i]$ is greater than s then set $a[j..i]$ as the optimal array and set $s = t$. If $t+a[i]$ is negative, however, the contiguity constraint means that we cannot include $a[j..i]$ in our subarray since any such subarray will have a smaller sum than a subarray without it. So, if $t+a[i]$ is negative set $t = 0$ and set the left-hand bound of the optimal subarray to $i+1$.

To illustrate, we consider the array [1, 2, -5, 4, 7, -2].

Set s = -infinity, $t = 0$, $j = 0$, bounds = (0, 0)

(1 2 -5 4 7 -2)

(1)| 2 -5 4 7 -2 (set $t = 1$. Since $t > s$, set $s = 1$ and bounds = (0, 0))

(1 2)|-5 4 7 -2 (set $t = 3$. Since $t > s$, set $s = 3$, and bounds = (0, 1))

1 2 -5(| 4 7 -2 (set $t = -2$. Since $t < 0$, set $t = 0$ and $j = 3$)

1 2 -5 (4)| 7 -2 (set $t = 4$. Since $t > s$, set $s = 4$ and bounds = (3, 3))

1 2 -5 (4 7)|-2 (set $t = 11$. Since $t > s$, set $s = 11$ and bounds = (3, 4))

1 2 -5 (4 7) -2| (set $t = 9$. Nothing happens since $t < s$)

This requires only one pass through the array and at each step we are only keeping track of three variables: the current sum from the left-hand edge of the bounds to the current point (t), the maximal sum (s), and the bounds of the current optimal subarray (bounds).

In this problem the "globally optimal" solution corresponds to a subarray with a globally maximal sum, but at each step we only make a decision relative to what we have already seen.

That is, at each step we know the best solution *thus far*, but might change our decision later based on our previous information and the current information. This is the sense in the problem has optimal substructure. Because we can make decisions locally we only need to traverse the list once, reducing the run-time of the solution to $O(n)$ from $O(n^2)$.

5.1 THE 0/1 KNAPSACK PROBLEM

What is a knapsack problem? We have a knapsack (bag) with capacity, $W = 20$. The weights and values of five items are given below.

Table 5.1: Knapsack example

item (i):	1	2	3	4	5
w_i:	3	4	7	8	9
v_i:	4	5	10	11	13

The objective of knapsack problem is to fill the knapsack with items to maximize the total value subject to its capacity. It is known as 0/1 knapsack problem, because we put one item into the knapsack or not (may not include a fraction of an item). The following decisions are taken to optimize the total value.

(1) Highest value, $v_5 = 13$, add $w_5 = 9$ to knapsack. Total value is 13 and knapsack remaining capacity is 11 (20 - 9).

(2) Next higher value, $v_4 = 11$, add $w_4 = 8$ to knapsack. Total value is 24 (13+11) and knapsack remaining capacity is 3 (11 - 8).

(3) Next higher value, $v_3 = 10$, we cannot add $w_3 = 7$ to knapsack. Because it exceeds the knapsack capacity ($9+8+7 = 24 > 20$).

(4) Next higher value, $v_2 = 5$, we cannot add $w_2 = 4$ to knapsack. Because it exceeds the knapsack capacity ($9+8+4 = 21 > 20$).

(5) Next higher value, $v_1 = 4$, add $w_1 = 3$ to knapsack. Total value is 28 (13+11+4) and knapsack remaining capacity is 0 (3 - 3).

(6) Maximum value is 28 (items included in knapsack: 1, 4, and 5).

The knapsack problem shows both overlapping subproblems and optimal substructure. Say there are n items with weights $w_1, \ldots, w_n$ and their values $v_1, \ldots, v_n$. In general, the 0-1 knapsack problem can be expressed as follows:

Maximize total value of items included in the knapsack: $v_1x_1 + v_2x_2 + \ldots + v_nx_n$

subject to the knapsack capacity constraint: $w_1x_1 + w_2x_2 + \ldots + w_nx_n \leq W$
where $x_1, x_2, \ldots, x_n$ take a value either 0 or 1.

The knapsack example given in Table 5.1 is formulated as follows:
Maximize: $4x_1 + 5x_2 + 10x_3 + 11x_4 + 13x_5$

Subject to: $3w_1 + 4w_2 + 7w_3 + 8w_4 + 9w_5 \leq 20$.
Optimal solution is: $x_1 = 1, x_2 = 0, x_3 = 0, x_4 = 1$, and $x_5 = 1$, with a maximum value of 28 (4 + 11 + 13).

To formulate the problem in terms of dynamic programming, we define a subproblem $S[k, u]$, which will be the optimal solution for the first k items, involving up to u weight. $S[k, u]$ is a recursive formula, which will specify how the subproblem can be solved. The real insight of dynamic programming is that we will take this recursive solution and convert it into an iterative solution, just as we did with Fibonacci numbers.

We will formulate this in terms of the solution that includes any of the items $1 \ldots k$-1. If we have the optimal solution for a given weight u for these k-1 items, then the optimal solution for the first k items will be described as follows: There are two main cases:

(1) Case: $w_k > u$. As the weight of item k is greater than the weight constraint that we are working with, item k cannot be included in the knapsack.

(2) Case: $w_k \leq u$. If item k is included, the value will be equal to the value of item k plus the maximum value of $k-1$ previous items, subject to a total weight of $u-w_k$, since we have to include w_k without exceeding the weight limit u. This is equivalent to $S[k-1, u-w_k] + v_k$. This leaves us two sub-cases.

  (a) If this total is less than the maximum for the first $k-1$ values, we will not include item k. The new value will be $S[k-1, u]$.

  (b) If it is larger, then we will include item k, and $S[k-1, u-w_k]+v_k$ will be the new value.

Thus, the recursive definition for the optimum is given as follows:

$$S[k, u] = \begin{cases} S[k-1, u] & \text{if } w_k > u \\ \max\{ S[k-1, u], S[k-1, u-w_k] + v_k \} & \text{otherwise} \end{cases}$$

We can store the subproblems in a two-dimensional array, with first subscript being the items that we choose from 1 to n, and the second being the weight that we fill from 0 to W. For any given k, we can find all of the values of $S[k, u]$ for $u = 0$ to W.

Algorithm 5.1: knapsack(w[1..n], v[1..n], W)

```
For u = 0 to W
      S[0, u] = 0
Endfor
For i = 0 to n
      S[i, 0] = 0
Endfor
For i = 0 to n
      For u = 0 to W
            If( w[i] ≤ u ) then       // item fits in knapsack
                  If( v[i] + S[i-1, u-w[i]] > S[i-1, u] ) then
                        S[i, u] = v[i] + S[i-1, u-w[i]]
                  Else  S[i, u] = S[i-1, u]
            Else  S[i, u] = S[i-1, u]
      Endfor
Endfor
Print S[n][W]              // max value of items included in the knapsack
// Find knapsack items
i = n,  k = W
While( i > 0 and k > 0)
      If( S[i][k] ≠ S[i-1][k] )
            Print i              // item i is in the knapsack
            k = k - w[i]
      Endif
      i = i - 1
Endwhile
```

Example 5.2: Let us trace this algorithm through the following example. Capacity of knapsack is 5.

Table 5.2: Knapsack example-2

item (i):	1	2	3	4
w_i:	2	3	4	5
v_i:	4	8	9	11

After the initialization step of the first row and first column, the matrix S will be completed as follows:

Table 5.3(a)	weight (u)					
item (i)	0	1	2	3	4	5
0	0	0	0	0	0	0
1	0					
2	0					
3	0					
4	0					

For $i = 1$, the computations for inner loop ($u = 0, 1, 2, 3, 4, 5$) are as follows:
$w[1] = 2$, $v[1] = 4$.
$u = 0$, $w[1] > u$, $S[1, 0] = S[0, 0] = 0$.
$u = 1$, $w[1] > u$, $S[1, 1] = S[0, 1] = 0$.
$u = 2$, $w[1] = u$ and $(v[1]+S[0, 0]) > S[0, 2]$, $S[1, 2] = v[1] + S[0, 0] = 4 + 0 = 4$.
$u = 3$, $w[1] < u$ and $(v[1]+S[0, 1]) > S[0, 3]$, $S[1, 2] = v[1] + S[0, 1] = 4 + 0 = 4$.
Similar results occur for $u = 4$, and $u = 5$, leaving us with the following table.

Table 5.3(b)	weight (u)					
item (i)	0	1	2	3	4	5
0	0	0	0	0	0	0
1	0	0	4	4	4	4
2	0					
3	0					
4	0					

For $i = 2$, the computations for inner loop ($u = 0, 1, 2, 3, 4, 5$) are as follows:
$w[2] = 3$, $v[2] = 8$.
$u = 0$, $w[2] > u$, $S[2, 0] = S[1, 0] = 0$.
$u = 1$, $w[2] > u$, $S[2, 1] = S[1, 1] = 0$.
$u = 2$, $w[2] > u$, $S[2, 2] = S[1, 2] = 4$.
$u = 3$, $w[2] = u$ and $(v[2]+S[1, 0]) > S[1, 3]$, $S[2, 3] = v[2] + S[1, 0] = 8 + 0 = 8$.
$u = 4$, $w[2] < u$ and $(v[2]+S[1, 1]) > S[1, 4]$, $S[2, 4] = v[2] + S[1, 1] = 8 + 0 = 8$.
$u = 5$, $w[2] < u$ and $(v[2]+S[1, 2]) > S[1, 5]$, $S[2, 5] = v[2] + S[1, 2] = 8 + 4 = 12$.

Table 5.3(c)	weight (u)					
item (i)	0	1	2	3	4	5
0	0	0	0	0	0	0
1	0	0	4	4	4	4
2	0	0	4	8	8	12
3	0					
4	0					

For $i = 3$, the computations for inner loop ($u = 0, 1, 2, 3, 4, 5$) are as follows:
$w[3] = 4$, $v[3] = 9$.
$u = 0$, $w[3] > u$, $S[3, 0] = S[2, 0] = 0$.
$u = 1$, $w[3] > u$, $S[3, 1] = S[2, 1] = 0$.
$u = 2$, $w[3] > u$, $S[3, 2] = S[2, 2] = 4$.
$u = 3$, $w[3] > u$, $S[3, 3] = S[2, 3] = 8$.
$u = 4$, $w[3] = u$ and $(v[3]+S[2, 0]) > S[2, 4]$, $S[3, 4] = v[3] + S[2, 0] = 9 + 0 = 9$.
$u = 5$, $w[3] < u$ and $(v[3]+S[2, 1]) < S[2, 5]$, $S[3, 5] = S[2, 5] = 12$.

Table 5.3(d)	weight (*u*)					
item (*i*)	0	1	2	3	4	5
0	0	0	0	0	0	0
1	0	0	4	4	4	4
2	0	0	4	8	8	12
3	0	0	4	8	9	12
4	0					

For $i = 4$, the computations for inner loop ($u = 0, 1, 2, 3, 4, 5$) are as follows:
$w[4] = 5$, $v[4] = 11$.
$u = 0$, $w[4] > u$, $S[4, 0] = S[3, 0] = 0$.
$u = 1$, $w[4] > u$, $S[4, 1] = S[3, 1] = 0$.
$u = 2$, $w[4] > u$, $S[4, 2] = S[3, 2] = 4$.
$u = 3$, $w[4] > u$, $S[4, 3] = S[3, 3] = 8$.
$u = 4$, $w[4] > u$, $S[4, 4] = S[3, 4] = 9$.
$u = 5$, $w[4] = u$ and $(v[4]+S[3, 0]) < S[3, 5]$, $S[4, 5] = S[3, 5] = 12$.

Table 5.3(e)	weight (*u*)					
item (*i*)	0	1	2	3	4	5
0	0	0	0	0	0	0
1	0	0	4	4	4	4
2	0	0	4	8	8	12
3	0	0	4	8	9	12
4	0	0	4	8	9	12

We have essentially found the maximum value that can be placed in the knapsack for any weight u, using all of the items up to i. To find the solution for the whole problem, we look at $S[n, W]$. In this case, the maximum value, $S[4, 5]$ from Table 5.3(e) is 12.

To reconstruct the solution, we note that if $S[i, k] \neq S[i\text{-}1, k]$, this happened because we added item i to the knapsack to increase the value. Thus, we can backtrack for $i = n$, $k = W$, adding an item to the list every time we see that $S[i, k] \neq S[i\text{-}1, k]$. Lines 18-25 of the Algorithm 5.1 give the second part.

For our example, we start with $i = 4$ and $k = 5$. Since $S[4, 5] = S[3, 5] = S[2, 5]$, we know that items 4 and 3 are not in the knapsack. However, when $i = 2$, $S[2, 5] \neq S[1, 5]$, so item 2 is in the knapsack, and we update k to be 3. When $i = 1$, $S[1, 3] \neq S[0, 3]$, so we add item 1, and we are done. The final knapsack contains items 1 and 2, for a total weight of 5 and a value of 12.

It should not be hard to see that the completion of the table takes $O(nW)$, while the reconstruction of the contents can be done in $O(n)$, both significant improvements on the enumeration of all possible subsets.

5.2 OPTIMAL BINARY SEARCH TREE

If we do not plan on modifying a search tree, and we know exactly how often each item will be accessed, we can construct an optimal binary search tree, which is a search tree where the average cost of looking up an item (the expected search cost) is minimized.

Assume that we know the elements and that for each element we know the proportion of future lookups which will be looking for that element. We can then use a dynamic programming solution to construct the tree with the least possible expected search cost.

Even if we only have estimates of the search costs, such a system can considerably speed up lookups on average. For example, if we have a BST of English words used in a spell checker, we might balance the tree based on word frequency in a text, placing words like "the" near the root and words like "rare" near the leaves. Such a tree might be compared with Huffman trees, which similarly seek to place frequently-used items near the root in order to produce a dense information encoding; however, Huffman trees only store data elements in leaves and these elements need not be ordered.

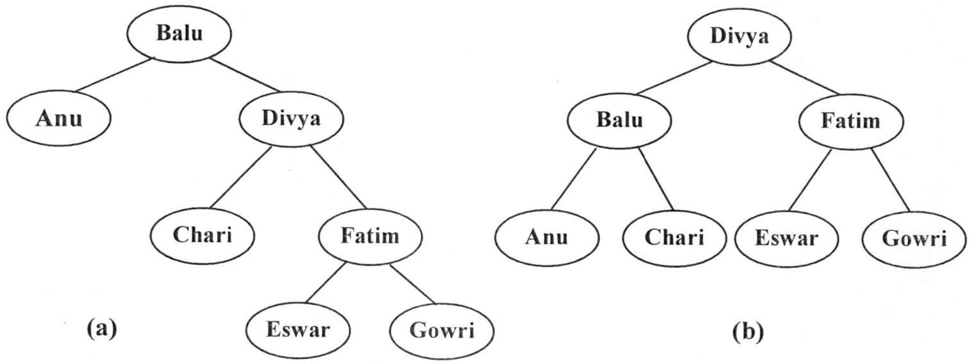

Figure 5.2: Examples of Binary Search Trees

A binary search tree is a tree where the key values are ordered lexicographically (alphabetically), that is, for each internal node all the keys in the left subtree are less than the keys in the node, and all the keys in the right subtree are greater. The inorder traversal of BST gives an ascending order of the keys. Figure 5.2 shows two binary search trees – one on the right is a balanced BST, and the left one is an unbalanced. A binary tree is called balanced if the depth of the two subtrees of every node never differs by more than 1. In Figure 5.2(a), the node containing "Fatim" has a depth of 2. Alternatively, we could say that the node is at level 2. The root has a depth of 0 and is at level 0.

When we know the frequency of searching each one of the keys, it is quite easy to compute the expected cost of accessing each node in the tree. An optimal binary search tree is a BST which has minimal expected cost of locating each node. An optimal BST is not equivalent to a balanced BST.

The search time for a given key is

$depth(key) + 1$,

where $depth(key)$ is the depth of the node containing the key. For example, the depth of the node containing "Fatim" is 2 in the Figure 5.2(a). The search time for "Fatim" is $depth$("Fatim") + 1 = 2 + 1 = 3.

Let $key_1, key_2, \ldots, key_n$ be the n keys in order and let p_i be the probability that key_i is the search key. If c_i is the number of comparisons required to find key_i in a given tree, the average search time for that tree is given by:

$$\sum_{i=1}^{n} c_i p_i$$

which is to be minimized.

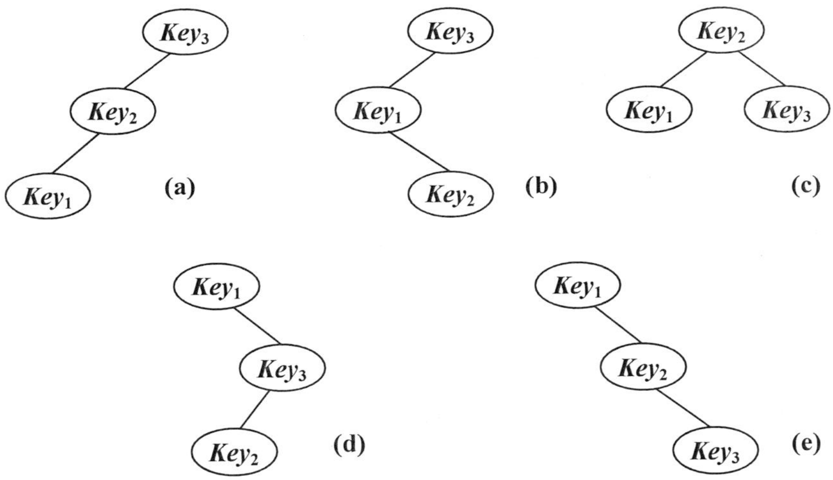

Figure 5.3: Five different Binary Search Trees

Example 5.3: Figure 5.3 shows five different trees when $n = 3$. The actual values of the keys are not significant. The only requirement is that they be ordered, if

$p_1 = 0.7, p_2 = 0.2$, and $p_3 = 0.1$,

the average search times for the trees in Figure 5.3 are:

(a) $3(0.7) + 2(0.2) + 1(0.1) = 2.6$

(b) $2(0.7) + 3(0.2) + 1(0.1) = 2.1$

(c) $2(0.7) + 1(0.2) + 2(0.1) = 1.8$

(d) $1(0.7) + 3(0.2) + 2(0.1) = 1.5$

(e) $1(0.7) + 2(0.2) + 3(0.1) = 1.4$

The fifth tree shown in Figure 5.3(e) is optimal.

In general, using brute-force method, we cannot find an optimal BST by considering all binary search trees because the number of such trees is at least exponential in n. Dynamic programming will be used to develop a more efficient algorithm. To that end, suppose that keys key_i through key_j are arranged in a tree that minimizes:

$$\sum_{m=i}^{j} c_m p_m$$

where c_m is the number of comparisons needed to locate key_m in the tree. We will call a tree *optimal* for those keys and denote the optimal value by $A[i][j]$. Because it takes one comparison to locate a key in a tree containing one key $A[i][i] = 1(p_i) = p_i$.

Considering the Example 5.3, we have three keys with probabilities: $p_1 = 0.7$, $p_2 = 0.2$, and $p_3 = 0.1$. To determine $A[2][3]$, we must consider two trees as shown in Figure 5.4. The average search times for the trees are:

(a) $1(p_2) + 2(p_3) = 1(0.2) + 2(0.1) = 0.4$

(b) $2(p_2) + 1(p_3) = 2(0.2) + 1(0.1) = 0.5$

The first tree is optimal and $A[2][3] = 0.4$.

Figure 5.4: Two different Binary Search Trees

Notice that the optimal tree obtained in this example (Figure 5.4) is the right subtree of the root of the optimal tree obtained in Figure 5.3(e). Even if this tree was not the exact same one as that right subtree, the average time spent searching in it would have to be the same. Otherwise, we could substitute it for that subtree, resulting in a tree with a smaller average search time. In general, any subtree of an optimal tree must be optimal for the keys in that subtree. Therefore, the principle of optimality applies.

Next, let tree 1 be an optimal tree given the restriction that key_1 is at the root, tree 2 be an optimal tree given the restriction that key_2 is at the root, . . ., tree n be an optimal tree given the restriction that key_n is at the root. For $1 \le k \le n$, the subtrees of tree k must be optimal, and therefore the average search times in these subtrees are as shown in Figure 5.5.

The Figure 5.5 also shows that for each $m = k$, it takes exactly one more comparison (the one at the root) to locate key_m in tree k than it does to locate that key in the subtree that contains it. This one comparison add 1 x pm to the average search time for key_m in tree k. The average search time for tree k is given by:

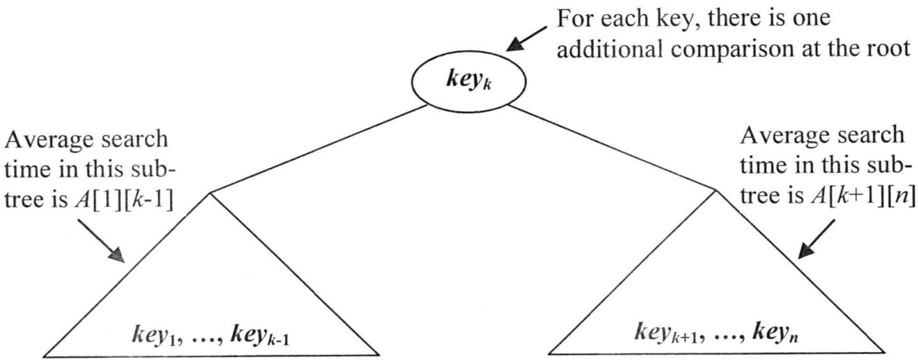

Figure 5.5: Optimal Binary Search Tree

$$\underbrace{A[1][k\text{-}1]}_{\text{Avg time in left subtree}} + \underbrace{p1 + \ldots + p_{k\text{-}1}}_{\text{Additional time comparing at root}} + \underbrace{p_k}_{\text{Avg time searching for root}} + \underbrace{A[k+1][n]}_{\text{Avg time in right subtree}} + \underbrace{p_{k+1} + \ldots + p_n}_{\text{Additional time comparing at root}}$$

which equals

$$A[1][k\text{-}1] + A[k+1][n] + \sum_{m=1}^{n} p_m$$

Because one of the k trees must be optimal, the average search time for the optimal tree is given by:

$$A[1][n] = \min_{i \le k \le j}(A[1][k-1] + A[k+1][n]) + \sum_{m=1}^{n} p_m$$

where $A[1][0]$ and $A[n+1][0]$ are defined to be 0. Although the sum of the probabilities in the last expression is clearly 1, we have written it as a sum because we now wish to generalize the result. It requires that the keys are key_1 through key_n. That is, in general, this pertains to key_i through key_j, where $i < j$. Therefore, we have:

$$A[i][j] = \min_{i \le k \le j}(A[i][k-1] + A[k+1][j]) + \sum_{m=i}^{j} p_m \qquad i < j$$

$A[i][j] = p_i$

$A[i][i\text{-}1]$ and $A[j+1][j]$ are defined to be 0.

We now determine an OBST for a set of keys, each with a given probability of being the search key.

Input: Let n be the number of keys and $p[i]$ the probability of searching for the ith key.

Output: *minavg* is a variable whose value is the average search time for an OBST. *R* is a matrix from which an OBST can be constructed. *R* has its rows indexed from 1 to *n*-1 and its columns indexed from 0 to *n*. *R*[*i*][*j*] is the index of the key in the root of an optimal tree containing the *i*th through the *j*th keys.

```
Algorithm 5.2: OBST(n, p[1..n])
For i = 1 to n
        A[i][i-1] = 0,  A[i][i] = p[i],  R[i][i] = i,   R[i][i-1] = 0.
Endfor
A[n+1][n] = 0,   R[n+1][n] = 0.
For d = 1 to n–1                        // d: diagonal
        For i = 1 to n–d
            j = i + d
            A[i][j] = min_{i≤k≤j}(A[i][k – 1] + A[k + 1][j]) + Σ_{m=i}^{j} p_m
            R[i][j] = a value of k that gave the minimum
        Endfor
Endfor
minavg = A[1][n]
```

Example 5.4: Consider the following values of the array key with probabilities.

key[*i*]:	*key*[1]	*key*[2]	*key*[3]	*key*[4]
Value:	Anu	Balu	Chari	Divya
p[*i*]:	3/8	3/8	1/8	1/8

The matrices *A* and *R* produced by Algorithm 5.2: OBST are shown in Figure 5.6 in stages. The following Table 5.4 illustrates the trace of the algorithm:

Table 5.4: Trace of Algorithm 5.2: OBST

d	*i*	*j*	*k*	$A_{i,k-1}$	$A_{k+1,j}$	$A_{i,k-1} + A_{k+1,j}$	$\sum_{m=i}^{j} p_m$	$A_{i,j}$	$R_{i,j}$
1	1	2	1	$A_{1,0} = 0$	$A_{2,2} = 3/8$	3/8 (**min**)	$p_1+p_2 = 6/8$	9/8	1
			2	$A_{1,1} = 3/8$	$A_{3,2} = 0$	3/8			
	2	3	2	$A_{2,1} = 0$	$A_{3,3} = 1/8$	1/8 (**min**)	$p_2+p_3 = 4/8$	5/8	2
			3	$A_{2,2} = 3/8$	$A_{4,3} = 0$	3/8			

	3	4	3	$A_{3,2} = 0$	$A_{4,4} = 1/8$	1/8 (**min**)	$p_3+p_4 = 2/8$	3/8	3
			4	$A_{3,3} = 1/8$	$A_{5,4} = 0$	1/8			
2	1	3	1	$A_{1,0} = 0$	$A_{2,3} = 5/8$	5/8	$p_1+p_2+p_3 = 7/8$	11/8	2
			2	$A_{1,1} = 3/8$	$A_{3,3} = 1/8$	4/8 (**min**)			
			3	$A_{1,2} = 9/8$	$A_{4,3} = 0$	9/8			
	2	4	2	$A_{2,1} = 0$	$A_{3,4} = 3/8$	3/8 (**min**)	$p_2+p_3+p_4 = 5/8$	8/8	2
			3	$A_{2,2} = 3/8$	$A_{4,4} = 1/8$	4/8			
			4	$A_{2,3} = 5/8$	$A_{5,4} = 0$	5/8			
3	1	4	1	$A_{1,0} = 0$	$A_{2,4} = 1$	1	$p_1+p_2+p_3+p_4 = 1$	14/8	2
			2	$A_{1,1} = 3/8$	$A_{3,4} = 3/8$	6/8 (**min**)			
			3	$A_{1,2} = 9/8$	$A_{4,4} = 1/8$	10/8			
			4	$A_{1,3} = 11/8$	$A_{5,4} = 0$	11/8			

$A =$

	0	1	2	3	4
1	0	3/8			
2		0	3/8		
3			0	1/8	
4				0	1/8
5					0

$R =$

	0	1	2	3	4
1	0	1			
2		0	2		
3			0	3	
4				0	4
5					0

Figure 5.6(a): Initialization (lines 1-4 of Algorithm 5.2)

$A =$

	0	1	2	3	4
1	0	3/8	9/8		
2		0	3/8	5/8	
3			0	1/8	3/8
4				0	1/8
5					0

$R =$

	0	1	2	3	4
1	0	1	1		
2		0	2	2	
3			0	3	3
4				0	4
5					0

Figure 5.6(b): when d (diagonal) = 1, the shaded cells are filled

$A =$

	0	1	2	3	4
1	0	3/8	9/8	11/8	
2		0	3/8	5/8	1
3			0	1/8	3/8
4				0	1/8
5					0

$R =$

	0	1	2	3	4
1	0	1	1	2	
2		0	2	2	2
3			0	3	3
4				0	4
5					0

Figure 5.6(c) : when $d = 2$, the shaded cells are filled

$A =$

	0	1	2	3	4
1	0	3/8	9/8	11/8	14/8
2		0	3/8	5/8	1
3			0	1/8	3/8
4				0	1/8
5					0

$R =$

	0	1	2	3	4
1	0	1	1	2	2
2		0	2	2	2
3			0	3	3
4				0	4
5					0

Figure 5.6(d) : when $d = 3$, the shaded cells are filled

The line-12 of the Algorithm 5.2 gives the minimal average search time which is $A[1][n] = A[1][4] = 14/8 = 7/4$. The index of the root for the OBST is $R[1][4] = 2$. That is, key_2 ("Balu") is the root of OBST. By recording every k during filling (backtracking k), we can obtain the OBST as shown in Figures 5.7 and 5.8.

$A =$

	0	1	2	3	4
1	0	(3/8)	9/8	11/8	(7/4)
2		0	3/8	5/8	1
3			0	1/8	(3/8)
4				0	(1/8)
5					0

$R =$

	0	1	2	3	4
1	0	(1)	1	2	(2)
2		0	2	2	2
3			0	3	(3)
4				0	(4)
5					0

Figure 5.7: Backtracking OBST

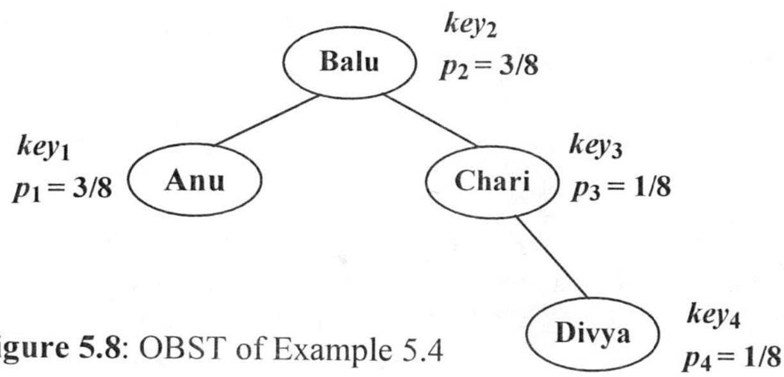

Figure 5.8: OBST of Example 5.4

We can verify the minimal average search time:

$$\begin{aligned} minavg &= 1(p_2) + 2(p_1) + 2(p_3) + 3(p_4) \\ &= 1(3/8) + 2(3/8) + 2(1/8) + 3(1/8) \\ &= 3/8 + 6/8 + 2/8 + 3/8 \\ &= 14/8 = 7/4. \end{aligned}$$

It is easy to see that the running time of OBST is $O(n^3)$, since its for-loops are nested three deep and each loop index takes on at most n values. The loop indices (*diagonal*, *i*, and *k*) in OBST do not have exactly the same bounds. They are within at most 1 in all directions.

5.3 MATRIX CHAIN MULTIPLICATION

Matrix chain multiplication is an optimization problem that can be solved using dynamic programming. Given a sequence of matrices, we want to find the most efficient way to multiply these matrices together. The problem is not actually to perform the multiplications, but merely to decide in which order to perform the multiplications.

Suppose that we want to multiply four matrices, $A \times B \times C \times D$, of dimensions 50 x 20, 20 x 1, 1 x 10, and 10 x 100, respectively (Figure 5.9). This will involve iteratively multiplying two matrices at a time. Matrix multiplication is not *commutative* (in general, $A \times B \neq B \times A$), but it is *associative*, which means for instance that $A \times (B \times C) = (A \times B) \times C$. Thus, we can compute our product of four matrices in many different ways, depending on how we parenthesize it. Are some of these better than others?

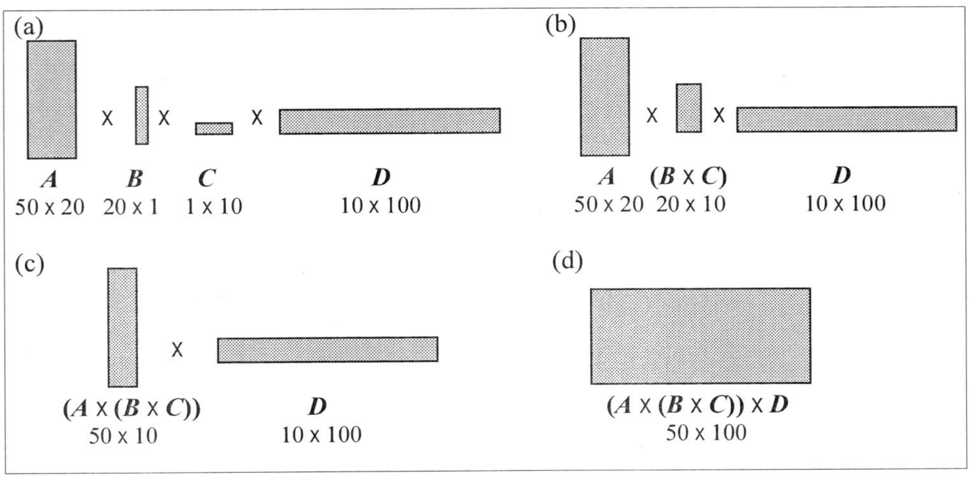

Figure 5.9: $A \times B \times C \times D = (A \times (B \times C)) \times D$

Multiplying an $m \times n$ matrix by an $n \times p$ matrix takes $m \times n \times p$ multiplications. Using this formula, let us compare several different ways of evaluating $A \times B \times C \times D$. The number of multiplications for the ordering: $A \times (B \times (C \times D))$ is computed as follows:

$C \times D = 1 \times 10 \times 100 = 1{,}000$ multiplications, result is 1×100.
$B \times (C \times D) = 20 \times 1 \times 100 = 2{,}000$ multiplications, result is 20×100.
$A \times (B \times (C \times D)) = 50 \times 20 \times 100 = 100{,}000$ multiplications, result is 50×100.
Total number of multiplications for this ordering is 103,000.

Table 5.4 shows five different orderings with five different parenthesizations.

Table 5.4: Five parenthesizations

Parenthesization		Total number of multiplications
(1)	$A \times (B \times (C \times D))$	103,000
(2)	$(A \times B) \times (C \times D)$	7,000
(3)	$((A \times B) \times C) \times D$	50,000
(4)	$(A \times (B \times C)) \times D$	60,200
(5)	$A \times ((B \times C) \times D)$	120,200

The order in which we parenthesize the product affects the number of simple arithmetic operations needed to compute the product, or the efficiency. How do we determine the optimal order, if we want to compute $A_1 \times A_2 \times \ldots \times A_n$, where the A_i's are matrices with dimensions $(p_0 \times p_1)$, $(p_1 \times p_2)$, …, $(p_{n-1} \times p_n)$, respectively? The first thing to notice is that a particular parenthesization can be represented very naturally by a binary tree in which the individual matrices correspond to the leaves, the root is the final product, and internal nodes are intermediate products (Figure 5.10). The possible orders in which to do the multiplication correspond to the various full binary trees with n leaves, whose number is exponential in n. We certainly cannot try each tree, and with brute force thus ruled out, we turn to dynamic programming.

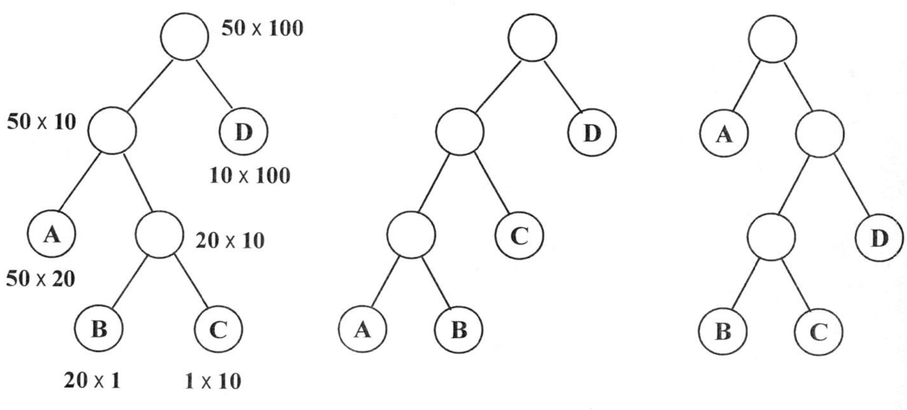

(a) $(A \times (B \times C)) \times D$ (b) $((A \times B) \times C)) \times D$ (c) $A \times ((B \times C) \times D)$

Figure 5.10: Binary tree representation of matrix multiplication

The binary trees of Figure 5.10 suggest that for a tree to be optimal, its subtrees must also be optimal. What are the subproblems corresponding to the subtrees? They are products of the form $A_i \times A_{i+1} \times \ldots A_j$. Let us see if this works: for $1 \le i \le j \le n$, define

$C[i][j]$ = minimum cost of multiplying $A_i \times A_{i+1} \times \ldots A_j$.

The size of this subproblem is the number of matrix multiplications, $|j-i|$. The smallest subproblem is when $i = j$, in which case there is nothing to multiply, so $C[i][i] = 0$. For $j > i$, consider the optimal subtree for $C[i][j]$. The first branch in this subtree, the one at the top, will split the product in two pieces, of the form $A_i \times \ldots \times A_k$ and $A_{k+1} \times \ldots \times A_j$, for some k between i and j. The cost of the subtree is then the cost of these two partial products, plus the cost of combining them: $C[i][k] + C[k+1][j] + (p_{i-1} \times p_k \times p_j)$. And we just need to find the splitting point k for which this is a minimum:

$$C[i][j] = \min_{i \le k < j} \{ C[i][k] + C[k+1][j] + (p_{i-1} \times p_k \times p_j) \}.$$

Algorithm 5.3: MatrixChain($p[0..n]$, n)

```
For i = 1 to n
        C[i][i] = 0.
Endfor
// "length" refers to the # of matrix multiplications in a subproblem.
For length = 1 to n–1
        For i = 1 to n – length
            j = i + length
            C[i][j] = min{ C[i][k] + C[k+1][j] + (p[i-1] x p[k] x p[j]) }, for i ≤ k < j
            s[i][j] = k    // k is at min of C[i][j]
        Endfor
Endfor
Return C[1][n]
```

In constructing an optimal solution, each entry $s[i][j] = k$ shows where to split the product $A_i \times A_{i+1} \times \ldots A_j$ for the minimum cost:

$$A_1 \ldots A_n = ((A_1 \ldots A_{s[i][n]}) (A_{s[i][n]+1} \ldots A_n))$$

To print the solution, the Algorithm 5.4 with parameters (s, 1, n) is invoked:

Algorithm 5.4: PrintOptimal($s[1..n]$, i, j)

```
If i = j then print "A"i
Else
        Call PrintOptimal( s, i, s[i][j] )
        Call PrintOptimal( s, s[i][j]+1, j )
```

Example 5.5 illustrates the construction of the order of matrix multiplication at the minimum cost.

Example 5.5: Consider the following four matrices. Show how to multiply this matrix chain optimally.

$$\begin{matrix} A_1 & \times & A_2 & \times & A_3 & \times & A_4 \\ (30 \times 1) & & (1 \times 40) & & (40 \times 10) & & (10 \times 25) \end{matrix}$$

The dimensions of four matrices are represented by the vector; p_i, for $i = 0$ to 4.

$p_0 = 30, p_1 = 1, p_2 = 40, p_3 = 10, p_4 = 25.$

(a) The entries in the Table 5.5(a) are generated when *length* = 1.

$C[i][j] = \min\{ C[i][k] + C[k+1][j] + (p_{i-1} \times p_k \times p_j) \}$, for $i \leq k < j$

$s[i][j] = k$ at minimum of $C[i][j]$.

$C[1][2] = C[1][1] + C[2][2] + p_0 \times p_1 \times p_2$
$= 0 + 0 + 30 \times 1 \times 40 = 1{,}200.$

$s[1][2] = 1.$

$C[2][3] = C[2][2] + C[3][3] + p_1 \times p_2 \times p_3$
$= 0 + 0 + 1 \times 40 \times 10 = 400$

$s[2][3] = 2.$

$C[3][4] = C[3][3] + C[4][4] + p_2 \times p_3 \times p_4$
$= 0 + 0 + 40 \times 10 \times 25 = 10{,}000$

$s[3][4] = 3.$

Table 5.5(a): when *length* = 1

i \ *j*	1	2	3	4
1	0	1,200 (1)		
2		0	400 (2)	
3			0	10,000 (3)
4				0

(b) The entries in the Table 5.5(b) are computed when *length* = 2.

$$C[1][3] = \min \begin{cases} C[1][1] + C[2][3] + p_0 \times p_1 \times p_3 = 0+400 + 30 \times 1 \times 10 = 700 \\ C[1][2] + C[3][3] + p_0 \times p_2 \times p_3 = 1200+0 + 30 \times 40 \times 10 = 13200 \end{cases}$$

$= 700$ and $s[1][3] = 1$.

$$C[2][4] = \min \begin{cases} C[2][2] + C[3][4] + p_1 \times p_2 \times p_4 = 0+10000 + 1 \times 40 \times 25 = 11000 \\ C[2][3] + C[4][4] + p_1 \times p_3 \times p_4 = 400+0 + 1 \times 10 \times 25 = 650 \end{cases}$$

$= 650$ and $s[2][4] = 3$.

Table 5.5(b): when *length* = 2

j / i	1	2	3	4
1	0	1,200 (1)	700 (1)	
2		0	400 (2)	650 (3)
3			0	10,000 (3)
4				0

(c) The entries in the Table 5.5(c) are calculated when *length* = 3.

$$C[1][4] = \min \begin{cases} C[1][1] + C[2][4] + p_0 p_1 p_4 = 0+650 + 30\text{x}1\text{x}25 = 1400 \\ C[1][2] + C[3][4] + p_0 p_2 p_4 = 1200+10000 + 30\text{x}40\text{x}25 = 41200 \\ C[1][3] + C[4][4] + p_0 p_3 p_4 = 700+0 + 30\text{x}10\text{x}25 = 8200 \end{cases}$$

= 1400 and $s[1][4] = 1$.

Table 5.5(c): when *length* = 3

j / i	1	2	3	4
1	0	1,200 (1)	700 (1)	1400 (1)
2		0	400 (2)	650 (3)
3			0	10,000 (3)
4				0

By Algorithm 5.4, the recursion tree is constructed as shown in Figure 5.11. Each node corresponds to the set of parameters. A_1 ((A_2 A_3) A_4) is the optimal order of four matrix multiplication. The total minimum cost is 1400. Let us verify the total number of multiplications with this order:

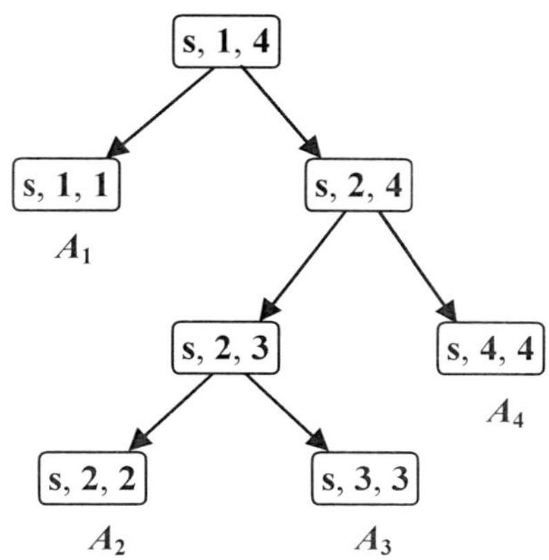

Figure 5.11:

$A_2 A_3 = 1 \times 40 \times 10 = 400$ multiplications, result is 1×10.
$(A_2 A_3) A_4) = 1 \times 10 \times 25 = 250$ multiplications, result is 1×25.
$A_1 ((A_2 A_3) A_4) = 30 \times 1 \times 25 = 750$ multiplications, result is 30×25.
Total number of multiplications $= 400 + 250 + 750 = 1400$.

A simple inspection of the nested loop structure of MatrixChain yields a running time of $O(n^3)$ for the algorithm. The loops are nested three deep, and each loop index (*length*, *i*, and *k*) takes on at most $n-1$ values.

5.4 ALL-PAIRS SHORTEST PATHS

The all-pairs shortest path problem involves finding the shortest path from each vertex in the graph to every other vertex in the graph. The problem occurs in many algorithms in communication, networking, and circuit design. For a map, it is to produce the (shortest) road distances between all cities, not which roads to take to get from one city to another. Using standard single-source algorithms, we can expect to get a naive implementation of $O(n^3)$. For example, Dijkstra algorithm does this.

Example 5.6: Consider the following weighted, directed graph (Figure 5.12). There are three paths from v_1 to v_3.

(v_1, v_2, v_3): path length $= 1 + 3 = 4$.
(v_1, v_4, v_3): path length $= 1 + 2 = 3$.
(v_1, v_2, v_4, v_3): path length $= 1 + 2 + 2 = 5$.
The shortest path from v_1 to v_3 is (v_1, v_4, v_3), with path length 3.

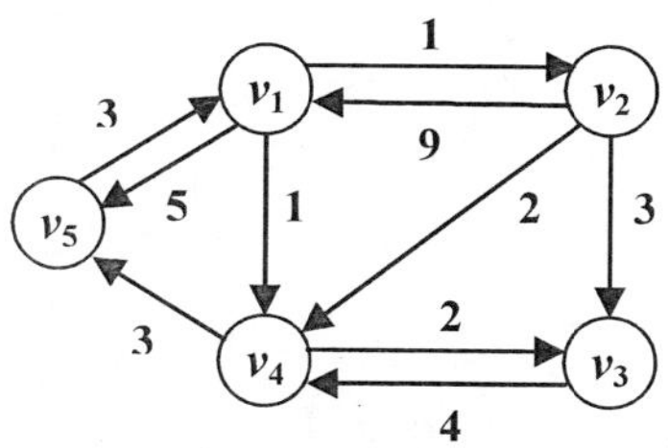

$W =$

	1	2	3	4	5
1	0	1	∞	1	5
2	9	0	3	2	∞
3	∞	∞	0	4	∞
4	∞	∞	2	0	3
5	3	∞	∞	∞	0

Figure 5.12: Weighted-directed graph and its adjacency matrix

Adjacency matrix of the graph is represented as follows:

$$W[i][j] = \begin{cases} \text{weight on edge} & \text{if there is an edge from } v_i \text{ to } v_j \\ \infty & \text{if there is no edge from } v_i \text{ to } v_j \\ 0 & \text{if } i = j \end{cases}$$

Storing all the paths explicitly can be very memory expensive indeed, as we need one spanning tree for each vertex. This is often impractical in terms of memory consumption, so these are usually considered as all-pairs shortest distance problems, which aim to find just the distance from each to each node to another. The result of this operation is an $n \times n$ matrix, which stores estimated distances to the each node. This has many problems when the matrix gets too big, as the algorithm will scale very poorly.

The *Floyd-Warshall* algorithm takes the dynamic programming approach. This essentially means that independent sub-problems are solved and the results are stored for later use. The algorithm allows negative edges, but no negative cycles, as per usual with such shortest path problems.

The basic concept is simple. If, for a path (i, j) and its length estimate $D[i][j]$, if we can take a detour via k and shorten the path, then it should be taken. This translates into the following equation:

$$D[i][j] = \min\{\ D[i][j], D[i][k] + D[k][j]\ \}.$$

The easiest way to calculate this is bottom up. We start with basic assumptions that can be made from the graphs connectivity, and correct those assumptions "n" times for each vertex pair and the results will converge.

The shortest path matrix of the graph is represented as:

$D^{(k)}[i][j] =$ length of a shortest path from v_i to v_j using only vertices in the set $\{v_1, v_2, \ldots, v_k\}$ as intermediate vertices.

Figure 5.13 shows the shortest path matrix of Figure 5.12. We will compute some typical values of $D^{(k)}[i][j]$ for the graph in Figure 5.12.

$D =$

	1	2	3	4	5
1	0	1	3	1	4
2	8	0	3	2	5
3	10	11	0	4	7
4	6	7	2	0	3
5	3	4	6	4	0

Figure 5.13

$D^{(0)}[2][5] = \text{length}(v_2, v_5) = \infty.$

$D^{(1)}[2][5] = \min\{\ \text{length}(v_2, v_5), \text{length}(v_2, v_1, v_5)\ \}$
$= \min\{\ \infty, 9 + 5\ \} = 14.$

$D^{(2)}[2][5] = D^{(1)}[2][5] = 14.$ → For any graph these are equal because a shortest path starting at v_2 cannot pass through v_2.

$D^{(3)}[2][5] = D^{(2)}[2][5] = 14.$ → For this graph these are equal because including v_3 gives no new paths from v_2 to v_5.

$D^{(4)}[2][5] = \min\{\ D^{(3)}[2][5], \text{length}(v_2, v_4, v_5)\ \}$
$= \min\{\ 14, 2 + 3\ \} = 5.$

$D^{(5)}[2][5] = D^{(4)}[2][5] = 5.$ → Length of a shortest path from v_2 to v_5 that is allowed to pass through any of the other vertices. This means that it is the length of a shortest path.

The Algorithm 5.5 computes the solution inplace from the weight matrix of the graph using a triple loop, but involving only additions and minimum operations, and with dependencies that restrict the ordering of the three loops (the k-loop has to be the outermost one).

```
Algorithm 5.5: All-pairsShortestPath ( W[1..n], n )
1.   Initialize matrix D with weight matrix W.
2.   For k = 1 to n
3.       For i = 1 to n
4.           For j = 1 to n
5.               D[i][j] = min{ D[i][j], D[i][k] + C[k][j] }
6.           Endfor
7.       Endfor
8.   Endfor
```

To simulate the Algorithm 5.5: All-pairsShortestPath, we consider our example graph given in Figure 5.12. The weight matrix, W is copied into matrix D. The initial D matrix, $D^{(0)}$, plus its values after 5 iterations (k = 1 to 5) $D^{(1)}$, $D^{(2)}$, $D^{(3)}$, $D^{(4)}$, and $D^{(5)}$ are given in Figure 5.14.

$D^{(0)}$	1	2	3	4	5
1	0	1	∞	1	5
2	9	0	3	2	∞
3	∞	∞	0	4	∞
4	∞	∞	2	0	3
5	3	∞	∞	∞	0

$D^{(1)}$	1	2	3	4	5
1	0	1	∞	1	5
2	9	0	3	2	14
3	∞	∞	0	4	∞
4	∞	∞	2	0	3
5	3	4	∞	4	0

$D^{(2)}$	1	2	3	4	5
1	0	1	4	1	5
2	9	0	3	2	14
3	∞	∞	0	4	∞
4	∞	∞	2	0	3
5	3	4	7	4	0

$D^{(3)}$	1	2	3	4	5
1	0	1	4	1	5
2	9	0	3	2	14
3	∞	∞	0	4	∞
4	∞	∞	2	0	3
5	3	4	7	4	0

$D^{(4)}$	1	2	3	4	5
1	0	1	3	1	4
2	9	0	3	2	5
3	∞	∞	0	4	7
4	∞	∞	2	0	3
5	3	4	6	4	0

$D^{(5)}$	1	2	3	4	5
1	0	1	3	1	4
2	8	0	3	2	5
3	10	11	0	4	7
4	6	7	2	0	3
5	3	4	6	4	0

Figure 5.14

The running time of the Floyd-Warshall algorithm for all-pairs shortest paths is determined by the triple nested for-loops of lines 2–7. Because each execution of line 5 takes $O(1)$ time, the algorithm runs in time $\Theta(n^3)$, where n is the number of vertices of the graph.

5.5 TRAVELLING SALESMAN PROBLEM

The Travelling Salesman problem (TSP) is a problem in combinatorial optimization studied in operations research/management science and theoretical computer science. Given a list of cities and their pairwise distances, the task is to find a shortest possible tour that visits each city exactly once. TSP is so easy to describe but so difficult to solve.

The TSP has several applications even in its purest formulation, such as planning, logistics, and the manufacture of microchips. Slightly modified, it appears as a sub-problem in many areas, such as genome sequencing. In these applications, the concept city represents, for example, customers, soldering points, or DNA fragments, and the concept distance represents travelling times or cost, or a similarity measure between DNA fragments.

In the theory of computational complexity, the decision version of TSP belongs to the class of NP-complete problems. Thus, it is assumed that there is no efficient algorithm for solving TSP problems. In other words, it is likely that the worst-case running time for any algorithm for TSP increases exponentially with the number of cities, so even some instances with only hundreds of cities will take many CPU years to solve exactly.

TSP can be modelled as a graph: the graph's vertices correspond to cities and the graph's edges correspond to connections between cities. The length of an edge is the corresponding connection's distance. A TSP tour is now a Hamiltonian cycle in the graph and an optimal TSP tour is a shortest Hamiltonian cycle.

Often, the underlying graph is a complete graph, so that every pair of vertices is connected by an edge. This is a useful simplifying step, because it makes it easy to find a solution, however bad, because the Hamiltonian cycle problem in complete graphs is easy. Instances where not all cities are connected can be transformed into complete graphs by adding very long edges between these cities, edges that will not appear in the optimal tour.

In the symmetric TSP, the distance between two cities is the same in each direction. Thus, the underlying structure is an undirected graph between; especially, each tour has the same length in both directions. This symmetry halves the number of feasible solutions.

In the asymmetric TSP, the distance from one city to the other need not equal the distance in the other direction, in general, there may not even be a connection in the other direction. Thus, the underlying structure is a directed graph. For example, the asymmetric case models one-way streets or air-fares that depend on the direction of travel.

The most direct solution would be to try all permutations (ordered combinations) and see which one is cheapest (using brute-force). The running time for this approach lies within a polynomial factor of $O(n!)$, the factorial of the number of cities, so this solution becomes impractical even for only 20 cities. One of the earliest applications of dynamic programming is an algorithm that solves the problem in time $O(n^2 2^n)$. The dynamic programming solution requires exponential space. The problem can be solved in time within a polynomial factor of 2^n and polynomial space.

Example 5.7: Consider the following weighted, directed graph (Figure 5.15). There are three tours starting from v_1. The lengths of these tours are given as:

length$[v_1, v_2, v_3, v_4, v_1] = 2 + 6 + 8 + 6 = 22$.
length$[v_1, v_3, v_2, v_4, v_1] = 9 + 7 + 4 + 6 = 26$.
length$[v_1, v_3, v_4, v_2, v_1] = 9 + 8 + 3 + 1 = 21$.

An optimal tour in a weighted, directed graph is a path of minimum length. The optimal tour of this graph is $[v_1, v_3, v_4, v_2, v_1]$ with length 21.

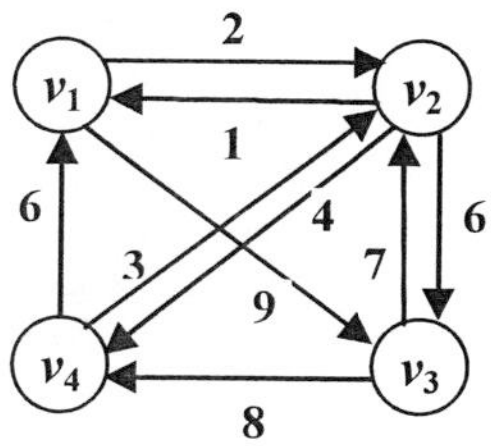

$$W = \begin{array}{c|cccc} & 1 & 2 & 3 & 4 \\ \hline 1 & 0 & 2 & 9 & \infty \\ 2 & 1 & 0 & 6 & 4 \\ 3 & \infty & 7 & 0 & 8 \\ 4 & 6 & 3 & \infty & 0 \end{array}$$

Figure 5.15: Weighted-directed graph and its adjacency matrix

We observe that if v_k is the first vertex after v_1 on an optimal tour, the sub-path of that tour from v_k to v_1 must be a shortest path from v_k to v_1 that passes through each of the other vertices exactly once. This means that the principle of optimality applies, and we can use dynamic programming.

Let V = set of all vertices, and S = a subset of V.

$D[v_i][S]$ = length of a shortest path from v_i to v_1 passing through each vertex in S exactly once.

For our example graph, $V = \{v_1, v_2, v_3, v_4\}$.

Notice that $\{v_1, v_2, v_3, v_4\}$ uses curly braces to represent set, whereas $[v_1, v_2, v_3, v_4]$ uses square brackets to represent a path. If $S = \{v_3\}$, then

$D[v_2][S] = \text{length}[v_2, v_3, v_1] = 6 + \infty = \infty$.

If $S = \{v_3, v_4\}$, then

$$D[v_2] = \min(\text{length}[v_2, v_3, v_4, v_1], \text{length}[v_2, v_4, v_3, v_1])$$
$$= \min([6 + 8 + 6], [4 + \infty + \infty]) = 20.$$

Because $V–\{v_1, v_j\}$ contains all vertices except v_1 and v_j and the principle of optimality applies, we have

$$\text{Length of an optimal tour} = \min_{2 \le j \le n}(W[1][j] + D[v_j][V\text{-}\{v_1, v_j\}]),$$

and in general for $i \neq 1$ and v_i not in S,

$$D[v_i][S] = \min_{j:\, v_j \in S}(W[i][j] + D[v_j][S\text{-}\{v_j\}]) \quad \text{if } S \neq \phi$$

$$D[v_i][\phi] = W[i][1].$$

We can create a dynamic programming algorithm for the TSP using the above equations. But first, let us illustrate how the algorithm would proceed.

We find an optimal tour for our example graph. First, we consider the empty set:

$D[v_2][\phi] = 1.$ **min**$(1 \rightarrow 3 \rightarrow 4 \rightarrow 2 \rightarrow 1)$
$D[v_3][\phi] = \infty.$
$D[v_4][\phi] = 6.$

Next, we consider all sets containing one item:

$$D[v_3][\{v_2\}] = \min_{j:\, v_j \in \{v_2\}} (W[3][j] + D[v_j][\{v_2\}-\{v_j\}])$$
$$= W[3][2] + D[v_2][\phi] = 7 + 1 = 8.$$

Similarly,

$D[v_4][\{v_2\}] = W[4][2] + D[v_2][\phi] = 3 + 1 = 4.$ **min**$(1 \rightarrow 3 \rightarrow 4 \rightarrow 2)$

$D[v_2][\{v_3\}] = W[2][3] + D[v_3][\phi] = 6 + \infty = \infty.$

$D[v_4][\{v_3\}] = W[4][3] + D[v_3][\phi] = \infty + \infty = \infty.$

$D[v_2][\{v_4\}] = W[2][4] + D[v_4][\phi] = 4 + 6 = 10.$

$D[v_3][\{v_4\}] = W[3][4] + D[v_4][\phi] = 8 + 6 = 14.$

Next, we consider all sets containing two items:

$$D[v_4][\{v_2, v_3\}] = \min_{j:\, v_j \in \{v_2, v_3\}} (W[4][j] + D[v_j][\{v_2, v_3\}-\{v_j\}])$$
$$= \min(W[4][2] + D[v_2][\{v_3\}],\ W[4][3] + D[v_3][\{v_2\}])$$
$$= \min(3 + \infty, \infty + 8) = \infty.$$

Similarly,

$$D[v_3][\{v_2, v_4\}] = \min(W[3][2] + D[v_2][\{v_4\}], W[3][4] + D[v_4][\{v_2\}])$$ **min**$(1 \rightarrow 3 \rightarrow 4)$
$$= \min(7 + 10, 8 + 4) = 12.$$
$$D[v_2][\{v_3, v_4\}] = \min(W[2][3] + D[v_3][\{v_4\}],\ W[2][4] + D[v_4][\{v_3\}])$$
$$= \min(6 + 14, 4 + \infty) = 20.$$

Finally, we compute the length of an optimal tour:

$$D[v_1][\{ v_2, v_3, v_4\}] = \min_{j:\, v_j \in \{v_2, v_3, v_4\}} (W[1][j] + D[v_j][\{v_2, v_3, v_4\}-\{v_j\}])$$
$$= \min(W[1][2] + D[v_2][\{v_3, v_4\}], W[1][3] + D[v_3][\{v_2, v_4\}], W[1][4] + D[v_4][\{v_2, v_3\}],)$$ **min**$(1 \rightarrow 3)$
$$= \min(2 + 20, 9 + 12, \infty + \infty) = 21.$$

Input to the Algorithm 5.6 (TSP) is adjacency matrix, W and number of vertices, n in the graph. The algorithm outputs *minlength* (length of an optimal tour), and matrix P from which an optimal tour can be constructed. P has its rows indexed from 1 to n and its columns indexed by all subsets of $V-\{v_1\}$. $P[i][S]$ is the index of the first vertex after v_i on the shortest path from v_i to v_1 that passes through all the vertices in S exactly once.

Trace of the algorithm:

minlength = $D[v_1][\{ v_2, v_3, v_4\}] = 21 \rightarrow$ this minimum is computed from

$W[1][\mathbf{3}] + D[v_3][\{v_2, v_4\}]$ at $j = \mathbf{3}$

$D[v_3][\{v_2, v_4\}] = W[3][\mathbf{4}] + D[v_4][\{v_2\}] \rightarrow$ minimum at $j = \mathbf{4}$

$D[v_4][\{v_2\}] = W[4][\mathbf{2}] + D[v_2][\phi] \rightarrow$ minimum at $j = \mathbf{2}$

$D[v_2][\phi] \rightarrow$ minimum with empty set (at $S = \phi$).

The optimal tour is: $[v_1, v_3, v_4, v_2, v_1]$ with length 21.

```
Algorithm 5.6: TSP( W[1..n], n )
1.  For i = 2 to n
2.      D[i][ϕ] = W[i][1]
3.  Endfor
4.  For k = 1 to n-2
5.      For(all subsets S ⊆ V-{v1} containing k vertices
6.          For(i such that i ≠ 1 and vi not in S)
7.              D[i][S] = min( W[i][j] + D[j][S-{vj}] )
                         j: vj ∈ S
8.              P[i][S] = value of j that gave the minimum.
9.          Endfor
10.     Endfor
11. Endfor
12. D[1][V-{v1}] = min( W[1][j] + D[j][V-{vj}] )
                  2 ≤ j ≤ n
13. P[1][V-{v1}] = value of j that gave the minimum.
14. minlength = D[1][V-{v1}].
```

Time complexity:

Basic operation: The time in both the first and last loops (lines 1-3, and line 12) is insignificant compared to the time in the middle loop, because the middle loop contains various levels of nesting. Therefore, we will consider the instructions executed for each value of v_j to be the basic operation. They include one instruction of addition.

For each set S containing k vertices, we must consider n-1-k vertices, and for each of these vertices, the basic operation is performed k times. Because of number of subsets S of V-$\{v_1\}$ containing k vertices is equal to $\binom{n-1}{k}$, the total number of times the basic operation is performed is given by:

$$T(n) = \sum_{k=1}^{n-2}(n-1-k)k\binom{n-1}{k} = (n-1)\sum_{k=1}^{n-2}k\binom{n-2}{k} = (n\text{-}1)(n\text{-}2)2^{n-3} \in \Theta(n^2 2^n).$$

The disadvantage of this dynamic programming solution is the space required, $O(n2^n)$. This is too large even for modest values of n.

CHAPTER SUMMARY

- *Dynamic Programming* is a technique for solving problems with overlapping sub-problems. Typically these subproblems arise from a recurrence relating a solution to a given problem with solutions to its smaller subproblems of the same type. Dynamic programming suggests solving each smaller subproblem once and storing the results in a table from which a solution to the original problem can then be obtained.
- Applicability of dynamic programming to an optimization problem requires the problem to satisfy the *principle of optimality*: an optimal solution to any of its instances must be up of optimal solutions to its sub-instances.
- Solving a knapsack problem by a dynamic programming algorithm illustrates an application of this technique to difficult problems of combinatorial optimization.
- Dynamic programming can be used for constructing an *optimal binary search tree* for a given set of keys and known probabilities of searching for them.
- *Matrix chain multiplication* is an optimization problem that can be solved using dynamic programming. Given a sequence of matrices, we want to find the most efficient way to multiply these matrices together. The problem is not actually to perform the multiplications, but merely to decide in which order to perform the multiplications.
- Floyd's algorithm for the *all-pairs shortest-paths* problem is based on the idea that can be interpreted as an application of the dynamic programming technique.
- *Travelling Salesman problem* (TSP): Given a list of cities and their pairwise distances, the task is to find a shortest possible tour that visits each city exactly once. A TSP tour is a Hamiltonian cycle in the graph and an optimal TSP tour is a shortest Hamiltonian cycle. By using dynamic programming, TSP can be solved in time within a polynomial factor of 2^n and polynomial space.

SELF-TEST QUIZ

5.1 Dynamic programming (DP) is an algorithm design method
  (a) which shows the characteristics of overlapping subproblems.
  (b) which demonstrates the characteristics of optimal substructure.
  (c) which can be viewed as a result of a sequence of decisions.
  (d) all of the above.

5.2 A problem is said to have overlapping subproblems if it can be broken down into subproblems which are reused multiple times. This is closely related to
  (a) iteration (b) recursion
  (c) divide-and-conquer strategy (d) greedy method

5.3 Consider the following two recursive functions:

```
int factorial(int n)
{   if (n == 0) return 1;
    return n*factorial(n-1);
}
```

```
int fib(int n)
{   if (n == 0) return 0;
    if (n == 1) return 1;
    return fib(n-1) + fib(n-2);
}
```

Which one of the following exhibits overlapping subproblems?

(a) factorial() (b) fib()
(c) both (a) and (b) (d) neither (a) nor (b)

5.4 If we can define a DP problem with overlapping subproblems recursively, then the technique will always _________ the execution time.

(a) reduce (b) increase
(c) either reduce or increase (d) reduce and increase

5.5 A problem is said to have optimal substructure if the globally optimal solution can be constructed from _______ optimal solutions to subproblems.

(a) locally
(b) globally
(c) locally or globally
(d) locally and globally

5.6 Assumptions made for dynamic programming method of evaluating lattices (sub-problems) are

(a) Seperabilility and Monotonicity
(b) Seperabilility and Enumeration
(c) Monotonicity and Enumeration
(d) Only Implicit Enumeration

5.7 Dynamic Programming is based on the Principle of ____.

(a) Equality (b) Similarity
(c) Optimality (d) Feasibility

5.8 In optimization procedure of dynamic programming problems is done with

(a) Seperabilility (b) Monotonicity
(c) Implicit Enumeration (d) Explicit Enumeration

5.9 Time Complexity for Dynamic Programming problems is ____.

(a) Logarithmic (b) Polynomial
(c) Quadratic (d) Exponential

5.10 In Dynamic Programming _________ is the advantage over Greedy Method.

(a) repeatedly solving sub-problems
(b) not repeatedly solving sub-problems
(c) generating one decision sequence as optimal solution
(d) many decision sequences are generated

5.11 The approach of reusing already computed solutions of sub-problems in computing the optimal solution is ______.

(a) memoization (b) overlapping

(c) recursion (d) optimal sub-structuring

5.12 Using top-down approach of solving problems in Dynamic Programming needs

(a) memoization & recursion

(b) overlapping & recursion

(c) memoization & overlapping

(d) optimal sub-structuring & recursion

5.13 Consider a 0/1 knapsack with capacity, $W = 20$. The weights and values of five items are given below.

item (i):	I_1	I_2	I_3	I_4	I_5
w_i:	3	4	7	8	9
v_i:	4	5	10	11	13

The objective of knapsack problem is to fill the knapsack with items to maximize the total value subject to its capacity.

What is the maximum value of knapsack subject to its capacity?

(a) 27 (b) 26 (c) 28 (d) none of these

5.14 Consider the above question: 5.6. What items constitute the maximum value of knapsack subject to its capacity?

(a) (I_1, I_3, I_5) (b) (I_1, I_4, I_5) (c) (I_2, I_3, I_4) (d) none of these

5.15 The knapsack problem shows

(a) overlapping subproblems.

(b) optimal substructure.

(c) overlapping subproblems and optimal substructure.

(d) neither overlapping subproblems nor optimal substructure.

5.16 The 0/1 knapsack algorithm takes _______ time (n: number of items, W: capacity).

(a) $O(nW)$ (b) $O(n+W)$ (c) $O(n^2W)$ (d) none of these

5.17 Consider the following two binary search trees:

A

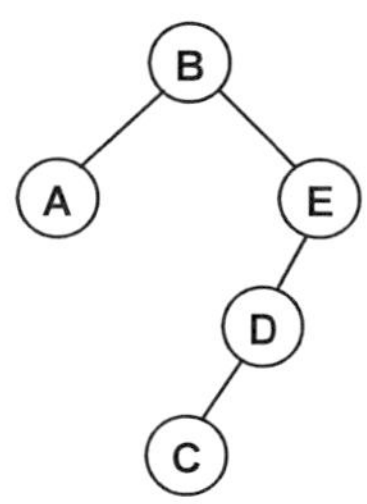

B

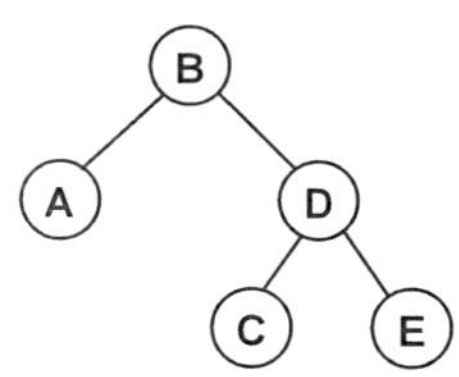

The tree of Figure A, in the worst case, requires ____ comparisons to find a key, whereas the tree of Figure B requires only _____.

(a) 4 … 3 (b) 3 … 4 (c) 3 … 2 (d) 2 … 3

5.18 Consider the trees of Figures A and B. On the average, the two trees need ____ and ____ comparisons, respectively. This calculation assumes that each key is searched for with equal probability and that no unsuccessful searches.

(a) 13/5 … 11/5 (b) 13/5 … 12/5
(c) 11/5 … 12/5 (d) 12/5 … 11/5

5.19 The running time of obtaining *OBST* using DP procedure is

(a) $O(n)$ (b) $O(n^2)$ (c) $O(n^3)$ (d) $O(n \log n)$

5.20 To multiply M×N, where matrix M is $p \times q$ and matrix N is $q \times r$, takes ____ operations if we use the "normal" matrix multiplication algorithm.

(a) $p \times q$ (b) $q \times r$ (c) $p \times r$ (d) $p \times q \times r$

5.21 If we have to compute the product P=ABCD where A, B, C and D are some given matrices with appropriate dimensions: A(3 x 5), B(5 x 8), C(8 x 3), D(3 x 4), then

A(B(CD)) = A((BC)D) = (A(BC))D = (AB)(CD) = ((AB)C)D

It is a fact of life that the total number of scalar products executed in the course of a chained matrix multiplication can vary significantly depending on how we parenthesize the sequence. Which one of these parenthesized schemes takes optimum number of calculations?

(a) A((BC)D) (b) (A(BC))D
(c) (AB)(CD) (d) ((AB)C)D

5.22 All pairs shortest-paths problem using Floyd's algorithm, the best case time complexity is _______.

(a) small-o(n^3) (b) big-O(n^3)
(c) $\Omega(n^3)$ (d) $\Theta(n^3)$

5.23 Space complexity for 0/1 knapsack algorithm is ______.

(a) $O(n^2)$ (b) $O(n^3)$ (c) $O(2^n)$ (d) none of these

5.24 Space complexity for TSP is ______.

(a) $O(n2^n)$ (b) $O(n^2 2^n)$ (c) $O(n^3 2^n)$ (d) none of these

5.25 Space complexity for Matrix Chain multiplication ______.

(a) $O(n^2)$ (b) $O(n^3)$ (c) $O(2^n)$ (d) none of these

EXERCISES

5.1 Find one problem for which the principle of optimality does not hold. Explain why the principle does not hold.

5.2 Explain the general dynamic programming problem.

5.3 What is the principle of optimality? Explain its significance.

5.4 Solve the following 0/1 knapsack problem using dynamic programming:
$m = 6, n = 3, (w_1, w_2, w_3) = (2, 3, 3), (p_1, p_2, p_3) = (1, 2, 4)$.

5.5 Solve the following 0/1 knapsack problem using dynamic programming:
$p = (11, 21, 31, 33), w = (2, 11, 22, 15), C = 40, n = 4$.

5.6 Explain the OBST algorithm.

5.7 Write a pseudocode of the dynamic programming algorithm for solving optimal binary search tree and determine its time and space efficiencies.

5.8 Determine the cost and structure of an optimal binary search tree for a set of keys (n = 5) with the following probabilities.

$p_1 = p_2 = 0.125, p_3 = p_4 = 0.0625, p_5 = 0.1875$
$q_0 = 0, q_1 = 0.1875, q_2 = q_3 = q_4 = q_5 = 0.0625$
The keys are: $a_1 < a_2 < a_3 < a_4 < a_5$.

5.9 Write a pseudocode for a linear time algorithm that generates the optimal binary search tree from the root table.

5.10 Explain matrix chain multiplication with an example.

5.11 Write an algorithm of matrix chain multiplication.

5.12 In how many ways, the following chain of matrices may be multiplied?

A	x	B	x	C	x	D
(2 x 5)		(5 x 3)		(3 x 6)		(6 x 4)

Find the number of multiplications required in each case.

5.13 Find minimum number of operations required for the following chain matrix multiplication using dynamic programming.

A(30, 40) * B(40, 5) * C(5, 15) * D(15, 6).

5.14 Write an algorithm of all pairs shortest path problem.

5.15 Solve the all pairs-shortest path problem for the following digraph with weight matrix.

0	2	∞	1	8
6	0	3	2	∞
∞	∞	0	4	∞
∞	∞	2	0	3
3	∞	∞	∞	0

5.16 Find the shortest path between all pairs of nodes in the following graph.

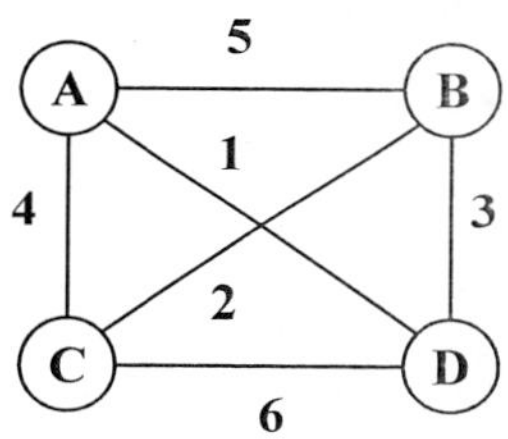

5.17 What is Traveling Sales Person problem and what are its applications.

5.18 For the Traveling Sales Person algorithm, show that the time complexity is $O(n^2 2^n)$ and space complexity is $O(n2^n)$.

5.19 Find the shortest tour of TSP for the following instance using dynamic programming.

	A	B	C	D
A	∞	12	5	7
B	11	∞	13	6
C	4	9	∞	18
D	10	3	2	∞

5.20 The edge lengths of a directed graph are given in the following matrix. Using TSP algorithm, calculate the optimal tour.

0	20	30	10	11
15	0	16	4	2
3	5	0	2	4
19	6	18	0	3
16	4	7	16	0

5.21 *Optimal binary search trees*: The frequency with which keywords in the programs of a certain language occur as follows:

keyword	frequency
begin	5 %
do	40 %
else	8 %
end	4 %
if	10 %
then	10 %
while	23 %

Calculate the total cost of the following two binary search trees.

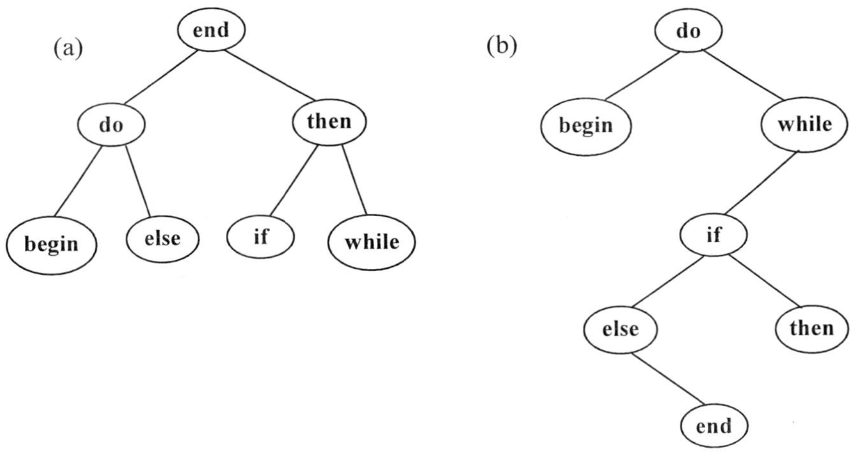

CHAPTER 6

BACKTRACKING

Backtracking is a general algorithm for finding all (or some) solutions to some computational problem that incrementally builds candidates to the solutions, and abandons each partial candidate *c* ("backtracks") as soon as it determines that *c* cannot possibly be completed to a valid solution. The term "backtrack" was coined by American mathematician D. H. Lehmer in the 1950s.

The classic textbook example of the use of backtracking is the eight queens puzzle, that asks for all arrangements of eight queens on a standard chessboard so that no queen attacks any other. In the common backtracking approach, the partial candidates are arrangements of *k* queens in the first *k* rows of the board, all in different rows and columns. Any partial solution that contains two mutually attacking queens can be abandoned, since it cannot possibly be completed to a valid solution.

Backtracking can be applied only for problems which admit the concept of a "partial candidate solution" and a relatively quick test of whether it can possibly be completed to a valid solution. It is useless, for example, for locating a given value in an unordered table. When it is applicable, however, backtracking is often much faster than brute force enumeration of all complete candidates, since it can eliminate a large number of candidates with a single test.

The backtracking algorithm enumerates a set of partial candidates that, in principle, could be completed in various ways to give all the possible solutions to the given problem. The completion is done incrementally, by a sequence of candidate extension steps.

Conceptually, the partial candidates are the nodes of a tree structure, the potential search tree. Each partial candidate is the parent of the candidates that differ from it by a single extension step; the leaves of the tree are the partial candidates that cannot be extended any further.

The backtracking algorithm traverses this search tree recursively, from the root down, in depth-first order. At each node *c*, the algorithm checks whether *c* can be completed to a valid solution. If it cannot, the whole sub-tree rooted at *c* is skipped (pruned). Otherwise, the algorithm (i) checks whether *c* itself is a valid solution, and if so reports it to the user; and (ii) recursively enumerates all sub-trees of *c*. The two tests and the children of each node are defined by user-given procedures.

Therefore, the actual search tree that is traversed by the algorithm is only a part of the potential tree. The total cost of the algorithm is basically the number of nodes of the actual tree times the cost of obtaining and processing each node. This fact should be considered when choosing the potential search tree and implementing the pruning test.

Consider a maze, shown in the Figure 6.1, where a player has to decide how to get from room A to room B. The player can move from room to room through the corridors provided, but has no way of telling how many corridors a room is connected to until he reaches that room. We will now see a sample procedure to understand the approach the player uses to solve the maze.

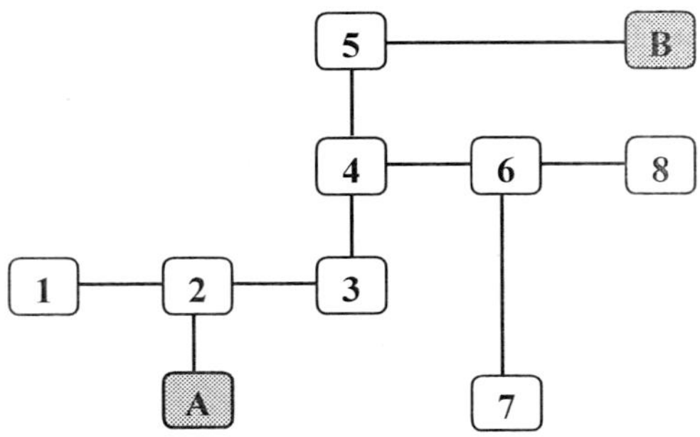

Figure 6.1: Sample Maze

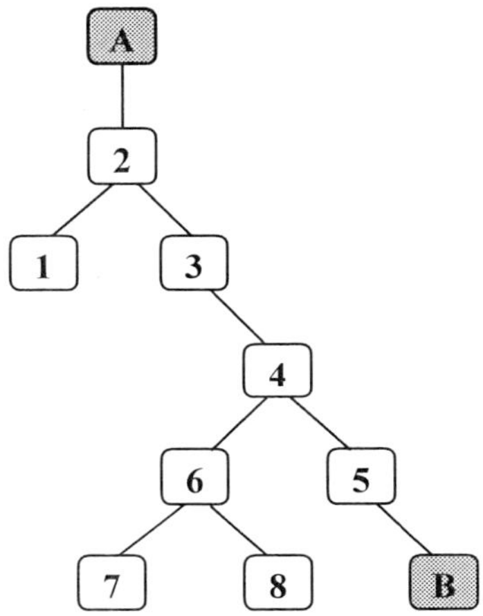

Figure 6.2: Maze as a tree

1. The player moves from room A to room 2.
2. From here he can move either to room 1 or 3. He chooses 1.
3. Dead End. He returns to room 2, then goes on to room 3.
4. He has no choice but to move to room 4.
5. Given a choice between rooms 5 and 6, he chooses 6.
6. Another choice between 7 and 8, he chooses 7.
7. Dead End. He returns to 6 and chooses 8.
8. Dead End again. He returns to 6 and sees that he has exhausted his choices.
9. He goes back to room 4, and chooses room 5.
10. He sees room B, moves to it, and solves the maze.

We will now examine Algorithm 6.1 which implements the procedure described above.

The algorithm takes care of rooms with dead ends, rooms with multiple corridors, and anything we care to throw at it. It has the elegant simple characteristic of all recursive procedures, but it differs slightly from the algorithms presented previously. It is a *backtracking* algorithm. How backtracking works – we shall consider maze as a tree (Figure 6.2).

Algorithm 6.1: CheckRoom(*RoomNumber*)

```
If RoomNumber has been visited, then
    Return
Endif
For each room connected to this room
    If ConnectedRoomNumber = B, then
        the maze has been solved
    Else CheckRoom(ConnectedRoomNumber)
    Endif
Endfor.
```

The sample maze, like all mazes, is essentially a tree, with room A at the root of the tree. Consequently, the backtracking algorithm discussed above is a tree-spanning algorithm. When it reaches a node like room 2, where it has more than one path to choose from, it picks one path (to room 1) which is a leaf node, or dead End. Finding that it can proceed no more, it unwinds to its previous execution, (back to room 2) and takes the other path, to room 3. Such an algorithm is known as a depth-first spanning algorithm, because it tends to follow a path right down to the bottom of the tree, before it gives up and unwinds to a previous execution in order to choose a different path. Manually apply the CheckRoom algorithm above to the tree to get a feel of how the algorithm works.

Backtracking algorithms are characterized by multiple recursive calls, typically within a loop (see the CheckRoom algorithm above). Unlike the simple recursion examples we had encountered in the previous chapters, a backtracking procedure goes through multiple winding and unwinding stages as it loops through the choices it has to make at every node. One of the most common applications of backtracking is in the evaluation of moves for strategy games like chess. We will look at *n*-queens problem, and see how a backtracking strategy can be used.

Backtracking algorithms try each possibility until they find the right one. It is a depth-first search of the set of possible solutions. During the search, if an alternative does not work, the search backtracks to the choice point, the place which presented different alternatives, and tries the next alternative. When the alternatives are exhausted, the search returns to the previous choice point and tries the next alternative there. If there are no more choice points, the search fails.

This is usually achieved in a recursive algorithm where each instance takes one more variable and alternatively assigns all the available values to it, keeping the one that is consistent with subsequent recursive calls. Backtracking is similar to a depth-first search but uses even less space, keeping just one current solution state and updating it. The Algorithm 6.2 demonstrates the concept. Let v be an unassigned variable for each possible value x of v.

Algorithm 6.2: BacktrackingSearch()

```
If all variables are assigned, then
        If the solution is valid, then
                return success and the solution
        Else return failure
        Endif
Else v = x
Endif
If BacktrackingSearch() succeeds, then
        return success and the solution
Endif
Un-assign v
Return failure.
```

In order to speed up the search, when a value is selected, before making the recursive call, the algorithm either deletes that value from conflicting unassigned domains (forward checking) or checks all the constraints to see what other values this newly-assigned value excludes (constraint propagation). This is the most efficient technique for certain problems like 0/1 knapsack and n-queen problem. It gives better results than dynamic programming for these problems.

6.1 N-QUEENS PROBLEM

The n-queens problem consists of placing n queens on an n-by-n chessboard so that no two queens attack each other by being in the same row or in the same column or on the same diagonal. This is a classical combinatorial problem. Figure 6.3 illustrates n-queens problem for n = 1, 2, 3.

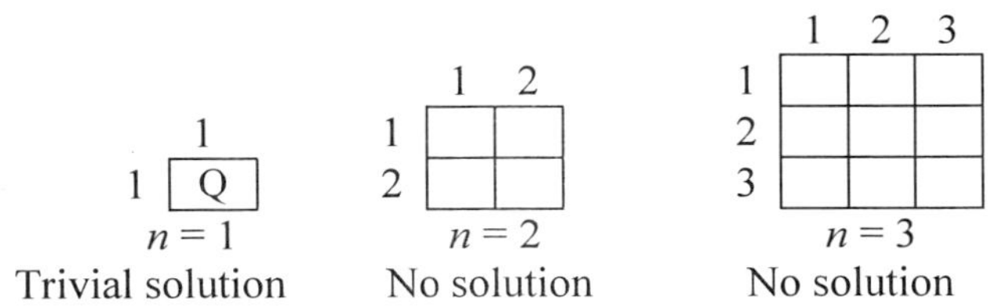

Figure 6.3: Examples of n-queens problem

Let us consider the 4-queens problem and solve it by the backtracking technique. Each queen has to be placed in its own row; all we need to do is to assign a column for each queen on the following board (Figure 6.4).

The 4 by 4 board (Figure 6.5: state space tree) shows a solution for n = 4. All nodes (boards) are numbered from 0 to 16. The numbers within parentheses indicate columns of the board. For example in board # 4, three queens are placed in columns 1, 4 and 2. Let us place 4th queen in column 3. If we place 4th queen in either row 1, 2, or 3, this will attack other three queens (already placed queens) row-wise. Also, 4th row does not permit, because it attacks diagonally queen at (3, 1). Therefore, there is no solution in this branch of tree (nodes: 1, 3, 4); it backtracks to node 5 and search for alternate solution. Now, we have two solutions: board # 8 and 12.

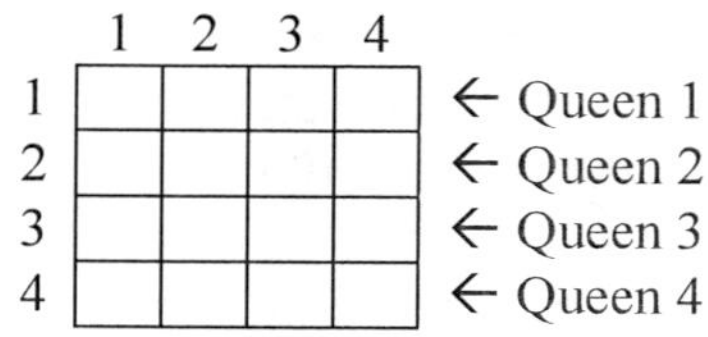

Figure 6.4: 4-queens problem

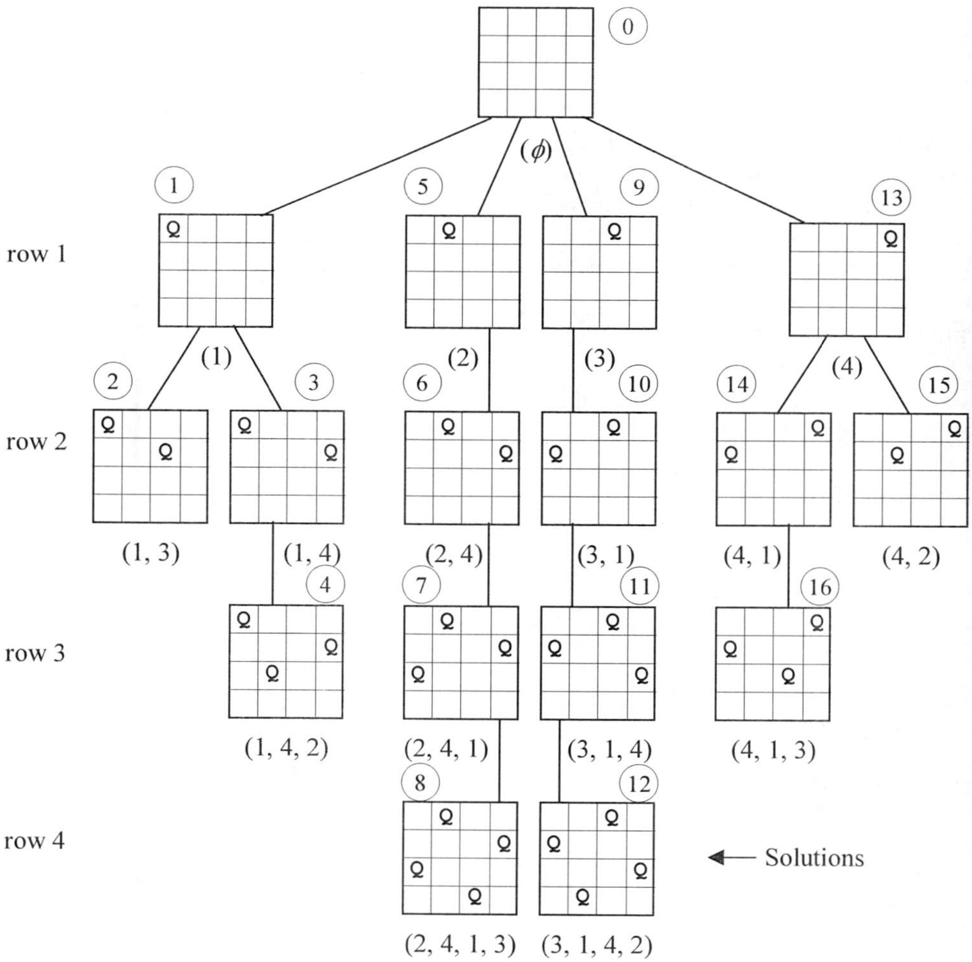

Figure 6.5: A complete backtrack search tree for 4-queens problem

We will introduce *backtracking* algorithm which can be used to construct all solutions for a given n.

- We could continue with the 4-queens example to obtain all possible solutions for $n = 4$.
- Our goal now is to convert this approach into an explicit algorithm.
- We track the position of the queens by using an array *row*.
- *row*[k] is the row in column k containing a queen.
- The main algorithm is the recursive algorithm *rn_queens*().
- When *rn_queens*(k, n) is called, queens have been successfully placed in columns 1 to k-1.
- The algorithm then attempts to place a queen in column k.
- If it is successful, then
  - if $k = n$, it prints the solution.
  - if $k < n$, it makes the call *rn_queens*(k+1, n).
  - it then returns to the call *rn_queens*(k-1, n).
- To test for a valid position for a queen in column k, we use an algorithm *position_ok*(k, n) which returns true if and only if the queen tentatively placed in column k does not conflict with the queens in positions 1 to k-1.
- The queens in columns i and k conflict if
  - they are in the same row: *row*[i] = *row*[k].
  - or in the same diagonal: absolute(*row*[k] - *row*[i]) = $k - i$.
- The algorithm is invoked with *rn_queens*(1, n).

Algorithm 6.3(a): rn_queens(k, n)

```
For row[k] = 1 to n
        If position_ok(k, n) = true, then
            If k = n, then
                Print solution
            Else
                rn_queens(k+1, n)
            Endif
        Endif
Endfor.
```

Algorithm 6.3(b): position_ok(k, n)

```
For i = 1 to k-1
        If (row[k] = row[i] or abs(row[k] – row[i]) = k–i ), then
            Return false
        Else
            Return true
        Endif
Endfor.
```

Time complexity: We will obtain an upper bound for the running time of the algorithm by bounding the number of times rn_queens(k, n) is called for each $k < n$. There are $n(n-1)\cdots(n-k+2)$ ways to place queens in the first k-1 columns in distinct rows. Ignoring recursive calls, rn_queens(k, n) executes in $\Theta(n)$ time for $k < n$. For $k = n$, there is at most one placement possible for the queen. Also, the loop in rn_queens executes in $\Theta(n)$ time. There are $n(n-1)\cdots 2$ ways for the queens to have been placed in the first n-1 columns, so the worst-case running time for rn_queens(n, n) is:

$$n[\, n(n-1)\cdots 2\,] = n \times n!$$

The algorithm runs in $O(n \times n!)$.

6.2 SUM OF SUBSETS PROBLEM

The *sum of subsets* problem consists of finding a subset of a given set $X = \{x_1, x_2 \ldots x_n\}$ of n distinct positive integers and a positive integer S. Find all subsets of $\{x_1, x_2 \ldots x_n\}$ that sum to S. For example, if $X = \{3, 5, 6, 7, 8, 9, 10\}$ and $S = 15$, there will be more than one subset whose sum is 15. The subsets are {7, 8}, {3, 5, 7}, {6, 9} and {5, 10}. On the other hand, if $X = \{1, 5, 6, 7, 11, 12, 13\}$ and $S = 15$, there will be no subset that adds up to 15.

We will assume a binary state space tree. The nodes at depth 1 are for including (*yes* = 1, *no* = 0) item 1, the nodes at depth 2 are for item 2, etc. The left branch includes x_i, and the right branch excludes x_i. The nodes contain the sum of the numbers included so far.

Backtracking consists of doing a DFS of the state space tree, checking whether each node is *promising* and if the node is *non-promising* backtracking to the node's parent. We call a node non-promising if it cannot lead to a feasible (or optimal) solution, otherwise it is promising. The state space tree consisting of expanded nodes only is called the *pruned* state space tree. The Example 6.1 shows the pruned state space tree for the sum of subsets problem.

Consider a node at depth i,

sumSoFar = sum of node – that is, sum of numbers included in partial solution node.
sumLeft = sum of the remaining items i+1 to n (for a node at depth i).

A node at depth i is non-promising:

If ((*sumSoFar* + *sumLeft* < *S*) or (*sumSoFar* + x[i+1] > *S*))

To be able to use this "promising function" the x_i must be sorted in increasing order.
The *include[1..n]* is a boolean array. If its value is true, then the node is included in the partial tree, else not included.

The Algorithm 6.4(a): sumOfSubsets(*i, sumSoFar, sumLeft*) is invoked with:
$i = 0$, *sumSoFar* = 0, and *sumLeft* $= x_1 + x_2 + \ldots + x_n$. The algorithm is called with sumOfSubsets(0, 0, 21) for our Example 6.1.

Algorithm 6.4(a): sumOfSubsets(*i, sumSoFar, sumLeft*)

```
If promising( i, sumSoFar, sumLeft ), then        //may lead to solution
    If ( sumSoFar = S ), then
        Print solution
    Else    //expand the node when sumSoFar < S
        include[i+1] = true                        // include x[i+1]
        sumOfSubsets( i+1, sumSoFar + x[i+1], sumLeft – x[i+1] )
        include[i+1] = false                       // exclude x[i+1]
        sumOfSubsets( i+1, sumSoFar, sumLeft – x[i+1] )
    Endif
Endif.
```

Algorithm 6.4(b): promising(*i, sumSoFar, sumLeft*)

```
If ( sumSoFar + sumLeft ≥ S) and
  ( sumSoFar = S or sumSoFar + x[i+1] ≤ S ) , then
    Return true
Else
    Return false
Endif.
```

Example 6.1: $X = \{3, 5, 6, 7\}$ and $S = 15$. There are only 15 nodes in the pruned state space tree (Figure 6.6). The full state space tree has 31 nodes ($2^{4+1} - 1$). Trace of the Algorithm 6.4 is given in Table 6.1. Nodes of the tree are shown by circled numbers. Notice that the x_1 is included at level 1 of the tree, x_2 at level 2, and so on. We have only one solution with subset {3, 5, 7}. This occurs at node 6 in Figure 6.6.

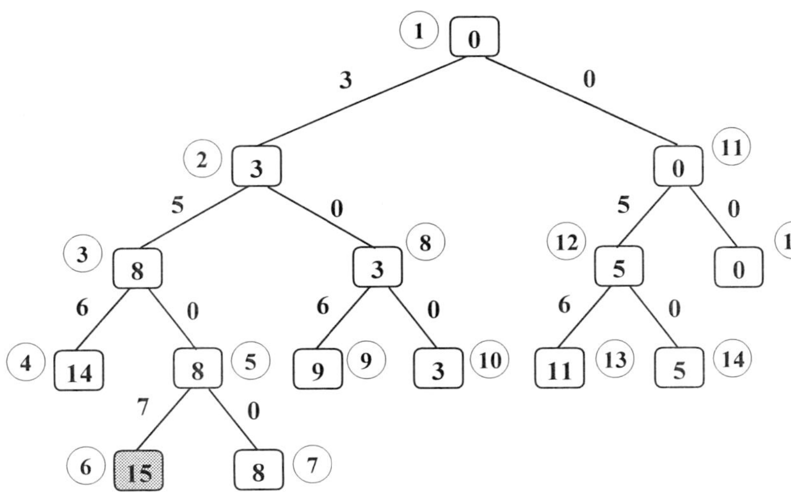

Figure 6.6: Pruned state space tree – Example 6.1

Table 6.1: Trace of sumOfSubsets – Example 6.1

i	*node*	*sumSoFar*	*sumLeft*	*Comment*
0	1	0	21	Start
1	2	3	18	include 3
2	3	8	13	include 5
3	4	14	7	include 6
3	5	8	7	exclude 6
4	6	15	0	include 7
			3 5 7	← Solution
4	7	8	0	exclude 7
2	8	3	13	exclude 5
3	9	9	7	include 6
3	10	3	7	exclude 6
1	11	0	18	exclude 3
2	12	5	13	include 5
3	13	11	7	include 6
3	14	5	7	exclude 6
2	15	0	13	exclude 5

6.3 GRAPH COLORING

Graph coloring is a way of coloring the vertices of a graph such that no two adjacent vertices share the same color. The convention of using colors originates from coloring the countries of a map, where each face is literally colored. This was generalized to coloring the faces of a graph embedded in the plane. By planar duality (x and y coordinates) it became coloring the vertices, and in this form it generalizes to all graphs.

Consider an undirected graph $G = (V, E)$ and an integer k. Assign one of k colors to each node, such that adjacent nodes get different colors.

For example, let $G = (V, E)$ where $V = \{1, 2, 3, 4\}$ and $E = \{(1, 2), (1, 3), (2, 3), (2, 4), (3, 4)\}$ and suppose that $k = 3$ (*Red*, *Green*, *Blue*). A valid coloring c of G is: $c(1) = R$, $c(2) = G$, $c(3) = B$, $c(4) = R$.

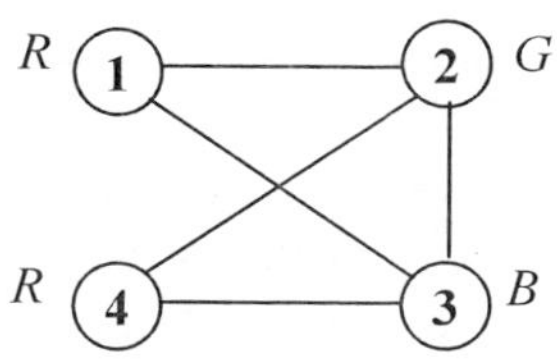

Figure 6.7: Graph coloring

Suppose that |V| = n. Then $(c_1, c_2, \ldots, c_n)$ is a possible coloring of graph where c_i is the color of i-node in the graph. Note that there are k^n possible colorings. A coloring is *feasible* or *valid* if no two adjacent nodes are given the same color, that is, if $(i, j) \in E$ then $c_i \neq c_j$.

Consider a graph shown in Figure 6.7 with k = 3. There are *six* valid colorings of graph given in the Table 6.2:

Table 6.2: Six valid colorings

node	(i)	(ii)	(iii)	(iv)	(v)	(vi)
1	*R*	*R*	*G*	*G*	*B*	*B*
2	*G*	*B*	*B*	*R*	*R*	*G*
3	*B*	*G*	*R*	*B*	*G*	*R*
4	*R*	*R*	*G*	*G*	*B*	*B*

Note that all these colorings are sort of equivalent. They all share the following structure:

- The same color is used for both node 1 and node 4. For colorings (i) and (ii), it is *R*, for colorings (iii) and (iv), it is *G*, and for colorings (v) and (vi), it is *B*.
- Nodes 2 and 3 must have distinct colors different from each other and from the color used for nodes 1 and 4.

By this observation, it follows that two colorings are equivalent if one can be transformed into another by permuting the k colors.

We will use the following strategy to find all valid colorings of a graph:

- Order nodes arbitrarily.
- Assign the first node a color.
- Given a partial assignment of colors $(c_1, c_2, \ldots, c_{i-1})$ to the first i-1 nodes, try to find a color for the i-th node in the graph.
- If there is no possible color for the i-th node given the previous choices, backtrack to a previous solution.

Consider a graph shown in Figure 6.7 with k = 3.

Step 1: Choose a color for node 1. It can be one of: *R*, *B* or *G*. Say we choose *R*.

Step 2: Given partial coloring (*R*), we choose a color for node 2. It can be one of: *G* or *B*. Say we choose *G*.

Step 3: Given partial coloring (*R*, *G*), we choose a color for node 3. It cannot be either *R* or *G*, so it must be *B* since k = 3.

Step 4: Given partial coloring (*R*, *G*, *B*), we choose a color for node 4. It cannot be *B* or *G*, so it must be *R*. This gives the coloring (*R*,*G*,*B*,*R*) which is coloring (i).

We have no more choices of colors in step 4, and in step 3. We have one choice in step 2.

Step 2: Given partial coloring (*R*), we choose a different color for node 2. We choose *B* for node 2.

Step 3: Given partial coloring (R, B), we choose a color for node 3. It cannot be R or B, so it must be G.

Step 4: Given partial coloring (R, G, B), we choose a color for node 4. It cannot be B or G, so it must be R. This gives the coloring (R,B,G,R) which is coloring (ii).

We have no more choices of colors in steps 4, 3 and 2. We go back to step 1.

Step 1: We choose a different color for node 1, say B. This will produce a branch in the tree equivalent to the first branch where R and B are switched. Thus, we will get the colorings (v) and (vi).

If we choose G for node 1 then, we will again get a branch equivalent to the first one with R and G swapped. This will produce the colorings (iii) and (iv).

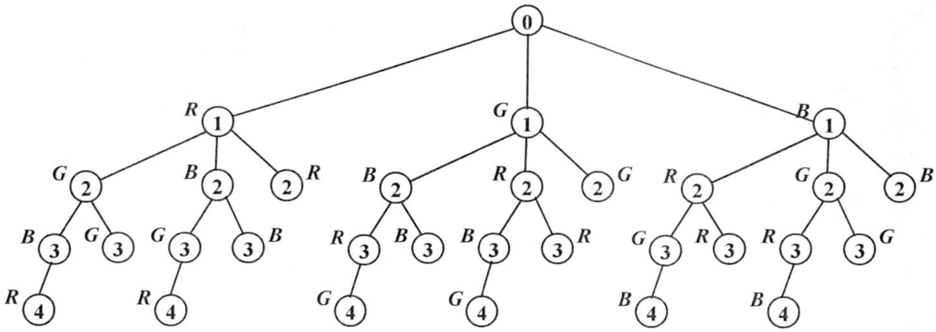

Figure 6.8: Graph coloring - state space tree

Algorithm 6.5 solves the graph coloring problem. It generates one solution (only).

$C[1..j\text{-}1]$:	a partial coloring for the first j-1 nodes of the graph.
$adj[1..n][1..n]$:	adjacency matrix for n-node graph.
k:	number of colors (labels).

We invoke the algorithm: Coloring(C, j, k, n), where j is the first node (j = 1).

Algorithm 6.5(a): Coloring($C[1..n]$, j, k, n)

```
If j = n+1, then
    Print C
Endif
For i = 1 to k
    C[j] = i
    If Valid(C, j, n) is true, then
        Coloring(C, j+1, k, n)
    Endif
Endfor.
```

Algorithm 6.5(b): Valid($C[1..n]$, j, n)

```
For i =1 to n          // for all adjacent nodes v of j with v < j
    If adj[j][i] ≠ 0, then
        v = i
        If C[v] = C[j], then
            Return false
        Endif
    Endif
Endfor
Return true.
```

We now trace the Coloring algorithm by considering the 4-node graph shown in Figure 6.7 with 3 colors (labels: 1 = Red, 2 = Green, 3 = Blue). Figure 6.9 shows the graph and its adjacency matrix.

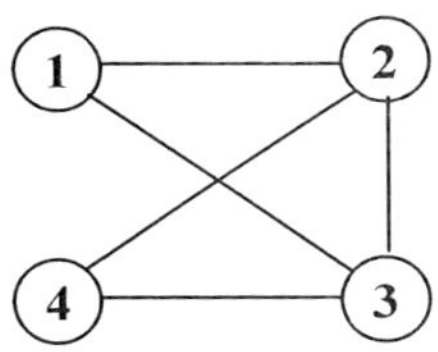

	1	2	3	4
1	0	1	1	0
2	1	0	1	1
3	1	1	0	1
4	0	1	1	0

Figure 6.9: Undirected graph and its adjacency matrix

Initially, the algorithm: (C, j, k, n) is called with $C = \{0, 0, 0, 0\}$, $j = 1$, $k = 3$, and $n = 4$. After first recursive call, $C = \{1, 0, 0, 0\}$ – that is, the node 1 is labeled with 1 (Red). After second call, $C = \{1, 2, 0, 0\}$ – the node 2 is labeled with 2 (Green). After third call, $C = \{1, 2, 3, 0\}$ – the node 3 is labeled with 3 (Blue). After fourth call, $C = \{1, 2, 3, 1\}$ – the node 4 is labeled with 1 (Red). It prints the labels: 1, 2, 3, 1.

After this, the algorithm backtracks, checks two more braches and terminates. The valid solution is: node 1 (label 1), node 2 (label 2), node 3 (label 3), and node 4 (label 1). This is one of the six valid colorings shown in column (i) of Table 6.2, and also notice the Figure 6.7.

The number of internal nodes in the state space tree is given by: $\sum_{i=0}^{n-1} k^i$. Valid routine takes $O(kn)$ time at each internal node to find the children corresponding to valid colorings. Hence, the total running time is bounded by:

$$\sum_{i=1}^{n} k^i n = n(k^{n+1} - 2)/(k-1) = O(nk^n).$$

6.4 HAMILTONIAN CYCLES

A *Hamiltonian cycle* in a connected graph is a cycle that passes through every vertex exactly once. The graph in Figure 6.10(a) contains the Hamiltonian cycle A, B, C, E, F, D, A. The graph in Figure 6.10(b) contains no Hamiltonian cycle.

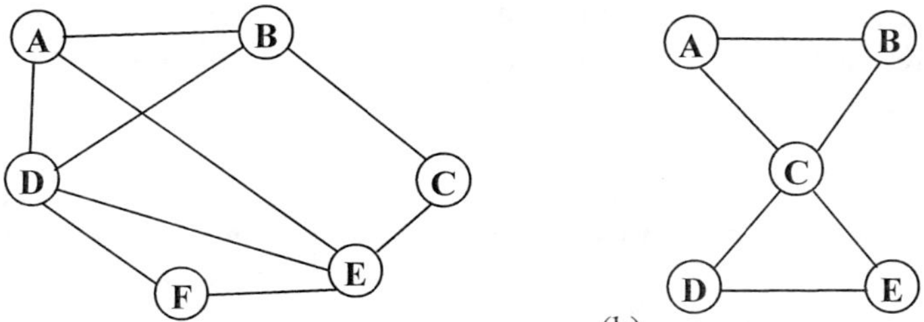

Figure 6.10: Undirected graphs

There is no known easy way to determine whether a given graph contains a Hamiltonian cycle. We now look at a backtracking algorithm that finds the Hamiltonian cycle in a graph. The graph may be directed or undirected. Let us apply the backtracking technique to find the Hamiltonian cycle in the following graph (Figure 6.11(a)), and obtain a Hamiltonian cycle as shown in Figure 6.11(b).

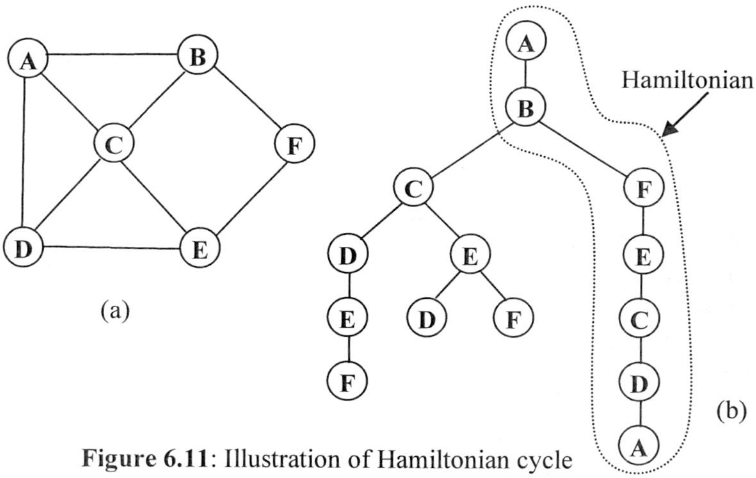

Figure 6.11: Illustration of Hamiltonian cycle

Example 6.4: Find a Hamiltonian cycle for the directed graph (Figure 6.12),

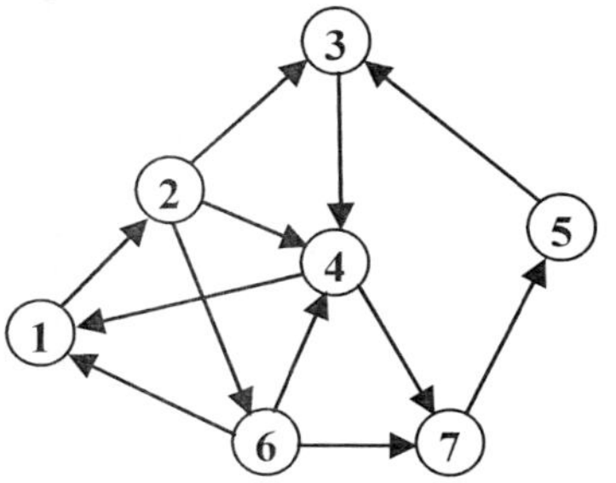

N 1 2 3

1 → 2
2 → 3 → 4 → 6
3 → 4
4 → 1 → 7
5 → 3
6 → 1 → 4 → 7
7 → 5

Figure 6.12: Directed graph and its adjacency list

Given a directed graph $G = (V, E)$. We store the graph as an adjacency list (for each vertex $v \in \{1, 2, \ldots, n\}$, and store a list of the vertices w such that $(v, w) \in E$). We store a Hamiltonian cycle as $A[1..n]$, where the cycle is:

$$A[n] \rightarrow A[n-1] \rightarrow \ldots . \rightarrow A[2] \rightarrow A[1] \rightarrow A[n]$$

We also set up an array D, the out-degree of each vertex. The values are tabulated as:

D	1	2	3	4	5	6	7
	1	3	1	2	1	3	1

Pruning: We keep a Boolean array $mark[1..n]$, where $mark[i]$ is 1 if vertex i is visited and 0 if vertex is unvisited (prune here).

To solve the Hamiltonian cycle problem, we use arrays N (adjacency lists) and D (degree) for the input graph, and execute the Algorithm 6.6 (given in three parts). Assume that $n \geq 2$.

Algorithm 6.6(a): Initialization()

```
For i = 1 to n-1
        mark [i] = 0
Endfor
mark [n] = 1;  A[n] = n
Hamilton(n-1)
```

Algorithm 6.6(b): Hamilton(k)

```
If k = 0 , then
        Process(A)
Else
        For j = 1 to D[A[k+1]]
                w = N[A[k+1]][j]
                If mark[w] = 0, then
                        mark[w] = 1;  A[k] = w
                Endif
        Endfor
        Hamilton(k-1)
        mark[w] = 0
Endif.
```

Algorithm 6.6(c): Process(A)

```
ok = 0
For j = 1 to D[A[1]]
        If N[A[1], j] = A[n], then ok = 1
Endfor
If ok = 1, then Print(A).
```

Let us simulate this algorithm. We build the array, $A[]$ progressively showing the status of the array *mark*[]. Finally $A[]$ contains the Hamiltonian cycle. Input to the algorithm is the adjacency list, $N[][]$ and degree $D[]$ of the graph.

After initialization, the arrays *mark*[] and $A[]$ are shown below and the algorithm Hamilton(n-1) is invoked.

mark	1	2	3	4	5	6	7
	0	0	0	0	0	0	1

A	1	2	3	4	5	6	7
							7

The for-loop (lines 4-10 in Algorithm 6.4(b)) checks whether a vertex is visited; if it is unvisited, then it marks visited and appends this vertex (w) to the array $A[]$. The for-loop is performed $D[A[k+1]]$ times. When $k = 6$, $A[k+1] = 7$, $D[A[k+1]] = 1$, and $w = 5$. We mark vertex 5 and append 5 to $A[6]$. The two arrays are updated (shown below):

mark	1	2	3	4	5	6	7
	0	0	0	0	1	0	1

A	1	2	3	4	5	6	7
						5	7

The subsequent steps are given in the following tables ($k = 5, 4, 3, 2, 1$):

mark	1	2	3	4	5	6	7
	0	0	1	0	1	0	1

A	1	2	3	4	5	6	7
					3	5	7

mark	1	2	3	4	5	6	7
	0	0	1	1	1	0	1

A	1	2	3	4	5	6	7
				4	3	5	7

mark	1	2	3	4	5	6	7
	1	0	1	1	1	0	1

A	1	2	3	4	5	6	7
			1	4	3	5	7

mark	1	2	3	4	5	6	7
	1	1	1	1	1	0	1

A	1	2	3	4	5	6	7
		2	1	4	3	5	7

mark	1	2	3	4	5	6	7
	1	1	1	1	1	1	1

A	1	2	3	4	5	6	7
	6	2	1	4	3	5	7

Finally, when $k = 0$, Hamilton(k) calls the algorithm Process(A) which checks that the cycle is closed. If it is ok, then the elements of array A (Hamilton cycle) will be printed.

Time complexity: Let $T(n)$ be the running time of Hamilton and d the maximum out-degree of the graph. For some b and c,

$$T(n) \le \begin{cases} b \times d & \text{if } n = 0 \\ d \times T(n-1) + c & \text{otherwise} \end{cases}$$

By repeated substitutions, $T(n) = O(d^n)$. The total running time on an n-vertex graph is $O(d^n)$ if there are no Hamilton cycles. The running time will be $O(d^n + d) = O(d^n)$ if there is one Hamilton cycle.

CHAPTER SUMMARY

- *Backtracking* is an intelligent exhaustive technique to solve some large instances of difficult combinatorial problems.
- Backtracking can be applied only for problems which admit the concept of a "partial candidate solution" and a relatively quick test of whether it can possibly be completed to a valid solution.
- The n-queens problem consists of placing n queens on an n-by-n chessboard so that no two queens attack each other by being in the same row or in the same column or on the same diagonal.
- The n-queens algorithm runs in $O(n\ n!)$.
- The *sum of subsets* problem consists of finding a subset of a given set $X = \{x_1, x_2 \ldots x_n\}$ of n distinct positive integers and a positive integer S. Find all subsets of $\{x_1, x_2 \ldots x_n\}$ that sum to S.
- *Graph coloring* is a way of coloring the vertices of a graph such that no two adjacent vertices share the same color. The convention of using colors originates from coloring the countries of a map, where each face is literally colored.
- The total running time of m-coloring of n-node graph is bounded by $O(nm^n)$.
- *Hamiltonian cycle* in a connected graph is a cycle that passes through every vertex exactly once.
- The total running time on an n-vertex graph is $O(d^n)$ if there is one Hamilton cycle, where d is the maximum out-degree of the graph.

SELF-TEST QUIZ

6.1 ____________ technique is an intelligent exhaustive technique to solve some large instances of difficult combinatorial problems.

(a) Backtracking (b) Divide and conquer
(c) Greedy (d) Dynamic programming

6.2 The 3-queens problem has ____________.

(a) trivial solution (b) optimal solution
(c) no solution (d) partial optimal solution

6.3 How many solutions the 4-Queens Problem has?

(a) one (b) two (c) four (d) sixteen

6.4 Suppose, if a particular node called 'c' is not leading to a valid solution, then backtrack will perform the following action.

(a) The whole sub-tree rooted at c is skipped.
(b) It will continue the sub-tree to lead a solution, leaving that invalid node.
(c) It will skip the entire tree and results to no solution.
(d) None.

6.5 Which statement is not true in case of backtracking method?

(a) Backtracking is a variation of the basic dynamic programming idea.
(b) Many problems which deal with searching for a set of solutions can be solved using the Backtracking method.
(c) Using backtracking method, we can solve problems in an efficient way, when compared to greedy method.
(d) For a given solution space a unique tree organization is possible..

6.6 Backtracking method follows _________ technique

(a) DFS (b) BFS (c) Binary search (d) Linear search

6.7 What is the problem statement of n-queens problem?

(a) n-queens are to be placed on a $n \times n$ chess board so that no two queens are on the same row, column or diagonal .
(b) n-queens are to be placed on a $n \times n$ chess board
(c) n-queens are to be placed on a 8×8 chess board
(d) n-queens are to be placed on a large chess board

6.8 Which of the following are suitable solutions for 4-queens problem?

(a) (2, 4, 1, 3) and (3, 1, 4, 2) (b) (1, 2, 3, 4) and (4, 3, 2, 1)
(c) (1, 1, 1, 1) and (2, 2, 2, 2) (d) (1, 2, 4, 3) and (2, 1, 3, 4)

6.9 Which of the following is a valid solution for 8-Queens problem?

(a) (7, 5, 3, 1, 2, 6, 2, 4) (b) (7, 5, 3, 1, 6, 8, 2, 4)
(c) (4, 5, 3, 1, 6, 8, 2, 7) (d) (7, 5, 4, 1, 6, 8, 2, 3)

6.10 The worst –case running time for n-queens algorithm is ________

(a) $O(n!)$ (b) $O(n \log n)$ (c) $O(\log n)$ (d) $O(n * n!)$

6.11 If $x = \{4, 5, 6, 7, 8, 9, 10\}$ and $s = 16$, total number of subsets (sum of subsets) are

(a) 2 (b) 3 (c) 4 (d) 5

6.12 In sum of subsets problem, if $x = \{1, 2, 3, 4\}$ and $s = 6$. The maximum number of nodes in a full state space tree is ___.

(a) 31 (b) 15 (c) 7 (d) 2

6.13 Which one of the following is true regarding graph coloring problem?

(a) No two adjacent vertices share the same color.
(b) Same color is shared by all the vertices.
(c) Different color shared to different vertices.
(d) Two adjacent vertices share the same color.

6.14 How many colors are required for the following graph?

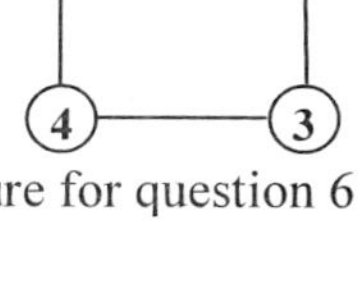

Figure for question 6.14

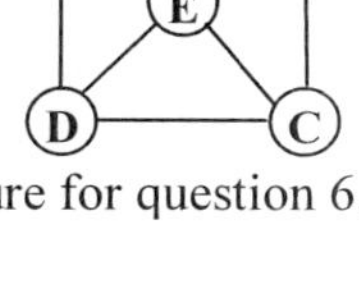

Figure for question 6.15

(a) 3 (b) 4 (c) 5 (d) 1

6.15 Which one of the following is a Hamiltonian cycle for the above figure?

(a) (A - B - C - E - D - A) (b) (A - C - B - E - D - A)

(c) (A - E - C - B - D - A) (d) (A - B - D - E - C - A)

EXERCISES

6.1 Write the control abstraction of backtracking.

6.2 Write a recursive backtracking algorithm.

6.3 Explain the applications of backtracking.

6.4 Compare and contrast brute-force approach and backtracking.

6.5 Draw the tree organization of 4-queen solution space. Number the nodes using DFS.

6.6 Describe the 4-queens problem using backtracking.

6.7 Write an algorithm of the 8-queens problem using backtracking.

6.8 Write an algorithm for n-queens problem.

6.9 Write a recursive backtracking algorithm for sum of subsets problem.

6.10 Let $w = \{15, 7, 20, 5, 18, 10, 12\}$ and $m = 35$. Find all possible subsets of w that sum to m. Draw the portion of the state space tree that is generated.

6.11 Draw the search tree to color the graph with three colors: red, blue, green.

6.12 Write an algorithm for finding all m-colorings of a graph.

6.13 Describe the graph coloring problem and its time complexity.

6.14 Apply backtracking to solve 3-coloring problem for the following graph.

6.15 Define Hamiltonian cycle. Apply backtracking to find the Hamiltonian cycle for the following graph. Write the implementation of the algorithm.

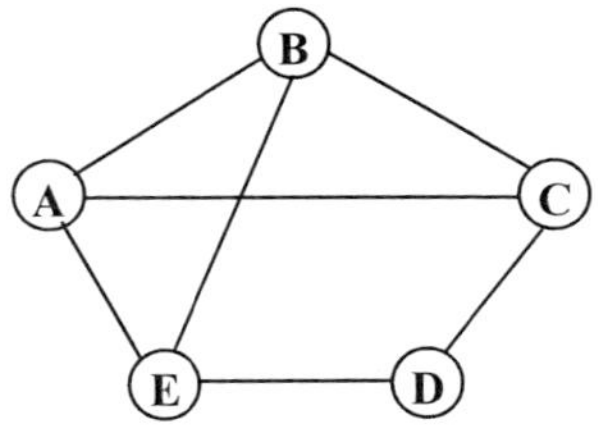

Figure for Ex: 6.14

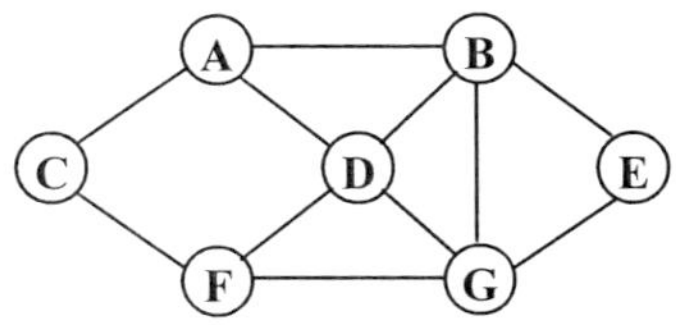

Figure for Ex: 6.15

CHAPTER 7

BRANCH AND BOUND

The branch-and-bound (B&B) design strategy is very similar to backtracking in that a state space tree is used to solve a problem. The differences are that the branch-and-bound method (1) does not limit us to any particular way of traversing the tree and (2) is used only for optimization problems.

Solving NP-hard discrete optimization problems to optimality is often an enormous job requiring very efficient algorithms, and the B&B paradigm is one of the main tools in construction of these. A B&B algorithm searches the complete space of solutions for a given problem for the best solution. However, explicit enumeration is normally impossible due to the exponentially increasing number of potential solutions. The use of bounds for the function to be optimized combined with the value of the current best solution enables the algorithm to search parts of the solution space only implicitly.

At any point during the solution process, the status of the solution with respect to the search of the solution space is described by a pool of yet unexplored subset of this and the best solution found so far. Initially only one subset exists, namely the complete solution space, and the best solution found so far is ∞. The unexplored subspaces are represented as nodes in a dynamically generated search tree, which initially only contains the root, and each iteration of a classical BB algorithm processes one such node. The iteration has three main components: selection of the node to process, bound calculation, and branching.

B&B is composed of two main actions, but there is an additional step. The first step is, as its name suggests, the *branching*. This is where we define the tree structure from the set of candidates in a recursive manner. The second action is called *bounding* since this procedure calculates the upper and lower bounds of each node from the tree.

Furthermore, there is the additional pruning step that we can add. In a nutshell, it means that if the lower bound for some node of the tree is greater than the upper bound of some other node of the tree, then the first node of the tree can be "discarded" from the search. A variable always holds the value of the global minimum upper bound.

All in all, B&B is very similar to backtracking. The main differences are that the former is used only in case of optimization problems, whereas backtracking cannot be, and B&B does not limit us to a particular way of traversing the tree (depth-first search / preorder as with backtracking). Backtracking always picks one single successor from the candidates, while B&B always has the entire list of successors in the queue.

A branch and bound algorithm is based on an advanced breadth-first search. The said BFS is done with a priority queue instead of the traditional list. We can imagine the priority queue as any other queue, except that it is sorted. This means that the highest priority element is always on the first position.

7.1 ASSIGNMENT PROBLEM

The assignment problem is one of the fundamental combinatorial optimizations. The problem consists of n persons and n jobs such that each can be assigned exactly one job. If i-th person is assigned j-th job, the cost is c_{ij}. Given the n x n cost matrix, C the problem is to assign n jobs to n persons such that the total cost is a minimum. We select one element in each row of the matrix so that no two selected elements are in the same column and their sum is the minimum. By applying branch-and-bound, we illustrate how to solve the assignment problem through an example.

Example 7.1: Let us consider the following instance of assignment problem. Persons are represented by A, B, C and D, and jobs by 1, 2, 3 and 4.

	1	2	3	4
A	7	3	8	9
B	4	5	2	6
C	5	7	9	4
D	7	8	6	5

	1	2	3	4
A	7	**3**	8	9
B	4	5	**2**	6
C	5	7	9	**4**
D	7	8	6	**5**

Figure 7.1: An instance of assignment problem

The cost of any solution cannot be less than the sum of minimum elements in each of the rows of the matrix. Even the optimal solution may not be less than this sum. In our example, the sum is 14 (3 + 2 + 4 + 5) as shown in second part of the Figure 7.1. We emphasize that this is not any valid solution – because (C, 4) and (D, 4) values (4 and 5) came from the same column, 4. It is just a lower bound on the cost of any selection. We can apply the same reasoning to obtain partial solutions. Partial solution consists of assigning a set of jobs (less than the total number of jobs to be assigned) to a set of distinct persons. For example, if we select 7 (A→1), the lower bound will be 7 + 2 + 4 + 5 = 18 as shown in node 1 of state space tree (Figure 7.2).

Construction of the state space tree involves the order in which the nodes of the tree will be generated. Rather than branching to a single node of the last promising node, we will branch to all promising nodes. We can do this by comparing the lower bounds of the live nodes.

We start with the root (no elements selected from the cost matrix). The lower bound, *lb* for the root is 14. The nodes on the first level of the tree relate to selection of an element in the first row of the matrix – that is, one job for a person A (Figure 7.2). First level contains four live nodes (1, 2, 3, and 4). As the node 2 has smaller lower bound compared to other three nodes (1, 3, and 4), we branch at node 2. Next, at level 2, three different jobs: 1, 3, and 4 are assigned to person B. Next, we branch at node 6 (minimum *lb* = 14 at level 3). First we consider assignment of person C to job 1; this leaves us with no choice but to assign person D to job 4. This yields node 8, which corresponds to the feasible solution: (A→ 2, B→ 3, C→ 1, D→ 4) with total cost of 15.

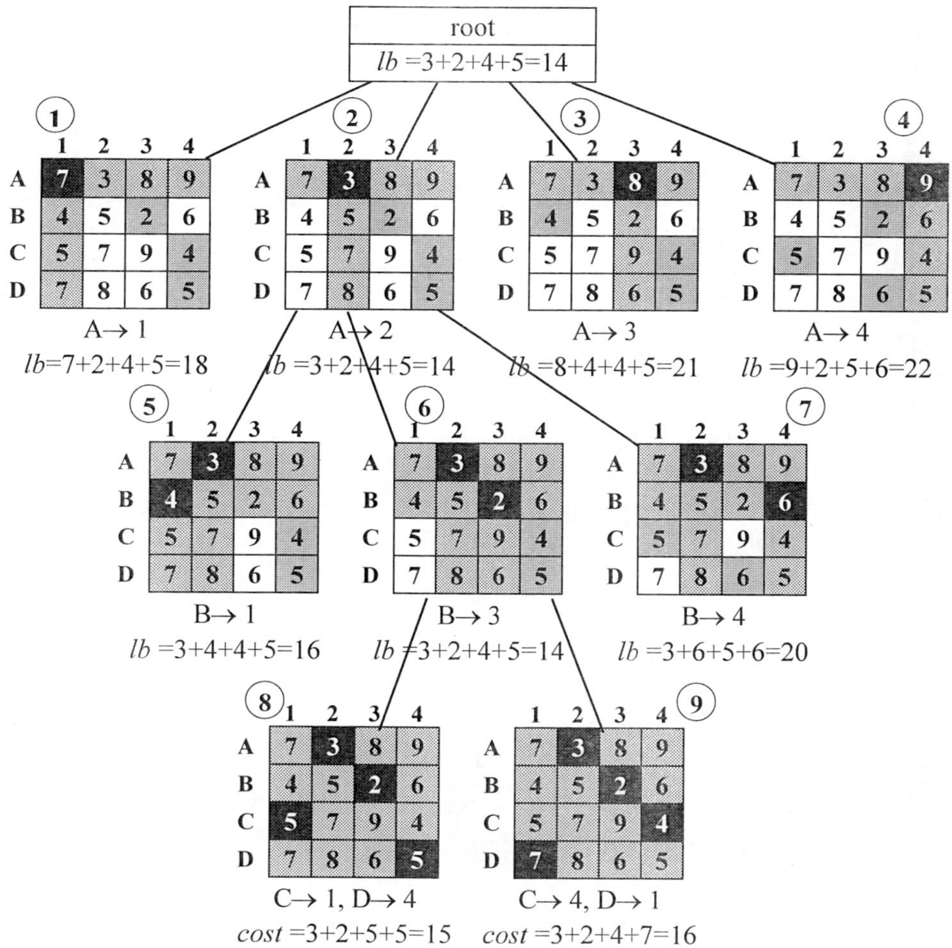

Figure 7.2: State space tree for assignment problem

Node 9 corresponds to feasible solution: (A→ 2, B→ 3, C→ 4, D→ 1) with total cost of 16. Since cost of node 9 is greater than that of node 8, we simply terminate node 9.
Now, as we inspect each of the live nodes of state space tree (nodes 1, 3, 4, 5, and 7), we find that their lower bound values are not less than 15, the value of the best selection seen so far (node 8). Hence, the optimal solution is (A→ 2, B→ 3, C→ 1, D→ 4) with minimum total cost of 15.

7.2 TRAVELING SALESMAN PROBLEM

The Traveling Salesman Problem (TSP) requires that we find the shortest path visiting each of a given set of cities once and returning to the starting point. In other words, the problem is to find, in an undirected graph with weights on the edges, a tour the sum of whose edge-weights is a minimum. A tour is a simple cycle that includes all the vertices. It is often called a Hamilton cycle.

The TSP is a famous example of a problem which can be solved by a branch-and-bound technique. Now let us consider how we might find the optimum tour by systematically considering all tours. One way is to consider all permutations of nodes, and evaluate the tour that visits the nodes in that order, remembering the best so far. The time for such an approach is $O(n!)$ on an n-node graph. Each permutation takes $O(n)$ time to evaluate.

The branch-and-bound technique produces the solution far more rapidly than the "try all permutations" method. We start constructing a tree, with a root that represents all tours (configurations). Each node has two children, and tours that a node represents are divided by these children into two groups – those that have a particular edge and those that do not.

Example 7.2: Consider the following instance of the traveling salesperson problem for five cities in which the symbol "∞" represents infinity.

	1	2	3	4	5
1	∞	17	7	35	18
2	9	∞	5	14	19
3	29	24	∞	30	12
4	27	21	25	∞	48
5	15	16	28	18	∞

	1	2	3	4	5	
1	∞	10	0	25	11	-7
2	4	∞	0	6	14	-5
3	17	12	∞	15	0	-12
4	6	0	4	∞	27	-21
5	0	1	13	0	∞	-15
				-3		

Figure 7.3: A TSP instance and its reduced matrix

A lower bound b is associated such that the cost of any complete tour that visits cities x_1, x_2, ..., x_k, in this order, must be at least b. Each complete tour must contain exactly one edge and its associated cost from each row and each column of the cost matrix. If a constant r is subtracted from every entry in a row or a column of the cost matrix, the cost of any tour under the new matrix is exactly r less than the cost of the same tour under the original matrix. We reduce the cost matrix so that each row or column contains at least one zero entry. Such a matrix is called a reduced matrix. In general, let $(r_1, r_2, ..., r_n)$ and $(c_1, c_2, ..., c_n)$ be the values subtracted from rows 1 to n and columns 1 to n, respectively, in an $n \times n$ cost matrix. Then

$$b = \sum_{i=1}^{n} r_i + \sum_{i=1}^{n} c_i$$

is a lower bound on the cost of any complete tour.

After computing the reduced matrix, the lower bound is computed. Initially, it is the value b of the reduced matrix. An edge (x, y) is chosen from the matrix. Two children of the current node are constructed where the right node represents all solutions that exclude edge (x, y). That is why the cost of (x, y) is set to ∞. The left node represents all solutions that include edge (x, y). The row x and column y are removed from the cost matrix, because the edge (x, y) will not appear again in the solution. Since all solutions use the edge (x, y), they will not use edge (y, x) and therefore the cost of (y, x) can be set to ∞. This is also applied for the current "paths". The lower bound in each child is computed by adding the current value of b into the current lower bound when computing the reduced matrix of each child. Choose the subtree with minimum bound in order to apply branch and bound.

Figure 7.4 illustrates a state space tree generated for the example TSP. Each node of the tree is represented by a circled number. Let us show the computation of few nodes. Node 1 represents the reduced matrix with lower bound of 63 (see Figure 7.3). With this bound, node 1 branches into two children – left one includes the edge (3, 5) whereas the right one excludes edge (3, 5).

Node 2 is generated by including edge (3, 5). We delete row 3 and column 5, because the edge (3, 5) will not appear again in the solution. As the entry (3, 5) is zero, the bound is 63 (63 + 0). Since all solutions use the edge (3, 5), they will not use edge (5, 3) and therefore the cost of (5, 3) can be set to ∞. Observe the reduced matrix at node 2.

By excluding edge (3, 5), we get node 3. Entry (3, 5) is set to ∞, because edge (3, 5) is not included in the partial tour. The bound is increased to 75 (63 + 12); 12 is the minimum cost in row 3. As the bound of node 2 is less than that of node 3, node 2 is being split. This process is continued until the reduced matrix contains one element. The minimum cost of tour is the bound at node 10 ($b = 67$). The final solution contains the following edges (arranged in order):

(1, 3), (3, 5), (5, 4), (4, 2), (2, 1) and the optimal tour is given as:

1 -> 3 -> 5 -> 4 -> 2-> 1.

Total cost of this tour = 7 + 12 + 18 + 21 + 9 = 67, which is same as the bound.

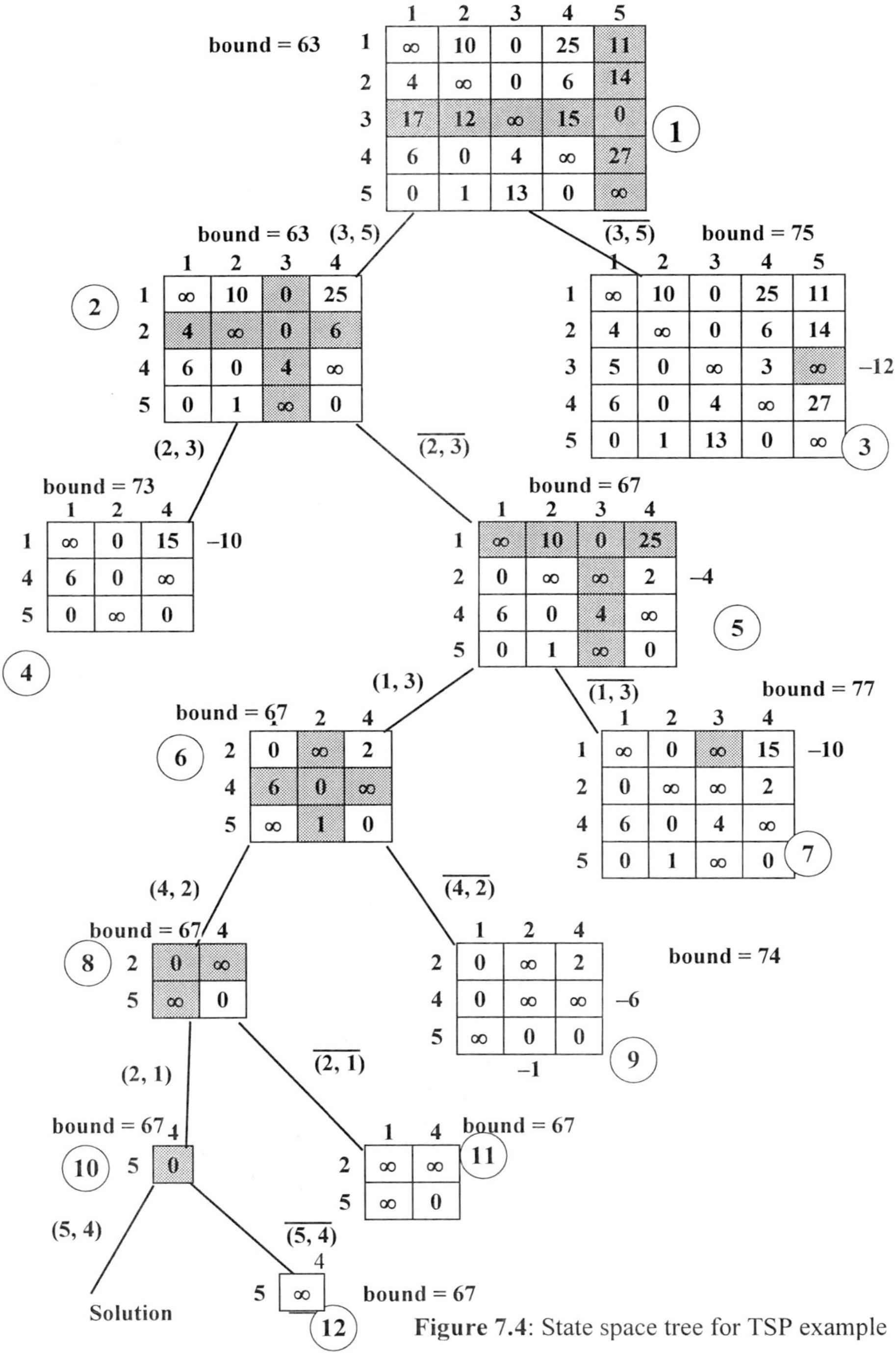

Figure 7.4: State space tree for TSP example

7.3 0/1 KNAPSACK PROBLEM

We have a knapsack (bag) with capacity, $W = 12$. The weights and values of four items are given below. The items are ordered in descending order of their value-to-weight ratios.

Table 7.1: A Knapsack example

item (i)	v_i (Rs)	w_i (Kg)	v_i/w_i
1	50	5	10
2	48	8	6
3	30	6	5
4	12	4	3

The objective of knapsack problem is to fill the knapsack with items to maximize the total value subject to its capacity. It is known as 0/1 knapsack problem, because we put one item into the knapsack or not (may not include a fraction of an item).

We will construct the state space tree where each node contains the total current value in the knapsack, the total current weight of the contents of the knapsack, and maximum potential value (upper bound) that the knapsack can hold. In the algorithm, we will also keep a record of the maximum value of any node (partially or completely filled knapsack) found so far. When we perform the breadth-first traversal of the state space tree, a node is "promising" if its maximum potential value is greater than this current best value.

We begin the state space tree with the root consisting of the empty knapsack. The current weight and value are obviously zero. To find the maximum potential value we treat the problem as if it were the fractional knapsack problem and we were using the greedy algorithmic solution to that problem. We have shown that the greedy approach to the fractional knapsack problem yields an optimal solution. We place each of the remaining items, in turn, into the knapsack until the next selected item is too big to fit into the knapsack. We then use the fractional amount of that item that could be included in the knapsack to determine the maximum potential value.

w = *totalWeight* = Weight of items included so far in the knapsack

v = *totalValue* = Total value of items so far included.

bound (maximum potential value or upper bound), b = *totalValue* + (W – *totalWeight*) x (value density of item that is partially placed).

In general, for a node at level i in the state space tree (the first i items have been considered for selection) and for the k-th item as the one that will not completely fit into the remaining weight (space) in the knapsack, these formulae can be written:

$$totalWeight,\ w = \sum_{i=1}^{k-1} w_i \qquad totalValue,\ v = \sum_{i=1}^{k-1} v_i$$

The bound at i-th level is given as:

$bound = v + (W - w) \times (v_k/w_k)$ where $k = i+1$.

For the root node, $totWeight, w = 0$, $totValue, v = 0$.

For $i = 0$ (level at the root),
$bound, b = v + (W - w) \times (v_1/w_1)$
$= 0 + (12 - 0) \times (10) =$ Rs 120.

Node 1: Left child of root represents the subsets that include item 1. Total weight = 5, value of items already included = 50, and value of bound = 50 + (12 – 5) x 6 = Rs 92.

Node 2: Right child of root represents the subsets that do not include item 1. Total weight = 0, value of items already included = 0, and value of bound = 0 + (12 – 0) x 6 = Rs 72.

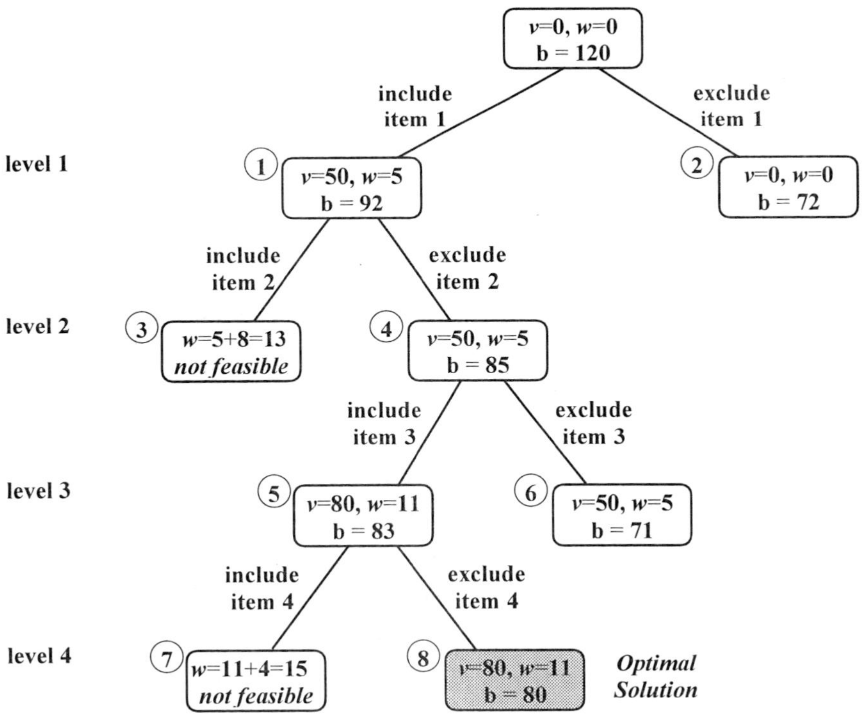

Figure 7.5: State space tree for the instance of the knapsack problem

Node 1 is more promising, because upper bound of node 1 is greater than that of node 2. Hence, we branch node 1 first. The children of node 1 are node 3 and node 4 representing subsets with item 1 and with and without item 2, respectively.

Node 3: By including items 1 and 2, the total weight is 13 (5 + 8) which is greater than knapsack capacity (W = 12). Hence, node 3 is not feasible.

Node 4: $v = 50$, $w = 5$, $b = v + (W - w) \times (v_3/w_3) = 50 + (12\text{-}5) \times (5)$ = Rs 85.

We select node 4 over node 2 for next branching, because the bound of node 4 is better than that of node 2. We get node 5 and node 6 by respectively including and excluding item 3.

Node 5: $v = 50 + 30 = 80$, $w = 5 + 6 = 11$, $b = v + (W - w) \times (v_4/w_4) = 80 + (12\text{-}11) \times 3$ = Rs 83.

Node 6: $v = 50$, $w = 5$, $b = v + (W - w) \times (v_4/w_4) = 50 + (12\text{-}5) \times 3$ = Rs 71.

Node 7 is infeasible.

As there are no additional items to consider, the upper bound for node 8 is simply equal to the total value of the items 1 and 3. The remaining live nodes 2 and 6 have lesser bound values than that of node 8. Hence, nodes 2 and 6 will be terminated. Finally, node 8 represents the optimal solution that has items 1 and 3.

Knapsack branch and bound algorithm uses queue as an auxiliary data structure. Elements of the queue are nodes. Each node contains level, weight, and profit. The variables u and v are node type.

Algorithm 7.1: Knapsack(p[1..n], w[1..n], W, n)

```
Initially Queue is empty
Insert v into Q
While Q is not empty
    Delete the next node and store it in v
    u->level = v->level + 1
    u->weight = v->weight + w[u->level]
    u->profit = v->profit + p[u->level]
    If u->weight ≤ W and u->profit > maxProfit, then
        maxProfit = u->profit
    Else
        If bound(u) > maxProfit, then
            Insert u into Q
        Else
            u gets v's weight and profit
        Endif
    Endif
    If bound(u) > maxProfit, then
            Insert u into Q
    Endif
Endwhile.
```

CHAPTER SUMMARY

- *Branch-and-bound* (B&B) is an algorithmic technique to find the optimal solution by keeping the best solution found so far. If a partial solution cannot improve on the best, it is discarded.
- B&B searches the set of all possible solutions embedded in a *state space tree* for a solution. The tree is a rooted tree where each level represents a choice in the solution space that depends on the level above and any possible solution is represented by some path starting out at the root (by definition the root has level zero and represents the state where no partial solution has been made) and ending at a leaf. A leaf has no children and represents the state where all choices making up a solution have been made.
- B&B can be applied to an *assignment problem* by assigning *n* persons to *n* jobs so that the total cost of assignment is a minimum. Each person can be assigned exactly one job.
- *Traveling Salesman Problem* (TSP) requires that we find the shortest path visiting each of a given set of cities once and returning to the starting point. In other words, the problem is to find, in an undirected graph with weights on the edges, a tour the sum of whose edge-weights is a minimum. A tour is a simple cycle that includes all the vertices and is often called a Hamiltonian cycle. TSP is a famous example of a problem which can be solved by a B&B.
- We can apply the B&B technique to solve the *knapsack* problem – given *n* items of known weights and values and a knapsack of capacity, find the optimum subset of items that fit in the knapsack.

SELF-TEST QUIZ

7.1 ___________ is a tree pruning technique for solving optimization problem using search technique.

(a) Backtracking (b) Branch-and-bound
(c) Greedy (d) Dynamic programming

7.2 _________ is a node that has been generated but whose children have not yet been generated.

(a) E-node (b) Live node
(c) Dead node (d) E-node or Live node

7.3 _________ is a generated node that is not to be expanded or explored any further.

(a) E-node (b) Live node
(c) Dead node (d) Dead node or E-node

7.4 A state space is

(a) part of RAM.
(b) one set of variable assignments.
(c) a set of possible arrangements of values.
(d) a graph.

7.5 Suppose you are given a TSP problem on 6 cities. There is a connection between every pair of cities in both directions. The cities are named A, B, C, D, E and F. Suppose that edges (A, B), (D, E), (E, C) and (F, A) have been included in a partial solution. Which edges can no longer be included in the solution because they will lead to a premature cycle?

(a) (D, E), (E, C) (b) (A, B), (D, E)
(c) (E, C), (F, A) (d) (A, B), (F, A)

7.6 BFS is a ______ search in terms of live nodes (list of live nodes is a queue).

(a) FIFO (b) LIFO
(c) Least-cost (d) Maxi-min

7.7 DFS is a ______ search in terms of live nodes (list of live nodes is a stack).

(a) FIFO (b) LIFO
(c) Least-cost (d) Maxi-min

7.8 What is the optimal tour for the following TSP defined by the following cost matrix?

	A	B	C	D
A	∞	3	2	7
B	4	∞	3	6
C	1	1	∞	3
D	1	6	6	∞

(a) A→B→D→C→A (b) A→C→B→D→A
(c) A→B→C→D→A (d) (b) and (c)

7.9 Considering the above question, what is the cost of optimal tour?

(a) 8 (b) 10 (c) 11 (d) 12

7.10 The knapsack problem searches

(a) a tree (b) a graph (c) an array (d) a state space

7.11 What is the optimal solution for the following 0/1 knapsack instance?
$n = 4$, $(p_1 \ldots p_4) = (10, 10, 12, 18)$, $(w_1 \ldots w_4) = (2, 4, 6, 9)$, and $m = 15$.

(a) subset (3, 4) (b) subset (1, 2, 3)
(c) subset (1, 2, 4) (d) subset (1, 3, 4)

7.12 Considering the above question, what is the maximum profit?

(a) 30 (b) 32 (c) 38 (d) 40

7.13 FIFO B&B uses ________ as an auxiliary data structure.

(a) stack (b) queue (c) priority queue (d) binary tree

7.14 Least Cost B&B uses ________ as an auxiliary data structure.

(a) stack (b) queue (c) priority queue (d) binary tree

EXERCISES

7.1 Explain the general method of branch-and-bound.

7.2 Describe the explicit constraints and implicit constraints.

7.3 Explain live node, E-node, and dead node with an example.

7.4 What is bounding? Explain how these bounds are useful in branch-and-bound methods.

7.5 Describe the problem state, solution state and answer state with an example.

7.6 Write an algorithm to solve the knapsack problem with branch-and-bound.

7.7 Differentiate between dynamic knapsack and branch-and-bound knapsack problem.

7.8 Write the LCBB algorithm for the 0/1 knapsack problem. Also analyze its complexity.

7.9 Write an algorithm of LCBB to find the minimum cost answer node.

7.10 Draw the portion of the state space tree generated by FIFO branch-and-bound for the following instance.

$n = 5$, $(p_1 \ldots p_5) = (10, 15, 6, 8, 4)$, $(w_1 \ldots w_5) = (4, 6, 3, 4, 2)$, and $m = 12$.

7.11 Draw the portion of the state space tree generated by LCBB for the following instance.

$n = 4$, $(p_1 \ldots p_4) = (10, 10, 12, 18)$, $(w_1 \ldots w_4) = (2, 4, 6, 9)$, and $m = 15$.

7.12 Describe the TSP in branch-and-bound.

7.13 Explain the method of reduction to solve TSP problem using branch-and-bound.

7.14 Explain the principles of LIFO branch-and-bound.

7.15 Solve the following TSP instance defined by the cost matrix.

	1	2	3	4	5
1	∞	7	3	12	8
2	3	∞	6	14	9
3	5	8	∞	6	18
4	9	3	5	∞	11
5	18	14	9	8	∞

7.16 Explain the principles of FIFO branch-and-bound.

CHAPTER 8

NP-COMPLETE PROBLEMS

Most algorithms we have studied so far have polynomial-time running times – that is, finding the shortest paths and minimum spanning trees in graphs, sorting of arrays, matrix multiplication, and so on. All these algorithms are efficient, because in each case their time requirement grows as a polynomial function (such as n, n^2, or n^3) of the size of the input.

This chapter gives a general introduction of P, NP and NP-complete problems. We will study the definition and some classic examples of NP-complete problems. More importantly, we will learn how to show that a problem is not easier than another problem by polynomial-time reduction. Polynomial-time reduction is the general method to prove that a new problem is NP-complete, so that we have an excuse not to find the optimal solution. As we encounter more NP-complete problems, we will learn some general techniques for reductions.

Polynomial-time algorithms can be considered tractable (easy or not so difficult) for the following reasons:

- Although a problem which has a running time of say $O(n^k)$ (for large value of k) can be called intractable (difficult), there are very few practical problems with such orders of polynomial complexity.
- For reasonable models of computation, a problem that can be solved in polynomial time in one model can also be solved in polynomial time on another.
- The class of polynomial-time solvable problems has nice closure properties (since polynomials are closed under addition, multiplication, etc.)

8.1 P, NP, and NP-complete

Somehow we believe that an efficient algorithm should run in polynomial time, that is, $O(n^k)$ for input size n and some constant k. Consequently, problems that can be solved in polynomial time are treated as "easy" problems (although k can be arbitrarily large), and we use P to denote the set of polynomial-time-solvable problems. Here is the formal definition:

P: the set of problems that can be solved in polynomial time.

Some examples in P:

(1) Finding the shortest-path in a graph between two vertices such that the sum of the weights of its constituent edges is minimized.
(2) Testing whether given number is prime.
(3) Finding the maximum element in a given array.

Some problems that we can not solve in polynomial time so far:

(1) Factorization: given n and m, determine whether n has any prime factors less than m. For example, let $n = 324$ and $m = 5$. 324 is the product of the prime factors 2 x 2 x 3 x 3 x 3 x 3 = $2^2 \times 3^4$. 2 and 3 are prime factors less than 5.
(2) Polynomial Identities Testing: determining whether a given multivariate polynomial is identically equal to 0. For example, consider a polynomial in two variables x and y: $x^3y^2 + xy - 10$. For $x = 2$ and $y = 1$, the value of this polynomial is 0. Hence,
(3) Graph Coloring: given k, determine whether a graph has a k vertex coloring.

The problems that can not be solved in polynomial time so far* are considered as "hard" problems. For the "hard" problems, if (say by guessing) we are given a solution for a problem, we may be able to check whether the solution is correct very efficiently (i.e. in polynomial time). This leads to the definition of NP problems:

> NP: the set of problems for which the "yes" answer (with a certificate – that is, a solution) can be verified in polynomial time. NP stands for "Non-deterministic Polynomial time".

One quick observation is that any problem in P is also in NP, because we can verify its answer by solving the problem (and so do not even need a certificate). On the other hand, many "hard" problems mentioned above are also in NP: although we do not have a polynomial-time algorithm for it, we can verify a solution in polynomial time. To understand the relation between P and NP, it is useful to have a "hardest" problem in NP. Here comes the definition for NP-completeness:

> A problem is NP-complete if (1) it is in NP; and (2) if it can be solved in polynomial time, then any problem in NP can be solved in polynomial time.

Generally NP-complete (NPC) problems are considered as the "hard" problems. The interesting thing is that we never say NPC problems can not be solved in polynomial time in the formal definition, because we do not have a proof for it. Instead, we use the second property in the definition to link all the NPC problems together: any NPC problem is at least not easier than any other NPC problem. The technique to show that a problem A is not easier than another problem B is Polynomial-time Reduction, which will be shown in next section.

Based on the above description (and our belief), the relation of P, NP and NPC problems are shown in Figure 8.1. Note that we do not know for sure whether NP or NPC problems are polynomial-time-solvable. This is the most famous open problem in theoretical computer science, and the Clay Mathematics Institute of Cambridge, Massachusetts, USA offers a million dollar for its solution.

---

* we almost believe that they can never be solved in polynomial time...

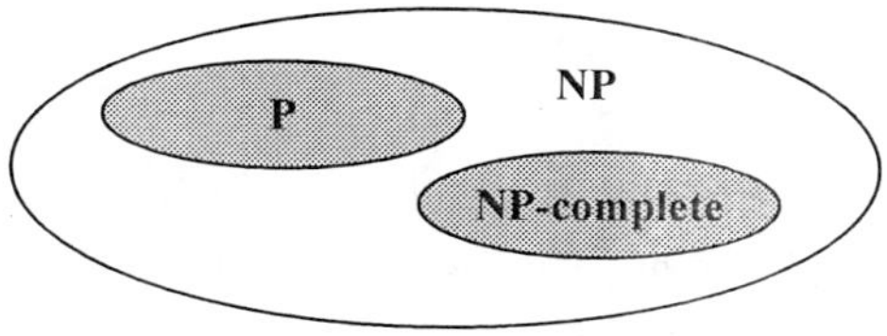

Figure 8.1: What we think the world looks like...

It is important to know the rudiments of NP-completeness for anyone to design "sound" algorithms for problems. If one can establish a problem as NP-complete, there is strong reason to believe that it is intractable. We would then do better by trying to design a good approximation algorithm rather than searching endlessly seeking an exact solution. An example of this is the Traveling Salesman Problem (TSP), which is intractable. A practical strategy to solve TSP therefore would be to design a good approximation algorithm. Another important reason to have good familiarity with NP-completeness is many natural interesting and safe-looking problems that on the surface seem no harder than sorting or searching, are in fact NP-complete.

8.1.1 Examples of some Intractable Problems

Before giving examples on intractable problems, let us define a decision problem. A *decision problem* determines whether or not there exists a decision procedure or algorithm for a class S of questions requiring a Boolean value (i.e., a true or false, or yes or no). These are also known as yes-or-no questions. For example, the decision problem for the class of questions "Does x divide y without remainder?" is decidable because there exists a mechanical procedure, which allows us to determine for any x and y whether the answer for "Does x divide y without remainder?" is yes or no.

Traveling Salesman Problem:
A Hamiltonian cycle in an undirected graph is a simple cycle that passes through every vertex exactly once. Optimization Problem: Given a complete, weighted graph, find a minimum-weight Hamiltonian Cycle. Decision Problem: Given a complete, weighted graph and an integer k, does there exist a Hamiltonian cycle with total weight at most k.

Subset Sum:
The input is a positive integer C and n objects whose values are positive integers $x_1, x_2, \ldots, x_n$. Optimization Problem: Among all subsets of objects with sum at most C, what is the largest subset sum? Decision Problem: Is there a subset of objects whose values add up to exactly C?

Knapsack Problem:
This is a generalization of the subset sum problem. Consider a knapsack of capacity C where C is a positive integer and n objects with positive integer weights $w_1, w_2, \ldots, w_n$ and positive integer profits $p_1, p_2, \ldots, p_n$. Optimization Problem: Find the largest total profit of any subset of the

objects that fits in the knapsack. Decision Problem: Given k, is there a subset of the objects that fits in the knapsack and has total profit at least k?

Satisfiability (SAT):
A propositional variable (Boolean variable) is one that can be assigned the value "true" or "false". A literal is a propositional variable or its negation (such as $\overline{p}$). A clause is a sequence of literals separated by the logical OR operator ($\vee$). A propositional formula is said to be in *conjunctive normal form* (CNF) if it consists of a sequence of clauses separated by the logical AND operator ($\wedge$). For example,

$$(p \vee q \vee s) \wedge (\overline{q} \vee r) \wedge (\overline{p} \vee \overline{q} \vee r \vee \overline{s})$$

This is a Boolean formula in CNF. A truth assignment for a set of propositional variables is an assignment of true or false value to each propositional variable. A truth assignment is said to satisfy a formula if it makes the value of the formula true. In other words, given a Boolean formula in CNF, either find a satisfying truth assignment or else report that none exists.

3SAT (Decision Problem): Given a CNF formula in which each clause is permitted to contain at most three literals, is there a truth assignment to its variables that satisfies it?

8.2 CLASSES P AND NP

An algorithm is said to be polynomially bounded if its worst-case complexity is bounded by a polynomial function of the input size. A problem is said to be polynomially bounded if there is a polynomially bounded algorithm for it.

P is the class of all decision problems that are polynomially bounded. The implication is that a decision problem $X \in$ P can be solved in polynomial time on a deterministic computation model (such as a deterministic Turing machine[♠]).

NP represents the class of decision problems which can be solved in polynomial time by a non-deterministic model of computation. That is, a decision problem $X \in$ NP can be solved in polynomial-time on a non-deterministic computation model (such as a non-deterministic Turing machine). A non-deterministic model can make the right guesses on every move and race towards the solution much faster than a deterministic model.

A deterministic machine, at each point in time, executes an instruction. Depending on the outcome of executing the instruction, it then executes some next instruction, which is unique. A non-deterministic machine on the other hand has a choice of next steps. It is free to choose any that it wishes. For example, it can always choose a next step that leads to the best solution for the problem. A non-deterministic machine thus has the power of extremely good, optimal guessing.

As an example, let us consider the decision version of TSP: Given a complete, weighted graph and an integer k, does there exist a Hamiltonian cycle with total weight at most k?

A smart non-deterministic algorithm for the above TSP problem starts with a vertex, guesses the correct edge to choose, proceeds to the next vertex, guesses the correct edge to choose there, etc. and in polynomial time discovers a Hamiltonian cycle of least cost and

---

♠ Devices with infinite memory used to model any computer.

provides an answer to the above problem. This is the power of non-determinism. A deterministic algorithm here will have no choice but take super-polynomial time to answer the above question.

Another way of viewing the above is that given a candidate Hamiltonian cycle (call it certificate), one can verify in polynomial time whether the answer to the above question is YES or NO. Thus to check if a problem is in NP, it is enough to prove in polynomial time that any YES instance is correct. We do not have to worry about NO instances since the program always makes the right choice.

It is easy to show that P $\subseteq$ NP. However, it is unknown whether P = NP. In fact, this question is perhaps the most celebrated of all open problems in computer science.

8.3 NP-COMPLETE PROBLEMS

We will look at a list of problems that are known to belong to NP but which might or might not belong to P. That is, they are easy to solve on a non-deterministic machine, but, despite considerable effort, no one has been able to find an efficient algorithm on a conventional machine (or prove that none exists) for any of them. These problems have an additional property that provides convincing evidence that P $\neq$ NP: if any of the problems can be solved in polynomial time on a deterministic machine, then so can all problems in NP (i.e., P = NP). That is, the collective failure of all the researchers to find efficient algorithms for all of these problems might be viewed as a collective failure to prove that P = NP. Such problems are said to be NP-complete. It turns out that a large number of interesting practical problems have this characteristic.

The primary tool used to prove that problems are NP-complete uses the idea of polynomial *reducibility*. We show that any algorithm to solve a new problem in NP can be used to solve some known NP-complete problem by the following process:

- transform any instance of the known NP-complete problem to an instance of the new problem,
- solve the problem using the given algorithm, then
- transform the solution back to a solution of the NP-complete problem.

By "polynomially" reducible, we mean that the transformations can be done in polynomial time: thus the existence of a polynomial-time algorithm for the new problem would imply the existence of a polynomial-time algorithm for the NP-complete problem, and this would (by definition) imply the existence of polynomial-time algorithms for all problems in NP.

The concept of reduction provides a useful mechanism for classifying algorithms. For example, to prove that a problem in NP is NP-complete, we need only show that some known NP-complete problem is polynomially reducible to it: that is, that a polynomial-time algorithm for the new problem could be used to solve the NP-complete problem, and then could, in turn, be used to solve all problems in NP. For an example of reduction, consider the following two problems:

Travelling Salesman Problem (TSP): Given a set of cities, and distances between all pairs, find a tour of all the cities of distance less than k.

Hamilton Cycle: Given a graph, find a simple cycle that includes all the vertices.

Suppose that we know the Hamilton cycle problem to be NP-complete and we wish to determine whether or not the TSP is also NP-complete. Any algorithm for solving the TSP can be used to solve the Hamilton cycle problem, through the following reduction:

Given an instance of the Hamilton cycle problem (a graph) construct an instance of the TSP (a set of cities, with distances between all pairs) as follows: for cities for the traveling salesman use the set of vertices in the graph; for distances between each pair of cities use 1 if there is an edge between the corresponding vertices in the graph, 0 if there is no edge. Then have the algorithm for the TSP find a tour of distance less than or equal to n, the number of vertices in the graph. That tour must correspond precisely to a Hamilton cycle. An efficient algorithm for the TSP would also be an efficient algorithm for the Hamilton cycle problem. That is, the Hamilton cycle problem reduces to the TSP, so the NP-completeness of the Hamilton cycle problem implies the NP-completeness of the TSP.

The reduction of the Hamilton cycle problem to the TSP is relatively simple because the problems are so similar. Actually, polynomial-time reductions can be quite complicated indeed and can connect problems which seem to be quite dissimilar. For example, it is possible to reduce the satisfiability problem to the Hamilton cycle problem. Without going into details, we can look at a sketch of the proof. We wish to show that if we had a polynomial-time solution to the Hamilton cycle problem, then we could get a polynomial-time solution to the satisfiability problem by polynomial reduction. The proof consists of a detailed method of construction showing how, given an instance of the satisfiability problem (a Boolean formula) to construct (in polynomial time) an instance of the Hamilton cycle problem (a graph) with the property that knowing whether the graph has a Hamilton cycle tells us whether the formula is satisfiable. The graph is built from small components (corresponding to the variables) which can be traversed by a simple path in only one of two ways (corresponding to the truth or falsity of the variables). These small components are attached together as specified by the clauses, using more complicated subgraphs which can be traversed by simple paths corresponding to the truth or falsity of the clauses. It is quite a large step from this brief description to the full construction: the point is to illustrate that polynomial reduction can be applied to quite dissimilar problems.

Thus, if we were to have a polynomial-time algorithm for the TSP, then we would have a polynomial-time algorithm for the Hamilton cycle problem, which would also give us a polynomial-time algorithm for the satisfiability problem. Each problem that is proven NP-complete provides another potential basis for proving yet another future problem NP-complete. The proof might be as simple as the reduction given above from the Hamilton cycle problem to the TSP, or as complicated as the transformation sketched above from the satisfiability problem to the Hamilton cycle problem, or somewhere in between. Literally thousands of problems have been proven to be NP-complete over the last ten years by transforming one to another in this way. Following is another example on reduction between *Clique* and *Independent Set*:

The Clique Problem is to determine whether a graph has a complete subgraph of size k (i.e. with k vertices); while the Independent Set Problem is to determine whether a graph has an independent set with k vertices. An independent set is a set of vertices such that there is no edge between any pair of vertices. Consider the example in Figure 8.2, where we show a graph G and its complement graph (in the complement graph of G, there is an edge between two vertices if and only if there is no edge between these two vertices in the original graph G). It is easy to see that each clique in G becomes an independent set in the complement graph. This leads to the easy reduction from Clique Problem to Independent Set Problem:

1. We are given an instance of Clique Problem: given a graph G and an integer k, determine whether it has a clique of size k.
2. In polynomial time, we construct G' which is the complement graph of G. Now the instance of Independent Set Problem is to determine whether G' has an independent set of size k.
3. Obviously G has a clique of size k if and only if G' has an independent set of size k.

Following similar steps, we can also reduce Independent Set Problem to Clique Problem. Based on the above discussion, the following statement holds:

- The Clique Problem can be reduced to the Independent Set Problem, and vice versa. We say these two problems are polynomially equivalent.

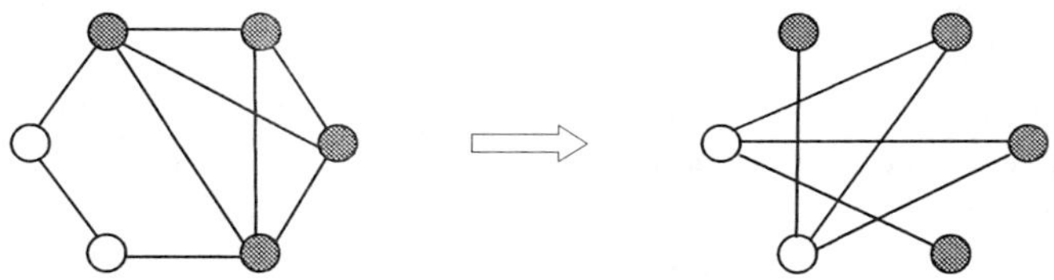

(a) Graph G – grey nodes form a clique of size 4

(b) Complement Graph of G – grey nodes form an independent set of size 4

Figure 8.2: Clique and independent set

8.3.1 NP-Hardness and NP-Completeness

NP-hard (Non-deterministic Polynomial-time hard) refers to the class of decision problems that contains all problems H such that for all decision problems L in NP there is a polynomial-time many-one reduction to H. Informally this class can be described as containing the decision problems that are at least as hard as any problem in NP. This intuition is supported by the fact that if we can find an algorithm A that solves one of these problems H in polynomial time then we can construct a polynomial time algorithm for every problem in NP by first executing the reduction from this problem to H and then executing the algorithm A.

Assuming language L to be NP-complete,

1. L is in NP
2. L' in NP, $L' \leq L$

NP-Hard assumes language L satisfies property 2, but not necessarily property 1.

The notion of NP-hardness plays an important role in the discussion about the relationship between the complexity classes P and NP. It is also often used to define the complexity class NP-complete which is the intersection of NP and NP-hard (see Figure 8.3). Consequently the class NP-hard can be understood as the class of problems that are NP-complete or harder.

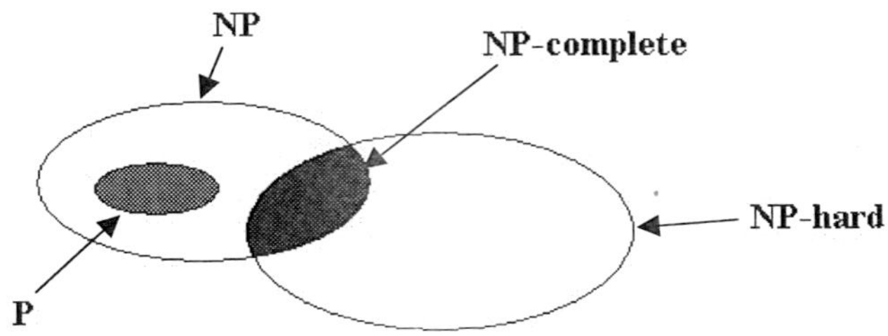

Figure 8.3: Relationship among P, NP, NP-complete, and NP-hard problems

A common mistake is to think that the "NP" in "NP-hard" stands for "non-polynomial". Although it is widely suspected that there are no polynomial-time algorithms for these problems, this has never been proven.

An example of an NP-hard problem is the decision problem Subset-Sum. Given a set of integers, does any non-empty subset of them add up to zero? That is a yes-or-no question, and happens to be NP-complete.

There are also decision problems that are NP-hard but not NP-complete, for example the *halting problem*. This is the problem "given a program and its input, will it run forever?" That is a yes-or-no question, so this is a decision problem. It is easy to prove that the halting problem is NP-hard but not NP-complete. For example the Boolean satisfiability problem can be reduced to the halting problem by transforming it to the description of a Turing machine that tries all truth value assignments and when it finds one that satisfies the formula it halts and otherwise it goes into an infinite loop. It is also easy to see that the halting problem is not in NP since all problems in NP are decidable and the halting problem is not.

8.4 COOK'S THEOREM

Before presenting Cook's theorem, let us state some of the related definitions, though we have defined previously: A decision problem is in NP if it can be solved by a non-deterministic algorithm in polynomial time. An instance of the Boolean satisfiability problem is a Boolean expression that combines Boolean variables using Boolean operators. An expression is satisfiable if there is some assignment of truth values to the variables that makes the entire expression true.

- Cook's Theorem states that any problem in class NP can be reduced to an instance of SAT in polynomial time.

Alternatively, it states that the Boolean satisfiability problem is NP-complete. That is, any problem in NP can be reduced in polynomial time by a deterministic Turing machine to a problem of determining whether a Boolean formula is satisfiable.

An important consequence of the theorem is this: if there were a deterministic polynomial time algorithm for solving Boolean satisfiability, then there would exist a deterministic polynomial time algorithm for solving all problems in NP. Crucially, the same follows for any NP complete problem as these are also in NP.

The question of whether such an algorithm exists is called the P = NP problem and it is widely considered the most important unsolved problem in theoretical computer science.

A decision problem is NP-hard if the time complexity on a deterministic machine is within a polynomial factor of the complexity of any problem in NP.

A problem is NP-complete if it is NP-hard and in NP.

Cook's theorem proved SATISFIABILITY was NP-hard by using a polynomial time reduction translating each problem in NP into an instance of SAT. Since a polynomial time algorithm for SAT would imply a polynomial time algorithm for everything in NP, SAT is NP-hard. Since we can guess a solution to SAT, it is in NP and thus NP-complete.

Figure 8.4

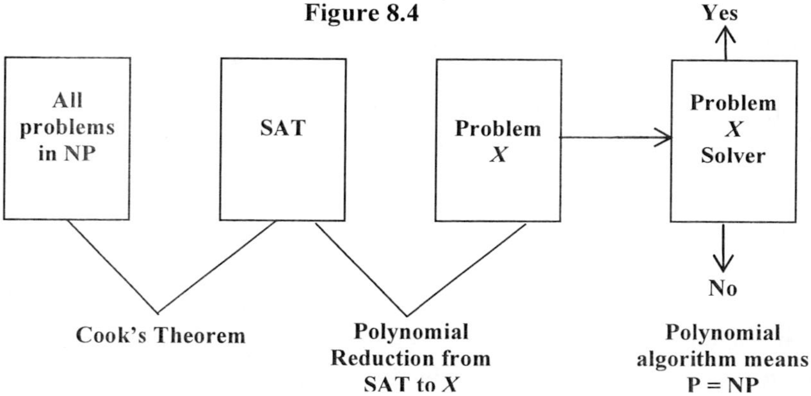

The proof of Cook's Theorem, while quite clever, was certainly difficult and complicated. We had to show that all problems in NP could be reduced to SAT to make sure we did not miss a hard one. But now that we have a known NP-complete problem in SAT. For any other problem, we can prove it NP-hard by polynomially transforming SAT to it!

Since the composition of two polynomial time reductions can be done in polynomial time, all we need show is that SAT, that is, any instance of SAT can be translated to an instance of *X* in polynomial time.

CHAPTER SUMMARY

- Complexity theory seeks to classify problems according to their computational complexity. The problems that can and cannot be solved in polynomial time are *tractable* and *intractable*, respectively. Complexity theory concentrates on *decision problems*, which are problems with yes-or-no answers.
- The *halting problem* is an example of an *undecidable* decision problem – that is, it cannot be solved by any algorithm.
- P is the class of all decision problems that can be solved in polynomial time. NP is the class of all decision problems whose randomly guessed solutions can be verified in polynomial time.

- Many important problems in NP, such as Hamiltonian cycle problem, are known to be NP-complete. All other problems in NP are reducible to such a problem in polynomial time.
- The first proof of a problem's NP-completeness was published by Stefan Cook for the *CNF-satisfiability problem.*
- It is not known whether P = NP or P is a subset of NP. This question is the most important unresolved issue in theoretical computer science. A finding of a polynomial time algorithm for any of the thousands known NP-complete problems would imply that P = NP.

SELF-TEST QUIZ

8.1 Uncomputable functions correspond to problems that are called

(a) undecidable (b) intractable
(c) P-time (d) optimization

8.2 Problems for which no polynomial-time solutions are known are called

(a) undecidable (b) intractable
(c) NP (d) optimization

8.3 The Halting Problem is

(a) undecidable (b) intractable
(c) NP-complete (d) optimization

8.4 The information-theoretic lower bound for a problem is given by the _____ height of the decision tree for the best algorithm that solves the problem

(a) maximum (b) minimum
(c) average (d) absolute (e) relative

8.5 The problem of sorting by comparisons is
(a) $O(n)$ (b) $O(n \lg n)$ (c) $O(n^2)$ (d) $(n \lg n)$

8.6 The Hamiltonian-cycle problem is considered

(a) intractable (b) undecidable
(c) tractable (d) decidable

8.7 The problem of evaluating a formula in propositional logic is

(a) intractable (b) undecidable
(c) tractable (d) exponential

8.8 Deciding whether a formula in propositional logic is satisfiable is

(a) intractable (b) undecidable
(c) tractable (d) decidable (e) polymorphic

8.9 If checking a given candidate solution to a problem is easy enough, then the problem is in

(a) P (b) NP (c) NPC (d) EXP (e) none of these

8.10 Problem A is reducible to problem B if there is an algorithm that can

(a) transform any instance of B to an instance of A

(b) transform any instance of A to an instance of B
(c) solve A
(d) solve B
(e) solve A as fast as B

8.11 Finding the maximum value in an array is ______ the sorting problem

(a) reducible to (b) harder than
(c) a subproblem of (d) equivalent to

8.12 SAT is the problem of deciding whether a formula in propositional logic

(a) holds
(b) has a set of variable assignments that make it true
(c) is not a contradiction
(d) is syntactically correct
(e) is probably true

8.13 Decision problems are equivalent to

(a) formulas in propositional logic
(b) assertions
(c) array manipulations
(d) languages

8.14 The Cook-Karp Thesis states that the problem of deciding membership of strings in a language is tractable only if the language is decidable in

(a) polynomial time (b) $O(n)$ (c) $O(2^n)$ (d) $O(\lg n)$

8.15 P is the set of

(a) algorithms that execute in O(n) time.
(b) problems decidable in $O(n^k)$ time for some constant k.
(c) problems not decidable in $O(n^k)$ time.
(d) intractable problems.
(e) exponential-time problems.

8.16 NP is the set of

(a) algorithms that execute in $O(n^k)$ time for some constant k.
(b) problems decidable in $O(n^k)$ time.
(c) problems for which possible solutions may be checked in $O(n^k)$ time.
(d) intractable problems
(e) exponential-time problems

8.17 NPC is a set of

(a) exponential-time problems.
(b) problems decidable in $O(n^k)$ time for some constant k.
(c) problems for which possible solutions may be checked in $O(n^k)$ time.
(d) intractable problems.

8.18 Problems to which SAT or similar problems are reducible are called

(a) P (b) NP (c) NP-complete (d) NP-hard

8.19 NP-complete problems are believed to have
(a) polynomial-time solutions
(b) no polynomial-time solutions
(c) no exponential-time solutions
(d) no solutions checkable in polynomial time

EXERCISES

8.1 Explain the classes of P and NP.

8.2 Explain NP-completeness reduction with an example.

8.3 Explain the satisfiability problem and write the algorithm for the same.

8.4 Explain the strategy to prove that a problem is NP-hard.

8.5 Sate and explain Cook's theorem.

8.6 Write a nondeterministic knapsack algorithm.

8.7 What is meant by Halting problem? Explain with an example.

8.8 Describe clique decision/optimization problem.

8.9 Differentiate between NP-complete and NP-hard.

APPENDIX-A

KEY TO SELF-TEST QUIZ

CHAPTER 1 Introduction to Algorithms

1.1 (a) 1.2 (b) 1.3 (d) 1.4 (d) 1.5 (d) 1.6 (b) 1.7 (a)

1.8 Consider $\sum_{1\le k\le n} O(n) = O(n) + O(n) + ...$ n terms

$$= n \times O(n) = O(n^2)$$

1.9 $O(1)$ – *constant*. The running time of the algorithm is constant. Since the index provides direct access into the array, the time it takes to complete this task is independent of the size n of the array.

1.10 $O(n)$ – *linear*. The linked list has to be searched from first item to the last element (if the target item is at the end of the list). Hence, the worst-case time is $O(n)$.

1.11 Minimum number of exchanges required in the worst-case is $n/2$ as the worst-case is the one where all the positive numbers occur before the negative ones.

1.12 $x * x = x^2$ $\log_2 2 = 1$ multiplication
$x^2 * x^2 = x^4$ $\log_2 4 = 2$ multiplications
$x^4 * x^4 = x^8$ $\log_2 8 = 3$ multiplications
$x^8 * x^8 = x^{16}$ $\log_2 16 = 4$ multiplications
. . .
$x^{n/2} * x^{n/2} = x^n$ $\log_2 n$ multiplications
Hence, the choice is: (a) $\log_2 n$

1.13 (d) $O(\log_2 n) < O(n) < O(n\log_2 n) < O(n^2) < O(2^n)$

1.14 $10 \times n \times \log_2 n > 2n^2$
$\log_2 n > 2n^2 / (10 \times n)$
$\log_2 n > n/5$

$n > 2^{n/5}$

Hence $0 < n$ £ 20

1.15 $f(n) = n^2\lg n$ and $g(n) = n(\lg n)^{10}$

$$T(n) = \lim_{n\to\infty}\frac{f(n)}{g(n)} = \lim_{n\to\infty}\frac{n^2\lg n}{n(\lg n)^{10}} = \lim_{n\to\infty}\frac{n\lg n}{(\lg n)^{10}} = \lim_{n\to\infty}\frac{n}{(\lg n)^9} \neq 1$$

Hence, $f(n) \neq O(g(n))$

By definition, we write $f(n) = O(g(n))$ to indicate that a function $f(n)$ is a member of the set $O(g(n))$ if and only if

$$\lim_{n\to\infty}\frac{f(n)}{g(n)} \to 1$$

1.16 (b) $(3^{k+1}-1)/2$

$T(2^k) = 3T(2^{k-1})+1,\ T(1) = 1$
$T(2) = 3T(2^0)+1 = 3T(1)+1 = 4$ for $k = 1$
$T(4) = 3T(2^1)+1 = 3T(2)+1 = 13$ for $k = 2$
$T(8) = 3T(2^2)+1 = 3T(4)+1 = 40$ for $k = 3$

$T(2^k) = T(2) = (3^{k+1}-1)/2 = (3^2-1)/2 = (9-1)/2 = 4$ for $k = 1$
$T(2^k) = T(4) = (3^{k+1}-1)/2 = (3^3-1)/2 = (27-1)/2 = 13$ for $k = 2$
$T(2^k) = T(8) = (3^{k+1}-1)/2 = (3^4-1)/2 = (81-1)/2 = 40$ for $k = 3$

1.17 (a) n

1.18 (d) $O(1)$. For large enough $n > 2^8$, the running time is constant.

1.19 The choice (a) I and II is correct.
$(n+k)^m = \Theta(n^m)$ is correct, because k is a constant and lower order terms with constant are omitted, except n^m. So, claim I is correct.
$2^{n+1} = O(2^n)$ since $2^{n+1} = 2 \times 2^n \leq 2 \times 2^n$
However 2^{2n} is not $O(2^n)$: by definition we have $2^{2n} = (2^n)^2$ which for no constant c asymptotically may be less than or equal to $c2^n$. Hence, claim II is correct.

1.20 $T(1) = 1$
$T(n+1) = T(n) + \lfloor\sqrt{n+1}\rfloor$ for all $n \geq 1$

$T(m^2) = T(m^2-1) + \lfloor m \rfloor$ for $n = m^2-1$ or $(m^2 = n+1)$

$T(2) = T(1) + \lfloor\sqrt{1+1}\rfloor = 1 + 1 = 2$ for $n = 1$
$T(3) = T(2) + \lfloor\sqrt{2+1}\rfloor = 2 + 1 = 3$ for $n = 2$

$T(4) = T(3) + \lfloor\sqrt{3+1}\rfloor = 3 + 2 = 5$ for $n = 3$

$T(5) = T(4) + \lfloor\sqrt{4+1}\rfloor = 2 + 5 = 7$ for $n = 4$

. . .

$T(9) = T(8) + \lfloor\sqrt{8+1}\rfloor = 13 + 3 = 16$ for $n = 8$

. . .

$T(15) = T(14) + \lfloor\sqrt{14+1}\rfloor = 31 + 3 = 34$ for $n = 14$

$T(16) = T(15) + \lfloor\sqrt{15+1}\rfloor = 34 + 4 = 38$ for $n = 15$

$T(m^2) = T(m^2\text{-}1) + \lfloor m\rfloor$

$T(4) = T(3) + \lfloor\sqrt{2}\rfloor = 3 + 1 = 4$ for $m = 2$

$T(9) = T(8) + \lfloor\sqrt{3}\rfloor = 13 + 1 = 14$ for $m = 3$

We will first verify alternative (a) $\frac{m}{6}(21m-39)+4$

For $m = 2$, $\frac{2}{6}(21\times 2-39)+4 = 1 + 4 = 5$

For $m = 3$, $\frac{3}{6}(21\times 3-39)+4 = 12 + 4 = 16$

For $m = 4$, $\frac{4}{6}(21\times 4-39)+4 = 30 + 4 = 34$

(b) $\frac{m}{6}(4m^2-3m+5)$

For $m = 2$, $\frac{2}{6}(4\times 2^2-3\times 2+5) = 5$ à $T(4) = 5$

For $m = 3$, $\frac{3}{6}(4\times 3^2-3\times 3+5) = 16$ à $T(9) = 16$

For $m = 4$, $\frac{4}{6}(4\times 4^2-3\times 4+5) = 38$ à $T(16) = 38$

Hence choice (b) satisfies the solution of $T(m^2)$ for $m \geq 1$

1.21 (c) $n \log n$

1.22 This algorithm finds the square root of m. The correct choice is (c) $m^{1/2}$.

1.23 This algorithm contains one for-loop which executes n times. As this is linear, its complexity is $\Theta(n)$.

1.24 This recursive function executes 2^n-1 times. Hence, complexity is the order of $2^n = O(2^n)$. Alternatively, we can analyze in the following way:
If we let $T(n)$ represent the number of recursive calls, the recurrence relation will be as follows:

$$T(n) = \begin{cases} 1 & \textit{if} \quad n = 1 \\ 2T(n-1)+1 & \textit{if} \quad n > 1 \end{cases} \qquad (1.3)$$

The solution of this recurrence relation is $T(n) = 2^n - 1$, for $n \geq 1$.

1.25 Using substitution method, we have:

$T(2) = 2T(2\text{-}1) + 2 = 2T(1) + 2 = 2 + 2 = 4$ for $n = 2$
$T(3) = 2T(3\text{-}1) + 3 = 2T(2) + 3 = 8 + 3 = 11$ for $n = 3$
$T(4) = 2T(4\text{-}1) + 4 = 2T(3) + 4 = 22 + 4 = 26$ for $n = 4$
$T(5) = 2T(5\text{-}1) + 5 = 2T(4) + 5 = 52 + 5 = 57$ for $n = 5$

(a) $2^{n+1}\text{-}n\text{-}2$
$2^2\text{-}1\text{-}2 = 4 - 3 = 1$ for $n = 1$
$2^3\text{-}2\text{-}2 = 8 - 4 = 4$ for $n = 2$
$2^4\text{-}3\text{-}2 = 16 - 5 = 11$ for $n = 3$
$2^5\text{-}4\text{-}2 = 32 - 6 = 26$ for $n = 4$
$2^6\text{-}5\text{-}2 = 64 - 7 = 57$ for $n = 5$

Hence, the choice (a) satisfies the recurrence equation.

1.26 The solution for this recurrence relation is given by $T(n) = n + n\log_2 n$.
In asymptotic notation, (a) and (d) are upper bounds and (c) is the lower bound. (b) $\Theta(n \log n)$ is false.

1.27 Suppose $n = 8$ ($i = n = 8$ initially)
$j = 8/2 + 4/2 + 2/2 = 4 + 2 + 1 = 7$ (3 terms)
$\log_2(8) = 3$

Suppose $n = 64$ ($i = n = 64$ initially) (6 terms)
$j = 64/2 + 32/2 + 16/2 + 8/2 + 4/2 + 2/2 = 32 + 16 + 8 + 4 + 2 + 1 = 63$
$\log_2(64) = 6$

Suppose $n = 512$ ($i = n = 512$ initially)
$j = 512/2 + 256/2 + \ldots + 2/2 = 256 + 128 + \ldots + 1 = 511$ (9 terms)
$\log_2(512) = 9$

If n is a power of 2, then 1/2 of n is added to j, 1/2 of previously reduced n is added, and so on up to $\log_2(n)$ terms.

In general, $j = n/2 + (n/2)/2 + ((n/2)/2)/2 + \ldots + 1$ $\log_2(n)$ terms.

If n is not a power of 2, then there will be minor difference.

Hence, the correct choice is (c) val(j) = $\Theta(n)$.

1.28 The variable j increases in power of 2. If statement $j = j*2$ executes k times, then

2^k **£** n
k **£** $\log_2 n$

Since k is an integer, total number of comparisons is $\lfloor \log_2 n \rfloor + 1$.

1.29 (c) $\Theta(\log_2 \log_2 n)$

1.30 (d) $\Theta(\log_2 \log_2 n)$

1.31 Upper bound may be $\sqrt{n}$ times that *for*-loop gets executed - i.e., $T(n) = O(\sqrt{n})$. Lower bound: for-loop is executed once or twice - hence, $T(n) = \Omega(1)$.

1.32 (b) $\Theta(\log n)$.

CHAPTER 2 Disjoint Sets

2.1 (c) 2.2 (b) 2.3 (d) 2.4 (a) 2.5 (d) 2.6 (a)

2.7 (c) For explanation, refer section 2.2.1

2.8 (c) For explanation, refer section 2.2.1

2.9 (b) $O(\log_2 n)$. Since n *Union* operations take $O(n\log_2 n)$, the amortized time of *Union* is = $O(n\log_2 n)/n = O(\log_2 n)$.

2.10(c) 2.11(c) 2.12(b) 2.13(a) 2.14(b) 2.15(c) 2.16(b)

2.17(a) Notice the following undirected graph and its spanning trees.

	Undirected graph	Spanning trees
$n = 3$	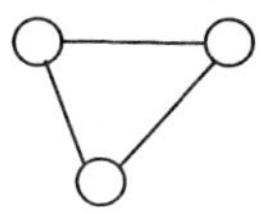	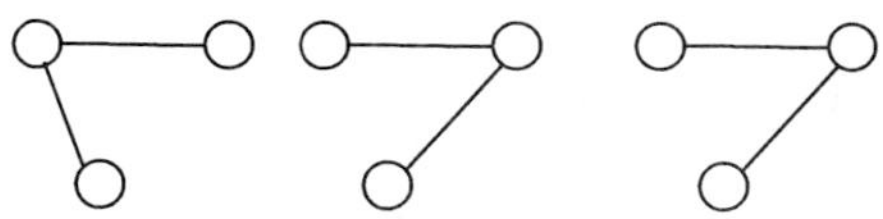 *edges* = n-1 = 2
$n = 4$	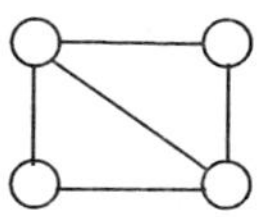	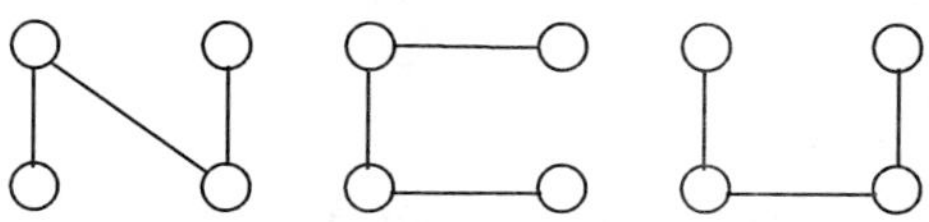 *edges* = n-1 = 3

2.18(c) 2.19(c) 2.20(b) 2.21(a) 2.22(a) 2.23(b) 2.24(b)

2.25(c) 2.26(b) 2.27(d) 2.28(c) 2.29(d) 2.30(a) 2.31(d)

2.32(c) 2.33(c) 2.34(d) 2.35(d) 2.36(b)

CHAPTER 3 Divide and Conquer

3.1 (c)	3.2 (d)	3.3 (c)	3.4 (d)	3.5 (d)	3.6 (b)	3.7 (d)
3.8 (b)	3.9 (c)	3.10(c)	3.11(a)	3.12(a)	3.13(a)	3.14(c)
3.15(d)	3.16(c)	3.17(c)	3.18(c)	3.19(a)	3.20(b)	3.21(c)
3.22(c)	3.23(a)	3.24(b)				

CHAPTER 4 Greedy Method

4.1 (b)	4.2 (a)	4.3 (c)	4.4 (b)	4.5 (c)	4.6 (a)	4.7 (c)
4.8 (b)	4.9 (b)	4.10(b)	4.11(d)	4.12(a)	4.13(c)	4.14(d)
4.15(a)	4.16(b)	4.17(b)	4.18(d)	4.19(a)	4.20(b)	4.21(b)
4.22(a)	4.23(a)	4.24(b)	4.25(d)			

CHAPTER 5 Dynamic Programming

5.1 (d)	5.2 (b)	5.3 (b)	5.4 (a)	5.5 (a)	5.6 (a)	5.7 (c)
5.8 (c)	5.9 (b)	5.10(d)	5.11(a)	5.12(a)	5.13(c)	5.14(b)
5.15(c)	5.16(a)	5.17(a)	5.18(d)	5.19(c)	5.20(d)	5.21(b)
5.22(b)	5.23(c)	5.24(a)	5.25(a)			

CHAPTER 6 Backtracking

6.1 (a)	6.2 (c)	6.3 (b)	6.4 (a)	6.5 (d)	6.6 (a)	6.7 (a)
6.8 (a)	6.9 (b)	6.10(d)	6.11(a)	6.12(a)	6.13(a)	6.14(a)
6.15(a)						

CHAPTER 7 Branch and Bound

7.1 (b)	7.2 (a)	7.3 (c)	7.4 (c)	7.5 (d)	7.6 (a)	7.7 (b)
7.8 (d)	7.9 (b)	7.10(d)	7.11(c)	7.12(c)	7.13(b)	7.14(c)

CHAPTER 8 NP-Complete Problems

8.1 (a)	8.2 (b)	8.3 (a)	8.4 (b)	8.5 (c)	8.6 (a)	8.7 (d)
8.8 (d)	8.9 (c)	8.10(b)	8.11(a)	8.12(b)	8.13(a)	8.14(a)
8.15(b)	8.16(b)	8.17(a)	8.18(c)	8.19(b)	8.20(c)	

APPENDIX-B

ANSWERS AND HINTS TO EXERCISES

CHAPTER 1 Introduction to Algorithms

1.1 An *algorithm* is a finite sequence of instructions, each of which has a clear meaning and can be performed with a fine amount of effort in a finite length of time. In addition, the algorithm must satisfy the following criteria (norms):

(1) *Input*: No input or more data items are supplied.
(2) *Output*: At least one data item is produced.
(3) *Definiteness*: Each instruction is clear and unambiguous.
(4) *Finiteness*: If we trace out the instructions of an algorithm, then for all cases, the algorithm terminates after a finite number of steps.
(5) *Effectiveness*: Every instruction must be basic so that a person using pencil and paper can carry it out, in principle. It is not enough that each operation is definite as in criterion (3); it also must be feasible.

1.3 The optimal computing time and storage requirements of an algorithm decide the better algorithm. Every algorithm must use some of a computer's resources to complete its task. The resources most relevant to efficiency are *central processor time* (CPU time) and *internal memory* (RAM). In other words, the two important ways to characterize the effectiveness of an algorithm are its space complexity and time complexity.

1.6 $f(n) = \frac{x^n}{n!} = \frac{x}{1} \times \frac{x}{2} \times \frac{x}{3} \times \ldots \times \frac{x}{n}$

B1.6: Algorithm(x, n)

```
1. fn = x
2. For k = 2 to n do
3.     fn = fn * x / k
4. Endfor
5. Return fn
```

Line-1 and line-5 count for one unit each. Line-3 counts for three units per time executed (one multiplication, one division, and one assignment) and is executed n-1 times, for a total of 3(n-1) units. Line-2 has the hidden costs of initializing k, testing $k \leq n$, and incrementing k. The total of all these is 1 to initialize, n for all the tests, and n-1 for all the increments, which is $2n$. Thus, the run time of this algorithm is given by: $T(n) = 2 + 3(n-1) + 2n = 5n-1$.

1.7 Algorithm to test whether a number n is a factorial number:

```
B1.7: Algorithm(n)
1.  Set fact, k to 1
2.  While( true )
3.      fact = fact * k
4.      If fact = n, then
5.          Print "n is a factorial number"
6.          Go to 14
7.      Endif
8.      If fact > n, then
9.          Print "n is not a factorial number"
10.         Go to 14
11.     Endif
12.     Add 1 to k
13. Endwhile
14. Return
```

1.8 *Refer* Algorithm 1.2.

1.9 Algorithm that inputs three integers and outputs them in ascending order.

```
B1.9: Algorithm()
Input a, b , c
If a > b, then
    Swap(a, b)
Endif
If( a > c ), then
    Swap(a, c)
Endif
If( b > c ), then
    Swap(b, c)
Endif
Print a, b, c
Return
```

1.10 Horner's rule is a means for evaluating a polynomial using a minimum number of multiplications.

$$P(x)=\sum_{k=0}^{n}a_kx^k=a_0+x(a_1+x(a_2+...+x(a_{n-1}+xa_n)...))$$

$P(x)$ is evaluated for given coefficients $a_0, a_1, \ldots, a_n$ and value x.

```
B1.10: Algorithm(a[1..n], x, n)
y = 0
i = n
While i ≥ 0
    y = a[i] + x * y
    i = i - 1
Endwhile
Return y
```

1.11 Testing a program consists of two phases: debugging and profiling (or performance measurement). *Debugging* is the process of executing programs on sample data sets to find whether wrong results occur and, if so, to correct them. Debugging can only point to the presence of errors. More than one programmer can develop programs for the same problem and verify the output with different input data sets.

Profiling is the process of executing a correct program on data sets and measuring its time and space. These timing figures are used to confirm the previous analysis and point out logical errors. This way, we can optimize the performance of algorithms.

1.12 In order to choose between data structures and algorithms, the efficiency of competing data structures (in terms of space required) and competing algorithms (in terms of time used) must be compared. The best test of a data structure or algorithm is to measure its efficiency. This is called a *posteriori* (after the fact) analysis. Since the choice of a data structure or algorithm is generally made before a program is written, a *priori* (before the fact) analysis is necessary.

The priori estimates refer to performance analysis and the posteriori analysis to performance measurement. A frequency count of statements executed is the most direct form of a priori analysis of the time used by an algorithm. A frequency count of data structure elements used is the most direct form of a priori analysis of data structures.

1.13 Omega-notation provides an *asymptotic lower bound.* Given functions $f(n)$ and $g(n)$, we say that $f(n)$ is $\Omega(g(n))$ if there are positive constants $c > 0$ and $n_0 \geq 1$ such that

$$f(n) \geq cg(n) \quad \text{for all } n,\ n \geq n_0$$

For example, let $f(n) = 2n^2 + 7n - 10$ and $g(n) = n^2$

Since with $c = 1$ and for $n \geq n_0 = 2$, we have $2n^2 + 7n - 10 \geq cn^2$.

Verification: $2(2^2) + 7(2) - 10 \geq 1(2^2)$.

$8 + 14 - 10 = 12 \geq 4$.

Hence, $f(n) \geq cg(n)$.

1.15

B1.15: Algorithm(n)	Count of primitive operations
$f_1 = 0;\ f_2 = 1$	2
Print f_1, f_2	1
For $i = 3$ to n do	$1 + (n\text{-}2) + (n\text{-}1)$
$f_3 = f_1 + f_2$	$2(n\text{-}2)$
Print f_3	$(n\text{-}2)$
$f_1 = f_2$	$(n\text{-}2)$
$f_2 = f_3$	$(n\text{-}2)$
Endfor	
Return	

Total number of primitive operations = $T(n) = 7n–9$ à $O(n)$

1.16 Algorithm that computes x^n for any real number x and integer n (where n is an integral power of 2).

```
B1.16: Algorithm(x, n)
k = log2(n)        // If n = 8 (or 2^3), then k = log2(8) = 3
y = x
For i = 1 to k do
      y = y * y
Endfor
Return y
```

If $n = 2^k$ for some integer k, then $k = \log_2(n)$. Hence, the running time of this algorithm is $\Theta(\log_2 n)$.

1.17 Derive the function $f(n) = 12n^2 + 6n$ is $o(n^3)$ and $\omega(n)$.

The function $f(n) = o(g(n))$ if and only if

$$\lim_{n\to\infty} \frac{f(n)}{g(n)} = 0$$

$f(n) = 12n^2 + 6n$ and $g(n) = n^3$

$$\lim_{n\to\infty} \frac{12n^2 + 6n}{n^3} = 0,$$ and also $f(n) < cg(n)$.

"$f(n) = o(g(n))$" means for all $c > 0$ there exists some $n_0 > 0$ such that $0 \leq f(n) < cg(n)$ for all $n \geq n_0$.

For $n \geq 7$ and $c = 2$, $f(n) = 12n^2 + 6n = 630$, and $cg(n) = 2n^3 = 686$.

Hence, $f(n) = 12n^2 + 6n$ is $o(n^3)$.

The function $f(n) = \omega(g(n))$ if and only if

$$\lim_{n\to\infty} \frac{g(n)}{f(n)} = 0$$

$f(n) = 12n^2 + 6n$ and $g(n) = n$

$$\lim_{n\to\infty} \frac{n}{12n^2 + 6n} = 0,$$ and also $f(n) > cg(n)$.

For $n \geq 2$ and $c = 18$, $f(n) = 12(2^2) + 6(2) = 60$, and $cg(n) = 18(2) = 36$.
Hence, $f(n) = 12n^2 + 6n$ is $\omega(n)$.

1.18 Show that $n^3\log_2 n$ is $\omega(n^3)$.

Let $f(n) = n^3\log_2 n$ and $g(n) = n^3$

$f(n)$ is $\omega(g(n))$ if and only if there exist positive constants c and n_0 such that $f(n) > cg(n)$, for all $n \geq n_0$. Alternatively, $f(n)$ is $\omega(g(n))$, if and only if

$$\lim_{n\to\infty} \frac{f(n)}{g(n)} = \infty$$

$$\lim_{n\to\infty} \frac{n^3\log_2 n}{n^3} = \lim_{n\to\infty} \log_2 n = \infty$$ for sufficiently large values of n

Hence, $n^3\log_2 n$ is $\omega(n^3)$.

1.19 Time complexity: The number of machine instructions which a program executes during its running time is called its *time complexity*. This number depends primarily on the size of the program's input. Time taken by a program is the sum of the compile time and the run time. In time complexity, we consider run time only. The time required by an algorithm is determined by the number of elementary operations.

The following primitive operations that are independent from the programming language are used to calculate the running time:

- Assigning a value to a variable
- Calling a function
- Performing an arithmetic operation
- Comparing two variables
- Indexing into an array or following a pointer reference
- Returning from a function

The following fragment shows how to count the number of primitive operations executed by an algorithm.

```
sum = 0;                // add 1 to the time count
for(i=0; i<n; i++)      // add n+1 to the time count
```

```
{   sum = sum + a[i]; }        // add n to the time count
print sum;                     // add 1 to the time count
```

This algorithm has the frequency count of $2n+3$ for time- that is, $T(n) = 2n+3$.

1.21 Consider a polynomial in n of the form

$$f(n) = \sum_{i=0}^{m} a_i n^i = a_m n^m + a_{m-1} n^{m-1} + a_2 n^2 + a_1 n + a_0, \text{ then } f(n) = O(n^m).$$

$$f(n) \le \sum_{i=0}^{m} |a_i| n^i$$

$$\le \sum_{i=0}^{m} |a_i| n^{i-m+m} \qquad m \text{ is added and subtracted to the power of } n.$$

$$\le \sum_{i=0}^{m} |a_i| n^{i-m} n^m$$

$$\le n^m \sum_{i=0}^{m} |a_i| n^{i-m}$$

$$\le n^m \left[|a_0| n^{-m} + |a_1| n^{1-m} + |a_2| n^{2-m} + \ldots + |a_m| n^{m-m} \right]$$

$$\le n^m \left[|a_0| + |a_1| + |a_2| + \ldots + |a_m| \times 1 \right] \quad n^{\text{-ve values}} \text{ are neglected for } n \ge 1.$$

$$\le n^m \sum_{i=0}^{m} |a_i|$$

Hence, $f(n) = O(n^m)$ assuming m is fixed.

1.22 Show that $f(n) = 8n+128 = O(n^2)$.
Given functions $f(n)$ and $g(n)$, we say that $f(n)$ is $O(g(n))$ if there are positive constants $c > 0$ and $n_0 \ge 1$ such that

$$f(n) \le cg(n) \text{ for all } n, n \ge n_0$$

Let $f(n) = 8n+128$, and $g(n) = n^2$
For $n \ge 16$ and $c = 1$, $f(n) \le g(n)$
We verify this by substituting for $n = 16$, we have

$$8(16) + 128 \le (16^2)$$

$$256 \le 256$$

We have $f(n) = O(g(n))$. Hence, $8n+128 = O(n^2)$.

1.23 Show that $f(n)+g(n) = O(n^2)$ where $f(n) = 3n^2 - n + 4$ and $g(n) = n\log n+5$.

$f(n) + g(n) = 3n^2 - n + 4 + n \log n + 5 = 3n^2 + (\log n - 1)n + 9$
By Big-Oh definition, we have $3n^2 + (\log n - 1)n + 9 \le cn^2$
This is true for $c = 4$ and $n_0 \ge 4$ à $3(4^2) + (2-1)4 + 9 \le 4(4^2)$ or $61 \le 64$.
Hence, $f(n)+g(n) = O(n^2)$.

1.24 Show that $f(n) = 4n^2 - 64n + 288 = \Omega(n^2)$.

Given functions $f(n)$ and $g(n)$, we say that $f(n)$ is $\Omega(g(n))$ if there are positive constants $c > 0$ and $n_0 \geq 1$ such that

$$f(n) \geq cg(n) \quad \text{for all } n, n \geq n_0$$

$f(n) = 4n^2 - 64n + 288$, and $g(n) = n^2$
This is true for $c = 1$ and $n_0 \geq 15$ à $4(15^2) - 64(15) + 288 \geq 1(15^2)$.
This is $228 \geq 225$. Hence, $f(n) = 4n^2 - 64n + 288 = \Omega(n^2)$.

1.25 Show that $f_1(n) + f_2(n) = O(\max(g_1(n), g_2(n)))$ where $f_1(n) = O(g_1(n))$ and $f_2(n) = O(g_2(n))$.

For all $n \geq 1$, $f_1(n) \leq \max(g_1(n), g_2(n))$ and $f_2(n) \leq \max(g_1(n), g_2(n))$. Therefore: $f_1(n) + f_2(n) \leq \max(g_1(n), g_2(n)) + \max(g_1(n), g_2(n))$

$f_1(n) + f_2(n) \leq 2 \max(g_1(n), g_2(n))$ By definition, $f(n) \leq cg(n)$

Thus, $f_1(n) + f_2(n) = O(\max(g_1(n), g_2(n)))$.

1.27 Prove that $f(n) = O(h(n))$ where $f(n) = O(g(n))$ and $g(n) = O(h(n))$.

Since $f(n) = O(g(n))$, there exists n_0 and c such that for all $n \geq n_0$, $f(n) \leq cg(n)$.
Similarly, since $g(n) = O(h(n))$, there exists n_0' and c' such that for all $n \geq n_0$', $g(n) \leq c'h(n)$. Therefore, for all $n \geq \max(n_0, n_0')$, $f(n) \leq cc'h(n)$.
Hence, $f(n) = O(h(n))$.

1.28 Let $f(n)$ and $g(n)$ be asymptotically nonnegative functions. Using the basic definition of Θ-notation, prove that $\max(f(n), g(n)) = \Theta(f(n) + g(n))$.

This means that there exists positive constants c_1, c_2 and n_0 such that,

$$0 \leq c_1(f(n) + g(n)) \leq \max(f(n), g(n)) \leq c_2(f(n) + g(n)) \quad \text{for all } n \geq n_0.$$

Selecting $c_2 = 1$ clearly shows the third inequality since the maximum must be smaller than the sum. c_1 should be selected as 1/2, since the maximum is always greater than the weighted average of $f(n)$ and $g(n)$. Note the significance of the "asymptotically nonnegative" assumption. The first inequality could not be satisfied otherwise.

1.29 Let $f(n)$ and $g(n)$ be asymptotically positive functions. Prove or disprove each of the following conjectures.

(a) $f(n) = O(g(n))$ implies $g(n) = O(f(n))$.
No. $f(n) = O(g(n))$ does not imply $g(n) = O(f(n))$.
Clearly, $n = O(n^2)$, but $n^2 \neq O(n)$.

(b) $f(n) + g(n) = \Theta(\min(f(n), g(n)))$.
No. $f(n) + g(n)$ is not $\Theta(\min(f(n), g(n)))$.
As an example, notice that $n+1 \neq \Theta(\min(n, 1) = \Theta(1)$.

(c) $f(n) = O(g(n))$ implies $\log_2(f(n)) = O(\log_2(g(n)))$, where $\log_2(g(n)) \geq 1$ and $f(n) \geq 1$ for all sufficiently large n.

Yes. $f(n) = O(g(n))$ implies $\log_2(f(n))=O(\log_2(g(n)))$, provided that $f(n)\geq 1$ and $\log_2(g(n)) \geq 1$. We have that:

$f(n) \leq cg(n) \Rightarrow \log_2(f(n)) \leq \log_2(cg(n)) = \log_2 c + \log_2 g(n)$

To show that this is smaller than $b\log_2 g(n)$, we set $\log_2 c + \log_2 g(n) = b\log_2 g(n)$. Dividing by $\log_2 g(n)$ yields:

$$b = \frac{\log_2 c + \log_2 g(n)}{\log_2 g(n)} = \frac{\log_2 c}{\log_2 g(n)} + 1 \leq \log_2 c + 1$$

The last inequality holds since $\log_2 g(n) \geq 1$.

(d) $f(n) = O(g(n))$ implies $2^{f(n)} = O(2^{g(n)})$.
No. $f(n) = O(g(n))$ does not imply $2^{f(n)} = O(2^{g(n)})$. If $f(n) = 2n$ and $g(n) = n$, we have that $2n \leq 2 \times n$, but not $2^{2n} \leq c2^n$ for any constant c.

(e) $f(n) = O((f(n))^2)$.
Yes and No. If $f(n) < 1$ for large n, then $f(n)^2 < f(n)$ and the upper bound will not hold. Otherwise $f(n) > 1$ and the statement is trivially true.

(f) $f(n) = O(g(n))$ implies $g(n) = \Omega(f(n))$.
Yes. $f(n) = O(g(n))$ implies $g(n) = \Omega(f(n))$. We have $f(n) \leq cg(n)$ for positive c and thus $(1/c)f(n) \leq g(n)$.

(g) No. $f(n)$ not $= \Theta(f(n/2))$.
Clearly 2^n not $\leq c2^{n/2} = c\sqrt{2^n}$ for any constant c if n is sufficiently large.

(h) Yes. $f(n) + o(f(n)) = \Theta(f(n))$.
Let $h(n) = o(f(n))$.
Since for all $n \geq 1$, $f(n) + h(n) \geq f(n)$, then $f(n) + h(n) = \Omega(f(n))$.
Since $h(n) = o(f(n))$, then there exists n_0 such that for all $n > n_0$,
$h(n) \leq f(n)$.
Therefore, for all $n > n_0$, $f(n) + h(n) \leq 2f(n)$ and so $f(n) + h(n) = O(f(n))$.

1.30 *Refer* Example 1.20

1.34 Monte Carlo algorithm for finding the majority element in an array.

An array a of n natural numbers has a *majority element* x, if the number of occurrences of x in a is greater than $n/2$. For example, the array: {3, 3, 4, 2, 4, 4, 2, 4, 4} has a majority element (4), whereas the array: {3, 3, 4, 3, 4, 4, 2, 4} does not.

Monte Carlo algorithm always returns a result, but the result may not always be correct. We attempt to minimize the probability of an incorrect result, and using the random element, multiple runs of the algorithm will reduce the probability of incorrect results.

By choosing an element at random and testing to see if it is a majority element we get a Monte Carlo (probabilistic or randomized) algorithm.

B1.34: Algorithm(a[1..n], n)

```
i = random(1..n)
x = a[i]
k = 0
For i = 1 to n do
      If( a[i] = x ) then
            k = k + 1
      Endif
Endfor
Return ( k > n/2 )
```

Here, random(1..n) is a uniform random selection of integers between 1 and n. Notice that this algorithm returns true exactly when it has selected a majority element, but that it may return false even if there is a majority element. However, if there is a majority element, then the probability of returning false is less than 1/2, since a majority element occupies more than half the array. Because of the random element, repeatedly running this algorithm will increase our confidence in the result: If it ever returns true, then there is a majority element. If after m runs every result is false, the probability of having a majority element is less than $1/2^m$.

CHAPTER 2 Disjoint Sets

2.3 (a) Unions are performed arbitrarily:

8 elements, initially in different sets

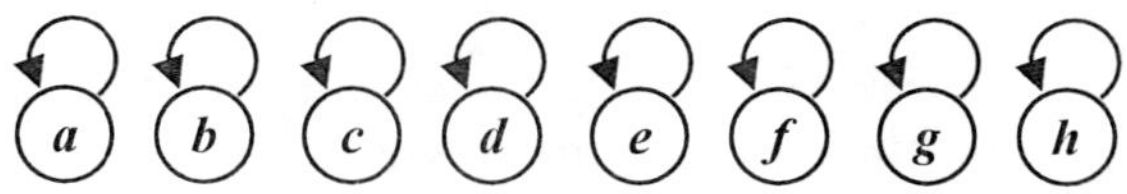

After *Union*(a, b), *Union*(e, f), *Union*(g, h).

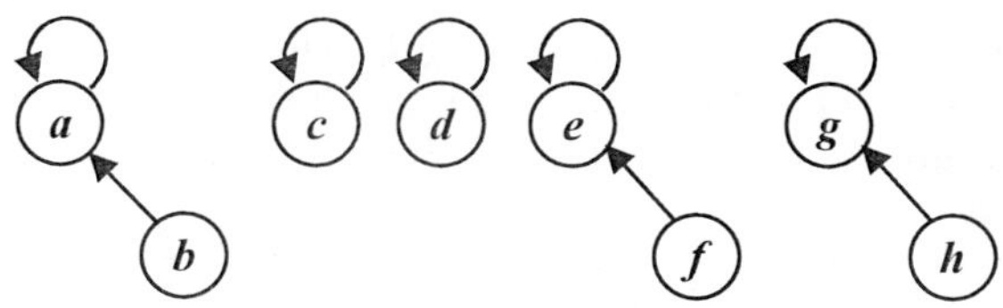

After *Union*(e, g).

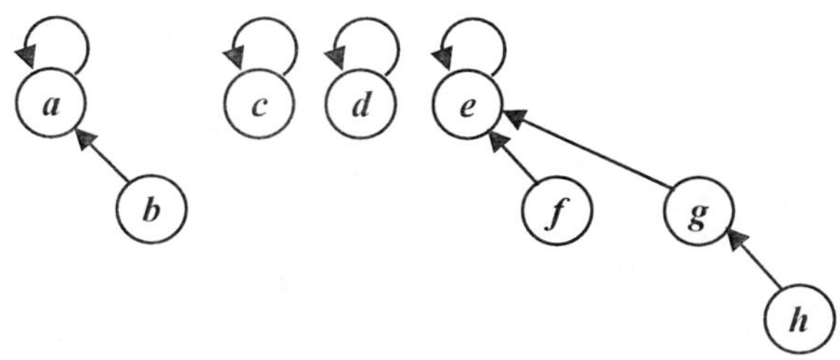

After
Union(*d*, *e*).

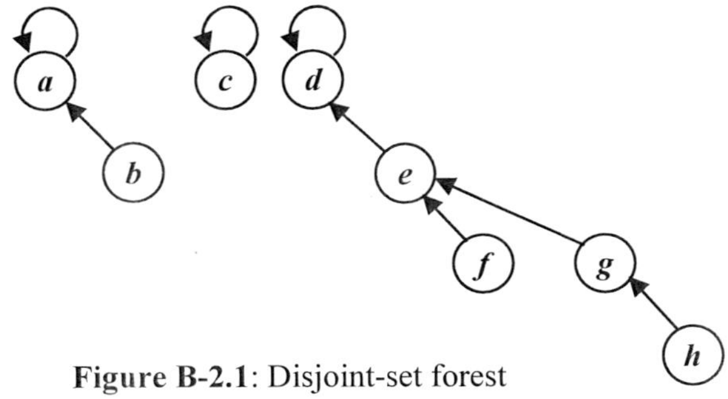

Figure B-2.1: Disjoint-set forest

(b) Unions are performed union-by-rank:
The tree formed by the set {*d*, *e*, *f*, *g*, *h*} is deeper as shown in the last part of Figure B-2.1. If the last operation *Union*(*d*, *e*) is performed by making smaller tree {d} as a subtree of {*e*, *f*, *g*, *h*}, then the tree height will be reduced as shown in Figure B-2.2.

Union-by-rank:
After *Union*(*d*, *e*).

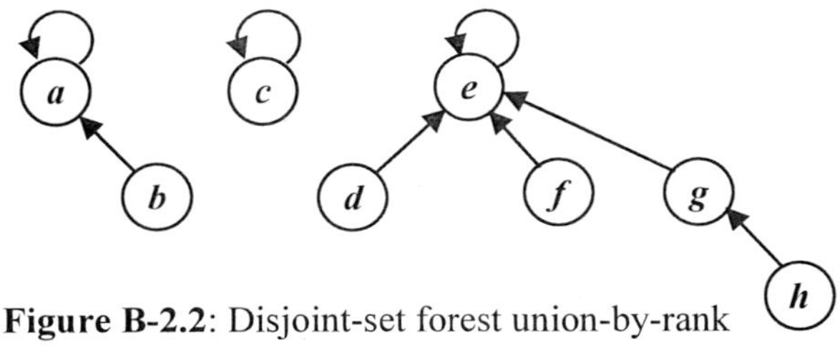

Figure B-2.2: Disjoint-set forest union-by-rank

(c) *Find* operation is performed with path compression on the deepest node. Path compression is performed during *Find* operation and is independent of the *Union* operations. In Figure B-2.2, '*h*' is the deepest node of the tree {*d*, *e*, *f*, *g*, *h*}. Suppose the operation is *Find*(*h*). Then the effect of path compression is that every node on the path from '*h*' to the root has its parent changed to the root. Figure B-2.3 illustrates the effect of path compression after *Find*(*h*).

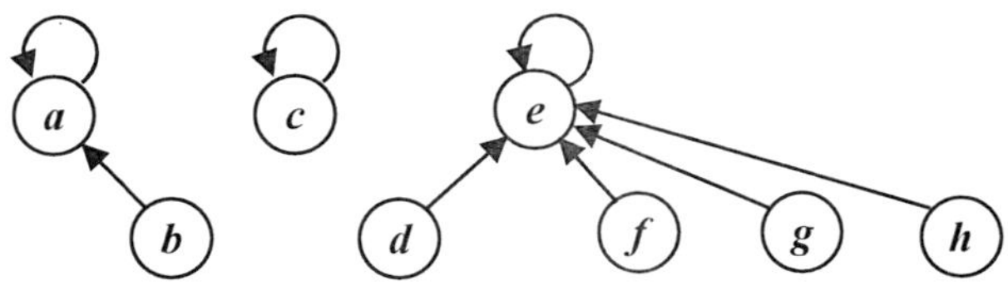

Figure B-2.3: Disjoint-set forest after path compression

2.4 Consider the following disjoint-set forest, perform *Find*(9) operation. Draw the resulting tree after path compression.

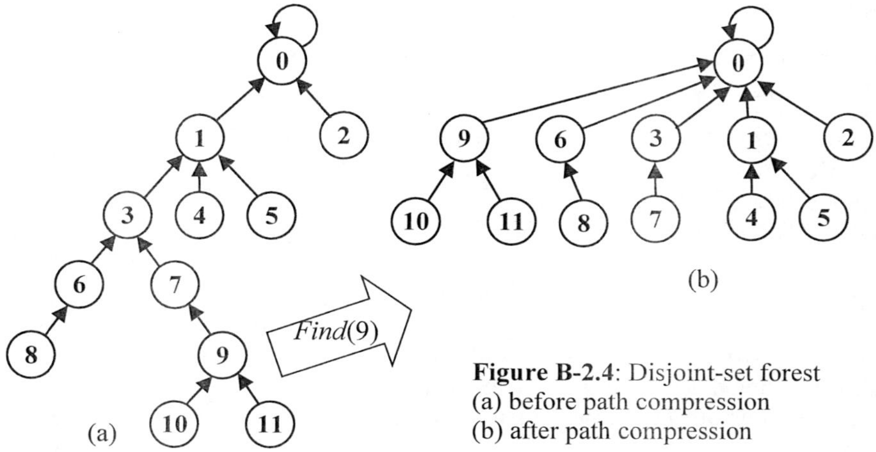

Figure B-2.4: Disjoint-set forest
(a) before path compression
(b) after path compression

2.5 Union-by-height: The root of the shorter tree is made a child of the root of the larger tree.

$$\text{height}_{x\cup y} = \begin{cases} \max(h_x, h_y) & \text{if } h_x \neq h_y \\ h_x + 1 & \text{otherwise} \end{cases}$$

Basis: When $k = 1$, height $= 1 \leq \log_2 1 + 1 \leq 0 + 1 \leq 1$.

Assume $h_k \leq \log_2 k + 1$, for all $1 \leq k < n$.

We show that $h_n \leq \log_2 n + 1$.

Suppose an n-node tree is formed by a-node tree and b-node tree, where $a + b = n$.

Case-1 ($h_a \neq h_b$): Then $h_n = \max(h_a, h_b) \leq \max(\log_2 a+1, \log_2 b+1) < \log_2 n+1$.

Case-2 ($h_a = h_b$): Then $h_n = h_a + 1 \leq (\log_2 a+1)+1 \leq \log_2 a + 2$.

Assume without loss of generality that $a \leq b$. Then, $2a \leq n$ (because $a+b = n$).

So that, $h_n \leq \log_2 a + 2 \leq \log_2(n/2) + 2 = \log_2 n - \log_2 2 + 2 = \log_2 n - 1 + 2 = \log_2 n + 1$.

Hence, a tree with k nodes has a height of at most $\log_2 k + 1$.

2.6 Suppose we have n distinct elements (1, 2, …, n) in n sets. Now let us process the following sequence of union/find operations:

Union(1, 2), *Union*(2, 3), *Union*(3, 4), *Union*(4, 5), …, *Union*(n-1, n), and *Find*(1), *Find*(2), …, *Find*(n-1), *Find*(n).

Since the time taken for a *Union* is constant, the n-1 unions can be processed in $O(n)$ time. However, each *Find* requires following a sequence of parent pointers from the element to be found to the root. Since the time required to process a *Find* for an element at level k of a tree is $O(k)$, the total time needed to process the n finds is $\sum_{k=1}^{n} k = n(n+1)/2 = O(n^2)$.

The total running time of union/find operations is $O(n) + O(n^2) = O(n^2)$.
If $m = n^2$, then the running time of m union/find operations is $O(m)$.

2.7 *Hint*: By taking union-by-rank heuristic, the total running time of union/find operations is $O(n\log_2 n)$.

2.8 (a) Suppose we have four disjoint sets containing each one distinct element.
$\{a\}, \{b\}, \{c\}, \{d\}$, We perform the following unions:

$Union(a, b) = \{a, b\}, \{c\}, \{d\}$
$Union(a, c) = \{a, b, c\}, \{d\}$
$Union(a, b) = \{a, b, c, d\}$

Here we performed 3 unions giving one disjoint set containing 4 elements. In general, if we have n disjoint sets containing each one distinct element: $\{1\}, \{2\}, \{3\}, \ldots, \{n-1\}, \{n\}$, then we will have one single set containing n elements after performing n-1 unions (see the exercise 2.6).

If u unions are performed, then no set contains more than u+1 elements – this is true.

Hint: With the same argument as above in (a), we can prove (b) and (c).

2.9 A spanning tree of a connected graph is a spanning subgraph that is a tree. A spanning tree is not unique unless the graph is a tree. Spanning trees have applications to the design of communication networks.

A *spanning tree* of an undirected graph of n nodes is a set of n-1 edges that connects all nodes. Consider the following connected, undirected graph and notice the number of edges. Also, each node is reachable from every other node. A spanning tree can be obtained by using either DFS or BFS.

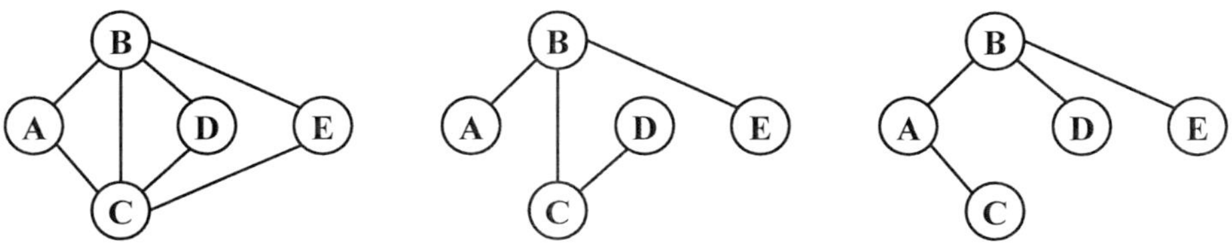

An undirected graph with its DFS and BFS spanning trees

For example, A is connected to B and E through path AàBàE, and C and D by path AàBàCàD.

2.10 (a)

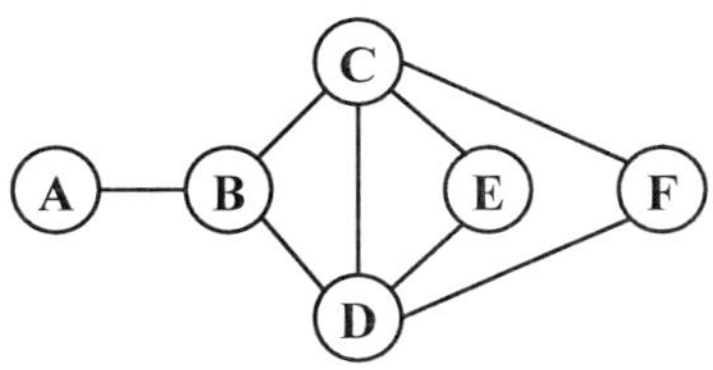

Adjacency lists:

AàBà null
BàAàCàDà null
CàBàDàEàFà null
DàBàCàEàFà null
EàCàDà null
FàCàDà null

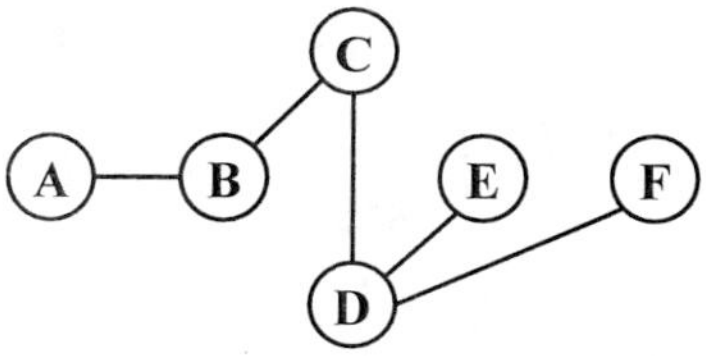

DFS spanning tree with root A

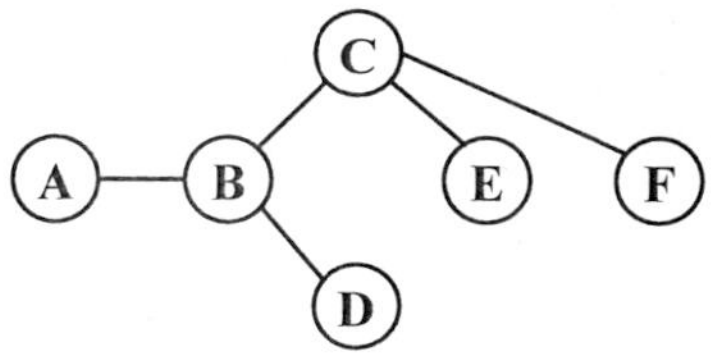

BFS spanning tree with root A

(b)

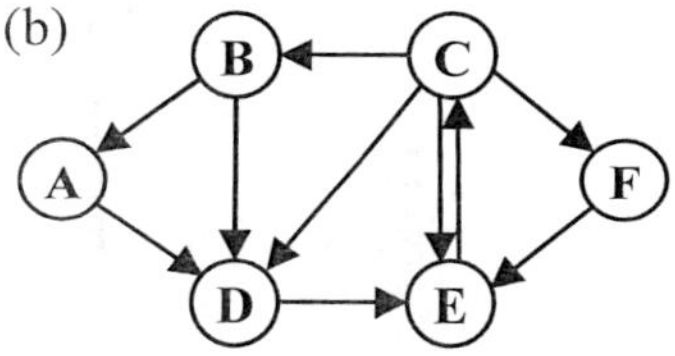

Adjacency lists:

AàDà null
BàAàDà null
CàBàDàEàFà null
DàEà null
EàCà null
FàEà null

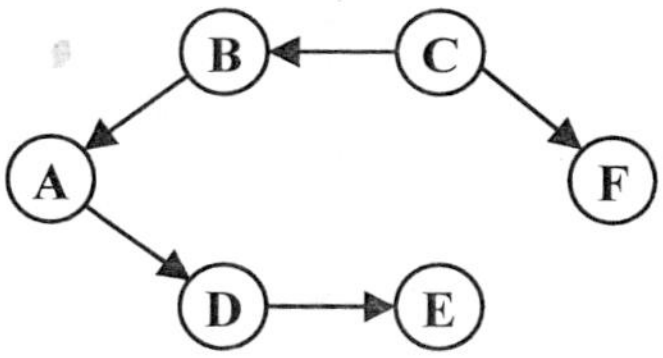

DFS spanning tree with root C

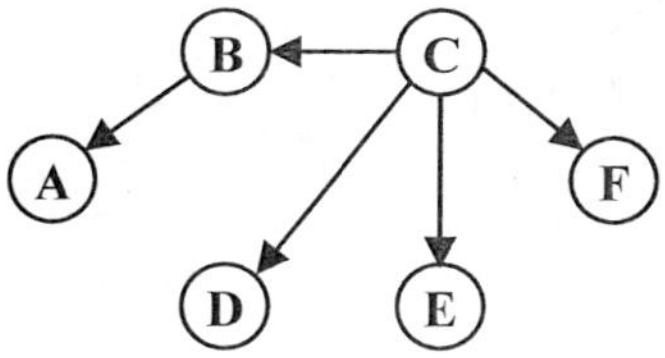

BFS spanning tree with root C

2.11 Let $G = (V, E)$ be a connected undirected graph. An articulation point (or cut vertex) of G is a vertex whose removal disconnects G. A biconnected graph G is a connected graph which has no articulation points. To disconnect a biconnected graph, we must remove at least two vertices. A biconnected component of a graph G is maximal biconnected subgraph (i.e., it is not contained in any larger biconnected subgraph) of G.

DFS can be used to find the articulation points of a graph, and hence the biconnected components. Suppose we run DFS on G, we get a DFS tree. If the root has two or more children, it is an articulation point. Moreover, a leaf is not an articulation point. Any other internal vertex v in the DFS tree, if it has one or more subtrees rooted at a child of v that does not have an edge which climbs higher than v, v is an articulation point.

The following figure illustrates these observations. B, D, F, and H are the articulation points which split the connected graph into six biconnected components.

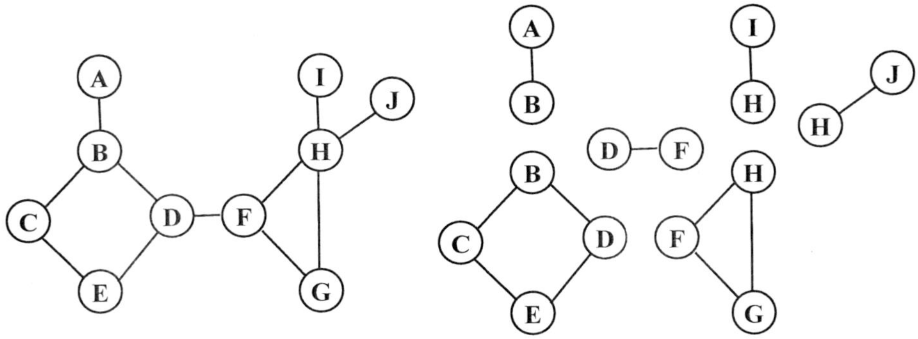

A connected graph with its biconnected components

2.12 If G is a connected undirected graph, then no edge of G can be in two different biconnected components. This can be noticed from the above figure (Ex: 2.11). For example, edge (B, D) is in the component {B, C, D, E}, edge (F, H) in {F, G, H}, and so on.

2.13

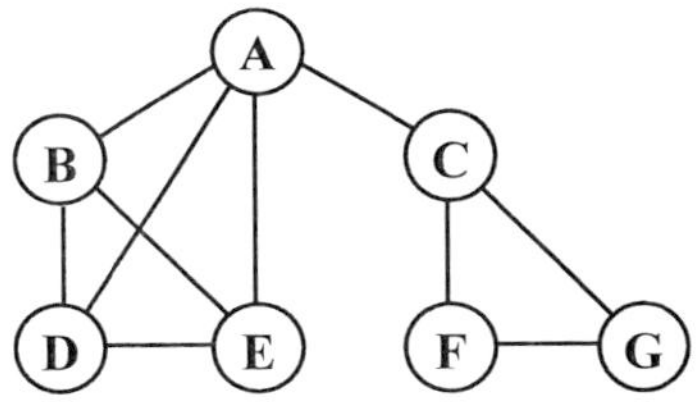

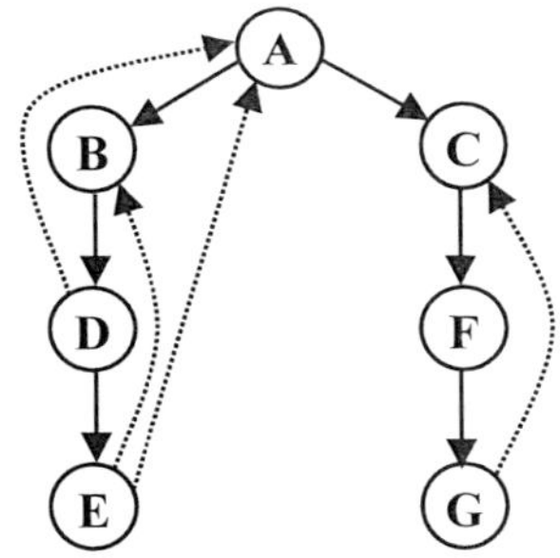

A graph and its DFS tree

By performing preorder traversal of the DFS spanning tree, we mark the *df-number* for each node. As the DFS started with node A, *dfn*(A) is 1. These *df-numbers* and *low* values are tabulated in the following table:

Table: *dfn* and *low* values generated by DFS

Node	A	B	C	D	E	F	G
dfn	1	2	5	3	4	6	7
low	1	1	5	1	1	5	5

By performing postorder traversal, the node E is visited first. At E, there are back edges (E, A) and (E, B). So, *low*(E) = min{*dfn*(E), *dfn*(A), *dfn*(B)} = min{4, 1, 2} = 1. Next node D is visited, and *low*(D) = min{*dfn*(D), *low*(E), *dfn*(A)} = min{3, 1, 1} = 1 (E is a child of D, and (D, A) is a back edge).

After computing *low* values, we consider each node. The root A is an articulation point, because it has two children. Node C is an articulation point, because it has a child F with *low*(F) ≥ *dfn*(C). The other nodes are not articulation points.

2.14 Strongly connected components of the directed graph.

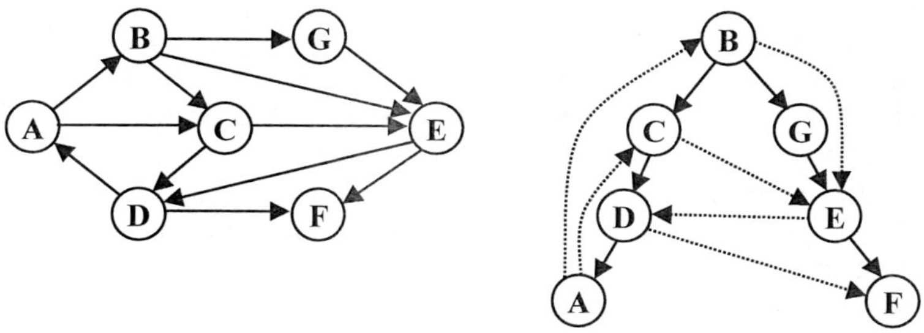

Directed graph and its DFS spanning tree with root B

Tree edges are actually part of the DFS forest. *Forward edges* lead from a node to a *non-child* descendant in the DFS tree. *Back edges* lead to an ancestor in the DFS tree. *Cross edges* lead to neither descendant nor ancestor; they therefore lead to a node that has already been completely explored (that is, already post-visited).

We start DFS at node B. This visits nodes B, C, D, A, G, E, and F. (A, C) and (A, B) are back edges. (B, E) is a forward edge that leads tree node to a descendent. (E, D) is a cross edge.

During DFS, the nodes of *G* are numbered by a postorder traversal of the DFS spanning tree, and all edges in original graph G are reversed, forming G_R. The following graph represents G_R; the numbers are shown against the nodes.

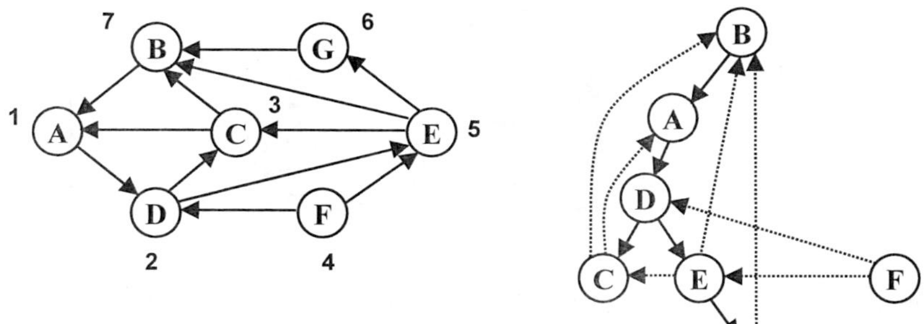

DFS of G_R – strong components are {B, A, D, C, E, G}, {F}

Each of the trees in this DFS spanning forest forms a strongly connected components - this is easier to see if we completely ignore all nontree edges. Thus, the strongly connected components are {B, A, D, C, E, G}, and {F}.

CHAPTER 3 Divide and Conquer

3.1 Control abstraction for Divide and Conquer:

Divide-and-conquer is a top-down technique for designing algorithms. These algorithms perform the following: (1) Divide the problem into several sub-problems that are similar to the original problem but smaller in size, (2) Solve the sub-problem (recursively, successively and independently), and (3) Then combine these solutions to sub-problems to create a solution to the original problem.

Control Abstraction is an algorithm-like structure. It is a procedure whose flow is clear but whose primary operations are specified elsewhere and hence unclear. Let us use a control abstraction to elaborate the idea behind the divide and conquer (dc) strategy

```
dc(P)
{   If (P is small)
        return SimpleFunc(P);     //Simple function that can solve P
    Else
    {   Divide P into smaller instances P1, P2, ..., Pk for k ≥ 1;
        Apply dc() to each instance;
        Return comb_instances(dc(P1), dc(P2), ..., dc(Pk));
    }
}
```

3.5 m = number of leaves in a full binary tree is 2^d where d is the depth of the tree.

$$\sum_{i=1}^{m} 2^{-d_i} = \left(\frac{1}{2^{d_1}} + \frac{1}{2^{d_2}} + \ldots + \frac{1}{2^{d_m}}\right) = \left(\frac{1}{2^d} + \frac{1}{2^d} + \ldots + \frac{1}{2^d}\right)$$

For full binary tree, $d = d_1 = d_2 = \ldots = d_m$

$$= \frac{1}{2^{\text{d}}}(1 + 1 + \ldots + m \quad 1\text{'s}) = \frac{m}{2^{\text{d}}} = \frac{m}{m} = 1$$

▶ $m = 2^d$

For example, a full binary tree of depth, 2 has 4 leaves.

$$\left(\frac{1}{2^2} + \frac{1}{2^2} + \frac{1}{2^2} + \frac{1}{2^2}\right) = \left(\frac{1}{4} + \frac{1}{4} + \frac{1}{4} + \frac{1}{4}\right) = 1$$

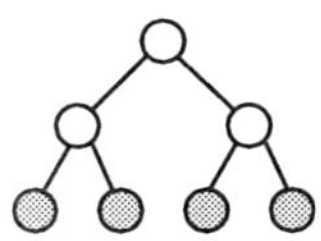

$m = 4$
$d = 2$

Other than full binary tree, the tree contains less than 2^d leaves.

Hence, $\sum_{i=1}^{m} 2^{-d_i} \leq 1$ and the equality is true for full binary tree.

3.6 The following is a modified binary search algorithm – if the search is successful, it returns *mid*, otherwise *high*. The index *high* (= i) satisfies the condition $A[i] < key <$

$A[i+1]$ for unsuccessful search. For unsuccessful case, the condition is: $low > high$ – that is, $A[high] < key < A[low]$.

```
BinarySearch (A[1..n], key)
low = 1;    high = n;
While (low ≤ high)
    mid = (low + high) / 2;
    If (A[mid] > key), then
            high = mid – 1;
    else If (A[mid] < key), then
            low = mid + 1;
    else
            return mid;          // found
    Endif
Endwhile
return high;                     // not found
```

3.7

```
TernarySearch (a[1..n], n, x, low, high)
1.  low = 1;
2.  high = n;
3.  While (low ≤ high)
4.      p = (low + high) / 3;
5.      If( p < low ), then
6.              p = low;
7.      Endif
8.      If (a[p] > x), then
9.              high = p – 1;
10.     else If (a[p] < x), then
11.             low = p + 1;
12.     else
13.             return p;          // found
14.     Endif
15. Endwhile
16. return -1;                     // not found
```

When the pointer p goes outside the range ($p < low$), the statements 5 and 6 adjust the pointer p ($p = low$). The worst-case running time, $T(n)$ of this algorithm occurs when the recursive call is on the larger $2n/3$-element partition.

3.8

```
BinarySearch(a[1..n], n, x, low, high)
low = 1
high = n
While (low ≤ high)
    mid = (low + high) / 2
    If (a[mid] > x), then
        high = mid –1
    else If (a[mid] < x), then
        low = mid +1
    else
        return mid            // found
    Endif
Endwhile
return mid                    // not found
```

Copy the diagonal elements of the *matrix* into one-dimensional array, and call the above BinarySearch(*a, n, x, low, high*) algorithm. '*x*' is the element to be searched. The algorithm returns *mid*. If(*matrix*[*mid*][*mid*] = *x*), then *x* is found at (*mid, mid*) position in the *matrix*. If the search fails, copy the row elements at *mid* (let this *mid* be *i*) and call the BinarySearch() algorithm. Note: we have to adjust the value of *mid* (or index, *i*) while copying the row values. It returns *mid* second time (let this *mid* be *j*). If(*matrix*[*i*][*j*] = *x*), then *x* is found at (*i, j*) position in the *matrix*. If the search is unsuccessful, then *x* is not found in the *matrix*. For these two BinarySearch() calls, the worst-case running time is $\log_2 n + \log_2 n = 2 \log_2 n$ which is less than *n*. Hence, the worst-case running time is $O(n)$.

Consider the following 6 x 6 matrix to search for the element 76.

	1	2	3	4	5	6
1	10	13	15	18	19	21
2	24	27	28	30	33	38
3	41	43	44	47	51	55
4	58	63	66	67	69	73
5	74	**76**	79	81	83	86
6	89	92	94	95	96	99

First call BinarySearch() with array {10, 27, 44, 67, 83, 99} – these are diagonal elements. Element 76 is not found in this vector. It returns *mid* = 5. Next call the algorithm with 5th row vector {74, **76**, 79, 81, 83, 86}. Now the search is successful.

3.9 Divide-and-conquer algorithm to find the maximum and minimum of an array A of n elements.

Suppose we know the maximum and minimum element in both of the $n/2$ sized partitions of an n-element ($n \geq 2$) array. Then in order to find the maximum and minimum element of the entire array we simply need to see which of the two maximum elements is the larger, and which of the two minimums is the smaller. We assume that in a 1-element array the only one element is both the maximum and the minimum element. Accordingly, we present the following algorithm for the maximum and minimum problem.

We assume the array, A is declared globally. The algorithm is invoked with *low* = 1 and *high* = *n* – that is, index of first element and index of last element respectively. And other two parameters are *max* and *min* which are initialized with first element.

```
MaxMin(low, high, max, min)
1.  If( low = high ), then                  // case when n = 1
2.        max = min = A[low];
3.  Else If( low = high-1 ), then           // case when n = 2
4.            If( A[low] > A[high] ), then
5.                max = A[low], min = A[high];
6.            Else max = A[high], min = A[low];
7.            Endif
8.        Else                              // case when n > 2
9.              mid = (low+high)/2;
10.             MaxMin(low, mid, maxleft, minleft);
11.             MaxMin(mid+1, high, maxright, minright);
12.             If(maxleft > maxright), then max = maxleft;
13.             Else max = maxright;
14.             If(minleft < minright), then min = minleft;
15.             Else min = minright;
16.       Endif
17. Endif
```

Let $T(n)$ be the number of comparisons performed by the MaxMin algorithm. When n = 1, there are no comparisons – that is, $T(1) = 0$. When $n = 2$, there is one comparison – that is, $T(2) = 1$. When $n > 2$, it is given as:

$$T(n) = 2T(n/2) + 2$$

MaxMin performs two recursive calls – one on left partition and another on right partition of the array, and then makes two further comparisons (steps 12 to 15) to arrange the maximum and minimum for the entire array.
Since we expect $T(n)$ to be a linear function, let $T(n) = an + b$.
We have $T(2) = 1$ and $T(4) = 2T(4/2) + 2 = 2T(2) + 2 = 2(1) + 2 = 4$,.

Hence, $2a+b = 1$ and $4a+b = 4$, from which we get $a = 3/2$ and $b = -2$.
So $T(n) = 3n/2 - 2$.

3.11 Stable sorting: Elements with the same value appear in the output array in the same order as they do in the input array. That is, ties between two elements are broken by the rule that whichever number appears first in the input array appears first in the output array. In other words, a sorting method is called stable if it preserves the relative order of equal keys in the array.

Example: Unsorted array: 22, 44_1, 77, 11, 44_2, 55, 66, 33.
Sorted array : 11, 22, 33, 44_1, 44_2, 55, 66, 77.

In this example, we have two equal keys (44). The relative positions of the keys 44_1 and 44_2 are retained in the sorted array.

Mergesort is stable. The elements comparison in merge includes equality so that the merge will be stable. Following figure illustrates the mergesort. Notice the elements: 44_1 and 44_2.

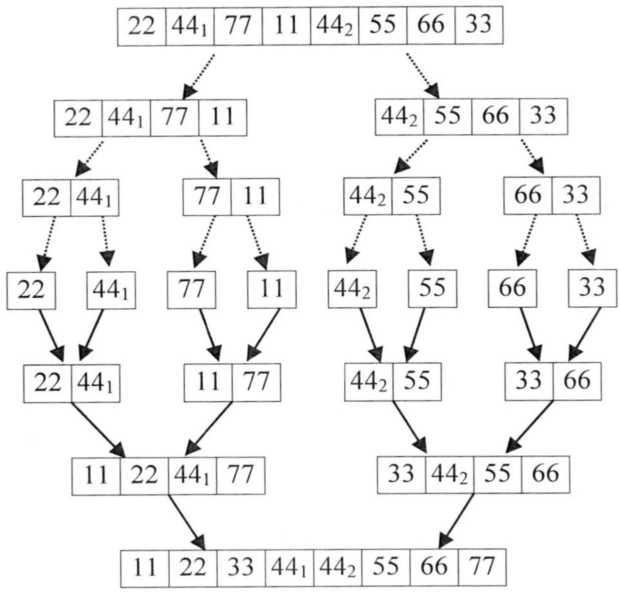

3.12 Mergesort sorts a given array into increasing order as follows:

- Divide the array of size n, into two parts. For example
  n_1 = the first $n/2$ elements in the array.
  n_2 = the remaining elements in the array.
- Sort n_1 and n_2 by recursively calling Mergesort with each one.
- Now we have two sorted arrays containing all the elements from the original array. Use *merge* procedure to combine them, put the result in the array.

Refer Algorithms 3.2 and 3.3. The best-case running time of mergesort is with sorted input array. The worst-case is with either reverse-ordered input or random-ordered input. The average-case is between best and worst cases. The running time of the mergesort is given by the following recurrence relation:

$T(1) = O(1)$ for $n = 1$

$T(n) = 2T(n/2) + O(n)$ for $n > 1$

- *Divide:* The divide step just computes the middle of the subarray, which takes constant time, $O(1)$.
- *Conquer:* We recursively solve two subproblems, each of size $n/2$, which contributes $T(n/2) + T(n/2)$ to the running time.
- *Combine:* The *merge* procedure on an n-element subarray takes time $O(n)$.

The time taken for *divide* and *conquer* steps is the same for sorted, reverse-ordered, and random-ordered input arrays – that is, $2T(n/2)$. We have slight difference in *merge* step – that is, $O(n)$. The complexity of *merge* is as follows:

- Every element in n_1 and n_2 is copied exactly once. Each copy is two accesses, so the total number of accesses due to copying is $2n$.
- The number of comparisons could be as small as $\min(n_1, n_2)$ or as large as $(n-1)$. Each comparison is two accesses.
- In the worst-case, the total number of accesses is $2n+2(n-1) = O(n)$.
- In the best-case, the total number of accesses is $2n + 2 \times \min(n_1, n_2) = O(n)$.
- The average-case is between the worst and best cases and is therefore also $O(n)$.

Hence, the recurrence relation is $T(n) = 2T(n/2) + O(n)$ for all the cases is the same. The running time of mergesort is $O(n\log_2 n)$.

3.13 The merge() procedure uses a local auxiliary array only and merges the two halves of the input array. The first two loops copy the halves into the auxiliary array in a particular manner. The first loop copies from the mid-point down to the first array position as normal. The second, however, copies from position mid+1 to the final position, but in reverse order. The last loop then does the sorted merging by taking care of the data checking at either end of the auxiliary array and moving the auxiliary array start and end pointers on as appropriate. The following is the in-place merge() routine:

```
merge(arr, left, mid, right)              // use local auxiliary: aux[]
{   For i = mid+1 downto left+1  // starts at the end and goes backwards
        aux[i-1] = arr[i-1]
    Endfor
    // go forwards but copies in reverse order
    For j = mid to right-1
        aux[right+mid-j] = arr[j+1]
    Endfor
    For k = left to right              // starting from left to right
        If aux[i] < aux[j] then        // compare 'start' and 'end' values
            arr[k] = aux[i]            // then put appropriate value back
```

```
            i = i + 1               // into our array, thus sorting and
        Else                        // merging. Then update appropriate
            arr[k] = aux[j]         // index pointer.
            j = j – 1
        Endif
    Endfor
}
```

Let us illustrate the merge() procedure by taking the following subarray and filling the auxiliary array with the contents of both subarrays in a specific order:

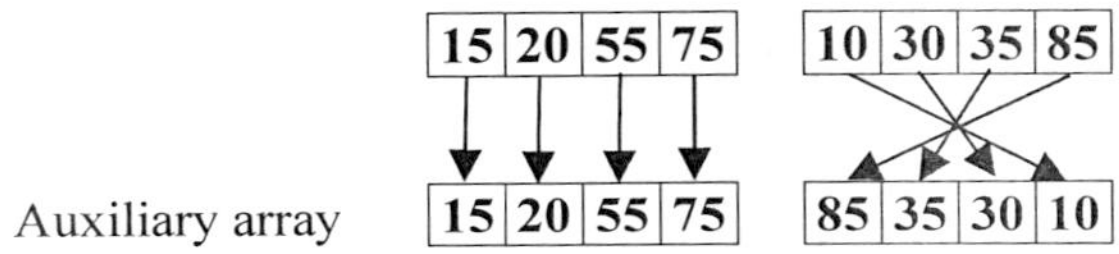

Now we go through auxiliary array at each end-point and do comparison to sort and merge into the original array.

3.14 Trace of the Quicksort: starting pivot = (1+7)/2 = 4

1	2	3	4	5	6	7	pivot	swap
C	**O**	L	L	E	G	**E**	L	O, E
C	E	**L**	L	E	**G**	O	L	L, G
C	E	G	**L**	**E**	L	O	L	L, E
C	E	**G**	**E**	L	L	O	G	G, E
C	E	E	G	L	L	O	Sorted	

The worst-case occurs if given array *arr*[1…*n*] is already sorted. The partitioning routine produces one subproblem with n-1 elements and one with 0 elements. The successive calls to partition will split arrays of length n, n-1, n-2, …, 2 and running time proportional to $n + (n-1) + (n-2) + \ldots + 2 = [(n+2)(n-1)]/2 = O(n^2)$. The worst-case also occurs if *arr*[1…*n*] starts out in reverse order.

3.18 Relative advantages and disadvantages of the partition algorithm:
The best-case behaviour of the quicksort algorithm occurs when in each recursion step the partitioning produces two parts of equal length. In order to sort n elements, in this case the running time is in $O(n\log_2 n)$. This is because the recursion depth is $\log_2(n)$ and on each level there are n elements to be treated.

The worst-case occurs when in each recursion step an unbalanced partitioning is produced, namely that one part consists of only one element and the other part consists of the rest of the elements. Then the recursion depth is n-1 and quicksort runs in time $O(n^2)$. Both the best-case and the average-case are the same - that is, $O(n\log_2 n)$.

The choice of the comparison element determines which partition is achieved. Suppose that the first element of the sequence is chosen as comparison element. This would lead to the worst-case behaviour of the algorithm when the sequence is initially sorted. Therefore, it is better to choose the element in the middle of the sequence as comparison element.

Even better would it be to take the $n/2$-th greatest element of the sequence (the median). Then the optimal partition is achieved. Actually, it is possible to compute the median in linear time. This variant of quicksort would run in time $O(n\log_2 n)$ even in the worst-case.

3.19

```
mergesort(a[1..n], n)

For i = 1 to n do            // Build the queue with array elements.
        insert_que(a[i])
Endfor
inc = 1;
While inc ≤ n
        j = 1;
        While j ≤ n
                For k = 1 to inc do
                        x[k] = delete_que();
                Endfor
                For k = 1 to inc do
                        y[k] = delete_que()
                Endfor
                k1=k2=0;                // Merge x, y
                For k = 1 to 2*inc do
                        If ( x[k1] < y[k2] ), then
                                insert_que(x[k1]);  k1++;
                        Else
                                insert_que(x[k2]);  k2++;
                Endif
                j = j + 2*inc;
        Endwhile
        inc = 2*inc;
Endwhile
For i = 1 to n do   // Copy the elements of queue into the array
        a[i] = delete_que();
Endfor
```

	F							R								
Queue:	10	30	45	15	35	25	20	40								
Delete 2 items			45	15	35	25	20	40								
Merge and insert			45	15	35	25	20	40	10	30						
Delete 2 items					35	25	20	40	10	30						
Merge and insert					35	25	20	40	10	30	15	45				
Delete 2 items							20	40	10	30	15	45				
Merge and insert							20	40	10	30	15	45	25	35		
Delete 2 items									10	30	15	45	25	35		
Merge and insert									10	30	15	45	25	35	20	40

	F							R								
Queue after 1st pass	10	30	15	45	25	35	20	40								
Delete 4 items					25	35	20	40								
Merge and insert					25	35	20	40	10	15	30	45				
Delete 4 items									10	15	30	45				
Merge and insert									10	15	30	45	20	25	35	40

	F							R								
Queue after 2nd pass	10	15	30	45	20	25	35	40								
Delete 8 items																
Merge and insert									10	15	20	25	30	35	40	45

	F							R								
Queue after 3rd pass	10	15	20	25	30	35	40	45								

3.21 Strassen's matrix multiplication:

$$A = \begin{bmatrix} 3 & 2 \\ 4 & 8 \end{bmatrix} \qquad B = \begin{bmatrix} 1 & 5 \\ 9 & 6 \end{bmatrix}$$

Solution: We set $C = A \times B$ and partition each matrix into four sub-matrices. Accordingly, $A_{11} = [3]$, $A_{12} = [2]$, $A_{21} = [4]$, $A_{22} = [8]$, $B_{11} = [1]$, $B_{12} = [5]$, $B_{21} = [9]$, and $B_{22} = [6]$, where

$$C = \begin{bmatrix} C_{11} & C_{12} \\ C_{21} & C_{22} \end{bmatrix}, \quad A = \begin{bmatrix} A_{11} & A_{12} \\ A_{21} & A_{22} \end{bmatrix}, \text{ and } \quad B = \begin{bmatrix} B_{11} & B_{12} \\ B_{21} & B_{22} \end{bmatrix}$$

Applying Strassen's algorithm, we compute the following products:

$P_1 = (A_{11} + A_{22}) \times (B_{11} + B_{22}) = ([3] + [8]) \times ([1] + [6]) = [77]$
$P_2 = (A_{21} + A_{22}) \times B_{11} = ([4] + [8]) \times [1] = [12]$
$P_3 = A_{11} \times (B_{12} - B_{22}) = [3] \times ([5] - [6]) = [-3]$
$P_4 = A_{22} \times (B_{21} - B_{11}) = [8] \times ([9] - [1]) = [64]$
$P_5 = (A_{11} + A_{12}) \times B_{22} = ([3] + [2]) \times [6] = [30]$
$P_6 = (A_{21} - A_{11}) \times (B_{11} + B_{12}) = ([4] - [3]) \times ([1] + [5]) = [6]$
$P_7 = (A_{12} - A_{22}) \times (B_{21} + B_{22}) = ([2] - [8]) \times ([9] + [6]) = [-90]$

From the above products, we can compute C as follows:

$C_{11} = P_1 + P_4 - P_5 + P_7 = [77] + [64] - [30] + [-90] = 21$
$C_{12} = P_3 + P_5 = [-3] + [30] = 27$
$C_{21} = P_2 + P_4 = [12] + [64] = 76$
$C_{22} = P_1 + P_3 - P_2 + P_6 = [77] + [-3] - [12] + [6] = 68$

$$C = \begin{bmatrix} 21 & 27 \\ 76 & 68 \end{bmatrix}$$

The correctness can easily be verified using the naïve algorithm.

CHAPTER 4 Greedy Method

4.2 *Optimization problem* is the one in which the objective function is to be optimized (usually minimized or maximized) subject to some constraints.
Feasible solution is a solution that satisfies the constraints.
Optimal solution is a feasible solution for which the objective function has the best possible value (maximum or minimum).
Example: Minimum Cost Spanning Tree (MST) - a spanning tree that has minimum cost.
Objective function: sum of edge costs.
Constraints: must select n-1 edges of the given n vertex graph, and the selected edges must form a tree.
Feasible solution: MST with less than n-1 edges of the given n vertex graph.

4.3 Most of the problems have n inputs and require us to obtain a subset that satisfies some constraints. Any subset that satisfies these constraints is called a feasible solution. We need to obtain a feasible solution that either maximizes or minimizes a given objective function. A feasible solution that does this is called an optimal solution. The greedy method suggests that one can devise an algorithm that works in stages considering one input at a time. At each stage decision is made regarding whether a particular input is in an optimal solution (using some selection procedure). If the inclusion of the next input into the partially constructed optimal solution will result in an infeasible solution, then this input is not added to the partial solution; otherwise it is added. This version of greedy method is called subset paradigm. For problems that do not call for the selection of an optimal subset in the greedy method, we make decisions by considering the inputs in some order. Each decision is made using an optimization criterion that can be computed using decision already made. Following is the greedy procedure control abstraction for the subset paradigm:

```
Greedy(input A)
    Output is empty;       // Output denotes the solution
    While (solution is not complete)
        Select the best element x in the remaining input A;
        If x is feasible
            Add x to the output;
            Remove x from the remaining input;
        Endif.
    Endwhile.
    Return output.
```

4.4 Optimal storage on tapes for the problem instance $n=3$, $(\ell_1, \ell_2, \ell_3) = (5, 10, 3)$.

Consider three files that are to be stored on a tape of length L. Each file i is of length ℓ_i where i lies between 1 and 3. All files can be stored on the tape if the sum of the lengths of the files is at most L. It is assumed that, whenever a file is to be retrieved the tape is initially positioned at the beginning of tape.

The time taken to access a file on the tape is called the mean retrieval time (MRT). Now the problem is to store the files on the tape so that MRT is minimized. The solution set obtained need not be a subset of data but may be the data set itself in a different sequence.

Length of files A, B and C are 5, 10 and 3 units respectively. All these three files are to be stored on to a tape in some sequence that reduces the average retrieval time. It is required to find a permutation for the three files so that when they are stored on the tape in the order the MRT is minimized. The following table shows the retrieval time for all possible orders.

Order of storage	Retrieval time			Total time	MRT
	A	B	C		
ABC	5	5+10	5+10+3	38	38/3
ACB	5	5+3	5+3+10	31	31/3
BAC	10	10+5	10+5+3	43	43/3
BCA	10	10+3	10+3+5	41	41/3
CAB	3	3+5	3+5+10	29	29/3
CBA	3	3+10	3+10+5	34	34/3

MRT can be minimized if the files are stored in an increasing order of their lengths. Hence, the ordering defined minimizes the retrieval time. The greedy procedure is as follows:

Make tape empty.
For $i = 1$ to 3 do
    Take the next shortest file
    Store it next on tape

The optimal ordering is C, A, B.

4.6 Job sequencing with deadlines: $n = 7$, $(p_1 \ldots p_7) = (3, 5, 20, 18, 1, 6, 30)$ and $(d_1 \ldots d_7) = (1, 3, 4, 3, 2, 1, 2)$.

The job sequencing with deadlines problem is stated as follows:

(1) Each ith job is associated with a deadline ($d_i \geq 0$), and a profit ($p_i > 0$).
(2) For any ith job, the profit p_i is earned, if job is completed by its deadline.
(3) To complete a job, it is processed on a processor for one unit of time.
(4) Only one processor is available for processing all jobs.
(5) Not all jobs have to be scheduled.

A feasible solution for this problem is a subset *list* of jobs such that each job in this subset can be completed by its deadline. The value of a feasible solution is the sum of the profits of the jobs in *list* ($\sum p_i$, where *list* contains ith job). An optimal solution is a feasible solution with maximum profit.

Job #	1	2	3	4	5	6	7
Profits:	3	5	20	18	1	6	30
Deadlines:	1	3	4	3	2	1	2

Sort the jobs in decreasing order of profit:

Job #	7	3	4	6	2	1	5
Profits:	30	20	18	6	5	3	1
Deadlines:	2	4	3	1	3	1	2

job (i)	p_i	d_i	profit	operation	*list*[1..7] initialized to 0
7	30	2	30	Assign job 7 to slot 2.	0 | 7 | 0 | 0 | 0 | 0 | 0
3	20	4	50	Assign job 3 to slot 4.	0 | 7 | 0 | 3 | 0 | 0 | 0
4	18	3	68	Assign job 4 to slot 3.	0 | 7 | 4 | 3 | 0 | 0 | 0
6	6	1	74	Assign job 6 to slot 1.	6 | 7 | 4 | 3 | 0 | 0 | 0

Optimal job sequence is 6 à 7 à 4 à 3 with maximum profit of 74.

4.8 (1) Greedy strategy on capacity utilization:
Greedy criterion: select items in increasing order of weight.
When $n = 2$, $c = 7$, $w = (3, 6)$, $p = (2, 10)$, if only item 1 is selected profit of selection is 2 - not the best selection. Better solution is item 2.

(2) Greedy attempt on profit earned:
Greedy criterion: select items in decreasing order of profit.
When $n = 3$, $c = 7$, $w = (7, 3, 2)$, $p = (10, 8, 6)$, if only item 1 is selected profit of selection is 10 - not the best selection. If items 2 and 3 are included in knapsack, then profit will be 14 (8+6) – this is a better solution satisfying the capacity restriction of 7 (total weight of items 2 and 3 is 5).

(3) Greedy strategy on profit density (p/w):
Greedy criterion: select items in decreasing order of profit density.
When $n = 2$, $c = 7$, $w = (1, 7)$, $p = (10, 20)$, if only item 1 is selected profit of selection is 10 - not the best selection.

(4) Another greedy attempt on profit density (p/w):
Works when selecting a fraction of an item is permitted
Greedy criterion: select items in decreasing order of profit density, and if next item does not fit, take a fraction so as to fill knapsack.
When $n = 2$, $c = 7$, $w = (1, 7)$, $p = (10, 20)$, item 1 and 6/7 of item 2 are selected. But this solution is not allowed in 0/1 knapsack. This is a greedy algorithm for fractional knapsack problem.

4.9

item (i):	1	2	3	4	5	6	7
p_i	10	5	15	7	6	18	3
w_i	2	3	5	7	1	4	1
p_i/w_i	5.0	1.7	3.0	1.0	6.0	4.5	3.0

We pack a fraction x_i of item i, where $0 \le x_i \le 1$. Arrange the items in ascending order of p_i/w_i.

item (i):	5	1	6	3	7	2	4
p_i	6	10	18	15	3	5	7
w_i	1	2	4	5	1	3	7
p_i/w_i	6.0	5.0	4.5	3.0	3.0	1.7	1.0

item (i) included in knapsack	p_i	w_i	Cumulative weight	x_i
5	6	1	1	1
1	10	2	3	1
6	18	4	7	1
3	15	5	12	1
7	3	1	13	1
2	5	3	15	2/3

Optimal solution: $x_1 = 1, x_2 = 2/3, x_3 = 1, x_4 = 0, x_5 = 1, x_6 = 1$, and $x_7 = 1$.

4.14 Counterexample to show that the greedy algorithm developed for the fractional knapsack problem does not work for the 0/1 knapsack problem.

The greedy algorithm for the fractional knapsack problem is defined as follows. We first compute the value per weight of each item (i.e., v_i/w_i). We then pack as much of the item with the greatest value-weight ratio into the knapsack. If the entire item is packed and there is still room left, we then pack as much of the item with the second greatest value-weight ratio, and so forth until the knapsack is filled to capacity.

In order to create a counterexample for the 0/1 Knapsack problem, consider the following setup. Let S denote the set of items, where $S = \{1, 2, 3\}$. Let the weight of the items be $w_1 = 10$, $w_2 = 20$, and $w_3 = 30$ kilograms, and let $M = 50$ denote the total weight that the knapsack can hold. Finally, let each item have a value in rupees of $p_1 = 60$, $p_2 = 100$, and $p_3 = 120$.

If we use the greedy strategy to solve the 0/1 Knapsack problem, we first need to calculate the value-weight ratio of each item; these ratios are 60/10 = 6, 100/20 = 5, and 120/30 = 4, respectively. We then pack the item with the greatest value-weight ratio into the knapsack. After packing the first item, the knapsack is not yet filled to capacity, so we pack the item with the second highest value-weight ratio. Observe that after packing the second item, we still have room left in our knapsack, but we can not pack the third and final item, because there is not sufficient space for the entire item. Adding the values of the two items in the knapsack, we have a total profit of 160, using the greedy strategy.

Now, consider what happens if we instead take the item with the greatest value first. We still have room in the knapsack; so we will take the item with the second greatest value. After packing these two items (items 2 and 3), we have reached the capacity and the total profit is 220, using this strategy.

We have a counterexample showing that the greedy strategy does not produce the optimal solution. Therefore, we conclude that the greedy strategy does not work for the 0/1 Knapsack problem.

4.15 A connected graph is a tree if and only if it has n vertices and n-1 edges. Assume there is an undirected, connected graph G. A spanning tree is a subgraph of G, is a tree, and contains all the vertices of G. A minimum spanning tree is a spanning tree, but has weights or lengths associated with the edges, and the total weight of the tree (the sum of the weights of its edges) is at a minimum. Following is an undirected, weighted graph with two *MST*s, each with a cost of 6:

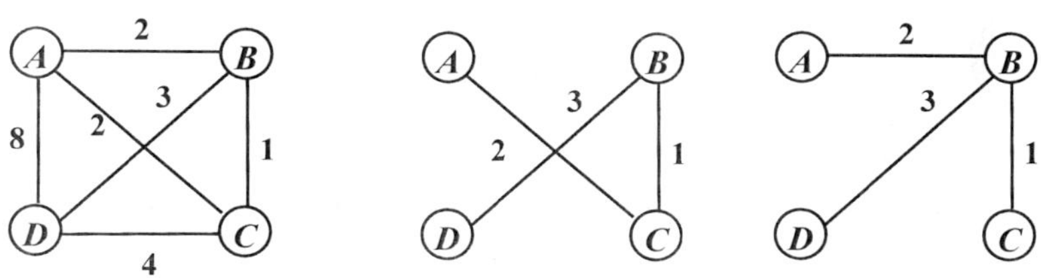

Minimum spanning trees have many applications. Some are:

- Building cable networks that join n locations with minimum cost.
- Building road network that joins n cities with minimum cost.
- Optimizing computer networks.
- Obtaining an independent set of circuit equations for an electrical network.
- In pattern recognition, MST can be used to find noisy pixels.

4.18 Edge with the smallest weight will be part of every minimum spanning tree.

Let *u-v* be the smallest weight edge. Pick any minimum spanning tree *T*. If the edge is in *T*, we are done. So assume that the edge is not in *T*. But then when we add *u-v* to *T*, we get a cycle. Pick any edge on the cycle other then *u-v* and remove the edge. The weight of the resulting subgraph is less than or equal to the weight of *T*. Moreover, the graph is a tree since it is connected and has *n*-1 edges (*n*: number of vertices in the graph). Kruskal's algorithm builds *MST*. The first edge that we add to *T* will be the smallest weight edge in the graph. Hence, the smallest weight will be part of every *MST*.

It is observed from the following figure that the minimum weight edge (weight = 2) of the graph is included in three minimum spanning trees.

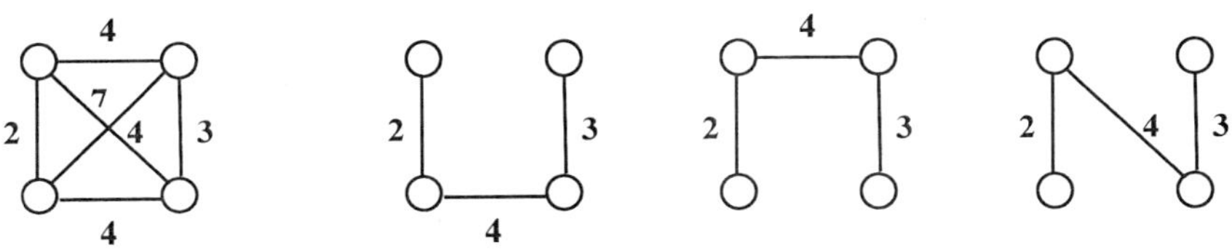

A Graph and three of its *MST*s

4.19 (a) False. For justification, refer Ex: 4.18.
(b) True. For justification, refer Ex: 4.18.
(c) True. For justification, refer Ex: 4.21.
(d) True. For justification, refer Ex: 4.21.

4.20 Let *G* = (*V*, *E*) which is represented by an adjacency list *Adj*.
d is an array of size |*V*|. Each *d*[*i*] contains the shortest distance for vertex *i*.
Q is a priority queue of UNKNOWN vertices.
p is an array of size |*V*|. Each *p*[*i*] contains the parent of vertex *i*.
s is the source vertex.

```
PRIM(G, s)
1. Initialize d[s] with 0, p[s] with 0, and all other d[i] (i != s) with a positive
   infinity and p[i] (i != s) with 0.
2. Q ß V          // initialize Q with all vertices as UNKNOWN.
3. While Q not empty do
4.      u ß DeleteMin(Q)          // Q is modified
5.      Mark u as KNOWN           // Dequeing u is the same as marking it
                                     as KNOWN
```

```
      For each vertex v in Adj[u] do
          If v is UNKNOWN and d[v] > weight(u, v), then
              d[v] = weight(u, v)    // update with smaller weight
              p[v] = u               // update v's parent as v
          Endif
      Endfor
Endwhile.
```

If a graph is represented by adjacency linked lists and priority queue is implemented as a min-heap, running time of the algorithm will be in $O(|E|\log|V|)$. Ex: 4.21 illustrates this algorithm.

4.21

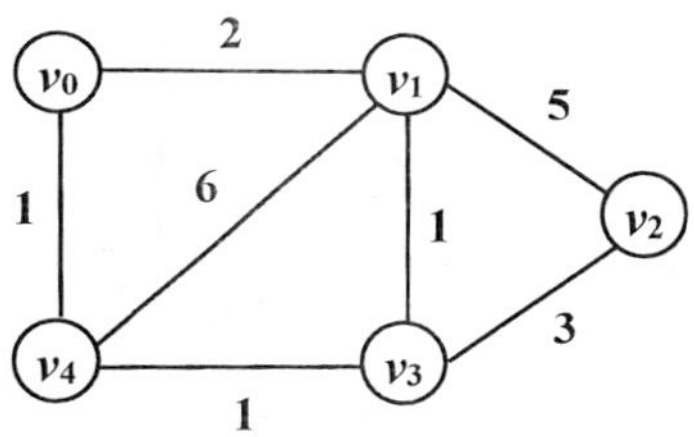

Adjacency list:

v_0 à v_1 à v_4à x x: null

v_1 à v_0 à v_2à v_3 à v_4à x

v_2 à v_1 à v_3à x

v_3 à v_1 à v_2à v_4à x

v_4 à v_0 à v_1à v_3à x

v_0 is the source vertex, and $d[i]$ for each vertex i is indicated at each node. The stages of Prim's algorithm are shown below:

(a)

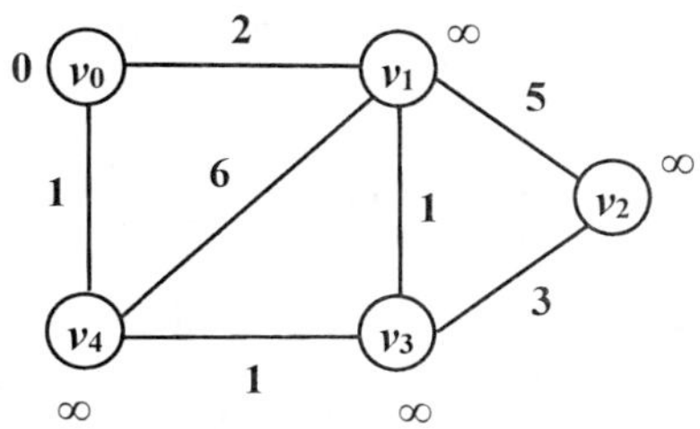

v	known	$d[v]$	$p[v]$
v_0	F	0	0
v_1	F	∞	0
v_2	F	∞	0
v_3	F	∞	0
v_4	F	∞	0

Q = { v_0, v_1, v_2, v_3 , v_4}

(b)

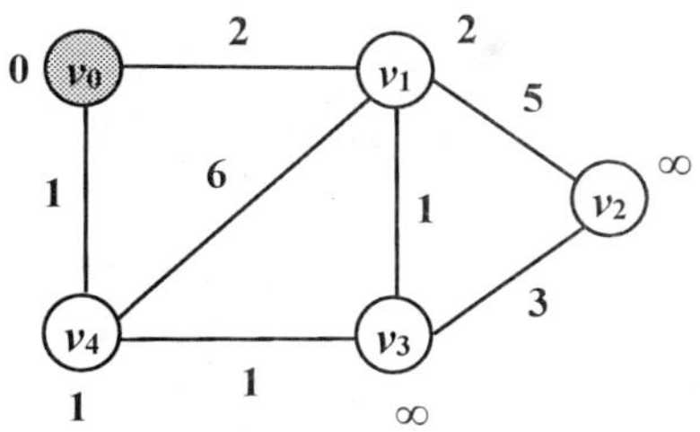

v	known	$d[v]$	$p[v]$
v_0	T	0	0
v_1	F	2	v_0
v_2	F	∞	0
v_3	F	∞	0
v_4	F	1	v_0

Q = { v_4, v_1, v_2, v_3}

(c)

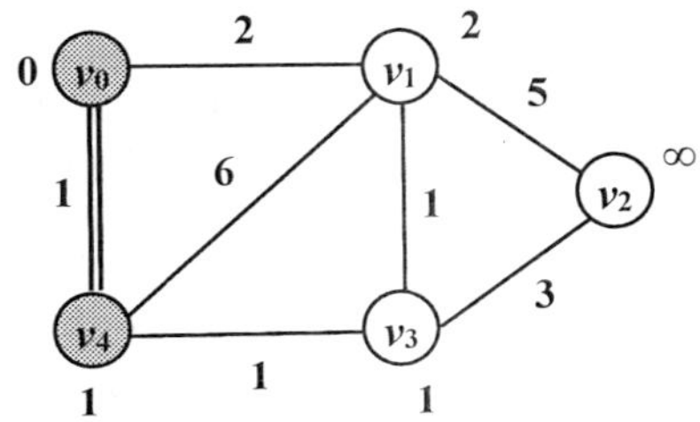

v	known	$d[v]$	$p[v]$
v_0	T	0	0
v_1	F	2	v_0
v_2	F	∞	0
v_3	F	1	v_4
v_4	T	1	v_0

Q = { v_3, v_1, v_2}

(d)

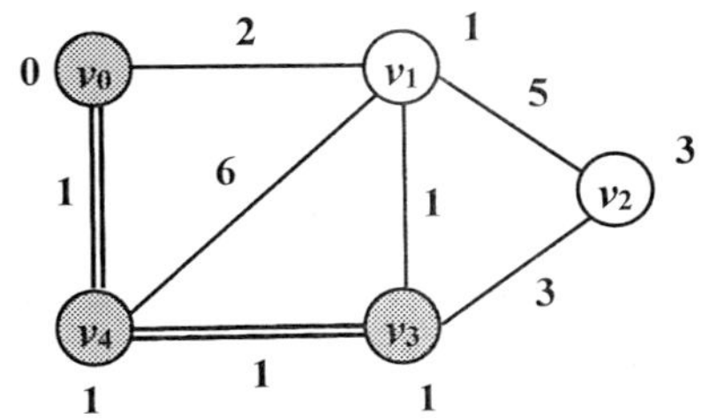

v	known	$d[v]$	$p[v]$
v_0	T	0	0
v_1	F	1	v_3
v_2	F	3	v_3
v_3	T	1	v_4
v_4	T	1	v_0

Q = {v_1, v_2}

(e)

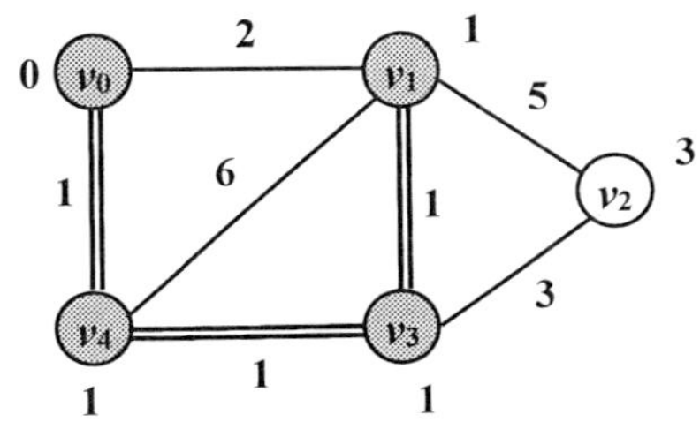

v	known	$d[v]$	$p[v]$
v_0	T	0	0
v_1	T	1	v_3
v_2	F	3	v_3
v_3	T	1	v_4
v_4	T	1	v_0

Q = {v_2}

(f)

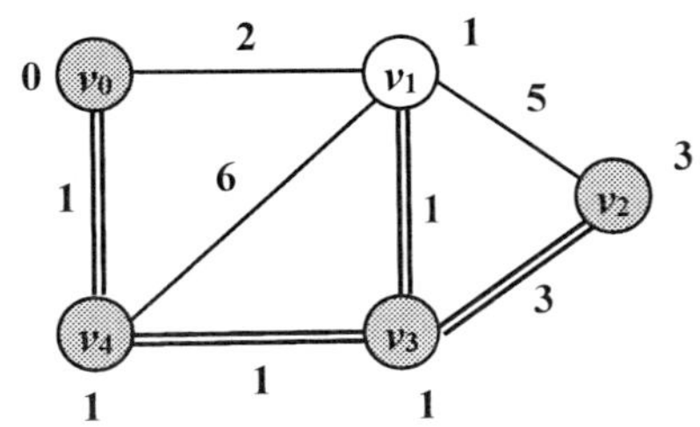

v	known	$d[v]$	$p[v]$
v_0	T	0	0
v_1	T	1	v_3
v_2	T	3	v_3
v_3	T	1	v_4
v_4	T	1	v_0

Q = {}

4.22 If the weights on edges of a connected undirected graph are distinct, then there is a unique minimum spanning tree.

If each edge has a distinct weight then there will only be one, unique minimum spanning tree. This can be proved by induction or contradiction. Say we have an algorithm that finds an *MST* (which we will call *A*) based on the structure of the graph and the order of the edges when ordered by weight. Assume for the moment that this

MST is not unique and that there is another spanning tree, *B*, with equal weight. If there are *n* vertices in the graph, then each tree has *n*-1 edges. There are some edges which belong to *B* but not to *A*. What happens if we decrease the weight of one of these edges by a small amount ε so that we do not change the overall ordering of all the edges of the graph when ordered by weight? (This is possible because all weights are separated by positive amounts.) It will not change the result of our algorithm, which still gives tree *A*. But tree *B* will now have a weight ε less than what it had before, which means that *A* is not minimal, contrary to assumption. Because of this contradiction, we conclude that the assumption that there can be a second *MST* was false.

Consider two different undirected connected graphs with distinct edge weights. The following figure shows two graphs with their unique minimum spanning trees.

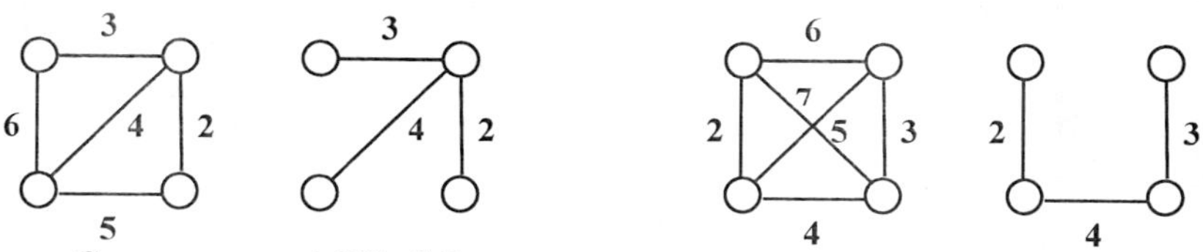

G_1 *MST* of G_1 G_2 *MST* of G_2

4.24

Prim's algorithm	Kruskal's algorithm
Build *MST* one vertex at a time. Start with one vertex tree *T*. Add the edge of minimum weight among those with one vertex in *T* and the other not in *T*.	Construct *MST* one edge at a time. Sort the edges by weight. Build a spanning forest (that eventually becomes a tree) by adding the edge of minimum weight which when added to those already chosen does not form a cycle.

The following figure shows the stages of Prim's MST algorithm (starting vertex is 1). Total minimum cost is 155.

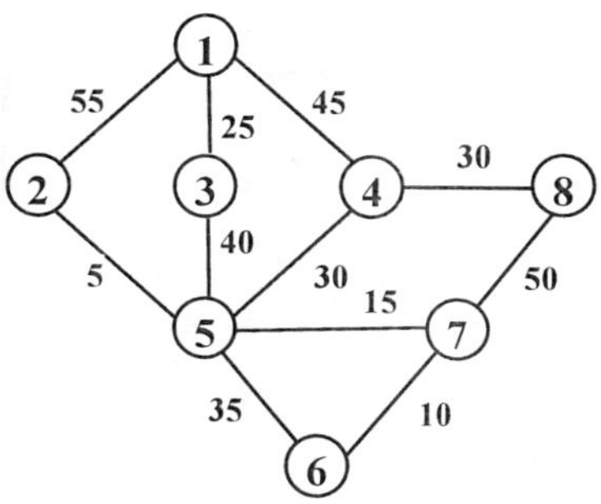

(a)

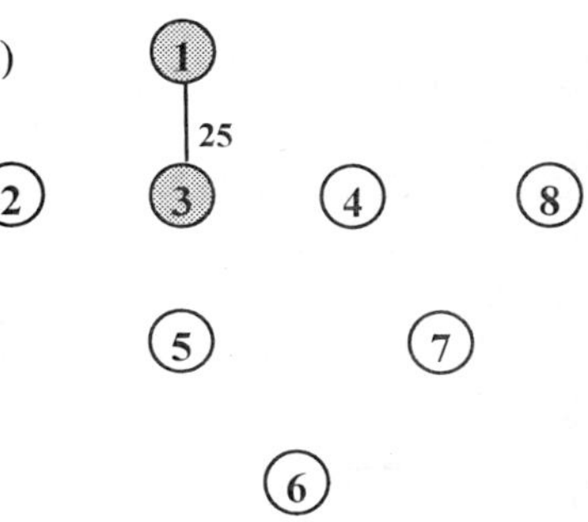

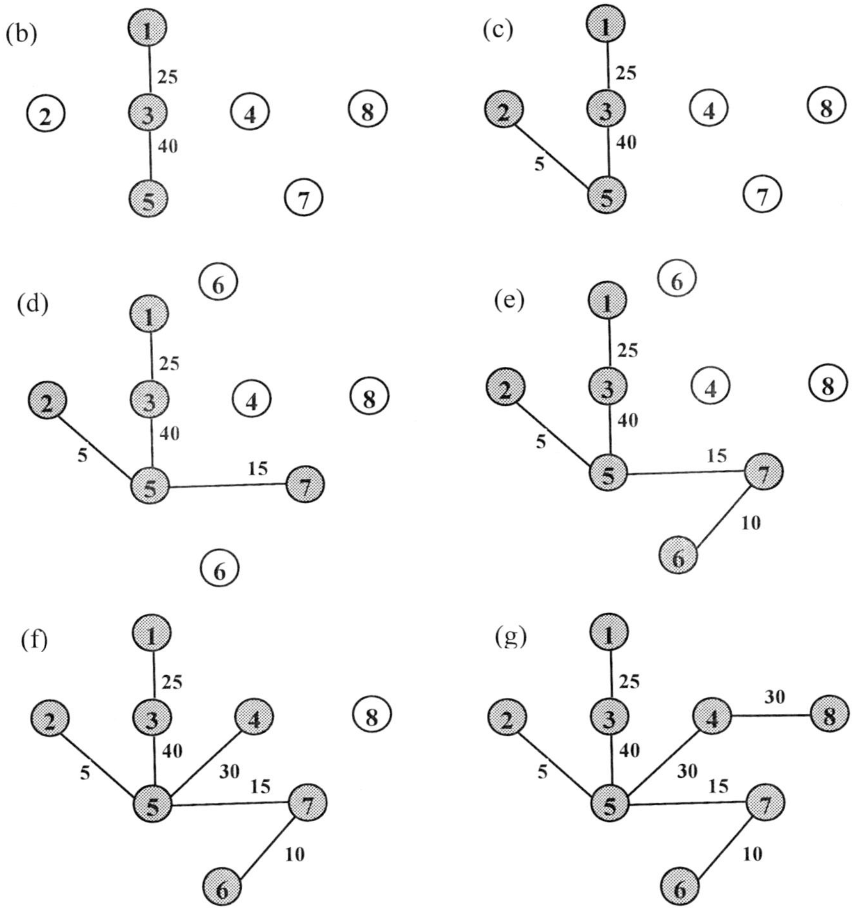

Kruskal's algorithm: Following table gives the construction of MST (edges are arranged in ascending order of edge weights): n = number of vertices = 8.

Edge	weight	Edge added in MST
(2, 5)	5	(2, 5)
(6, 7)	10	(6, 7)
(5, 7)	15	(5, 7)
(1, 3)	25	(1, 3)
(4, 5)	30	(4, 5)
(4, 8)	30	(4, 8)
(5, 6)	35	Forms cycle
(3, 5)	40	(3, 5)
(1, 4)	45	*Stop*: MST contains (n-1) = 7 edges.
(7, 8)	50	
(1, 2)	55	

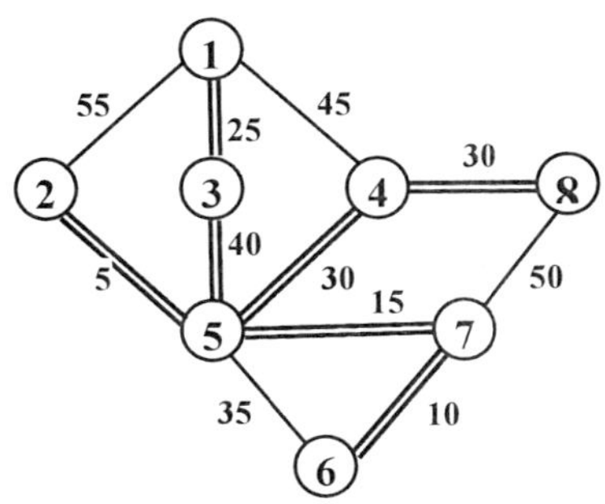

4.27 (a) Arrange the characters in ascending order of frequency. Build the Huffman tree with lowest frequency characters step-by-step (left-to-right)

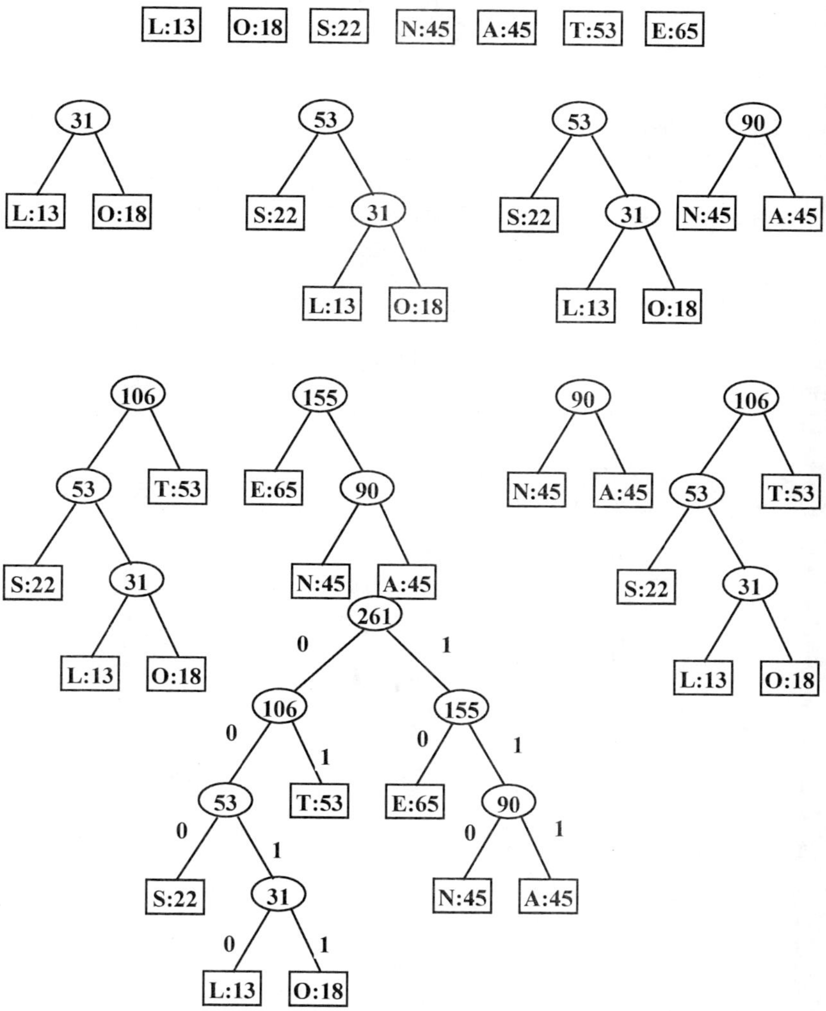

The sequence of zeros and ones that are the edges in the path from the root to each leaf node are the desired codes:

Character:	A	E	L	N	O	S	T
Codeword:	111	10	0010	110	0011	000	01
Frequency:	45	65	13	45	18	22	53

(b) If we assume the message consists of only the characters A, E, L, N, O, S, T, then the number of bits transmitted will be:
3*45 + 2*65 + 4*13 + 3*45 + 4*18 + 3*22 + 2*53 = 696 bits
If the message is sent uncompressed with 8-bit ASCII representation for the characters, we have 261*8 = 2088 bits, that is, we saved about 70% transmission time.

(c) Data encoded using Huffman coding is uniquely decodable. This is because Huffman codes satisfy the prefix property. This property guarantees that no codeword is a prefix of another Huffman codeword. For example, 10 and 101 cannot simultaneously be valid Huffman codewords because the first is a prefix of the second. Thus, any bitstream is uniquely decodable with a given Huffman code. We can see by inspection that the generated codewords are valid Huffman codewords.

4.28 Symbols *A*, *B*, *C*, *D*, *E*, *F* are being produced by the information source with probabilities (in percentages) 30, 40, 6, 10, 10, 4 respectively. What is the binary Huffman code?

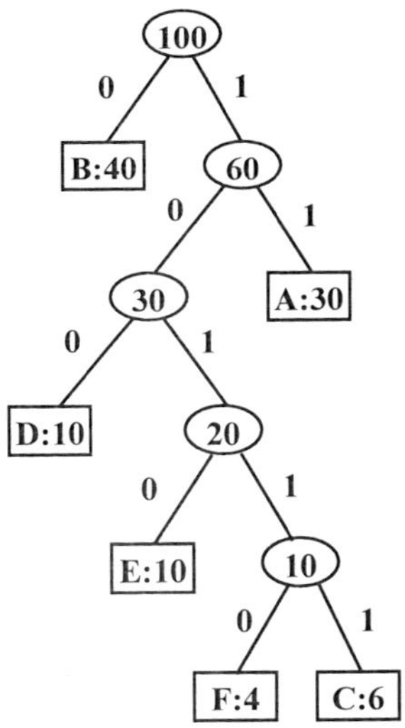

A: 11
B: 0
C: 10111
D: 100
E: 1010
F: 10110

CHAPTER 5 Dynamic Programming

5.4 $p = (2, 3, 3)$ $w = (1, 2, 4)$ $m = 6$, $n = 3$

$f_n(m) = \max \{f_{n-1}(m), f_{n-1}(C\text{-}W_n + P_n\}$ where, $f_0(x) = 0$, *for any* x

$f_0(x) = -\infty$, *for* $x < 0$

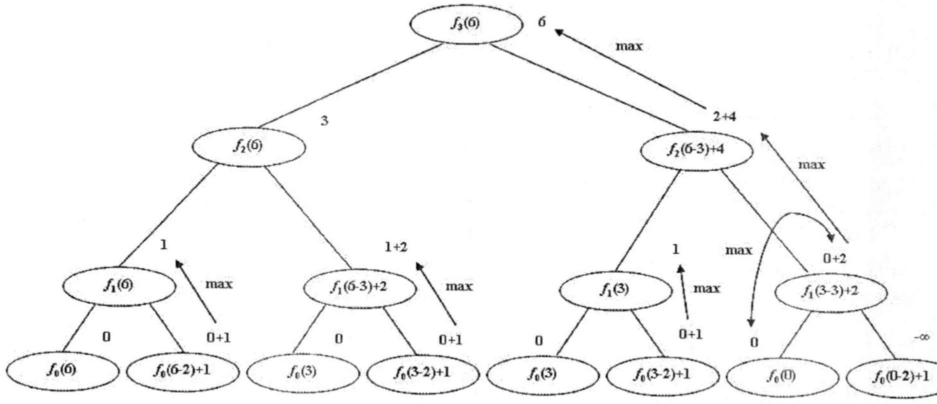

for maximizing knapsack value i.e., $f_3(6)$:
Weights taken into knapsack are w_2=3 and w_3=3 i.e., total of 6, then maximum value becomes 2 + 4 = 6.

5.5 $p = (11, 21, 31, 33)$ $w = (2, 11, 22, 15)$
$C = 40, n = 4$
$F_n(C) = \max \{f_{n-1}(C), f_{n-1}(C-W_n + P_n\}$ where, $f_0(x) = 0$, *for any* x
$f_0(x) = -\infty$, *for* $x < 0$

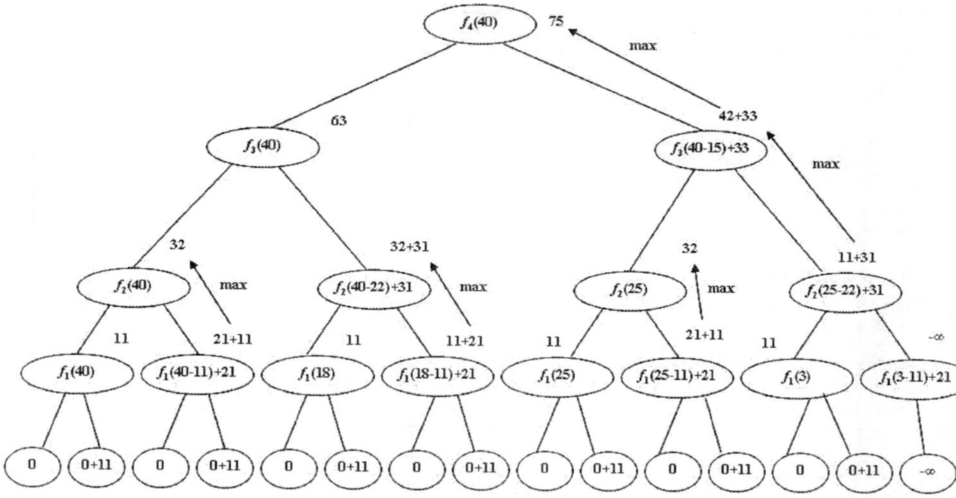

So, for maximizing knapsack value i.e., $f_4(40)$:

Weights taken into knapsack are 15,22 and 2 i.e., total of 39, then maximum value becomes 33+31+11=75.

5.8 Consider the following values of the array key with probabilities:

Since, 1/8=0.125, 1/16=0.0625 & 3/16=0.1875, given values are:

key[*i*]:		*key*[1]	*key*[2]	*key*[3]	*key*[4]	*key*[4]
Value:		a1	a2	a3	a4	a5
p[*i*]:		p_1 = 1/8	p_2 = 1/8	p_3 = 1/16	p_4 = 1/16	p_5 = 3/16
q[*i*]:	q_0 = 0	q_1 = 3/16	q_2 = 1/16	q_3 = 1/16	q_4 = 1/16	q_5 = 1/16

$$Wi,j = Pj + Qj + Wi,j\text{-}1$$

$$A_{i,j} = W_{i,j} + \min_{i<k\leq j} A_{i,k-1} + A_{k,j}$$

d	*i*	*j*	*k*	$W_{i,j} = P_j + Q_j + W_{i,j-1}$	$A_{i,j} = W_{i,j} + \min_{i<k\leq j} A_{i,k-1} + A_{k,j}$	$A_{i,j}$	$R_{i,j}$
1	0	1	1	1/8+3/16+0= 5/16	5/16+[0+0]	5/6	1
	1	2	2	1/8+1/16+3/16=6/16	6/16+[0+0]	6/16	2
	2	3	3	1/16+1/16+1/16=3/16	3/16+[0+0]	3/16	3
	3	4	4	1/16+1/16+1/16=3/16	3/16+[0+0]	3/16	4
	4	5	5	3/16+1/16+1/16=5/16	5/16+[0+0]	5/16	5
2	0	2	1	1/8+1/16+5/16=8/16	8/16+[0+6/16]	14/16	2
	0	2	2	1/8+1/16+5/16=8/16	8/16+[5/16+0] (min)	13/16	
	1	3	2	1/16+1/16+6/16=8/16	8/16+[0+3/16] (min)	11/16	2
	1	3	3	1/16+1/16+6/16=8/16	8/16+[6/16+0]	14/16	
	2	4	3	1/16+1/16+3/16=5/16	5/16+[0+3/16] (min)	8/16	3
	2	4	4	1/16+1/16+3/16=5/16	5/16+[3/16+0]	8/16	
	3	5	4	3/16+1/16+3/16=7/16	7/16+[0+5/16]	12/16	5
	3	5	5	3/16+1/16+3/16=7/16	7/16+[3/16+0] (min)	10/16	
3	0	3	1	1/16+1/16+8/16=10/16	10/16+[11/16+0]	21/16	2
	0	3	2	10/16	10/16+[5/16+3/16] min	18/16	

	0	3	3	10/16	10/16+[13/16+0]	23/16	
	1	4	2	1/16+1/16+8/16=10/16	10/16+[0+8/16] (min)	18/16	2
	1	4	3	10/16	10/16+[6/16+3/16]	19/16	
	1	4	4	10/16	10/16+[11/16+0]	21/16	
	2	5	3	3/16+1/16+5/16=9/16	9/16+[0+10/16]	19/16	
	2	5	4	9/16	9/16+[3/16+5/16] (min)	17/16	4
	2	5	5	9/16	9/16+[8/16+0]	17/16	
4	0	4	1	1/16+1/16+10/16=12/16	12/16+[0+18/16]	30/16	2
	0	4	2	12/16	12/16+[5/16+8/16] min	25/16	
	0	4	3	12/16	12/16+[13/16+3/16]	28/16	
	0	4	4	12/16	12/16+[18/16+0]	30/16	
	1	5	2	3/16+1/16+10/16=14/16	14/16+[0+17/16]	31/16	3
	1	5	3	14/16	14/16+[6/16+16/16]min	30/16	
	1	5	4	14/16	14/16+[11/16+5/16]	30/16	
	1	5	5	14/16	14/16+[18/16+0]	32/16	
5	0	5	1	3/16+1/16+12/16=16/16	16/16+[0+30/16]	46/16	2
	0	5	2	16/16	16/16+[5/16+17/16]min	38/16	
	0	5	3	16/16	16/16+[13/16+10/16]	39/16	
	0	5	4	16/16	16/16+[18/16+5/16]	39/16	
	0	5	5	16/16	16/16+[25/16+0]	38/16	

OBST Table from $R_{i,j}$ values:

	0	1	2	3	4	5
0	0	(1)	2	2	2	(2)
1		0	2	2	2	3
2			0	(3)	3	(4)
3				0	4	5
4					0	(5)
5						0

5.12 A (2 x 5) x B(5 x 3) x C(3 x 6) x D(6 x 4)

A (B (C D)) = (3 x 6 x 4) + (5 x 3 x 4) + (2 x 5 x 4)
= 72 + 60 + 40 = 172

(A B) (C D) = (2 x 5 x 3) + (3 x 6 x 4) + (2 x 3 x 4)
= 30 + 72 + 24 = 126

(A (B C)) D = (5 x 3 x 6) + (2 x 5 x 6) + (2 x 6 x 4)
= 90 + 60 + 48 = 198

A (B C) D = (5 x 3 x 6) + (5 x 6 x 4) + (2 x 5 x 4)
= 90 + 120 + 40 = 250

((A B) C) D = (2 x 5 x 3) + (2 x 3 x 6) + (2 x 6 x 4)
= 30 + 36 + 48 = 114

In this problem, 114 number of iterations are required for order: ((A B) C)D.

5.13 A(30,40) x B(40,5) x C(5,15) x D(15,6)

A (B (C D)) = (5 x 15 x 6) + (40 x 15 x 6) + (30 x 40 x 6)
= 450 + 1200 + 7200 = 8850

(A B) (C D) = (30 x 40 x 5) + (5 x 15 x 6) + (30 x 5 x 6)
= 6000 + 450 + 900 = 7350

(A (B C)) D = (40 x 5 x 15) + (30 x 40 x 15) + (30 x 15 x 6)
= 3000 + 18000 + 900 = 21900

A (B C) D = (40 x 5 x 15) + (40 x 15 x 6) + (30 x 40 x 6)
= 3000 + 3600 + 7200 = 13800

((A B) C) D = (30 x 40 x 5) + (30 x 5 x 15) + (30 x 15 x 6)
= 6000 + 2250 + 2700 = 10950

Here, total number of iterations for chain matrix multiplication is calculated in the sequence respectively. Among them least no. of iterations are done is the solution.
So, 7350 number of iterations are required for multiplication to be done in the order: (A B) (C D).

5.16 $A^k(i,j) = \min_{k=1,2,3,4} \{ A^{k-1}(i,k) + A^{k-1}(k,j) , C(i,j) \}$ where $n = 4$, no. of nodes

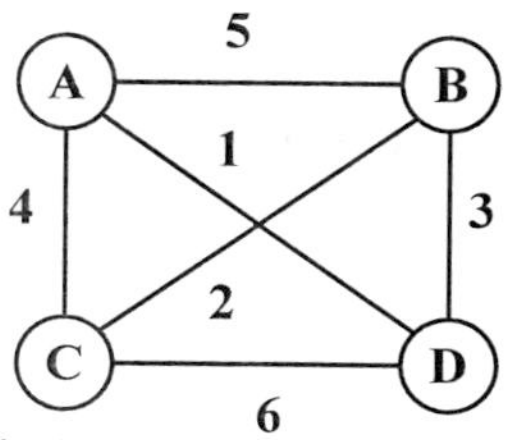

A^0

	1	2	3	4
1	0	5	4	1
2	5	0	2	3
3	4	2	0	6
4	1	3	6	0

for k=1

1	1	$A^1(1,1) = \min [A^0(1,1)+ A^0(1,1) , C(1,1)] = \min [0+0, 0] = 0$
1	2	$A^1(1,2) = \min [A^0(1,1)+ A^0(1,2) , C(1,2)] = \min [0+5, 5] = 5$
1	3	$A^1(1,3) = \min [A^0(1,1)+ A^0(1,3) , C(1,3)] = \min [0+4, 4] = 4$
1	4	$A^1(1,4) = \min [A^0(1,1)+ A^0(1,4) , C(1,4)] = \min [0+1, 1] = 1$

Similarly, for other values need to compute like-wise, for those values that are changed have been done as

3	4	$A^1(3,4) = \min [A^0(3,1)+ A^0(1,4) , C(3,4)] = \min [4+1, 6] = 5$
4	3	$A^1(4,3) = \min [A^0(4,1)+ A^0(1,3) , C(4,3)] = \min [1+4, 6] = 5$

A^1

0	5	4	1
5	0	2	3
4	2	0	5
1	3	5	0

Thus, A^1 matrix is obtained will be the input for A^2.
In this iteration values of matrix doesn't change but needs to compute for next iteration i.e., $k = 2$

A^2

0	5	4	1
5	0	2	3
4	2	0	5
1	3	5	0

In this iteration values of matrix doesn't change but needs to compute for next iteration i.e., $k = 3$

A^3

0	5	4	1
5	0	2	3
4	2	0	5
1	3	5	0

Finally, A^3 is the resultant values for *all pair shortest path.*

5.19 $T(A, V) = \min_{k=2,3,4,5} \{C_{1k}+T(k, V-\{k\})\}$ where, V = {B, C, D}

C_{Ak} is Cost between A and k nodes
T (A,{B,C,D}) is the minimal value from those values obtained as of the given table

k	$C_{Ak}+T(k, V-\{k\})$
B	$C_{AB}+T(B,\{C,D\})$
C	$C_{AC}+T(C,\{B,D\})$
D	$C_{AD}+T(D,\{B,C\})$

for T (B,{C,D})

k	$C_{BK}+T(k, V-\{B,k\})$		
C	$C_{BC}+T(C,\{D\})$	= 13 + 28	= 41
D	$C_{BD}+T(D,\{C\})$	= 6 + 6	= 12

Since, $T(C,\{D\}) = C_{CD}+T(D, \emptyset) = C_{CD}+C_{DA} = 18+10 = 28$
$T(D,\{C\}) = C_{DC}+T(C, \emptyset) = 2+4 = 6$

for T(C, {B,D})

k	$C_{Ck}+T(k, V-\{C,k\})$		
B	$C_{CB}+T(B,\{D\})$	= 9 + 16	= 25
D	$C_{CD}+T(D,\{B\})$	= 18 + 14	= 32

Since, $T(B,\{D\}) = C_{BD}+T(D,\emptyset) = C_{BD}+C_{DA} = 6+10 = 16$
$T(D,\{B\}) = C_{DB}+T(B,\emptyset) = 3+11 = 14$

for T(D,{B,C})

k	$C_{Dk}+T(k, V-\{D,k\})$		
B	$C_{DB}+T(B,\{C\})$	= 6 + 17	= 23
C	$C_{DC}+T(C, \{B\})$	= 18 + 20	= 38

Since, $T(B,\{C\}) = C_{BC}+T(C,\emptyset) = C_{BC}+C_{CA} = 13+4 = 17$
$T(C,\{B\}) = C_{CB}+T(B,\emptyset) = 9+11 = 20$

Now, the Initial table becomes:

k	C_{Ak}+T (k, V-{k})	Min = 24
B	C_{AB}+T (B,{C,D})	12+12
C	C_{AC}+T (C,{B,D})	5+25
D	C_{AD}+T (D,{B,C})	7+23

So, the solution for the given TSP is
=> A -> T (B,{C,D})
=> A -> B -> T (D,{C})
=> A -> B -> D -> C -> A
=> 12 + 6 + 2 + 4 = 24

5.20 $T(1, V) = \min_{k=2,3,4,5} \{C_{1k}+T(k, V-\{k\})\}$ where, V = {2, 3, 4, 5}

C_{1k} is Cost between 1 and k nodes
T (1,{2,3,4,5})

Need to compute,

k	C_{1k}+T (k, V - {k})
2	C_{12}+T (2, {3,4,5})
3	C_{13}+T (3, {2,4.5})
4	C_{14}+T (4, {2,3,5})
5	C_{15}+T (5, {2,3,4})

for T(2, {3,4,5})

k	C_{2k}+T (k, V - {2,k})		
3	C_{23}+T (3, {4.5})	= 16+min{C_{34}+T(4,{5});C_{35}+T(5,{4})} = 16+min(2+19,4+35) = 16+9	= 37
4	C_{24}+T (4, {3,5})	= 4+min{C_{43}+T(3,{5});C_{45}+T(5,{3})} = 4+min(18+20,3+10) = 4+13	= 17
5	C_{25}+T (5, {3,4})	= 2+min{C_{53}+T(3,{4});C_{54}+T(4,{3})} = 2+min(7+21,16+21) = 2+28	= 30

Since, T(4,{5}) = C_{45}+T(5,ø) = C_{45}+C_{51} = 3+16 = 19
T(5,{4}) = C_{54}+T(4,ø) = 16+19 = 35
T(3,{5}) = C_{35}+T(5,ø) = 4+16 = 20
T(5,{3}) = C_{53}+T(3,ø) = 7+3 = 10
T(3,{4}) = C_{34}+T(4,ø) = 2+19 = 21
T(4,{3}) = C_{43}+T(3,ø) = 18+3 = 21

for T(3, {2,4,5})

k	C_{3k}+T (k, V - {3,k})		
2	C_{32}+T (2, {4.5})	= 5+min{C_{24}+T(4,{5});C_{25}+T(5,{4})} = 5+min(4+19,2+35) = 5+23	= 28
4	C_{34}+T (4, {2,5})	= 2+min{C_{42}+T(2,{5});C_{45}+T(5,{2})} = 2+min(6+18,3+19) = 2+22	= 24
5	C_{35}+T (5, {2,4})	= 4+min{C_{52}+T(2,{4});C_{54}+T(4,{2})} = 4+min(4+23,16+21) = 4+27	= 31

Since, T(2,{5}) = C_{25}+T(5,ø) = C_{25}+C_{51} = 2+16 = 18
T(5,{2}) = C_{52}+T(2,ø) = 4+15 = 19
T(2,{4}) = C_{24}+T(4,ø) = 4+19 = 23
T(4,{2}) = C_{42}+T(2,ø) = 6+15 = 21

for T(4, {2,3,5})

k	C_{4k}+T (k, V - {4,k})		
2	C_{42}+T (2, {3.5})	= 6+min{C_{23}+T(3,{5});C_{25}+T(5,{3})} = 6+min(16+20,2+10) = 6+12	= 18
3	C_{43}+T (3, {2,5})	= 18+min{C_{32}+T(2,{5});C_{35}+T(5,{2})} = 18+min(5+18,4+19) = 18+23	= 41
5	C_{45}+T (5, {2,3})	= 3+min{C_{52}+T(2,{3});C_{53}+T(3,{2})} = 3+min(4+19,7+20) = 3+23	= 26

Since, T(2,{3}) = C_{23}+T(3,ø) = C_{23}+C_{31} = 16+3 = 19
T(3,{2}) = C_{32}+T(2,ø) = 5+15 = 20

for T(5, {2,3,4})

k	C_{5k}+T (k, V - {5,k})		
2	C_{52}+T (5, {3,4})	= 4+min{C_{53}+T(3,{4});C_{54}+T(4,{3})} = 4+min(7+21,16+21) = 4+28	= 32
3	C_{53}+T (3, {2,4})	= 7+min{C_{32}+T(2,{4});C_{34}+T(4,{2})} = 7+min(5+23,2+21) = 7+23	= 30
5	C_{54}+T (4, {2,3})	= 16+min{C_{42}+T(2,{3});C_{43}+T(3,{2})} = 16+min(6+19,18+20) = 16+25	= 41

Now, the Initial table becomes,

k	C_{1k}+T (k, V - {k})	Min = 28
2	C_{12}+T (2, {3,4,5})	20 + 17 = 37
3	C_{13}+T (3, {2,4.5})	30 + 24 = 54
4	C_{14}+T (4, {2,3,5})	10 + 18 = 28

5	C_{15}+T (5, {2,3,4})	11 + 30 = 41

So, the solution for the given TSP is
=> 1 -> T (4,{2,3,5})
=> 1 -> 4 -> T (2, {3.5})
=> 1 -> 4 -> 2 -> T(5,{3})
=> 1 -> 4 -> 2 -> 5 -> 3 -> 1 = 10+6+2+7+3 = 28

5.21 Answers: (a) cost = 2.42 (b) cost = 2.18

CHAPTER 6 Backtracking

6.1 The Control Abstraction in backtracking can be stated by the following guidelines

In the backtracking method

1. The desired solution is expressible as an n tuple($x_1,x_2......x_n$) where x_i is chosen from some finite set Si
2. The solution maximizes or minimizes or satisfies a criterion function C ($x_1,x_2......x_n$).

The problem can be categorized into three.
For instance – For a problem P let C be the set of constraints for P. Let D be the set containing all solutions satisfying C, then finding whether there is any feasible solution? – is the decision problem.
What is the best solution? – is the optimization problem.
Listing of all the feasible solutions – is the enumeration problem.

The basic idea of backtracking is to build up a vector, one component at a time to test whether the vector being formed has any chance of success. The major advantage of this algorithm is that we can realize the fact that the partial vector generated does not lead to an optimal solution. In such a situation the vector can be ignored.

6.3 Backtracking is one of the most general techniques, in which we search for the set of solutions or optimal solution which satisfies some constraints. Concept of Backtracking is used in many applications such as:

- N-Queens problem
- Sum of subsets
- Graph colouring
- Hamiltonian cycle

N-Queens Problem:

As an example of *n*–queens problem we will consider 8–queens problem which can be stated as follows:

Consider a chessboard of order 8 x 8.The problem is to place 8 queens on this board such that no two queens can attack each other. That means no two queens can be placed on the same row, column or diagonal.
The solution to 8-queens problem can be obtained using back tracking method. The solution can be given as below:

	1	2	3	4	5	6	7	8
1							Q	
2					Q			
3			Q					
4	Q							
5						Q		
6								Q
7		Q						
8				Q				

Sum of subsets:

There are n positive numbers given in a set. The desire is to find all possible subsets of this set, the contents of which add onto a predefined value M. In other words, Let there be n elements given by the set $w = (w_1, w_2, w_3, \ldots w_n)$, then find out all the subsets from whose sum is M.
For example:
Consider $n = 6$ and $(w_1, w_2, w_3, \ldots w_6) = (25, 8, 16, 32, 26, 52)$ and $M = 59$, then we will get the desired sum of subset as (25, 8, 26).

Graph Coloring Problem:

Graph Coloring is a problem of coloring each vertex in a graph in such a way that no two adjacent vertices have same color and yet m-colors are used. This problem is also called m-coloring problem. If the degree of given graph is d then we can color it with d+1 colors. The least number of colors needed to color the graph is called its *chromatic number*.
For example, consider the following graph; chromatic number of the given graph is 3.

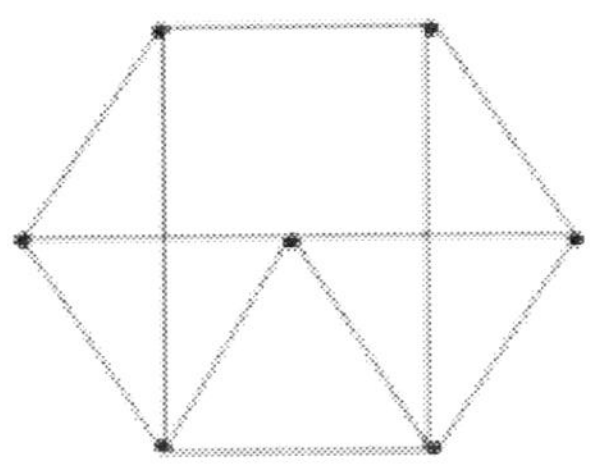

Hamiltonian Cycle:

Hamiltonian cycle is the problem which can be solved by using backtracking. The Hamiltonian cycle is defined as that passes through all vertices of the graph exactly once.

6.4

Backtracking	Brute-force Technique
Solution for Backtracking is traced using Depth First Search	This technique uses Breadth First Search in finding the solution
Typically Decision Problems can be solved using backtracking	Typical Decision Problems cannot be solved using backtracking
Bad choices can be made while finding solution to the problem	Bad choices cannot be made while finding solution to the problem
The problems which can be solved in polynomial time can be solvable using backtracking	The problems which cannot be solved in polynomial time can be solvable using Brute-force technique
It is possible to solve only small problems using this technique	It is possible to solve large problems using this technique
Cannot Estimate runtime	Used in Estimating Runtime

6.14 Graph Coloring: Convert the graph into the following form.

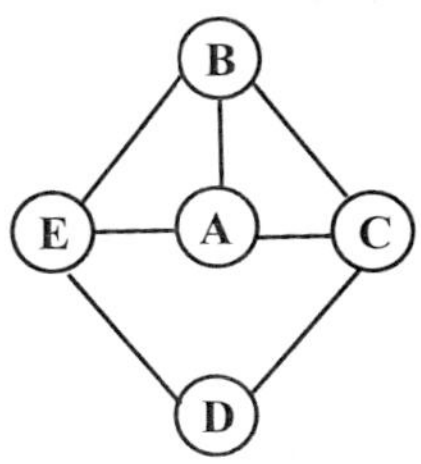

A Graph consists of vertices from A to E. There are three colors used Red, Blue and Green. We will number them out. That means 1 indicates Red, 2 indicates Blue and 3 indicates Green.

Step 1: Choose a color for node B. It can be one of: 1(Red), 2(Blue) or 3(Green). Say, we choose 1.

Step 2: Given partial coloring (1), we choose a color for node E. It can be one of: 2 or 3. Say we choose 2.

Step 3: Given partial coloring (1, 2), we choose a color for node A. It cannot be either 1 or 2, so it must be 3.

Step 4: Given partial coloring (1, 2, 3), we choose a color for node C. It cannot be 1or 3, so it must be 2.

We have no more choices of colors in step 4, and in step 3. We have one choice in step 2.

After performing the above steps, the graph will be as shown in (a):

(a)

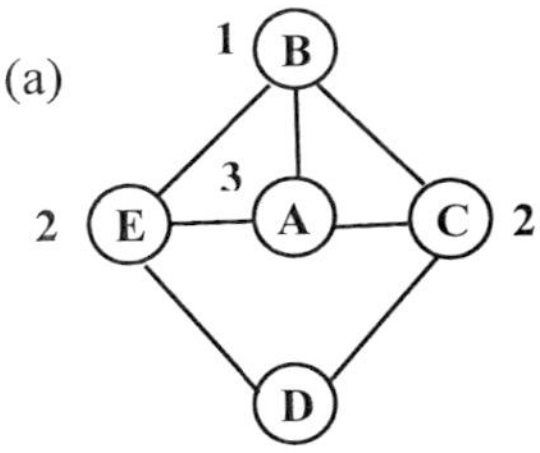

Now we have to choose color for node D. We can choose either 1(Red) or 3(Green). Say we choose 1(Red). And the resultant graph is shown in (b).

(b)

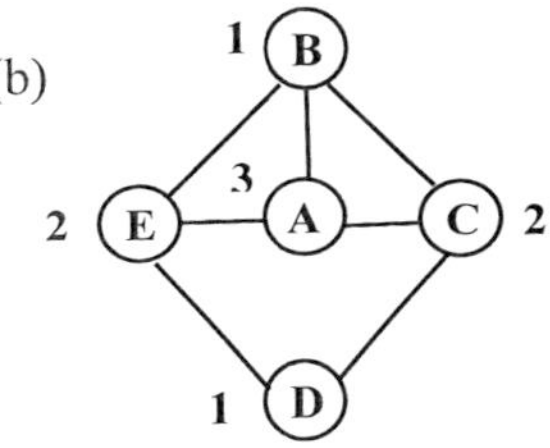

Thus, the graph coloring problem is solved.

We can also color the above graph in different color combinations. Consider graph G having vertices B, E, A, C and D, such that G = {B, E, A, C, D} and we will call the colors Red, Blue and Green as 1, 2 and 3. Now assign each number to each vertices of a graph such that no two adjacent vertices share the same color.

node	(i)	(ii)	(iii)	(iv)
B	1	1	1	1
E	2	3	2	3
A	3	2	3	2
C	2	3	2	3
D	1	1	3	2

These are the color combinations for the above graph, if we start with the Red color. In the same way we can get some more different combinations, if we start with the Blue and Green color.

6.10 Sum of subsets: W = {5, 7, 10, 12, 15, 18, 20} and m = 35. Notice that the w_1 is included at level 1 of the tree, w_2 at level 2, and so on. The possible subsets of w that sum to m are: {5, 12, 18}, {5, 10, 20}, {15, 20}.

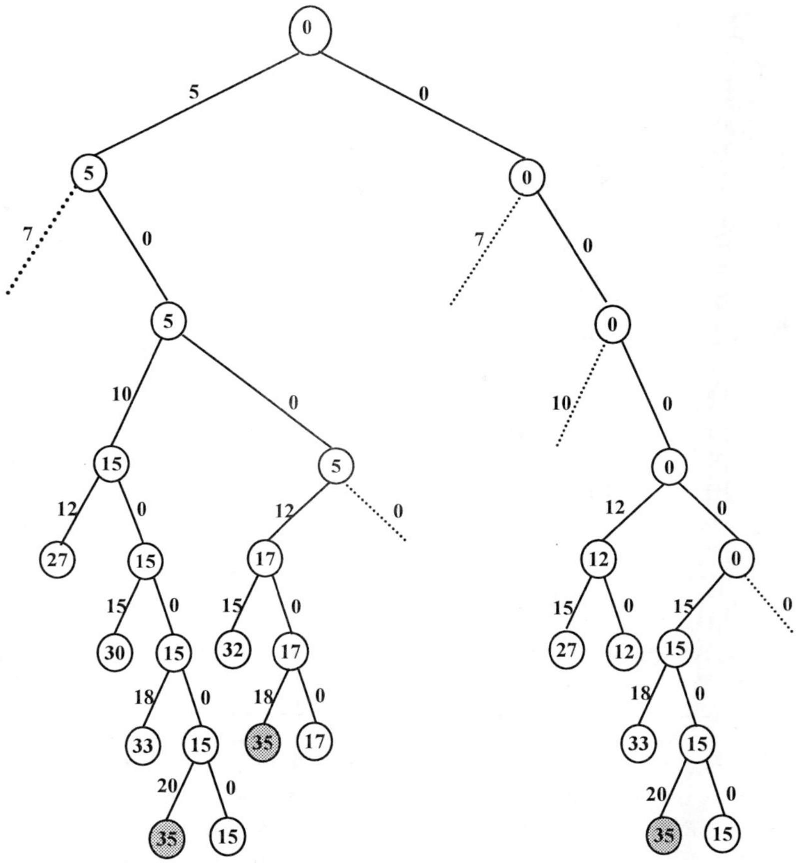

CHAPTER 7 Branch and Bound

7.1 In branch and bound method a state space tree is built and all the children of E-nodes are generated before any other node can become a live node. For exploring new nodes either a BFS or D-search technique can be used. In Branch and Bound technique, BFS-like state space search will be called FIFO search. This is because the list of live node is First-In-First-Out list (Queue). On the other hand the D-search like state space search will be called LIFO search because the list of live node is Last-In-First-Out list (Stack). In this method, a space tree of possible solutions is generated. Then partitioning is done at each node of the tree. We compute lower bound and upper bound at each node. This computation leads to selection of answer node. Bounding functions are used to avoid the generation of sub-trees that do not contain an answer node. Following is a general algorithm for Branch And Bound:

```
Algorithm BranchBound()
// E  is a node pointer;
E=new(node);  //This is root node which is the dummy start node
// H is heap for all the live nodes
// H is a min-heap for minimization problems,
// H is a max-heap for maximization problems
While (true)
      If (E is a final leaf) then,     //E is an optimal solution
            Write(path from E to the root);
            return;
      Endif
      Expand(E);
      If (H is empty) then,
          write(" there is no solution");
          return;
      Endif
      E = delete_top(H);
Endwhile.
```

```
// Expand() is for generating state space tree.
Generate all the children of E;
Compute the approximate cost value of each child;
Insert each child into the heap H;
```

7.2 *Explicit constraints* are defined to be constraints that will require procedures for recognition as an integral part of the branch-and-bound algorithm. Explicit constraints are the rules that restrict each x_i to take on values only from a given set.
Implicit constraints are constraints that will be satisfied by the manner in which the branch-and-bound algorithm is constructed.

7.3 *Live node* is a node that has been generated but whose children have not yet been generated.
E-node is a live node whose children are currently being explored. In other words, an E-node is a node currently being expanded.
Dead node is a generated node that is not to be expanded or explored any further. All children of a dead node have already been expanded.

Example: 4-queens problem. Branch-and-bound refers to all state space search methods in which all children of an E-node are generated before any other live node can become the E-node. Initially, (in FIFO branch-and-bound algorithm), there is only one live node; no queen has been placed on the chessboard. The only live node becomes E-node. We expand and generate all its children; children being a queen in column 1, 2, 3, and 4 of row 1 (only live nodes left). Next E-node is the node with queen in row 1 and column 1. We expand this node, and add the possible nodes to the queue of live nodes, and bound the nodes that become dead nodes.

7.4 *Bounding and its uses*

As we know that the bounding functions are used to avoid the generation of subtrees that do not contain the answer nodes. In bounding, lower bounds and upper bounds are generated at each node

A cost function $\hat{c}(x)$ is such that $\hat{c}(x) \leq c(x)$ is used to provide the lower bounds on solution obtained from any node x.

Let *upper* is an upper bound on cost of minimum – cost solution. In that case, all the nodes with $\hat{c}(x)$ > upper can be discarded.

At the start, the upper is usually set to ∞.After generating the children of current E-node, *upper* can be updated by minimum cost answer node. Each time a new answer node can be obtained

7.10 Portion of the state space tree generated by FIFO branch-and-bound for the following instance.

$n = 5$, $(p_1 \ldots p_5) = (10, 15, 6, 8, 4)$, $(w_1 \ldots w_5) = (4, 6, 3, 4, 2)$, and $m = 12$.

Upper bound of each node of the state space tree is computed as:

$b = p + (m\text{-}w) \times (p_{i+1}/w_{i+1})$

where b = upper bound,

p = total profit of the items already selected,

w = total weight of the items already selected,

m = capacity of the knapsack, and

(p_{i+1}/w_{i+1}) = best per unit payoff among the remaining items.

item (i)	p_i	w_i	(p_i / w_i)
1	10	4	2.5
2	15	6	2.5
3	6	3	2.0
4	8	4	2.0
5	4	2	2.0

The nodes are computed as follows:

Node 0 (root): total profit, $p = 0$, total weight, $w = 0$.
$b = p + (m\text{-}w) \times (p_1/w_1) = 0 + (12 - 0) \times 2.5 = 30.$

Node 1 (include item 1): $p = 10$, $w = 4$.
$b = p + (m\text{-}w) \times (p_2/w_2) = 10 + (12 - 4) \times 2.5 = 30.$

Node 2 (exclude item 1): $p = 0$, $w = 0$.
$b = p + (m\text{-}w) \times (p_2/w_2) = 0 + (12 - 0) \times 2.5 = 30.$

Node 3 (include item 2): $p = 25$, $w = 10$.
$b = p + (m\text{-}w) \times (p_3/w_3) = 25 + (12 - 10) \times 2.0 = 29.$

Node 4 (exclude item 2): $p = 10$, $w = 4$.
$b = p + (m\text{-}w) \times (p_3/w_3) = 10 + (12 - 4) \times 2.0 = 26$.

Similarly, the remaining nodes are calculated. The following figure shows a portion of the state space tree:

Optimal solution: Include items 1, 2 and 5 with total weight of 12 (4 + 6 + 2) and total profit of 29 (10 + 15 + 4). This solution matches with the shaded node.

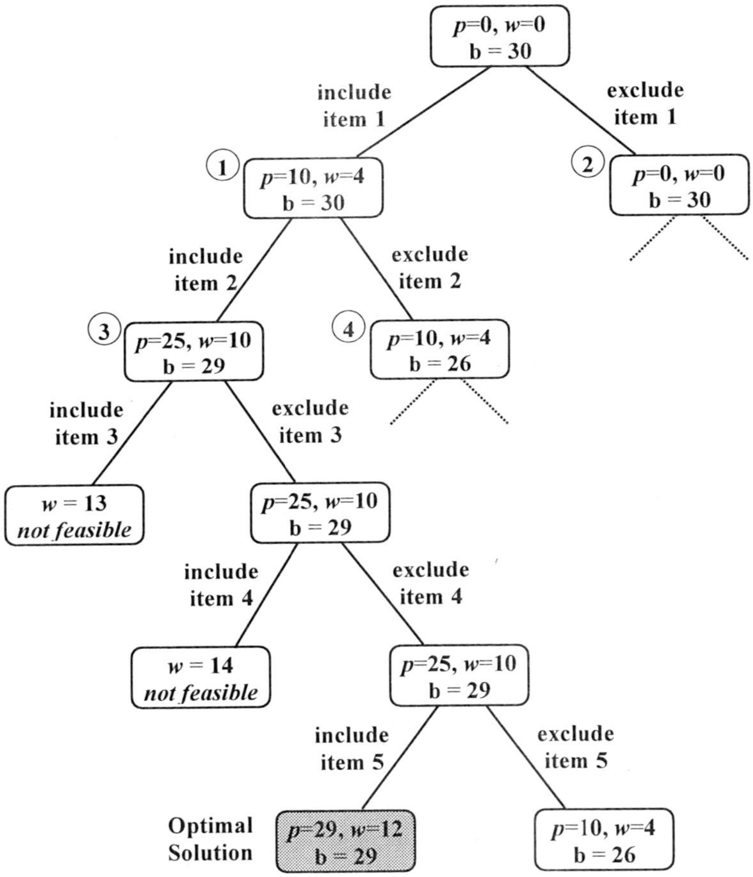

7.12 The Traveling Salesman Problem (TSP) requires that we find the shortest path visiting each of a given set of cities once and returning to the starting point. In other words, the problem is to find, in an undirected graph with weights on the edges, a tour the sum of whose edge-weights is a minimum. A tour is a simple cycle that includes all the vertices. It is often called a Hamilton cycle.

The TSP is a famous example of a problem which can be solved by a branch-and-bound technique. Now let us consider how we might find the optimum tour by systematically considering all tours. One way is to consider all permutations of nodes, and evaluate the tour that visits the nodes in that order, remembering the best so far. The time for such an approach is $O(n!)$ on an n-node graph. Each permutation takes $O(n)$ time to evaluate.

The branch-and-bound technique produces the solution far more rapidly than the "try all permutations" method. We start constructing a tree, with a root that represents all tours (configurations). Each node has two children, and tours that a node represents are divided by these children into two groups – those that have a particular edge and those that do not.

7.14 Principles of LIFO branch-and-bound:
The LC branch and bound can be obtained using fixed tuple size formulation.
The steps to be followed for LCBB solution are

1. Draw state space tree
2. Compute $\hat{c}(.)$ and $u(.)$ for each node
3. If $\hat{c}(x) >$ upper then, discard node x
4. Otherwise the minimum cost $\hat{c}(x)$ becomes E-node. Generate children for E-node
5. Repeat steps 3 and 4 until all the edges get covered
6. The minimum cost $\hat{c}(x)$ becomes the answer node. Trace the path in backward direction from x to root for solution subset.

7.15 The minimum cost of tour is the bound at node 10 ($b = 30$). The final solution contains the following edges (arranged in order):

(1, 5), (5, 4), (4, 2), (2, 3), (3, 1) and the optimal tour is given as:

1 -> 5 -> 4 -> 2 -> 3-> 1.

Total cost of this tour = 8 + 8 + 3 + 6 + 5 = 30, which is same as the bound.

	1	2	3	4	5
1	∞	7	3	12	8
2	3	∞	6	14	9
3	5	8	∞	6	18
4	9	3	5	∞	11
5	18	14	9	8	∞

	1	2	3	4	5	
1	∞	4	0	9	0	-3
2	0	∞	3	11	1	-3
3	0	3	∞	1	8	-5
4	6	0	2	∞	3	-3
5	10	6	1	0	∞	-8
					-5	

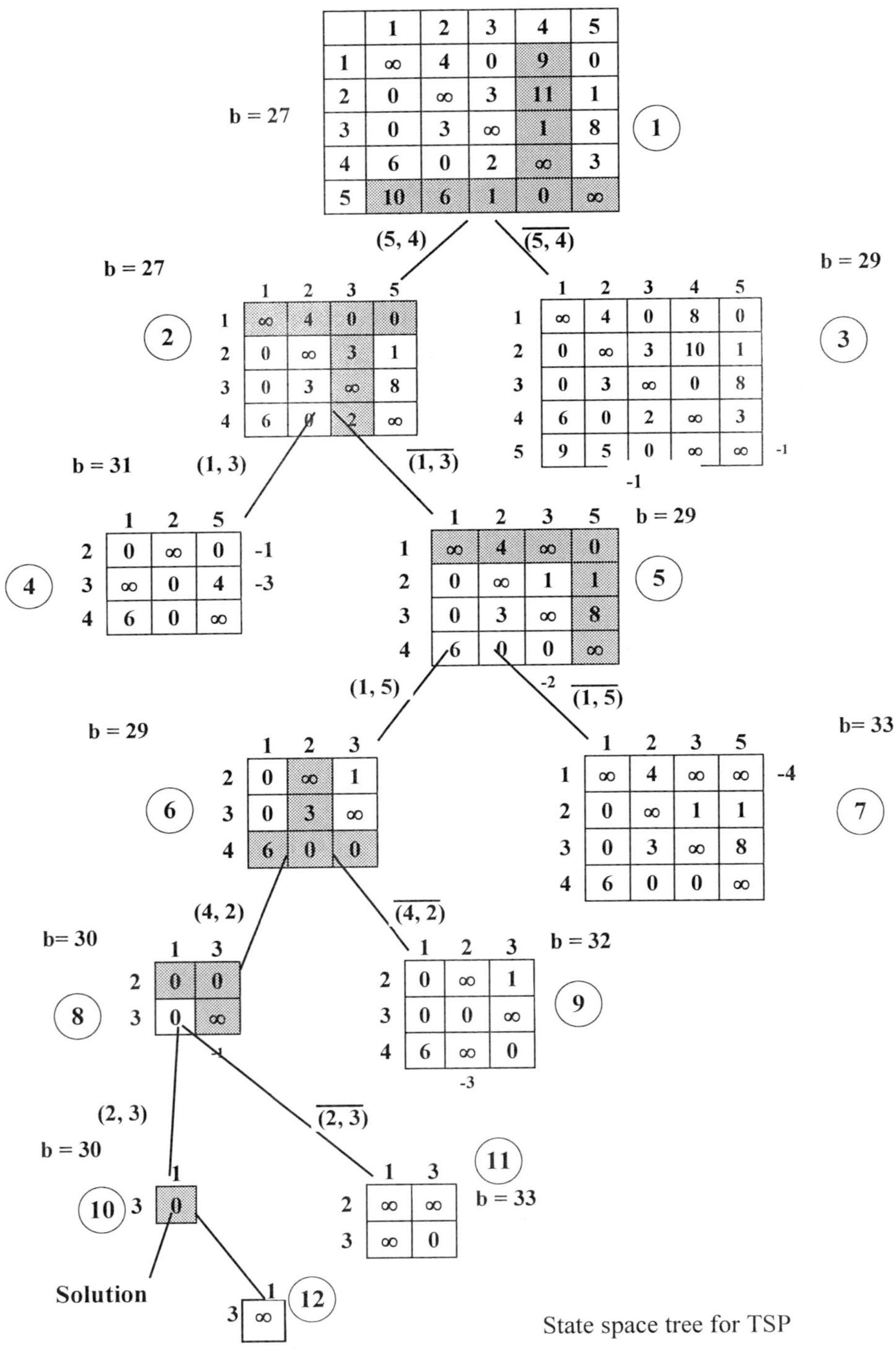

State space tree for TSP

7.16 FIFO branch-and-bound

- FIFO branch-and-bound for job sequencing problem can begin with
  $U = \infty$ or $(U=\sum_{1\le i\le n} p_i)$ as an upper bound
  on the cost of a minimum-cost answer node.
- Start with node 1 as the E-node in the variable tuple formulation of the state space tree
  Nodes 2, 3, 4, and 5 are generated in that order
  $u(2) = 19$, $u(3) = 14$, $u(4) = 18$, and $u(5) = 21$
- Variable U is updated to 14 when node 3 is generated
- Since $\hat{c}(4)$ and $\hat{c}(5)$ are greater than U, nodes 4 and 5 get killed (or bounded)
- Only nodes 2 and 3 remain alive
- Node 2 becomes the next E-node; its children are generated as nodes 6, 7, and
- $u(6) = 9$ and so, U is updated to 9
- $\hat{c}(7) = 10 > U$ and so, node 7 gets killed
- Next node 3 becomes E-node; generating node 9 and 10
- $u(9) = 8$ updating U to 8

CHAPTER 8 NP-Complete Problems

8.2 NP-completeness reduction with an example:
We consider an NP problem and call it *X*. We show that solving *X* in polynomial time allows us to solve SAT in polynomial time. Then since we can use a polynomial SAT algorithm to solve any NP problem, we can also use a polynomial *X* algorithm to solve any NP problem; so X is also NP-complete. This is an NP-completeness reduction.

If *X* is known to be NP-complete, then we can reduce another NP problem *Y* to *X*, and then *Y* is NP-complete:

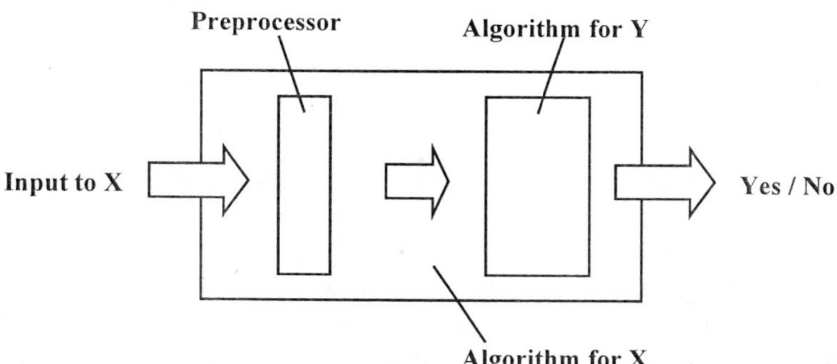

Note that the output of the preprocessor must be a valid input to *Y*. Now if the preprocessor is polynomial time, then if *Y* were in P, *X* would also be in P. And if *X* is NP-complete then its membership in P implies all problems in NP are in P, that is P = NP. So then *Y* must be NP-complete as well.

To show that Y is NP-complete from knowledge that X is NP-complete we have to describe the preprocessor algorithm, but the algorithm for Y (the box on the right in the above figure) is purely hypothetical. And the proof then must show each of the following: that Y is in NP, that the preprocessor is in polynomial time, and that the algorithm for Y when run on the instance outputted by the preprocessor will say "yes" if and only if the answer for the original instance of X should be "yes".

8.3 SATISFIABILITY (SAT) is a decision problem: Given a Boolean formula in conjunctive normal form (CNF), return "yes" if the formula has a satisfying assignment and "no" otherwise. SAT plays a crucial role in the theory of NP-completeness. Also, algorithms solving SAT are important in practice and are routinely used, for instance, for hardware verification. Thus, SAT is important from a theoretical as well as from a practical perspective.

By Cook's theorem, SAT is NP-complete. Thus, under the assumption $P \neq NP$, SAT does not have a polynomial algorithm. By making a somewhat stronger, but still very reasonable assumption, a stronger conclusion can be made. Following is an algorithm for SAT:

```
Boolean SAT(CNFformula f)
f = Simplify(f)
If f does not contain any variables, then
        return Evaluate(f)
Else
        Pick a variable x in f
        f0 = f[x ß false]
        If SAT(f0) = true, then
                return true
        Else
                f1 = f[x ß true]
                return SAT(f1)
        Endif
Endif
```

Note that a formula containing no variables but only constants can be readily evaluated to either true or false by doing the necessary Boolean operations; this is the intended semantics of the expression "Evaluate(f)". By $f[x$ ß true$]$ we mean the formula obtained by replacing all occurrences of the literal x with true and all occurrences of the literal x with false. We define f[x ß false] similarly. If we ignore the first line f = Simplify(f) for a moment, we see that the algorithm decides if a formula is satisfiable by first recursively deciding if it is satisfiable by an assignment making a particular variable false, and if not, recursively deciding if it is satisfiable by an assignment making the same variable true. Simplify is intended to be an auxiliary method in the algorithm. Intuitively, we want Simplify(f) to return a "simplified" version of f with fewer clauses or variables, so that our job is made easier.

8.4 Strategy to prove that a problem is NP-hard:
A problem is NP-hard if having a polynomial-time solution to it would give us a polynomial solution to every problem in NP. The usual strategy is to find a polynomial-time reduction of a known NP-hard problem - say P1 to the problem in question (say P2). The goal is to show that P2 is at least as hard (in terms of polynomial versus super-polynomial time) as P1. If P1 can be translated to an equivalent problem P2 in polynomial time, then a polynomial-time solution to P2 would also give a polynomial-time solution to P1: First reduce P1 to P2, then solve it. Make sure we are reducing the known problem to the unknown problem. In practice, there are now thousands of known NP-complete problems. A good technique is to look for one similar to the one you are trying to solve.

8.6 Knapsack problem can be solved using the following non-deterministic algorithm:

v_i = value of i-th item, w_i = weight of i-th item, for $i = 1$ to n items.
C = knapsack capacity.
K = minimum value to be taken in the knapsack.
totalWeight = Weight of items included so far in the knapsack
totalValue = Total value of items so far included.
S denotes the set of items to be included in the knapsack.
found is a Boolean variable.

```
Knapsack(v[1..n], w[1..n], W, K, n)
totalWeight = totalValue = 0
Initially S is empty;  found = false.
For i = 1 to n do
     Add i-th item to S
     Add w[i] to totalWeight
     Add v[i] to totalValue
     If totalWeight > C, then fail
     Else If totalValue ≥ K, then
               found = true
               succeed
          Endif
     Endif
Endfor.
```

8.7 The *halting problem* is a decision problem which can be stated as follows:

> Given a description of an algorithm and its initial input, determine whether the algorithm, when executed on this input, ever halts (completes). The alternative is that it runs forever without halting.

Alan Turing proved that a general algorithm to solve the halting problem for all possible inputs cannot exist. We say that the halting problem is *undecidable*.

Let us construct an algorithm A whose input is a prepositional formula X. Suppose X has n variables. Algorithm A tries out all 2^n possible truth assignments and verifies if X is satisfiable.

If it is NP-hard then A stops.
If X is not satisfiable, then A enters an infinite loop.

Hence A halts on input if X is satisfiable. If we had a polynomial time algorithm for the halting problem, then we could solve the satisfiability problem in polynomial time using A and X as input to the algorithm for the halting problem. Hence, the halting problem is an NP-hard problem which is not in NP. So it is not NP-complete.

8.8 A *clique* in a graph is a set of pairwise adjacent vertices, or in other words, an induced subgraph which is a complete graph. In the graph at the right, vertices 1, 2 and 5 form a clique, because each has an edge to all the others.

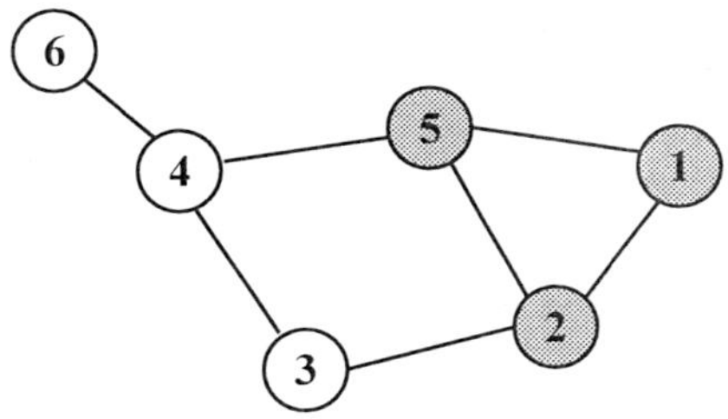

Then, the clique problem is the problem of determining whether a graph contains a clique of at least a given size k. This is a decision problem. Once we have located k or more vertices which form a clique, it is trivial to verify that they do, which is why the clique problem is in NP. The corresponding optimization problem, the maximum clique problem, is to find the largest clique in a graph.

The NP-completeness of the clique problem follows trivially from the NP-completeness of the independent set problem, because there is a clique of size at least k if and only if there is an independent set of size at least k in the complement graph. This is easy to see, since if a subgraph is complete, its complement subgraph has no edges at all.

8.9 NP-complete and NP-hard:

A problem that is NP-Complete has the property that it can be solved in polynomial time if all other NP-Complete problems can also be solved in polynomial time. If an NP-Hard problem can be solved in polynomial time, then all NP-Complete problems can be solved in polynomial time. All NP-Complete problems are NP-Hard, but not all NP-Hard problems are NP-Complete.

REFERENCES

1 Aho, Hopcroft, Ullman, Data structures And Algorithms, Pearson, Delhi, 2001.

2 Baase, Sara., "Computer algorithms : introduction to design and analysis", Reading, Mass : Addison-Wesley Pub. Co., 1978.

3 Brassard, Gilles, Fundamentals of algorithmics, Englewood, N.J. : Prentice Hall, 1996.

4 Bruno R. Preiss , Data Structures and Algorithms with Object-Oriented Design Patterns in CPlusPlus.

5 Cook Stephen. The complexity of theorem proving procedures. Proceedings of the Third Annual ACM Symposium on Theory of Computing, 1971.

6 Cormen, Thomas H, et al, Introduction to algorithms", Cambridge, Mass : MIT Press ; New York : McGraw-Hill, 1990.

7 Dasgupta, Papadimitriou, Vazirani, Algorithms, Tata Mcgraw-Hill, New Delhi, 2008.

8 Garey M.R and Johnson D.S, Computers and Intractability : A Guide to the Theory of NP-completeness. W.H. Freeman, 1979.

9 Horowitz E, Sahni S and Rajasekharan S, Fundamentals of Computer Algorithms, Galgotia Publishing Pvt. Ltd, New Delhi, 1999.

10 Horowitz E, Sahni S, Mehta D and Freeman W H, Fundamentals of Data Structures in C++, New York, NY, 1994.

11 Knuth D E, Fundamental Algorithms, Vol. 1, The Art of Computer Programming, Third Edition, Pearson Education, New Delhi, 2007.

12 Knuth D E, Seminumerical Algorithms, Vol. 2, The Art of Computer Programming, Third Edition, Pearson Education, New Delhi, 2007.

13 Knuth D E, Sorting and Searching, Vol. 3, The Art of Computer Programming, Third Edition, Pearson Education, New Delhi, 2007.

14 Kruse R L, Data Structures and Program Design, Prentice-Hall of India, New Delhi, 2002.

15 Kruse, Robert L., "Data Structures and Program Design", second edition Prentice-Hall, 1996.

16 Levitin, An Introduction to Design and Analysis of Algorithms, Pearson, Delhi, 2009.

17 Manber U, Introduction to Algorithms: A Creative Approach, Addison-Wesley, 1989.

18 Mark Allen Weiss, Data Structures and Problem Solving Using C++, Addison Wesley, 1999

19 Polya G, How to Solve It, Princeton University Press, Princeton, N.Y, 1971.

20 Robert L. Kruse , Data Structures and Program Design in C++, Prentice Hall,1998

21 Robert Lafore, SAMS Teach Yourself Data Structures And Algorithms In 24 hours, Pearson Education , 2000

22 Sartaj Sahni, Data Structures, Algorithms, And Applications In C++, 2nd Edition, Silicon Press , 2004

23 Sedgewick R and Flajolet P, An Introduction to the Analysis of Algorithms, Reading, Mass., Addison-Wesley, 1996

24 Storer, An Introduction to Data Structures and Algorithms, Springer (India), New Delhi, 2009.

25 Tremblay J P and Bunt R B, An Introduction to Computer Science: An Algorithmic Approach, McGraw-Hill Book Co, New York, 1979.

26 Tremblay J P and Sorenson P G, An Introduction to Data Structures with Applications, Tata McGraw-Hill, New Delhi, 2004

27 Watkins R P, Computer Problem-Solving, Wiley, Hong Kong, 1974.

28 Wirth N, Algorithms + Data Structures = Programs, Prentice Hall, Englewood Cliffs, 1976.

29 Wirth N, Systematic Programming: An Introduction, Prentice-Hall, Englewood Cliffs, N.J, 1973.

INDEX